Alternative Assets and Strategic Allocation

Alternative Assets and Strategic Allocation

Rethinking the Institutional Approach

JOHN B. ABBINK

BLOOMBERG PRESS
An Imprint of
WILEY

For Carol

CONTENTS

PART FOUR | PORTFOLIO CONSTRUCTION

LIST of ILLUSTRATIONS

Figures

---

* Russell Investments is the owner of the trademarks, service marks, and copyrights related to their indices. The indices are unmanaged and cannot be invested in directly.
† "Dow Jones" and "Dow Jones Select REIT Index" are service marks of Dow Jones & Company, Inc. The Dow Jones Select REIT Index is published by and proprietary to Dow Jones & Company, Inc.

* Provided as a courtesy by Chicago Board Options Exchange, Inc.

† The source of this illustration is a Staff Report of the Federal Reserve Bank of New York. This paper presents preliminary findings and is being distributed to economists and other interested readers solely to stimulate discussion and elicit comments. The views expressed in the paper are those of the authors and are not necessarily reflective of views at the Federal Reserve Bank of New York or the Federal Reserve System. Any errors or omissions are the responsibility of the authors.

Tables

ACKNOWLEDGMENTS

I have never been as punctilious a scholar as I should be, and in any case most of what I think I know about finance has been acquired through osmosis rather than formal study. I cannot believe that all of the observations I make in this volume, but for which I lack a reference, are original to me, and I am fairly certain that much that I have gained through experience or conversation has occurred to and been published by others. While I attempt to reference them where I can, I apologize to those who deserve a citation but have not received one. If my readers are kind or indignant enough to help me with references and my effort is fortunate enough to achieve a second edition, I will attempt to give credit where it is due to those whom I have unintentionally slighted.

Although I accept full responsibility for the errors and omissions I have doubtless made, I have benefited from conversations with numerous friends and colleagues as well as comments on drafts of my text from many others. I am indebted to Wally Anders, Jeffrey Boardman, William Hayes, Stephen Hoedt, Richard Katz, Michael Mainelli, Steven Resnick, Ferenc Sanderson, Andre Sharon, Timothy Swanson, and Gary Zdolshek as well as my editors at Bloomberg Press for their criticisms and suggestions. I would also like to thank my wife for her patience with a project that consumed many evenings and weekends.

I am grateful to my sources, in particular the Federal Reserve Bank of New York for permission to use the illustrations in Figure 17.1 and to the CFA Institute for permission to quote at length from one of their publications in Chapter 17. I would like to thank the data providers Baltic Exchange Information Services, Barclays Capital, the Chicago Board Options Exchange, Dow Jones & Co., FactSet Mergerstat, Hedge Fund Research, IntercontinentalExchange, NASDAQ OMX Group, the National Council of Real Estate Investment Fiduciaries, the Russell

Investment Group, and Standard & Poor's Financial Services for permission to use their data. Bloomberg Finance L.P. has provided me with currency, spot commodity, and equity price data, as well as permitting me to use its Bloomberg Professional® service to obtain convenient access to the data of several of the other providers already mentioned, for which I am also grateful.

Introduction

There is a wealth of literature on alternative investments, ranging from collections of admiring interviews with the various wizards and rocket scientists whom the media seem to think populate the industry, to detailed strategy-by-strategy guidebooks and an ever-mounting corpus of densely argued academic discussion. Although there is considerable chaff among the wheat in all this mass of material, alternative investments are certainly not in want of attention, and by now many of the requirements of serious investors who are new to the topic, let alone those of sensation-seekers, have been quite fully addressed. There is little need for yet another introduction to alternative investments or yet another encyclopedic handbook to guide newcomers through the luxuriant profusion of different alternative investment techniques.

The literature on what to do with alternative investments—how they fit into portfolios and their role in an investment allocation that includes traditional investments as well—is much thinner on the ground. This is not to say that no useful work has been done in this area, and this volume relies on a number of authors who have made important contributions to the study of the portfolio function of alternative investments, as witnessed by my references to them. However, it remains somewhat puzzling that there are not more studies of this kind—after all, institutional interest in the area has been extremely lively for several years. On reflection, it seems that there are three influences that discourage significant progress on this front. One is an intense focus on the role of

1

talent in investment management, to the exclusion of virtually all other possible influences on the ability of alternative investment managers to generate returns. The second is the fairly widespread view—almost but not quite the consensus—that alternative investments are something radically different from conventional investments, so conceptually distinct that they cannot usefully be discussed in the same context, using similar terms and comparable analytic techniques. Finally, there is an intractable problem deriving from the woefully inexact terminology of alternative investments, which constantly forces commentators into problems of definition, resulting in yet more encyclopedic surveys of the territory simply to achieve some clarity about what exactly it is that is being discussed.

Talent is a great discussion stopper: once it is accepted as essentially the only explanation for investment performance, then there is not a great deal more that can usefully be said. It is God-given and inherently mysterious. While talented investors clearly share with each other certain characteristics, such as insightfulness and decisiveness, talent of any kind is fundamentally opaque to further analysis. There are no handy touchstones or interview techniques that can assure us that we are in its presence. It is only somewhat helpful that, unlike God's grace (at least according to St. Paul), we can recognize talent by its works, but even then it is usually very difficult to distinguish the products of skill from those of luck and hard work. The fact that the managers of alternative investments have an interest in maintaining the mystique of talent does not help matters.

The contribution of talent to good investment performance is undeniable. Where numerous highly trained and diligent professionals have access to much the same information required to support their decision-making, luck and relentless dedication alone cannot account for the investment successes of the few compared to the mediocre performance of the many. However, there is a tendency in far too much of the literature on alternative investments to identify talent with α (excess risk-adjusted return). In fact, α is often treated explicitly as though it were somehow a quantitative measure of skill. This neglects Edison's analysis of the relative contributions of inspiration and perspiration to genius, but it also discourages analysis of the risk-taking that is the ultimate source of all returns. We can give talent its due—and no one should dream of denying its importance in investment or in other walks of life—while still finding useful things to say about how talent, hard work, and luck conspire to generate investment returns in an environment of uncertainty.

This focus on talent is most pronounced in the hedge fund arena. It is possible to read entire volumes on private equity or real estate investment without encountering much, if any, name-dropping, but this is not the case with any but the driest and most scholarly writing on hedge funds. An important contributor to this cult of personality is almost certainly hedge funds' near-universal lack of transparency. Although the enhanced performance that derives from active management of private equity or real estate investments may not receive much press attention, the primary investment activities—the purchases and disposals—that are executed by managers of these types of assets are carried out very much in the open. The lack of similar transparency for hedge funds seems to have driven their chroniclers to concentrate on the managers themselves, rather than their activities and the decision-drivers that motivate them.

The second unfortunate influence on the literature of alternative investments is the very widespread tendency to treat them as though they belong to a separate asset class, something completely different from conventional investment vehicles. This is another discussion stopper: to insist on radical difference is to insist on entirely different terms of reference. It is an impediment to comparative analysis, and, if taken to an extreme, it implies that it is not possible to adopt a rational approach to allocation between conventional and alternative investment categories or even within the alternative category. In fact, most alternative investments employ the same assets as conventional investment vehicles, and few of their trading practices are completely unique to alternative investments alone. The fairly rare exceptions are far outnumbered by alternative investment vehicles that use publicly traded equity and fixed income or something very similar to them as the fundamental sources of their returns. It would seem unlikely on the face of it that alternative investments' differences from conventional ones place them in a category entirely apart from them.

The content of the term "alternative investment" has been lost if it does not make sense to ask the question, "Alternative to what?" If the question is still meaningful, then we are forced to conclude that alternative investments must be analyzed as part of a continuum of investment opportunities stretching from savings accounts through the wilder regions of venture capital, commodity speculation, statistical arbitrage, and so on. Unless we regard alternative investments as completely exogenous return generators, analogous to "investing" in lottery tickets, then we must be able to analyze them with the same sorts of tools that are used in thinking about conventional investments—perhaps not identically the same tools, but at least very similar ones. If alternative investments were truly members of one or more distinct asset classes, quite separate from conventional investments, then it is not clear that they would be amenable to comparative analysis at all. In that case an investigation of the grounds for making allocations to them, such as is attempted in this volume, would be largely beside the point.

Apart from tone and an artificial segregation of alternative investments from investments generally, the third aspect of the way that alternative investments are discussed that has interfered with institutionally oriented examination of them is rampant terminological inexactitude. There are many occasions when knowledgeable professionals have to nail down the definition of commonly used terms simply to hold a meaningful conversation about alternatives with each other. The confusion fostered by loose terminology may enhance the crepuscular allure of alternative investments and may in some cases be helpful to funds' marketing efforts, but it unquestionably interferes with any attempt to understand them. When every term needs to be defined, it is difficult to get past the starting gate of discussion, and I believe that this accounts for most of the difficulty that the literature faces in attempting to progress much beyond general introductions to the topic.

However, the battle to achieve precise nomenclature has long been lost, so there is little point in attempting to offer a new taxonomy of alternative investments, because it would only add to the muddle. And perhaps a certain amount of imprecision is appropriate to the discussion of alternative investments. In a field where creativity is so rife and nuance so important to differentiating among the various approaches to investment, a rigid system of terminology might well constitute a greater barrier to understanding than allowing for a certain amount of interpretive ambiguity in the terms of reference. Constant retracing of steps to concrete examples and clarifying definitions may be a tiresome impediment to progress, but perhaps that is the price required to make any progress at all. While I discuss the classification of investments in Part IV, the intention there is to offer an aid to thinking about allocation, rather than a fixed and exhaustive scheme of categories, and what I offer is intended to be quite flexible.

Throughout this book, my intention is to examine alternative investments as investments. Their strategies are explored in the context of strategies that are applied to conventional investments, and their risks are examined from the standpoint of where any investment's risks come from. What results turns out to be a comparatively colorless treatment of the topic, lacking in "war stories," gossip, and hyperbole, but I do not believe that an attempt to understand alternative investors' remarkable creativity detracts from or trivializes their undeniable accomplishments. While I hope that my remarks can be of some value to any investor who has acquired an interest in these vehicles, they are directed primarily at plan sponsors, trustees, managers of funds of funds, and others with the responsibility for forming investment policies that employ these vehicles. The ranks of institutional investors who are confronted by allocation decisions involving alternative investments have swelled rapidly over the last decade or so, and may continue to do so despite recent disappointments. In my view, their needs for a functional understanding of these investment vehicles have only occasionally been well served by what has been written about them. This volume will by no means succeed in filling that gap, but in conjunction with the contributions of others, it endeavors to push that project forward.

What Is Alternative about Alternative Investments?

It is not unreasonable to expect that something that is generally identified as "alternative" should in some sense be different, and many alternative investments truly are. By this, presumably everyone who uses the term means that they are different from conventional investments in cash, stocks, and bonds. However, much to the bewilderment of the uninitiated, their difference is not usually to be found in their choice of investment instruments—some truly strange alternative specimens nevertheless restrict their attentions to familiar assets. In this respect, at the very least, alternative investments as a group certainly do not inhabit a separate asset class.

The majority of hedge funds trade exclusively in stocks and bonds, perhaps with some options and futures thrown in for variety's sake. Private equity is first and foremost equity, whereas real estate assets are, at bottom, either equity or debt. Direct financing strategies differ fundamentally from purchasing certificates of deposit only insofar as they may include an equity "kicker" apart from their basic structure as loans. Commodities, foreign currencies, art, and collectibles are noticeably different from the assets held by conventional investment vehicles, and there are a handful of true exotica of the alternative investment world that are completely unfamiliar to conventional investment practice. By and large, however, it is impossible to conclude that the assets employed in alternative investment products are what make them "alternative."

Alternative investments may be leveraged or activist, they may be hedged, operate over unusual time horizons, or be parts of an arbitrage strategy. *Any of these may also be true of conventional investments*:

❑ The Investment Company Act of 1940 permits mutual funds to leverage themselves up to 50 percent of the value of their assets, and increasing numbers of funds make at least partial use of this permission. Although use of leverage in other regulated investment contexts such as ERISA pensions or IRAs is more restricted, it is not impossible to find ways to introduce leverage into them, too.

❑ Activism, such as initiating proxy contests and similar initiatives to encourage managements to pursue a desired course of action, has become a common technique among many conventional investors, including mutual funds and, in a very high profile way, certain states' retirement plans. Arguably, it was conventional investors who introduced alternative managers to the idea of such activism.

❑ Hedging is by no means absent from conventional investing—notably currency hedging in cross-border products, but also position and transaction hedging activities that make use of futures or options in fixed-income mutual funds and domestic equity vehicles.

❑ Time horizons can also be quite varied in conventional investment vehicles—although very short-term trading strategies may not be so common, they are not unknown. There are equity managers with annual turnover well in excess of 200 percent and a large number of bond funds with twice and even three times that level. These amounts of trading turnover may not rival some of the most active Commodity Trading Advisors (CTAs) or high-frequency hedge funds, but they are certainly enough to keep their trading desks very busy. At the other extreme, there are numerous conventional managers that hold equity positions for five years or more, approaching the average holding periods of private equity vehicles.

❑ Participation in arbitrage is fairly unique to alternative investors, but there are arbitrage-like aspects to many conventional investment techniques—particularly those encountered in bond markets—and by no means all alternative strategies engage in arbitrage or anything that resembles it.

In each of these respects, the difference between alternative investment vehicles and conventional ones seems to be a matter of degree rather than a difference in kind. No radical change is encountered in moving from the sphere of one to that of the other. We could be tempted to conclude that alternative investments are in fact just like conventional investments—only more so. Reaching a similar destination by a quite different route, Bookstaber (2007) writes,

> The hedge funds/alternative investments moniker is a description of what an investment fund is not, rather than what it is. The universe of alternative investments is just that: the universe. It encompasses all possible investment vehicles and all possible investment strategies minus the traditional investment funds and vehicles. (244)

Cynics might argue that what truly makes alternative investment vehicles different is their fee structure, and like all competent cynics, they have a point. It has been suggested, I think by Warren Buffett, that hedge funds in particular are less an investment category than a compensation scheme. Although performance-related fee structures are permitted to conventional investment managers, few in fact adopt them. And the often breathtaking generosity of the fees charged even for very simple investment vehicles that are hardly even "alternative" (2 percent management fee and a 20 percent incentive fee for an index buy/ write option strategy!) are unknown among conventional investment managers, whose charges generally bear at least a vague relationship to the cost of offering their services. However, their fee structures can hardly be regarded as a fundamental, distinguishing characteristic of alternative investments. These structures are external to the investment program, and although they have proven highly resistant to change, it is not inconceivable that an alternative investment vehicle could charge economically justifiable fees and still be regarded as "alternative." Various products of this kind have in fact found their way into the marketplace: no one regards them as conventional simply because they are comparatively affordable.

Most alternative investment vehicles also share various features of legal structure and regulatory oversight that differentiate them from typical conventional investment instruments. But again, these are external differences rather than characteristics inherent to these products, and in many cases there are conventional vehicles that have chosen to adopt the same or similar structures. Most alternative investments are structured as Limited Partnerships, and most of them impose some form of lockup on their investors' commitments. Most of them are lightly regulated if at all, and if they are subject to U.S. regulation, it may be through the

Commodity Futures Trading Commission or even the Small Business Administration (in the case of some mezzanine funds) rather than the Securities and Exchange Commission (SEC), which oversees most U.S. conventional managers. These characteristics may not be distinguishing features of alternatives in the sense that we are looking for, but they do account for a number of important differences between alternative and conventional investment products, including minimum net wealth requirements, maximum numbers of investors, restrictions on solicitation, the blithe vagueness of offering memoranda, and so on. However, alternativeness seems to have created a conventionality of its own. For certain forms of investment, these inconvenient structures are unnecessary—vehicles making these sorts of investments could be structured in a way that was much less of an imposition on their investors. When their managers are asked why they have chosen the less convenient structure, they invariably reply that it is what customers for that type of investment expect. Having steeled themselves to the nuisance of this or that structure, the customers would presumably be disappointed not to have the opportunity to demonstrate the sophistication implied by their tolerance for its inconvenience.

In alternative investments' heroic period, during the late 1980s and early 1990s, they were notable for their sheer, swashbuckling aggressiveness. When "macro" hedge fund managers were Kings of the Street and buyout firms were Barbarians, it was common practice to characterize investment strategies as "alternative" simply on the basis of their voracious risk appetites. Yet even in that fabled Golden Age, this characterization failed to encompass the entire alternative investment universe—some investors were concerned with market neutrality, the pursuit of "absolute return," and similarly less-than-gun-slinging risk profiles even then—but it was a widespread view amply reflected in the media. The environment has changed considerably since then, both because the returns to swashbuckling are no longer as great as they once were, and because the entry of institutional investors into the alternative investment arena has encouraged a different attitude toward risk. Since the 1990s, this sort of aggressiveness has become much less characteristic of alternative investment managers, although it persists in isolated spots and experiences the occasional revival. The media have yet to notice, and continue to regard all alternative investors as inveterate risk-takers, when they are not otherwise engaged in fawning on or vilifying them.

A feature of many alternative investment vehicles that is related both to their colorful pasts and to their legal and regulatory status is their lack of a specified investment discipline. General Partners frequently grant themselves extremely wide latitude in the sorts of assets they may hold and the techniques that they may employ to select and exploit them. It is not uncommon, for example, for a hedge fund's or commodity pool's private placement memorandum to neglect to mention even in the most general terms which types of instruments it will employ, what trading signals will motivate its activities or the time horizon(s) over which it will trade. Alternatively, the permissions a General Partner grants itself may be specified at excruciatingly pedantic length, but so encyclopedically as to impose no effective restraint on its activities whatsoever. For example, one such document I encountered recently lists, in exhaustive detail, thirty classes of instruments that the fund might choose to employ ("...collars, floors, warrants, swaps, swaptions...") and, on the off chance that any possible investment vehicle was overlooked, concludes with "...and any other interest or instruments on a cleared and non-cleared basis as determined by the Portfolio Manager in its sole discretion." However, the growing presence and influence of institutional investors in the alternative investment arena, with their desire to allocate among identifiably different investment vehicles, has tended to encourage greater style purity among alternative investment managers. In this respect, alternative investments are arguably becoming *less* "alternative," and in certain respects they increasingly resemble conventional, institutionally oriented investment products in their concern with consistency and predictability.[1] And in any case, indiscipline has never been unique to alternative investments: even in these Style Box–obsessed times, there are still plenty of mavericks among conventional equity and fixed-income managers who invest more or less as the spirit moves them and in the assets that attract their momentary fancy.

There is also what might be regarded as a counter-trend underway, toward the creation of explicitly multi-strategy vehicles. This does not actually represent a "renaissance of indiscipline," as multi-strategy managers clearly require at least the same degree of style transparency in their underlying investments that institutions demand, in order to inform their allocation decisions among them. And because they manage the underlying investments themselves, they can be certain of obtaining it. Rather, it is motivated by the perception that returns to tactical allocation can be

---

1. A useful discussion of hedge fund transparency as it relates to the needs of institutional investors can be found in Anson (2002), Chapter 9. In the course of his discussion there he mentions still another form that the lack of hedge fund transparency can take, when he informs us that Long-Term Capital Management carried some 60,000 positions in its portfolio.

attractive, as well as the potential that a multi-strategy format offers to compete for investors' assets with funds of hedge funds. However, the trend creates a sort of second-order opacity: while the underlying strategies may be style-pure, the techniques these funds employ for allocating among them are not likely to be transparent at all. It is the goal of this book to shed some light on such allocation procedures, but it is worth noting that in some cases, multi-strategy funds employ no top-down allocation procedure whatsoever. Instead, their portfolios are built from the bottom up in conformity with risk parameters placed on the individual investment disciplines, and investment allocation is determined entirely by the investment choices made by those disciplines' individual portfolio managers, without any coordination or selection from "on high."

Perhaps in reaction to the reputation that they have acquired for uncontrolled indiscipline, these days the managers of many alternative investment vehicles take great pains to stress their risk aversion and their attentiveness to issues of risk management. Increasingly, they describe themselves as seeking "absolute return." However, not all alternative investment managers would describe their strategies as "absolute return"–oriented. And in any case, "absolute return" is not a property that is unique to the vehicles that lay claim to it: a certificate of deposit offers absolute returns, as does cash in a mattress. Arguably, all modern investment thinking that insists upon the central importance of portfolio diversification to sound investment practice is driven by the desire to achieve "absolute return," or at least something that comes as close to it as possible.

However, aggressiveness, comparative indiscipline, and an attraction to "absolute return" provide an indication of what it is that distinguishes alternative from conventional investments. Alternative investors seek to generate returns that do not correlate closely with those offered by conventional investment strategies. In other words, their difference consists largely in their desire to be different. Given that any investment technique seeking excess returns, whether alternative or conventional, must depart from the risks inherent to the broad aggregate of the assets in which it invests—usually, if slightly inaccurately, identified as their β—any actively managed return-seeking technique seeks non-correlation to a greater or lesser extent. Thus, at the end of the day, what distinguishes alternative from conventional investment managers seems to be the lengths to which the former will go in seeking return, and thus the lengths to which they will go in seeking ways to invest that have little or no correlation with conventional approaches to investing. This is clearly a matter of degree rather than a difference in kind—as already suggested, a matter of "only more so." It is likely that a great deal of the "gee whiz" factor that attaches to the practitioners of alternative investing derives from their obsession with being different from the crowd.

So I have become comfortable in the prejudice that alternative investments should be considered in the context of conventional approaches to investing, because there is little evidence that alternative investments are so radically distinctive that they require a completely different analytic framework. Every investment of any kind claims a spot on the continuum of investment risks. As I will argue in my first chapter, this continuum results from a fairly simple observation about investments—that, at bottom, there is a rather narrowly restricted number of return-generating risks that any investment manager can take.

The Plan of This Book

This volume is addressed to investment policymakers who are confronted with the task of making investment allocation decisions that embrace both conventional and alternative assets. In deference to this audience, I have assumed that my readers are fairly sophisticated about investments generally, but to the extent that I have been able to, I avoid highly technical discussion and financial mathematics, and I have attempted to isolate the technical material in Chapter 3, where it can be safely ignored by those who dislike such matters. I have chosen not to dwell on issues that affect taxable investors, since it seems very likely that changes in the Tax Code will soon render stale most comments that might be specifically relevant to them. And I have not addressed the other issues that are peculiar to high net worth investors, since in most respects the concerns of those who are able to allocate across several categories of alternative investments resemble those of institutional investors in any case.

The bias of the discussion is toward the practical and empirical rather than the theoretical, not least because the devil's primary residence is in the details rather than the broad principles of investment allocation. Further, the state of research and the data available afford relatively few opportunities for truly meaningful application of mathematical modeling to many of the issues discussed here, and I do not believe that formalization that is then dismissed as approximate adds a great deal of value to such a discussion. I regret that the discursive approach I have adopted demands some patience: if what this book attempts to accomplish ever becomes clear to the reader, it will probably not do so until its final section.

The first section lays out an analytical toolkit that amounts to a way of thinking about any investment product, as well as some criteria by which commonality or distinctiveness among them can be discerned. Readers with a keen appreciation for nuance may find my approach reductionist, but I appeal to a comment from one of my university professors, who grouped cognitive styles into two camps—"splitters" and "lumpers." "Splitters" look for distinguishing features in whatever absorbs their attention, while "lumpers" seek a common thread that binds their experience together. Neither is a superior mode of thought, and there is considerable power in both approaches, although each is better- or worse-suited to some varieties of inquiry than others. The project of integrating all investment categories into a reasonably consistent allocation framework of necessity implies a cognitive bias toward finding commonality. But I endeavor nevertheless to pay due attention to important nuances, and to help assure this, Part II adopts something resembling a case study approach to examining various approaches to alternative investing.

Given the comments made above regarding the vagaries of alternative investment terminology, some discussion of examples is in any case probably unavoidable, to lend my discussion concreteness. The maxim that "concepts without percepts are empty, percepts without concepts are blind" applies to investing as well as to most other spheres, but especially where the received nomenclature threatens "emptiness" at every turn. So although this volume makes no attempt to offer a comprehensive guide to the vast array of alternative investment techniques that is available, its second part examines various investment approaches to illustrate the application of the analytic framework laid out in Part I. These chapters provide illustrations rather than proper case studies, in that they still deal generally with various investment approaches rather than examining specific vehicles and actual managers in the act of making "live" investment decisions. Because this portion of the book is not intended as a general guide, I have not included in it many of the metrics, such as maximum drawdown, and so on, that an institution actively engaged in a manager search would no doubt want to examine. By restricting the discussion to operational and more formal considerations, the examples discussed in Part II are meant to provide the "percepts" that I hope will give meaning to the "concepts" that are developed in the final two sections of the book.

My choice of examples is idiosyncratic, intended to provide interesting illustrations of the application of the analytic framework rather than to cover any prescribed portion of the investment universe. Inclusion in the set of examples does not imply any judgment of this or that investment technique's importance or value. Nor does exclusion imply that an investment category is unimportant or in any way flawed—it only indicates my failure to find anything useful to say about it in the context of what I am attempting to accomplish with these examples.

The order in which the examples are presented is not dictated by any internal logic or system of classification. Rather, Part II traces out what are, in effect, a couple of *tours d'horizon*, covering the alternative investment territory and then re-visiting it to examine it from different perspectives that are informed by an accumulating view of the whole. This is my attempt to deal with what Swensen calls the "complex simultaneity of the asset management process" (2000, 3; 2009, 4).[2] Although Swensen was writing about the specific problems of disentangling top-down from bottom-up influences on security selection in the context of choosing investment managers, his phrase can aptly be applied to the whole range of challenges that allocation among investment categories presents. Investment allocation is not a linear process, but involves complicated feedback loops and a certain circularity of logic that is easier to illustrate than to articulate. Part III attempts to draw these various strands of inquiry together and erect some generalizations about the material discussed in Part II.

Part IV is entitled "Portfolio Construction," because any title incorporating the term "theory" would be a misuse of too good a word for my attempts to build toward generality. What results is neither grand nor elegant, and although it should be of general application, it is more empirical than conceptual. Even inattentive readers will notice the lack of mathematics in what attempts to be a serious investment discussion—a confirmation, if one were needed, that this volume stops far short of theory in any formal sense. Although I hope to offer something more than just handy tips, cautionary advice, anecdotes, and a few rules of thumb, I do not pretend that my efforts make any great contribution to science. But the allocation of portfolio investments

---

2. I quote from Mr. Swensen in several places in this volume, and his publisher has requested that I provide the following acknowledgment: *Pioneering Portfolio Management: An Unconventional Approach to Institutional Investing* by David F. Swensen. Copyright © 2000, 2009 by David F. Swensen. Reprinted with permission of the Free Press, a division of Simon & Schuster, Inc. All rights reserved.

is first and foremost a practical activity, something that needs to be accomplished whether it has strong theoretical underpinnings or not. After all, the foundations of investment theory are barely fifty years old, but investment activity has gone on since time immemorial. If readers indulge me with their patience and come away from this volume with a clearer sense of how to approach the investment problems that it addresses, even though the problems are by no means definitively solved, then I will have achieved everything that I can reasonably hope to.

PART I

ANALYTIC TOOLS

CHAPTER 1

Risk and Return

The reader for whom this volume is intended is no doubt already thoroughly aware of the intimate relationship between risk and return, so there is no need to rehearse the usual clichés about the availability of free lunch, the obverse and reverse of coins, the relationship between timber growth and the sky, and so forth. The analyses found here rely on the premise that understanding the returns that investment vehicles produce means understanding the risks that they take. My contention that the palette of available return-generating risks is fundamentally the same for all investment vehicles, and that the risks are quite limited in number, informs my expectation that it will be possible to uncover some useful continuity of analysis between conventional and alternative investments.

This book seeks the common features that permit comparison and, ultimately, a rationally grounded approach to allocation among a range of investment opportunities that includes both conventional and alternative investments within its scope. In this endeavor, it is useful to draw a distinction between investment strategies, return enhancers, and volatility generators. Investment strategies are the fundamental sources from which investment returns derive—they are the risks that investment managers must take in order to generate any return at all. I have been able to identify only three of them, although they frequently operate in combinations that produce the wide variety of very differently structured return streams available to investors. This chapter will examine these investment strategies and the two quite distinct roles that time plays in the context of investment.

Return enhancers are applied to investment strategies in order to make their return streams more attractive, whether from a risk or a return perspective. Almost all of them involve risks of their own, as the most notable and common of them—leverage and tactical allocation or style rotation—certainly do. However, they do not themselves produce the returns that investors seek but rather accentuate the returns generated by one of the investment strategies (although this requires some footnoting in the case of tactical allocation). The strategies to which return enhancement techniques are applied provide the targeted returns, and in most cases one can regard return enhancers as overlays on those strategies.

Volatility generators are uses of investment assets for purposes other than generating return: they generally employ one of the investment strategies, but for the purpose of trading around its volatility rather than, or at least more than, for capturing those returns themselves. In fact, those who exploit volatility generators (typically investment banks) usually sell those underlying returns to other investors, retaining for their own purposes only the exposure to the tradable volatility that they provide. Return enhancers and volatility generators will be discussed in the following chapter.

The Three Sources of Investment Returns

There is a wild profusion of investment techniques, whether conventional or alternative—a thicket of investment styles that is an affront to tidy minds and an impediment to new initiates' understanding. It does not help that the nomenclature for distinguishing among them is shifting and unruly. However, just three investment strategies underlie the many approaches to investing; all investments derive their returns from one or—as often if not more frequently—a combination of them. As would be expected, each strategy represents a distinct risk. The interplay among them can be complex, and they sometimes appear in unexpected guises. Investment managers may even be unconscious of the fact that several distinct strategies contribute to their returns, and it may be difficult for analysis to determine precisely which strategy is contributing what to returns in any given market circumstance. The pursuit of just these strategies, sometimes amplified through the use of return enhancers, accounts for all the many different ways of confronting the challenges of investment.

The numerous investment styles and disciplines are, at bottom, different approaches to these strategies:

❑ *Directional strategies* purchase or sell short to capture anticipated price changes. Their trades may last seconds or years, and their exposure may be naked or partially hedged. However, any hedge used in conjunction with a directional trade cannot be a complete one, as the returns to this strategy derive from the transaction having at least some net exposure to price movements in the underlying asset or some other changeable factor such as volatility that can provide the source of such a return. A perfect hedge against a purely directional trade would result in no net investment exposure at all, only a loss due to transaction costs.

❑ *Cash flow strategies* seek returns from the ownership of cash-generating assets. In principle, these strategies are unconcerned with price changes in those assets, and in some circumstances may even achieve their owners' investment objectives without the asset ever being realized. The cash flows anticipated may be regular and specifiable in advance, or they may be intermittent and quite variable in size. These trades can, at least in principle, be perfectly hedged against price movement in the instruments employed while remaining productive of returns, although in most cases hedging is likely to sacrifice a sizable share of those returns.

❑ *Arbitrage strategies* exploit discrepancies between related prices, generally through pairing long and short exposure to the related instruments. They succeed whether the short position's price rises toward the long position's, the long falls toward the price of the short, or their prices meet anywhere in between. An arbitrage is market-neutral—fully hedged against price movements—provided that the relationship of counter-correlation between the legs of the trade is strong and persistent. Arbitrages are, in the final analysis, exposed to the price convergence of the legs of the trade rather than to the price movement of either leg separately.

It is impossible to prove a negative existential proposition of the form "No other investment strategy exists," so there is no way to guarantee the completeness of this list, but I know of no investment technique that cannot be reduced to these strategies, although occasionally doing so may require a little imagination. Based on this negative evidence, we can be fairly certain that the list is complete. However, as has become a truism, the belated discovery of black swans (*Cygnus atratus*, taxonomically described in 1790) indicates that negative empirical generalizations are vulnerable to counter-example. There are certainly other sources of return, such as engaging in games of chance, treasure-hunting with a metal detector, and (if all else fails) work. However, it is appropriate to respond to claims for any of them by employing terminological sleight-of-hand—that is, by simply refusing to regard them as investing activities. If they are not investments, then clearly they cannot deliver investment returns. Investment, according to this view, involves purchase or short sale of one or more assets to exploit its (their) economic characteristics. This might raise the question whether day-trading qualifies as a form of investment, but the fact that price volatility is an economic characteristic, too, ensures that it does.

Three strategies form a small toolkit, but as we will see in Part II of this volume, there is considerable nuance in each of them, and each can be applied quite flexibly whether alone or in combination. Further, they are not asset-specific, and in some cases each can be applied separately to the same asset in order to generate quite different sorts of return streams. Consider distressed debt—a periodically fashionable category of investment that is sometimes (but not exclusively) classified among alternative investments. Arbitrageurs may buy it and take a short position in some other portion of the issuer's capital structure against it, cash flow investors may hold it to maturity to capture its yield, and directional investors may hold it for some part of its life in the expectation that its credit rating and thus its price will improve: one asset, three investment strategies, and three quite different patterns of return generation. A wide range of assets may be profitably exploited using each of the three strategies.

Directional Strategies

The purest forms of directional strategies are cash purchase of long positions in physical commodities, collectibles, and equities that do not pay dividends. As it is usually unleveraged, venture capital may also qualify as similarly "pure." The returns on these investments consist of sale price less purchase price, commissions and storage, or custody costs.[1] The risk to them is an incorrect forecast of the price development of these assets, compounded, as is the case for all investments of any type, by a virtual and unquantifiable factor: opportunity cost. As opportunity

---

1. Note that even the "purest" forms of an investment strategy have a cash flow element to them, although it is a negative one. The only investment strategies that are truly "pure" are those not involving acquisition, storage or custody costs, such as keeping the gift of a few gold coins in a dresser drawer. But for the purposes of the discussion here, these negative cash flow elements can be ignored.

cost attaches to every investment except the single best-performing one in any given time period, I will not discuss it further here, but as it is such a universal feature of investment activity, I will return to it later in this volume.

A critical reader may grant physical commodities and collectibles but may object that the value of an equity (and venture capital) is derived from some form of discounting model. This implies that the analysis includes a cash flow element, if only virtual cash flows in the case of equities without earnings or dividends. In response to such an objection, there is clearly no point in denying the point that equity analysis generally does include some form of cash flow modeling. However, note that the actual returns on venture investments or equities that do not pay dividends, as opposed to their expected returns, do not depend on cash flows (virtual or otherwise) generated by the investment. In these cases, the return computation above is unaffected by in- or out-flows of investors' cash apart from those involved in the purchase and sale of the investments, so the return on investment is due solely to price change less costs.

That is, there is a real and potentially very powerful distinction between the *value* or expected return of such an investment and its *price*. Valuation involves discounting, but price is simply what the market delivers (or what can otherwise be negotiated) at any given moment. If price were always identical to value, there would be no opportunities for directional investment—or arbitrage, for that matter. The only possible investment strategy would be the pursuit of cash flow, and assets such as bullion, raw land, or rare postage stamps that do not distribute cash flows to investors could not be regarded as investments at all—thus Black (1976).

The purity of the strategy is reduced as soon as cash flow considerations enter the picture, regardless of whether the cash flow is positive or negative. Consequently, the use of leverage in any form adds an element of cash flow strategy to the investment mix. For example, short sales of any asset are directional strategies with a cash flow admixture, due to negative cash flow incurred in borrowing the assets to permit delivery. If put options or short futures positions are used to establish the short position, an examination of the relevant pricing formulae makes quite clear that there is an interest-rate element involved in those cases as well. Financing a short position that takes either form creates a drag on performance—a negative cash flow—and occasionally an acute one. For example, in the summer of 2008, when it was difficult to locate bank stocks to borrow for the purposes of delivery on short sales, borrowing rates in some cases exceeded 10 percent *per annum*, which is a hefty performance hurdle. By the fourth quarter of that year, the general availability of credit to hedge funds, for short sales or other purposes, was drying up significantly: see Pulliam and Strasburg (2009).

Ownership of dividend-producing equities quite explicitly includes a positive cash flow element, regardless of whether the dividends are regularly scheduled payments or special dividends that issuers occasionally volunteer or that are extracted from them through investor activism. Cash flows extracted from leveraged buyouts prior to their initial public offerings are another example. Fixed-income instruments purchased in anticipation of yield-curve or credit-rating changes offer an even more cash flow–oriented mixture of strategies. Raw land that has been purchased with cash and that remains undeveloped is a purely directional speculation (apart from the negative cash flows demanded by tax authorities), but returns on undeveloped real estate are unlikely to be compelling without the enhancements of leverage or improvement, which introduce negative cash flow elements. Note, however, that compelling returns on an investment in raw land can be achieved if someone other than its owner—say, a turnpike authority—plans to make those enhancements. The improvement, rather than its underwriter, generates any appreciable directional return on raw land. This wrinkle is the source of some extraordinary directional returns on what would otherwise be a rather unpromising investment category.

The risk to directional strategies is simply that the forecast price movement is not achieved, although this may occur for any of a thousand reasons, some of which may be quite complex and entirely unexpected. Analyzing the factors that might contribute to forecast failure is among directional traders' primary risk-control activities. While this may seem trivial, it further illustrates the distinction between price and value. There is no reason to research the source of directional trades' returns: it is known in advance to be price activity. The *causes* of that price activity give rise to the multimillion-dollar question, keep numerous analysts employed, and are by no means a simple matter.

Hedging a directional strategy does not fundamentally change the strategy, provided that the hedge is imperfect or partial. A perfectly, completely hedged directional strategy is, in effect, no strategy at all: since the returns on directional strategies derive from price exposure, completely vitiating the exposure hedges away the strategy. Imperfect hedges involve elements of arbitrage. The extent to which a short position in a Standard & Poor's 500 Index future hedges a position in an individual equity is a function of the volatilities of the equity and the index future as well as the relationship of correlation between their price movements. These relationships are subject to constant change, introducing a correlation risk that was not inherent in the original, unhedged directional trade. But partial (rather than imperfect) hedging need not entail arbitrage risk—buying individual-equity put options against a specific security position reduces potential exposure below the option's exercise price without adding any appreciable element of correlation risk. Note the qualifier: no *appreciable* risk, but there is a small amount of arbitrage risk nonetheless, as will be discussed below.

When they run into trouble, all investment strategies become directional, and their direction is never the desired one. Thus, if a loan becomes questionable, the value of the lender's asset plummets even if the lender continues to receive cash flow from it—an experience that has recently become all-too-familiar to holders of mortgages. If an arbitrage relationship weakens, then one or both legs of the trade are likely to move against the trader, and the resulting loss can be expected to be considerably greater than the gain that their convergence was forecast to generate when the trade was initiated. As we will see in the next chapter, when return enhancements go wrong, most of them also become unfortunate directional speculations.

Cash Flow Strategies

Cash purchase of bonds held to maturity is probably the most familiar form of cash flow investment. Although the bonds' price will fluctuate over the life of the investment, traditional wealth managers have a lot of practice assuring nervous clients that they can ignore that volatility because, barring default, the bond will return to par at maturity. Total return approaches to fixed-income are foreign to their clientele, not least because wealth managers have little incentive to inform them about them. Provided that they always purchase bonds at or below par and avoid fatal credit mishaps, they have a ready if somewhat specious reply to clients who are concerned about declines in the value of their accounts.

Real estate held for income rather than speculative resale also lends itself to cash flow strategies, as aristocrats have known for millennia. The Grosvenor estate, the most valuable portions of which came into his family in the seventeenth century, provides the current, sixth Duke of Westminster with the third-largest fortune in Britain as well as his title. Private equity held for income can also be an excellent cash flow generator. For example, S. C. Johnson & Son, should by rights be called

"S.C. Johnson & Great-Great-Grandson," while Mars has been closely held for four generations, producing what family members apparently consider satisfactory returns without any recourse to the proceeds that might be generated by exiting the position. Any asset that produces cash flow, from legal settlements and lottery proceeds to life insurance policies on third parties, is suitable for use in this investment strategy.

Use of leverage does not bring a "foreign" element into cash flow strategies—its cost just offsets a portion of their returns. As further exploration of the examples of both the Grosvenor estate and S.C. Johnson & Son would illustrate, borrowing may be in support of development, which will result in higher future cash flow returns if the additional investment proves to be well judged. However, where cash flow distributions are variable in size or in their timing, as in the case of many real assets that generate cash flows, excessive leverage can be quite risky. And the profitability of a trade in which funds are borrowed short-term to lend medium- to long-term is dependent on the persistence of a relationship between interest rates that is arbitrage-like. In effect these trades involve a short position in nearby maturities and a long position in distant maturities. This sort of trade is pursued routinely by banks and direct lending hedge funds and incorporates the risk that the arbitrage may collapse if financing costs rise, if the short-term financing cannot be renewed, or if returns on the loans that are made to third parties decline.

In contrast to assets employed in directional strategies, value and price are identical for assets with stable and predictable cash flows—assuming efficient markets for them. The credit crisis of 2007 to 2009 witnessed wide divergences between the prices and values of such assets, precisely because the disappearance of market liquidity rendered the market inefficient even for many good quality instruments of this type. I am aware of bonds that were quoted at 4000 basis-point bid/ask spreads and bonds that were priced within a 3500 basis-point range depending on which dealer was consulted. This created arbitrage opportunities that alternative investment vehicles, ranging from bond arbitrageurs to lever-aged buyout firms, were quick to exploit, to the extent that the restricted liquidity of the relevant markets permitted them to do so.

The risk to cash flow strategies is that the cash flows fail to meet return requirements. This may be due to underperformance by the asset—if, for example, targeted lease or occupancy levels are not obtained or corporate cash flow generation is not as great as anticipated—or due to default in the case of fixed income instruments or other types of loans. As suggested above, their yield-curve exposure is essentially a directional feature of bonds, but when paired with a mismatched liability, yield-curve exposure can become an arbitrage risk.

In almost all cases, assets suitable for use in cash flow strategies are also suitable for use in directional ones. The principal exceptions are variable-rate and other cash-like instruments, where value and price are even more likely to maintain their identity than they are for fixed-payment instruments. Their lack of directional risk is precisely what makes these instruments appealing as stores of value, as collateral for debt obligations and to risk-averse investors that have not been per-suaded to ignore fluctuations in the value of their principal, although various U.S. municipalities have discovered to their cost that even these instruments become directional when their default risk manifests itself.

It has been possible to hedge default risk through insurance ever since insurance began, and latterly it has become possible to hedge credit-market default risk through credit-default swaps and options on swaps. Unlike directional hedges, these instruments offer the possibil-ity of an at least theoretically perfect and complete hedge against issuer default, while in most cases leaving an investor with some cash flow, because swap prices relate to short-term interest rates. As an example, and making some sweeping assumptions on swap pricing, the investor swaps the returns on risky credit for Treasury returns, and consequently retains income, but at a much lower effective rate. However, if the origi-nal, risky credit position was financed or if the swap was purchased after the credit's quality had already deteriorated, the cost of the swap may eliminate return or even drive it into negative territory. Default cover-age on other cash flow–generating instruments may be negotiated, at considerable cost, with insurers.

Arbitrage Strategies

Arbitrages involve owning an asset and a complementary short position: acquirers with their targets, derivatives with their underlying, equity with its issuer's other securities, and so forth. Where the values of two assets are related to each other—whether they move in lockstep or are reliably out of step—but market forces have caused their pricing to depart from their theoretical relative values, arbitrage exploits the divergence in their prices. Note, once again, the distinction between "value" and "price." Arbitrage involves going long the asset that is valued too cheaply and selling short the asset that is too dear, and thus is reliant on a perception of where their values "should" be relative to each other. Because they hedge away any directional exposure to the assets' price changes, arbitrages succeed regardless of how the values converge—whether the cheap asset's price rises, the dear asset's price falls, or their prices converge somewhere in between, the return is the same.

Arbitrage is a finite or bounded trade in terms of its absolute returns and also in time. The return that can be extracted from it is a fixed-dollar amount that is known at the time that the trade is put on. Once the valuation gap that the arbitrage seeks to exploit is closed, there is no incremental return to be had from holding onto the positions that constitute the strategy; while occasionally such trades overshoot in the snap back to "fair value," this is neither something to be relied upon nor a source of much potential return, because the new value discrepancy that results will itself be arbitraged away. Once the point of "fair value" has been reached, the trade reverts to the market correlations of its components (if it is an imperfect arbitrage) and may begin to lose money due to the negative cash flow from financing the short sale. When full convergence is reached, the trade offers only interest expenses and the risk that the valuation gap will re-open. While the time that it will take for a valuation discrepancy to close is in many cases unpredictable, the time that an arbitrageur can wait for that to occur is known at the time the trade is put on, as it is a function of the potential return and the cost of financing the position.

In so-called riskless arbitrages,[2] the link between the instruments traded is systematic. Commodities and cross-listed equities offer riskless opportunities for locational arbitrage because they are fungible—gold is gold is gold, regardless of whether it is traded on the New York Mercantile Exchange or the London Metals Exchange, and American Depositary Receipts are nothing other than receipts for the underlying equity traded on a non-U.S. exchange. Derivatives and American Depository Receipts offer riskless arbitrages with their underlying because they convert into them. Barring a major dislocation, such as the failure of a central counterparty or depositary, the correlation between the value of a derivative and its underlying is fixed at identity (1.0000 or,

---

2. There is no such thing as a riskless trade. These arbitrages earn that description because there is essentially no risk that the trade's return driver—the correlation between the two assets—will fail the trader. In fact, these trades carry significant risk, but it is operational rather than economic. What keeps such arbitrageurs awake at night is worry about the failure of one leg of their trade: if one of their orders is not filled or is only partially filled, they find themselves with naked and highly leveraged directional exposure. If trade reporting is slow, or if the liquidity needed to reverse their trade(s) has meanwhile disappeared, they will be in this unhappy condition far longer than they would like to be.

where the derivative and its underlying counter-correlate, −1.0000). As would be expected from their description as "riskless," these trades offer low returns and are generally not worth pursuing unless they can be very substantially leveraged. Consequently, participation in these trades is largely restricted to firms with exchange memberships. Their minimal transaction costs and access to abundant and cheap clearing credit make the trades attractive for these firms to pursue although they generate returns of only pennies on tens of thousands of dollars of capital committed.

Merger arbitrage is often called risk arbitrage because the counter-correlations it exploits are neither fixed nor as low as −1.0000. By bidding for the target, an acquirer establishes a relationship based on fungibility between its share price[3] and that of its target, which is defined by the terms of its bid. The arbitrage opportunity the acquirer thus creates has the risk that the assets will not remain complementary—that the proposed merger will collapse and the counter-correlation between the bidder's share price and the position in the target's share price created by the merger announcement will disappear. Over the course of the acquisition process, the price divergence will narrow or widen depending on the market's perception of the likelihood and timing of completion or the possibility that the acquirer will have to increase its bid. Not surprisingly, merger arbitrageurs tend to be connoisseurs of competition regulation and other noninvestment disciplines that can determine the success or failure of a proposed acquisition, as these are among the causes of the less-than-perfect counter-correlation that is the source of their risk and their returns.

Statistical arbitrages[4] rely on observed correlations between different assets, for which the link is neither systematic nor artificially created through merger activity. In the summer of 2008, just about everyone believed that oil and the U.S. dollar exchange rate counter-correlate.

---

3. "Classic" merger arbitrage is a pair trade between the equities of the bidder and its target, but if the target carries a lower credit rating than the bidder, or if completion of the transaction will result in a downward revision of the credit rating on the target's debt, an arbitrage between their publicly traded debt may also open up, and there are investors who exploit such opportunities.

4. Confusingly, this term is also used for a pair-trading technique employing only roughly correlated equities, primarily practiced by investment banks' trading desks (see Bookstaber (2007), p. 184 and following). It is also sometimes used to describe market-neutral strategies. In these cases, the trade is more properly regarded as a hedged transaction than a true arbitrage. Chapter 2 will discuss this rather fine distinction.

It was such generally received wisdom that one of that year's presidential candidates mentioned it as though it were a matter of fixed economic truth. This is the type of relationship that a statistical arbitrageur exploits. But the history of the relationship between oil and the dollar, as illustrated in **Figure 1.1**, indicates that the price correlation between them has been quite unstable and often not very significant. Although the aggregate statistic for the period shown there, at −0.0603, indicates marginal counter-correlation, it is hardly of very great significance. Their correlation reached a negative extreme in the third quarter of 2008, but it recovered sharply from there to the bottom of its apparently normal range. It remains to be seen whether it has permanently readjusted or will return to the range it has historically occupied. Statistical arbitrage entails the risk that the correlations it seeks to exploit could, as this one may, turn out to be transitory or even specious. Figure 1.1 shows that even well-established relationships between price series are subject to dramatic change, indicating that this risk is always present where causation cannot be conclusively demonstrated. Arguably, extremely high oil prices *do* have a causal relationship with the dollar's value, but that cannot explain the continued strength of the counter-correlation between them after oil prices began to drop sharply in July, 2008. Correlation is easy to data-mine, but not always easy to explain.

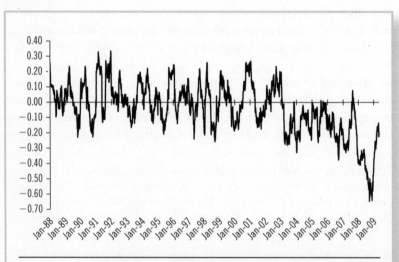

FIGURE 1.1   *The Dollar and Oil: 90-Day Trailing Coefficient of Correlation: ICE Dollar Index, Bloomberg WTI Cushing Spot Crude Oil*

Source: Interncontinental Exchange, Bloomberg Finance L.P.

The risk to arbitrage strategies is precisely this sort of reversal—that the correlation upon which the trade relies for its returns fails to persist for the life of the trade. Arbitrages are regarded as riskless when this cannot happen for economic reasons and the only danger that the riskless relationship could break down is due to the irreducible risk of systemic failure of some sort. In merger arbitrage, correlation failure occurs when a deal collapses, for instance, because the acquirer's or target's shareholders successfully oppose it. In statistical arbitrage, correlation failure may happen for any number of reasons, not the least of which is that the correlation may have been a specious artifact of data-mining in the first place—an accident of statistics—rather than a relationship grounded in economic reality. As with cash flow trades, when arbitrages collapse, they become unfortunate directional speculations, and because arbitrage is in almost all cases fairly highly leveraged, the results are often considerably worse than just "unfortunate."

Academic discussions of finance make frequent reference to arbitrage, where it often serves as a sort of *deus ex machina* to save theory from inconvenient empirical observations. How often do we read that this or that counter-example derived from actual market behavior is "an anomaly that will be arbitraged away"? In fact, this never happens except by mistake. Arbitrage may reduce anomalies, but it cannot both make them completely disappear and still be a profitable activity. Arbitrageurs who close a valuation gap completely find themselves with positions that offer few attractions to other traders and can close out their positions only by giving up some of what they have gained. Arbitrageurs who intend to remain in business for any length of time always leave something on the table. Arbitrage is a commercial activity like any other, carried out for return-seeking purposes rather than to lend elegance to a theoretical model. If practitioners believe that the returns offered by a potential arbitrage trade are inadequate, the trade will not get done, even if theory demands it. This accounts for the stubborn persistence of pricing anomalies that academics contend that arbitrageurs should eliminate, as I will discuss below.

Time, Return, and Risk

Returns are measured over time. If someone offers to double our money, before jumping at the chance we should ask, "Over what period?" If the answer is a day, then the return on the investment would be so extraordinary—3.76×10^{109}% over a 365-day year—that we should immediately be suspicious and probably should call the police. If the answer is fifty years, we can ignore the offer: during our lifetimes, a 1.4 percent *per annum* return has not been much to get very excited about.

Investors with actuarial issues, such as pension funds, must be able to estimate returns in order to determine their future funding requirements. If they invest in private equity (as many of them do), this presents them with some significant challenges. Internal rates of return are freely bandied about by private equity firms, but in instruments with lives of ten years or more, their value as an investment metric is questionable. A high internal rate of return achieved from an investment held only briefly represents an enormous loss of opportunity for such a fund's Limited Partners. Examination of **Figure 1.2** indicates that a 20 percent return over ten years is much more attractive to long-term investors than a 100 percent return in one year, unless a new, high-return investment can reliably and immediately be found to replace the investment that was returned to them along with its 100 percent profit. Reinvestment risk and the costs of carrying out new manager searches are fairly certain to offset much of the good fortune of achieving an extraordinary return in the short -term.

The role of time as the denominator of returns affects all investments, and it is highly erosive, as anyone who is conversant with any form of discounting model is quite aware. Parts of the next chapter discuss ways

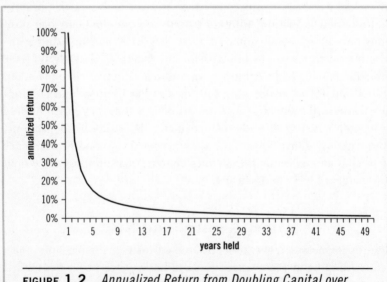

FIGURE 1.2 *Annualized Return from Doubling Capital over Different Holding Periods*

that investment managers attempt to reduce this denominator. The erosive effects of time are magnified for investments that are leveraged or when other forms of borrowing are involved, as in short selling. Financing costs compound, and over time they can erect a significant performance hurdle. For less rich trades, such as perfect arbitrages, they are often the primary determinant of whether the trade is worth pursuing at all. Long-term investments such as leveraged buyouts and leveraged real estate investment, which make substantial use of borrowed funds, rely on cash extraction from their assets, the tax efficiencies of debt and the limited partnership structure, and, ultimately, high exit multiples to overcome this hurdle. Long-term investors in these sorts of assets who do not foresee an exit as a contributor to their returns, such as the Mars or Grosvenor families, tend to leverage them much less highly than directional investors do.

At the extremes, investment time horizon dictates strategy. Over very short time horizons—the seconds or minutes over which some hedge funds and many CTAs operate—cash flow strategies are out of the question. If these traders receive a distribution or capture any positive roll yield, it is probably by accident rather than design. Over horizons of five years or more, receiving cash flows from the investment in the interim between purchase and liquidation is in most cases essential to the economics of the trade. In this respect as in many others, venture capital investing is the high-risk exception.

An anomaly that has attracted considerable comment and lured not a few investors into quixotic efforts to exploit it is the discount at which Italian savings shares trade relative to the common shares of the same issuer. This should be a riskless arbitrage, and an unusually rich and liquid one, that virtually cries out for exploitation. For 57 percent of the observations shown in **Figure 1.3**, the valuation gap between these instruments was greater than 20 percent, and at its richest it reached 58 percent. So the failure of arbitrageurs to trade it away is a major irritant to academics, who cannot tolerate anomalies unless they are small enough to be ascribed to market friction (that is, ignored). There is certainly market friction in this trade—Fiat's savings shares' daily liquidity averaged just 11.3 percent of that of its common shares for the period shown—but that is not sufficient to account for such an enormous and persistent premium in the common stock relative to the savings shares. However, it would be unfair to single out academics for criticism in this instance, since numerous practitioners, who ought to have foreseen the risk, have been enticed by its illusory attractions into what is, in fact, a classic value trap.

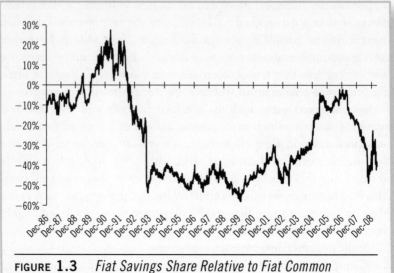

Source: Bloomberg Finance L.P.

FIGURE 1.3   *Fiat Savings Share Relative to Fiat Common*

The problem with this trade is time. As there is no conversion feature attached to the savings shares, there is nothing to catalyze price convergence, as there is for derivative or merger arbitrage trades. Although Figure 1.3 clearly indicates that the prices of regular and savings shares *can* converge, there is no force acting on the shares' prices other than the activities of arbitrageurs themselves that would cause them to do so. Too aggressive an attempt to bring about convergence would (1) probably constitute illegal market manipulation, and (2) leave the arbitrageur with a position that would be impossible to unwind without giving back essentially all the gains achieved. The short leg of an arbitrage requires financing and consequently has negative cash flow that eats steadily into return until the trade is closed out, so holding onto the position indefinitely in the entirely understandable expectation that the valuation gap will one day close is not an economically viable option. Despite academic cheerleading and some not inconsiderable periods of profitability, putting on a convergence trade in Italian savings shares has mostly proven to be an excellent way to lose money.

There are other commercial aspects to the arbitrage business that academic research tends to neglect, including the costs of information gathering and the value of traders' time. For example, there are riskless arbitrage opportunities among cross-listings of shares on different exchanges. On exchanges where the cross-listing rarely trades, the opportunities can sometimes be very rich, usually due to neglect on the part of the cross-listing's assigned market maker. But this does not happen often enough to make trolling through the price feeds from obscure exchanges a good use of traders' time, and obtaining the necessary price feeds is costly. Most of the time this sort of mispricing is likely to persist until the market makers notice and correct their error. Traders who engage in arbitrage of cross-listings restrict all but a very small fraction of their attention to liquid cross-listings that offer continual, but much less rich, opportunities to trade.

Timing

Chapter 3 will discuss the relationship between volatility and compounding, which provides one of the foundations for portfolio theory by explaining why investors should shun volatility. But quite apart from holding periods, time enters into investment thinking in another very important way. The timing of a trade is not itself an investment strategy in the sense I have laid out, but it is a fundamental driver of the returns that most strategies will achieve. To paraphrase Gloucester in *King Lear*, "a trade may rot" if it remains unproductive for too long, to which Edgar replies, "Ripeness is all." Given the arithmetic of percentages, a trade that is perfectly timed will capture the maximum performance offered by the opportunity it is designed to exploit. This is obvious in the case of directional trades, but Figure 1.3 shows that it is equally true of arbitrages. Timing also affects cash flow strategies, but somewhat less markedly, because their returns are not entirely derived from the price movements that occur between purchase and sale. For cash flow investments where price and value are (or should be) identical, such as floating rate notes, timing risk is at a minimum, approaching but not quite reaching immateriality, because the rates offered by such instruments are reset periodically rather than adjusted continuously.

Time horizon does little to alter the importance of timing to returns—it is just as possible to make dreadful mistakes over ten years as it is over a period of as many seconds. Long-term directional investments that permit active management of the asset subsequent to its purchase (real estate, private equity, and a wide variety of real assets) allow their managers some opportunity to offset (or at least obfuscate) timing errors through improvements in cash flow generation and better timing at the exit. But their returns are ultimately no less affected by unfortunate transaction timing. The ability that active management offers to reduce the magnitude of these errors through postacquisition management may in practice create considerable moral hazard, if it encourages investors to pay less than appropriate attention to considerations of value at the time of purchase.

Because timing can drive returns, it is a risk. While academics and practitioners have devoted an enormous amount of attention to risk reduction through diversification of positions, relatively little has been written about temporal diversification. Even time-honored practices such as bond laddering and dollar-cost averaging have received only modest amounts of formal analysis. A partial exception is offered by the private equity and venture area, where investors became acutely aware of the need for vintage diversification after the collapse of the Technology Bubble, and my discussions with people in the real estate industry suggest that vintage is becoming more of a concern to investors in that investment category, too.

But perhaps this neglect of temporal diversification is not really so surprising. Time is stubbornly resistant to analysis—as St. Augustine wrote, "If no one asks me, I know what time is. If someone asks, I know not." At bottom, the result of what little thinking of which I am aware about the role of temporal risk in investing boils down to two frequently repeated cautions:

❑ Where investment is "lumpy"—that is, where large commitments are demanded over discrete time periods, as in private equity—it should be made according to a schedule. This will generally involve continuously repeated periodic commitments to diversify exposure to the market conditions prevailing at any given time of entry or exit; and

❑ Avoid market-timing: rather than complete exit from a market segment that is out of favor, investors should maintain some level of residual exposure to capture the maximum return from that segment, if there is any reason to believe that it will eventually recover. In keeping with this maxim, formal limits on minimum sectoral exposure are a common risk-management tool in conventional equity and fixed income investment.

Neither piece of advice embodies any extraordinary investment insight, and in fact closer analysis shows that they are essentially the same piece of advice and that they represent two sides of the familiar justifications for dollar-cost averaging. But it is hardly news that these admonitions are regularly, even routinely ignored. Private equity and venture firms despair over the failure of investment policymakers to adopt (and stick with) disciplined plans of vintage diversification, while the constant temptation to override minimum exposure levels is familiar to every manager that operates within such constraints.

Hedge funds, CTAs, and a vocal minority of conventional managers glory in their refusal to hug benchmarks—a freedom that renders it impossible for them to set minimum exposure limits. They argue that, because timing imposes risk it offers returns: the risk should not be avoided if it can be exploited successfully. And the risk is worth taking because the arithmetic of percentages offers the largest slice of the performance pie to those who enter a trade at precisely the right moment. But there is the rub: exploiting timing on a consistent basis is very difficult to do, and timing errors can be extremely costly. Many of the most successful market-timers use technical and momentum indicators, often embodied in trading algorithms and implemented by computers, to avoid the entry of cognitive biases into timing-related transaction decisions. Chapters 8, 16, and 18 will discuss related matters in more detail.

Effective or not, market-timers pose an enormous quandary for those who must determine investment policy. While slavish attention to "Style Box" categories attracts ample criticism, such slavishness at least helps organize and limit an investment committee's task. And it offers not unreasonable assurance of some level of performance consistency within any segment of the Box. Managers who flout its disciplines are difficult for investment policymakers to incorporate into their thinking. They are idiosyncratic and neither amenable to analysis as a group nor easily placed in the context of more disciplined (the managers themselves would argue, "blinkered") approaches to investing even in the same asset class. The difficulties of deciding whether and where in a portfolio to place these vehicles and those of other practitioners of investment techniques that depend on timing, recur throughout this volume.

CHAPTER 2

Return Enhancement

A n investment strategy's returns can be improved upon in various ways, and many investment techniques need the boost. Where unassisted returns are low, as in riskless arbitrages, leverage is required or the trade is simply not worth the trouble and risk of pursuing. Use of hedges can change a strategy's risk characteristics, often in ways that make an otherwise excessively speculative strategy a tolerable risk, and may also provide investors with a source of leverage. Deliberate use of illiquid instruments in directional and cash flow strategies can exploit the illiquidity discount attached to certain instruments as a way of increasing the returns of the primary investment technique.

Tactical allocation and investor activism do not alter the characteristics of an investment technique. Tactical allocation seeks to boost returns through timing of exposure to different techniques, while activism seeks to accelerate the occurrence of an event that will crystallize a gain. Four of these techniques involve investment risks of their own. Of the return enhancers discussed here, only activism is risk-neutral, although it may entail a risk to the reputation of the investment manager who applies it, may create moral hazard, and in fact does usually involve some monetary costs. But there are some return enhancers that will not be discussed here, such as call-writing and other forms of securities hypothecation that, while not exactly free of risk (ask anyone who used Lehman Brothers as a prime broker in London), may or may not entail investment risks.

Volatility generators are strategies employed for their ability to create trading opportunities rather than for the returns that the strategy might generate. Their inclusion in this chapter is somewhat parenthetical, but the digression explores some themes to which later chapters will return.

Leverage

Borrowing allows us to acquire more of something than we could otherwise afford. In most cases, leveraging an investment serves no other purpose than this. Buying more does not affect the investment's returns—0.7 percent is 0.7 percent whether it is on $1,000 or on $10 million—but it magnifies the return on investors' own capital. Neglecting borrowing costs, if they participate in the trade with, say, twenty times their own capital commitment, they still receive a 0.7 percent return on their aggregate exposure, but with 20:1 leverage (i.e., 95.2 percent debt financing) they enjoy or suffer a 14 percent change in the value of the capital they commit.

None of which should come as startling news, but it is worth rehearsing in order to emphasize that leverage is not an investment strategy in the sense outlined in the previous chapter. The return on the investment strategy to which leverage is applied is generated in the same way and is the product of the same market forces whether the trade is leveraged or not. Borrowing is an overlay on an investment strategy rather than a strategy in itself, but for trades that do not offer substantial returns, it is often the enabler that makes it interesting to pursue the investment at all. Leverage does not alter the nature of the risk being taken by choosing to make this or that particular investment, but because it changes the potential return, it changes the magnitude of that risk to the investor proportionately. And it contributes some risks of its own.

Leverage is the mirror image of a cash flow investment strategy. When we are paying rather than receiving interest, the "magic" of compound interest is black magic. No one borrows for the untrammeled pleasure of being in debt, and if borrowing per se were an investment strategy, it would reliably end in tears. Investors tolerate its cost and the additional risks it entails for the opportunity to gain greater exposure to an investment strategy. The risk that leverage itself contributes to the transaction—independent of what it does to the risk of the underlying strategy—is due to the time denominator of returns. Interest charges of, say, 3 percent per annum for our 20:1 leveraged trade would completely absorb its 0.7 percent return in eighty-nine days, putting a definite, fixed limit on the profitable duration of the leveraged investment that follows from the fixed return I ascribed to it in the first place.

For many investments, the potential return cannot be predicted so precisely, but leverage always imposes a limit on the longevity of directional or arbitrage strategies, which is a function of the cost of leverage and the return that can be expected from the trade. For cash flow strategies, if the cost of leverage is lower than the anticipated cash flow distributions, then leverage need not impose a time limit on the trade's profitability. Where cash flows are regular, reliably specifiable in advance, and larger than borrowing costs, they in effect hedge away the longevity risk created by leverage. I am aware of a fund that, for tax and regulatory reasons, must be more leveraged than its manager actually wishes to be. To address the problem, part of the portfolio is held in floating rate notes, which effectively hedge or defease the (changeable) portion of its borrowing (which is floating rate and generally lower cost than the notes) that the manager believes to be excessive. Magnified returns still imply magnified losses if the leveraged cash flow asset fails to deliver the anticipated cash flows, but the leverage does not limit the trade's time horizon unless borrowing costs change and begin to exceed income.

However, if the cash flows from the investment are irregular in their timing or amount, leverage adds a timing risk that is otherwise absent from such trades. In these cases, timing not only affects initial purchase or final sale decisions regarding the position but may compel sale or forfeiture of the investment in the interim because of the uneven match between cash flow receipts and obligations. This is an inherent drawback to leverage in such circumstances that can be mitigated only by leveraging conservatively relative to the minimum expected cash flow distribution, or not at all.

Where holding periods are lengthy and the General Partner who is managing the investment controls its capital structure, the return-enhancing contribution of leverage goes beyond just its role in magnifying the return on capital committed. It may then include the tax efficiency of debt and also the contribution that indebtedness makes to management discipline in the target investment. Leverage in a corporate financing context has elements of capital structure arbitrage, so it introduces the correlation risk associated with all arbitrages. The parts of the structure may not work together as intended. Cerberus seems to have experienced something of the sort with its Chrysler investment—a "one damned thing after another" proliferation of tangentially connected financial difficulties arising from a highly complex balance sheet that included leases as both assets and liabilities and a near-endless variety of debt covenants.

Leverage can be raised in any number of ways. Hedge funds for the most part rely on credit from their prime brokers and the leverage that is embedded in the instruments they employ—be they futures, options, short sales, or what-have-you. Investors in longer-tail assets may use collateral-based financing such as leases or mortgages, as well as bank credit lines and privately placed or publicly traded bonds. In the commercial mortgage area, relatively short-term (five-year) balloon structures are common, reducing payments relative to lease receipts at the cost of significant refinancing risk. Early stage venture capital is not usually leveraged, but in a later stage—when an IPO is fairly realistically within sight—the firms (as opposed to the investment funds that control them) may have recourse to mezzanine finance. This is usually in the form of hybrid debt instruments with warrants attached.

Leverage enters into investment activities in other ways than as a return enhancer. When it does so, in all but the case of cash flow strategies with regular and fixed distributions, it contributes an element of additional trade longevity or cash flow timing risk to the trade. Acquiring short exposure always involves leverage—explicitly if securities are borrowed to effect delivery and implicitly if derivatives are employed (recall that interest rates and remaining time to expiry feature in the pricing formulae for derivatives of all types). Although it is seldom commented upon, securities lending is a significant source of credit to the economy: one estimate places its contribution at 6 percent of outstanding U.S. credit in 2008 (see Bridgewater Associates 2009, p. 1). Making use of the leverage obtained in this way can be a significant risk, as many investors discovered in the summer of 2007. Funds raised through short sales were used to acquire additional long exposure, and when, in a general market downdraft, the equities held short outperformed the equities in which these managers were long, short squeezes developed, and some very messy forced liquidation ensued. Several hedge funds and 130/30 vehicles were forced out of business as a result.[1]

---

1. The problem was exacerbated by the high degree of overlapping exposure among many funds managed along low frequency quantitative lines, which crowded the exits simultaneously when forced to liquidate their holdings to cover their shorts. According to Rothman (2008), 38 percent each of both the long and short exposure of a sample of these funds was identical. Detailed analysis of this episode can be found in Lo (2008) Chapter 10 and Daniel (2009), but naïve quantitative managers seem to have drawn few lessons from it, at least in the twelve months immediately following (see Madigan 2008), and many trades favored by such managers remained heavily overcrowded.

Where derivatives are used to create short positions, as in "portable α" techniques, they create so-called notional leverage, which can be extremely deceptive to quantitative analysis, to which it is largely opaque. An optimizer will net this exposure against what it is being used to hedge, but can take no account of the fact that correlation between the underlying positions, and their respective standard deviations, may not turn out to be as expected. In that case "merely notional" leverage can manifest itself as very real and much greater than superficial analysis might have suggested, with disastrous results. As Dorsey (2007) notes,

> While cash leverage enables the purchase of a greater amount of an investment, notional leverage represents the embedded price multiplier for an underlying security. As such, notional leverage can be associated with potentially greater volatility than cash leverage. Notional leverage also may not be as readily apparent as cash leverage. (211)

Quantitative analyses' tendency to overlook this source of leverage is behind many of the largest accidents that corporations and others have experienced with their hedging programs. This was particularly the case in the early days of structured derivative products, accounting for a number of high profile losses by Bankers Trust's clients, the liability risk from which ultimately forced it to seek a buyer, but the risk remains and continues to be underappreciated.

Hedging

Hedging has become a portmanteau term—a concept that has gradually been made to carry so much freight that it has become very difficult to unpack. A hedge is a position that is put on to offset the volatility of another. This can lead to equivocation over which is the position and which is the hedge. Human nature being what it is, managers sometimes claim that the successful legs of hedged trades were invariably the investment positions, reflecting their sagacity, while the losses on the other legs of the trades "just reflected unavoidable hedging costs."

There are services that overlay hedging strategies on portfolios that are managed by a separate firm from that which manages the portfolio itself. They are found most frequently in the international investment arena, where currency overlay is a reasonably well-established product niche. The manager of the overlay receives the geographic exposures from the manager of the underlying portfolio and trades currencies around them. Given the commercial imperative for any investment manager to add value, the equivocation between hedge and return-seeking trades is perhaps strongest in the case of this sort of overlay. Although their purpose is not primarily to hedge, "portable α" services may be offered through similar structures.

Because the effectiveness of a hedge relies on the counter-correlation between its price and that of the position that is being hedged, there is an arbitrage element to the activity of hedging. Consequently, unless the hedge is perfect—that is, involves a riskless arbitrage—the activity of hedging introduces the risk to a portfolio that the counter-correlation will disappear, or at any rate become less negative. When a riskless arbitrage collapses, the results can be dramatic, as the experience of October 19, 1987, suggests. In the overwhelming flood of trading volume that accompanied the Crash, option pricing became disconnected from the price of the underlying equities due to the different execution speeds in the option pits compared to the equity markets. As I recall, at one juncture the Consolidated Tape was delayed four and a half hours, while option markets continued to trade more or less in real time. Hedgers using Δ-hedges (dynamic option strategies) for the purpose of "portfolio insurance" exacerbated an already ugly situation. A useful summary account of this episode can be found in Bookstaber (1999, 11–12), and is elaborated with considerable anecdote in Bookstaber (2007) Chapter 2. For a more formal discussion of what occurred in connection with option pricing on October 19, 1987, see Wilmott (1998) Chapter 29.

The "classic" hedge matches a short position to a long position, but long-only hedges are also possible, such as the hedge achieved by holding a long position in an airline's equity to offset the price behavior of a long position in an oil producer's. Looking through the trade to the fundamentals of its component legs reveals the same long/short structure, however, as an airline is operationally short what an oil producer is operationally long. A barbell structure in bonds (concentrating holdings at the near and distant maturity ends of the yield curve while under-weighting exposure in the middle) provides an effective hedge against duration-induced volatility, but can be understood as a hedge only with reference to a benchmark: relative to the benchmark, the structure is long the long and short ends of the yield curve and short the middle. These examples of long-only hedges raise the question of how much of a distinction there is between hedging and diversification.

Diversification is often caricatured in "eggs in one basket" terms, but the idea goes deeper than simply reducing risk by increasing the denominator over which it is spread. It is rare for security price movements to be completely independent of each other, and the extent to which they correlate or counter-correlate with each other is an important consideration in portfolio construction. That is, diversification can reduce the numerator as well. In a naïve implementation of Modern Portfolio Theory, correlations and forecast returns are in fact the *only* considerations of portfolio construction. At its foundation, a diversified portfolio is an arbitrage, although typically a long-only one. Does this mean that we should regard diversification as a hedging trade?

In important respects, diversification should be regarded as such, which explains why the portmanteau is so heavily packed, to the point that the term "hedge" threatens to burst a seam and lose any specific content. To rein in a concept that is in danger of becoming completely amorphous, it is useful to emphasize a distinction between trades that are return-seeking and those that are risk-avoiding, however weak the distinction and however easy it is to equivocate between them. Thus, a trade for which a successful outcome could equally be a gain or a loss is a hedge, while a trade that is said to fail because it generates less than its required return is return-seeking. Thus, what qualifies as a hedge is a matter of the trader's intentions, not a property inherent in the investment itself. This preserves at least a minor distinction between hedging and diversification. The managers of diversified portfolios generally choose each position in anticipation that it will contribute to return, and overlay diversification requirements as a risk control measure. According to this distinction, then, they are not hedgers.

Hedging may be a tactical maneuver, or it may be inherent to the pursuit of an investment strategy. Many hedgers are occasional, opportunistic, and unsystematic—when they identify a risk of sufficient magnitude, they may or may not choose to hedge it. Others, such as equity market-neutral hedge funds, are quite systematic in their approach to hedging, maintaining to the extent possible a constant and fixed hedge ratio against their β exposure and often against other risk factors (sector exposure, etc.) as well. Arbitrage is, by definition, a consistently hedged trade. A minority of international equity managers hedges currency exposure consistently, but most are opportunists if they engage in currency hedging at all.

The fact that hedging is essential to arbitrage does not, in my opinion, detract from the status of hedging as a return enhancer rather than a strategy in itself. In principle, the valuation discrepancies that give rise to arbitrages could be exploited through unhedged directional trades—provided that the trader has reliable forecasts of which leg of the trade will rise or fall. By hedging, an arbitrageur obviates any need for such forecasts and also obtains higher returns in the (frequent) circumstance that both legs of the arbitrage, rather than just one of them, move toward convergence. In arbitrage, equivocation between risk-avoidance and return-seeking is probably unavoidable, but provided that the trader's intention to exploit convergence in the prices of related assets is explicit, in the case of arbitrage equivocation is unlikely to lead to confusion. Arbitrageurs generally regard their trades as aggregated structures of their long and short positions and will often refer to the two-legged structures they create as a single trade.

The failure to recognize that a hedge is a trade in its own right, and thus has risks associated with it, is the root of many spectacular corporate accidents—spectacular because in most cases they seem to have come as bolts out of the blue. This occurs because hedges frequently have a leveraging function, and it is not uncommon for their users to neglect this notional leverage or to equivocate between their hedges' risk reduction and financing roles. This failure seems to lie behind the demise of Long-Term Capital Management. A more subtle instance was the collapse of the German energy and materials conglomerate Metallgesellschaft in 1993. One of its U.S. subsidiaries, Metallgesellschaft Refining and Marketing, hedged its effective long-term short position using Over-the-Counter swaps and by rolling ("stacking") futures. This strategy was successful as long as oil was in backwardation (i.e., prices were higher for the front month than subsequent months) but encountered difficulties when the market became contangoed (the front month became cheaper than later months). The subsidiary was unable to meet the resulting margin calls, and its bankruptcy brought down its parent, too.

Some—most notably Merton Miller—have contended that given sufficient time and access to credit, Metallgesellschaft's trade would ultimately have been successful (see the summary of various debates over Metallgesellschaft in Krapels 2001). But their case relies on the highly debatable contention that backwardation is the "natural" state of futures markets. And in any event that "given" is a huge one, as John Maynard Keynes' witticism about our long-run mortality would suggest. In a world where margin calls have to be met, where credit is not infinitely available, and where losses of $1.75 billion cannot simply be ignored, claims about the theoretical long run are beside the point. The hedge rested on assumptions about the behavior of futures contracts that proved faulty, or at any rate vulnerable to exceptions, and the management of Metallgesellschaft apparently had such faith in its subsidiary's risk management capabilities that it was willing to take enormous exposures (154 million barrels equivalent in September, 1993) based upon them.

Or perhaps not: as is usual in these cases and regardless of plausibility, when called to account, Metallgesellschaft's management claimed to have been unaware of the risk and blamed the fiasco on its traders. Readers are invited to decide for themselves, although I believe that it is probably a relevant datum that the firm's 1881 Articles of Incorporation specified commodity trading as one of its principal activities.

Hedges may counter-correlate continuously with the position hedged, or their counter-correlation can be variable and nonlinear but will offset the risk of the position hedged over the life of the trade. If the hedges are financed, those with variable correlation entail a significant risk from margin calls. The opposite situation—where an effective short-term hedge becomes progressively less effective as the holding period increases—also occurs. Short-exposure Exchange-Traded Funds correlate fairly precisely to the inverse of their underlying indices on a day-to-day basis, but over longer periods compounding effects on their returns cause their counter-correlation to the positions they would seem to hedge to decrease. These instruments re-base daily to the index, causing their volatility to influence their compounding over periods of numerous days, a phenomenon that will be discussed in the next chapter. Prospective hedgers who are not completely clear about the nature of the correlation risk that they are taking should become so before they proceed—unintended consequences are far from uncommon in this area, and notional leverage can magnify them disastrously.

This risk can manifest itself in unanticipated ways. For example, many investment vehicles make use of index products—be they futures, options, or Exchange-Traded Funds—to reduce the market risk (β) of directional strategies. Their intention is usually to isolate the excess return (α) generated by their security selection from the influence of general market movements. In most circumstances this technique works well. But recall that a directional strategy becomes no strategy at all—simply a source of transaction costs and interest charges—if its exposure to price movements is completely hedged. In a strongly declining market,[2] correlations tend to collapse (in the common wisdom, "correlations go to one," and "in a crash the only thing that goes up is correlation"), so all or close to all of the α in the trade may have been sold short. The phenomenon of market-wide correlations coalescing on identity—what Lo (2008) calls

2. The effect can be symmetrical. In strongly rising markets, event-driven trades often tend to underperform, because they offer a finite, specifiable return based on the "event" rather than general market correlation. Consequently, in these conditions the short position may over-hedge the long one.

"phase-locking behavior" (18)—first came to the fore in the Crash of 1987. Although there has been a certain amount of debate over whether this is a consistent phenomenon, I believe that Campbell et al. (2002) have put that debate definitively to rest. The October 17, 1987, data point was so extreme that it significantly distorted all volatility statistics and thus all correlation series that did not remove it as an outlier for years thereafter.

It is worth noting that the economics of hedging for an investment bank's or other securities firm's trading desks are diametrically opposed to what they are for institutional investors. For a "sell-side" trading desk, the *long* positions require financing, while the short positions that generate "carry." This asymmetry does much to keep markets liquid, but it also results in mutual incomprehension during times of crisis, where these contrasting situations are most likely to come into high relief. In an effort to encourage economical use of the firm's resources, most trading firms charge their traders a use-of-capital levy for their long positions, which is netted against the income received from investing the proceeds generated by their shorts.

Tactical Allocation

Investment allocation may be a matter of policy or tactics, and as just about everyone who has experience with investing is aware, the line between the two can be difficult to discern. The reason is that we tend to talk about them both in terms of asset classes, because for most market participants, the instruments they trade inform their intuitive understanding of risk and patterns of return. That is, a trader in the $/¥ spot market is likely the have a different perception of "normal" and "exceptional" volatility than, say, a trader of options on biotechnology stocks. In other endeavors—say warfare, where the distinction arose—tactics are more clearly identifiable as the means by which policy is implemented. For instance, a policy to wage war of attrition against a superior invading force might dictate tactics such as ambush and poisoning the wells. In investments we tend to specify a return objective in terms of the means we will use to achieve it (60/40 or what-have-you), which also provides us with a convenient shorthand for our risk tolerance. The *locus classicus* for investment allocation contrasts policy and tactics as follows: the former involves "deciding upon the normal, or long-term, weights for each of the asset classes allowed in the portfolio" while tactics involve "strategically altering the investment mix weights away from normal . . ." (Brinson et al. 1986, 43). This does little to resolve any confusion between the two.

Most of us probably have a vague notion that the distinction between policy and tactics somehow involves a difference in time horizons, but insofar as we think about it at all, that is about as deeply into the matter as we generally go. However, this vague notion provides a key to distinguishing between them reasonably clearly. The previous chapter discussed how time imposes a risk to returns due to its erosive effect and offers an opportunity for return through compounding, while timing entails risks and return potential of a different sort. I propose a distinction in which investment policy seeks to exploit the returns to time, while tactics seek to exploit the returns to timing. Policy takes maximum advantage of compounding over long periods, and thus much of the thinking underlying policy is devoted to identifying the allocation that will deliver the required return while minimizing volatility, as volatility reduces compounding effects. Policy-making is a matter of ensuring that the required return is achieved. Tactics exploit volatility for the purposes of return maximization rather than achieving a specified level of return. Without price movements there would be no timing trades to be made. So we specify a policy as, say, 60/40—indicating a tolerance of some volatility in pursuit of the required return, while we say we are overweight fixed income relative to policy to indicate a tilt of exposure that we currently (but probably temporarily) regard as opportune.

Anson (2004) arrives at a fairly similar analysis by a completely different route. He contends that the concern of investment policy is β, while the concern of tactical allocation is α. In particular, he contends that "The long-term nature of strategic asset allocation is not designed to beat the market . . . the long-term funding goals of an organization should not be derailed by financial market cycles." By contrast, "Tactical asset allocation attempts to beat the market" (10). This leads Anson to make some interesting observations about the optionality (and thus return asymmetry) of the α-seeking investment techniques that he regards as the proper domain of tactics, in contrast to the linearity of the relationships with which be believes that investment policy should concern itself, although I am not entirely convinced by them. The differences between Anson's approach and mine involve some fairly subtle distinctions to which I will devote more attention at various points later in this volume.

Neither investment policy nor tactical allocations among investment strategies affect the strategies themselves, although there may be exceptions to this generalization. The entry of gargantuan investors such as Anson's former employer, CalPERS, into a strategy is often, and probably with considerable justice, believed to have negative effects on a strategy's return potential. The earlier discussion of overcrowding in quantitative equity hedge-fund management provides another example where allocation decisions appear to affect the underlying returns of the technique to which excessive allocation has been made, as does the familiar claim that traders will arbitrage away this or that discrepancy in valuations. By and large, however, a trade will proceed to do whatever it is that it does regardless of our decision to participate in it or not. With these provisos, tactical allocation affects the returns we achieve from a strategy through the fortune or misfortune of the timing of our entry into it, rather than affecting the strategy's returns themselves.

At its core, tactical allocation is a directional overlay on the trades among which it allocates, dependent on the accuracy of the manager's forecasts of relative returns among those trades. As Tokat and Stockton (2008) write, "The first step in developing an overall [tactical allocation] model is to forecast excess returns . . ." (3). This is true in essence even if the investment techniques among which the manager allocates include nondirectional cash flow or arbitrage trades. Assuming that the tactical allocator's tactics include seeking diversification, tactical allocation has an element of hedging and thus of arbitrage to it. Managers of funds of hedge funds may be explicit about this hedging aspect, for example, using dedicated short sellers or short-bias funds as hedges against a portion of the risk embedded in their long-bias exposure. Less sophisticated funds of funds managers may simply follow the generally accepted wisdom that exposures should be diversified without considering the ways in which they can hedge each other. This can lead to unintentional hedging away of return potential. While it is arguable whether there is such a thing as "hedge fund β," there is unquestionably such a thing as self-defeating over-diversification of hedge fund holdings (see Lhabitant and Learned 2002). Attention to how managers of funds of hedge funds analyze the interactions among the return characteristics of their investments is an important consideration in performing due diligence on them.

With some exceptions, multi-strategy hedge funds do not behave significantly differently in their tactical allocation procedures from the way funds of hedge funds do, although they are less diversified by manager because (by definition) they manage the different strategies themselves. Both advantages and disadvantages arise from this choice. On the positive side, the managers of multi-strategy funds have full transparency as to what is going on in their portfolios, which is valuable information to inform their allocation decisions. It would be difficult, for instance, for them to fail to recognize the extent to which one trade hedges another. On the other hand, it is arguable whether a single firm is likely to have the best available implementation of all the investment techniques that a multi-strategy manager might wish to exploit. In many cases, the factor that drives investors' choice of multi-strategy funds over style-diversified funds of funds is that the former do not entail a second layer of fees and performance incentives, but the transparency issue should probably be the more decisive one, which investment policymakers should not neglect. A multi-strategy manager that employs position analysis as a part of its risk monitoring discipline has, at least in principle, an ability to add value through tactical allocation that is denied to funds of funds managers who must rely exclusively on *ex post* multi-factor analysis of returns. Further, the timeliness of multi-strategy managers' allocation decisions is not constrained by the only periodic availability of fund liquidity with which most fund of funds managers are forced to contend.

Tactical allocation is probably best understood as an "overlay" on investment strategy, but there are some investment managers who would look upon it as central to their investment technique. A later chapter will discuss long/short equity hedge funds. While many of these are, as a matter of policy, permanently biased toward long, short, or neutral β exposure, imposing strict limits on the degree to which they can depart from it, many others shift between net long or net short exposure opportunistically, and even those with a permanent bias usually have the discretion to adjust their net market exposure to some extent in the interest of return-seeking. For analytic purposes it is convenient to regard this freedom to adjust net exposure as an "overlay," even if many of these traders would probably regard the ability to do this as an inherent component of their core investment processes. Their argument has special force in the case of "pure" tactical allocation, which allocates among passive investment instruments and thus derives its α entirely from timing. However, even this technique is still reliant on the β of the underlying passive instruments to generate any returns at all—*nihil ex nihilo fit*, and no amount of allocation among asset categories that produce zero return can produce a return. Consequently, it seems reasonable to regard even such allegedly "pure" tactical allocation as an overlay that affords the manager real options to adjust exposure which are the source of its value added. Portable α techniques—in which the β exposure of a manager is hedged away and the proceeds used to invest in another investment category entirely—make this characteristic explicit, although arguably at a strategic rather than a tactical level of implementation.

If (against all advice and the overwhelming weight of received wisdom) tactical allocation is performed at the investment policy level, it takes on a somewhat different character that resembles relative value arbitrage. If it is made in the context of an established allocation target—say, 60 percent equities and 40 percent fixed income—a decision to overweight one asset class is, in effect, a decision to be short the other—the funds required to build the overweight exposure are "borrowed" from the effective short position. This has implications for investment policy that will be explored in more detail in Part IV, but this description explains why received opinion is opposed to the idea. The institution is making a notionally leveraged speculation relative to its benchmark, and while there is nothing in principle wrong with doing this, investment policymakers should examine their consciences to determine whether they really believe that they have the expertise to enter such trades.

Activism

As I have stressed, time erodes returns, and its erosiveness is magnified through the use of leverage. Time allegedly waits for no man, but activist investors are unwilling to wait for time. While activism may take various forms, including the promotion of political, social, or environmental causes that an investor may espouse, the activism that is relevant to this discussion is in the cause of maximizing returns. On occasion it is useful for activists of this sort to wrap themselves and their activities in other, more apparently altruistic mantles, but their primary motivation is usually so transparent that it requires no cynicism to discern it. Barv et al. (2008) find that activism (specifically attempts to influence management on financial and strategic matters) is successful in enhancing returns in two-thirds of cases, and that abnormal equity returns from the public disclosure of activism (i.e., the use of the media as a "bully pulpit") are approximately 7 percent, with no reversal during the subsequent year.

There are measures such as securities repurchases or spinning off a division that a corporate issuer of securities can take that crystallize value for its investors, and these are what activists seek to hurry along. Using whatever forum is available to them, they seek to persuade, cajole, or otherwise encourage managements to take the measures that are in the interest of the activists and—at least allegedly—other investors in the same instrument. The platforms available to activists vary depending on circumstances and the instrument involved—proxy contests, pointed questions at annual meetings, and even service on the issuer's board of directors are all fairly common for activist equity investors, while creditor committees provide an influential forum for investors in debt default situations. Recourse to the law is not infrequent, but given the painful slowness with which the wheels of justice grind, this stratagem can often be counterproductive for managers whose intention is to accelerate progress toward their return-seeking goal. Grandstanding in the media is not universal, but is common enough that the *Wall Street Journal* no doubt makes a reasonable living from full-page advertisements taken out by activists—not least because they often elicit full-page responses from management, unions, or other interested parties.

Activism in a debt-workout situation is a somewhat different matter than trying to persuade or force the management of a public company to take a desired action. If there are many creditors involved in a Chapter XI process and the seniority of claims is debatable—if some claimants have very large exposure or if suppliers, pensions, and other interests are involved—there may be considerable scope for negotiation. Exploiting the opportunity for value creation that this can offer requires an investment approach where legal expertise, bargaining skill, and, occasionally, sharp elbows are as important to achieving the desired return as valuation techniques or forecasting ability. For example, I am aware of a hedge fund that bought deeply discounted preferred equity late in a multi-year proceeding, which it was able to redeem near par within a few months, largely because it threatened to delay the bankruptcy process even further.

Activism has its costs—in addition to the expense of *Journal* pages and the value of the investment manager's time, it can also generate significant legal expenses. And activists certainly run risks to their reputations—many are routinely vilified as locusts, vultures, and worse, particularly if they choose to operate in Germany. No one is much persuaded by their professions of altruistic service to capitalism, although the fact that their protestations are self-serving does not in itself make them untrue. However, it is noticeable that CalPERS, TIAA-CREF, and the Council of Institutional Investors, which are vocal activists in the cause of sound corporate governance, rarely attract such opprobrium, although they are quite forthcoming about the fact that the motives underlying their activism are by no means purely altruistic (see Anson 2002, Chapter 22). But activism is different from the other return enhancers discussed in this chapter because it entails no additional investment risk of its own. The trade contains all the investment risk, which activism seeks to reduce by noninvestment means. Activism may occasionally tempt a manager into taking an unfortunate risk, if the manager acquires a position in the belief that its efforts can sway a management that proves to be obdurate, but the risk is in the position, not in the enhancement, even if the perceived opportunity for enhancement is what tempted the manager into the position. Activism is effective as a return enhancer only in circumstances that are propitious for it. But I have seen a well-known activist in private interaction with corporate boards, and the mixture of sweet reason, suave persuasion, and implied threat can be very powerful. Greenwood and Schor (2007, 23*f*) find evidence of this power and its consequences for investment performance in a comparison of the outcomes of a sample of activist situations with similar investment opportunities where activism was absent.

There is an element of activism to any investment in which a General Partner takes a role in the operational management of the asset in which it invests—even if it is only non-member observer status on the investment's board of directors. General Partners are expected to take on such non–executive oversight roles in private equity and real estate investments. In venture capital and occasionally in buyouts, participation in the management of investments may be much more hands-on than that, involving an executive role that may include arranging the appointment of managers and close engagement, at the very least, in the setting of corporate strategy. A member of the General Partner (often a "special" or "entrepreneurial" partner who is only indirectly affiliated with the general partner) is not infrequently appointed as CEO. The venture capital arena is quite clubby (not to say incestuous), and it is common for General Partners to help the companies in which they invest on a variety of matters, including commercial contacts, introductions to sources of additional capital or financing, negotiations, and other matters that go well beyond filling out their executive suites. In these cases, too, the purpose of activism is to accelerate events that will result in crystallizing the value of the General Partner's investment, although it does not require the manager to grab a spotlight in the public arena to accomplish this.

Unlike activism in the public securities sphere, activism in private assets may not be without risk. As board members or even officers of the firm in which they invest, general partners acquire liability for the activities of the firm, for instance, if it violates labor, securities, or environmental statutes. However, this liability does not pass through to their limited partners, so that from an investor's standpoint, such activism is also risk-free return enhancement, although limited partners can expect to pay for the general partner's time and liability insurance. They may also pay the consequences of hiring an agent to perform their management for them. While agency risk arises whenever an institution turns to third parties to manage its assets, it is more extreme in the case of private assets than most others.

Accepting Liquidity Risk

In principle, investors should demand a higher return from investments that do not offer the opportunity of an easy exit to allow for reallocation. This follows from the general principle that no risk should be taken without a return. In most cases an investment manager is unable to transform a liquid position into an illiquid one for the purpose of capturing the associated increase in return, but there are occasions when it is possible. For example, participation in the PIPE (Private Investment in Public Equity) market[3] is made attractive to investors precisely because the issuer offers the investment at a discount to market, in return for investors' acceptance of the prohibition on near-term sale that attaches to restricted equity issues of this kind. Investors who already hold an instrument for which a related PIPE becomes available may decide to capture this discount by switching their exposure to the PIPE. Although I am not aware of anyone who does so as their primary return generator, in principle a directional strategy of capturing these illiquidity premia could be constructed by hedging away the directional exposure of the position with a counterbalancing short position in the unrestricted equity. But PIPE's discounts and availability are not generally so great as to make this a very attractive technique, and deliberate participation in illiquid instruments is more usually an enhancement of an unhedged directional trade that relies on the appreciation in the liquid underlying instrument as well as capturing the illiquidity premium for its return. However, where the underlying instrument is dividend-paying, PIPEs may also be used to enhance cash flow returns.

Investment in private placements of fixed-income instruments is a practice of long standing, particularly among institutions, such as insurance companies, that tend to take a buy-and-hold approach to their

---

3. That is, participation in this market by public market investors. Venture capitalists have begun to penetrate this market (see Tam 2009), for whom it performs the quite different role of offering them the potential for greater liquidity than their accustomed trades. Whether the expertise required for venture capital investment will be successfully transferable to the PIPE arena remains to be seen.

fixed-income exposure. These instruments have no precise counterparts in the public markets, so unlike PIPEs, they do not eventually become readily marketable. They are, however, strongly analogous to publicly traded fixed-income securities, making pricing in this market a comparatively easy negotiation. Investors who make significant use of this market tend to be actuarially driven (explaining insurers' enthusiasm), and in many cases employ these instruments for purposes other than just return enhancement. Rather than incremental yield, the benefit that may be of primary concern to them in this instance is just as likely to be customization of terms to match their actuarial or distribution requirements. Characteristics of the bond that can be customized, such as its duration or coupon, may be of more importance to these investors than capturing the better-than-market yield that would be implied by an illiquidity discount. The privately placed debt market is very large, with numerous participants, but use of these instruments is usually restricted to a relatively small portion of any individual institution's portfolio, in order to prevent its aggregate illiquidity risk from becoming too great.

The risk attached to employing illiquid instruments is probably immaterial if the portfolio manager would otherwise have held its liquid counterpart over the long-term in any case, as most such institutions typically do. But illiquid securities obviously create timing risk if the manager's convictions change.[4] And if they constitute too substantial a portion of a portfolio, they can contribute to the risk that arises from the need to comply with regulatory capital requirements as well as (in some cases) the possibility of investor withdrawals, margin calls, or other unexpected demands on the portfolio's liquidity. Further, even without consideration of unforeseen liquidity needs, liquidity discounts can be suffered rather than enjoyed. A manager's initially liquid positions can for any of a number of reasons become illiquid, in which case these risks are taken on unintentionally, resulting in a loss on the position and sometimes entailing additional, very unfortunate consequences.

---

4. A less-than-honorable means of escaping this risk is sometimes encountered in the private equity area. If, after an IPO, the fund finds itself holding restricted stock, the General Partner may transfer this to its Limited Partners as a distribution in kind. The distribution is marked to market at the time it is distributed, locking in the performance achieved to that date for the benefit of the fund's track record. Any subsequent decline in the stock's price is for the account of the Limited Partners and does not affect the fund's reported performance.

Volatility Generators

No trader is a solipsist: without a counterparty there can be no trading whatsoever. Exchanges—whether they are physical trading pits or a Web address—are gathering places where potential counterparties can easily find each other. But traders have long recognized the advantages of doing at least a portion of their business off-exchange. Competition for transactions is reduced, as are execution costs, given that the fees that exchanges charge for providing a trading venue can be avoided. Difficult executions can often be carried out more easily away from the competitive bidding process, and internalization of trades increases the economies of scale that brokerage firms can draw from their very substantial sunk costs in trading and marketing infrastructures. A familiar example is trading against proprietary order flow.

Rather than routing its order stream to an exchange, a firm may match orders internally and act as principal against those that do not find a match with another customer's order. But even at large wire houses with order flow from many thousands of customers, order flow can be sporadic and its composition—its mix of buy and sell orders—unattractive to the firm's trading desk. A regular, orderly flow of the "right" kind of orders cannot reliably be obtained from proprietary flow, but it can be engineered. Note that the "right" kind of order can include orders that do *not* arrive, such as orders to sell shortly before the market's close, if a trader has more short exposure than is desirable from a risk management perspective.

The synthetic instruments that provide investment banks' and other trading firms' trading desks with these permanent trading counterparties are swap agreements, structured notes, and various forms of over-the-counter hedging products. The refined product contracts mentioned above, that Metallgesellschaft's U.S. subsidiary sold primarily to distributors of home heating oil, provide an example of the latter. Perhaps too good an example: Metallgesellschaft was forced to settle with the Commodity Futures Trading Commission when the regulator found that it had sold what it deemed to be illegal futures contracts (see Commodity Futures Trading Commission 1995). In the case of a swap, the trader's firm enters into an agreement with a counterparty that requires regular cash in- or outflows, and its dealers can position their trading books in the knowledge that these trades will arrive at prearranged times. These are directional trades, which are reliant on price volatility to generate returns. The more volatile the asset underlying the structured product, the more attractive the product's virtual order stream is to trade against, and this is—or at least should be—reflected in the terms offered to potential customers for structured products.

From the perspective of purchasers of these products, they are buying directional exposure to whatever underlying is chosen—perhaps with bells and whistles such as buffers or leveraged upside attached, but directional exposure nonetheless. From the standpoint of the issuing firm, sale of the product is not so much a directional exposure—on the short side—as a way of acquiring orderflow in a volatile and therefore tradable asset. Returning once again to the by now rather tired example of Metallgesellschaft, the firm's underlying reason for selling the contracts in the first place was not to acquire short exposure to petroleum products, but to finance trading in them. In particular, its strategy was to capture the positive roll on backwardated futures—a cash flow strategy. When the market in the futures shifted into contango, the carry on this hedge became a negative cash flow, so as losses inexorably mounted, the trade (and thanks to the size of its exposure, the firm) ultimately collapsed.

A purer example of a volatility generator is any underlying that is selected for use in an option straddle. Here a trader simultaneously purchases puts and calls with identical strikes and dates of expiry on some volatile underlying security or index. As the option payoff diagram in **Figure 2.1** indicates, this fully hedged trade will produce a return provided that the price of the underlying changes in either direction sufficiently to offset the premia paid to obtain the options as well as the trade's other transaction costs. The trader is essentially indifferent to the fundamental nature of the underlying and to the price direction that it takes, provided

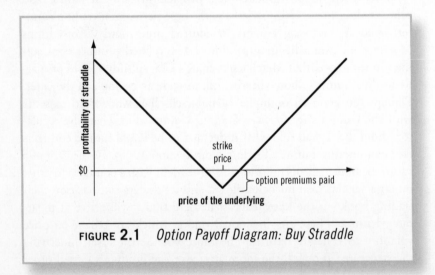

FIGURE **2.1** *Option Payoff Diagram: Buy Straddle*

that it exhibits the necessary price volatility. Return derives from the volatility of the underlying rather than its direction, since the holder of the strategy is equally long and short. Holders of buy (or "long") straddles are said to be long volatility and holders of short straddles (in which a similar but inverted structure is created) have short exposure to this virtual quantity.

This digression into investment banks' trading activities is not entirely beside the point, as will become apparent in later chapters. But it also illustrates that one market participant's strategy need not be the same as its counterparty's. An investor's directional trade can serve the purposes of another's cash flow strategy. In principle, and perhaps not so infrequently in fact, it is possible that one leg of an arbitrageur's pair trade could be employed by an investor pursuing a directional strategy and the other by a counterparty pursuing a cash flow strategy. It is a cliché that disagreements make horse races, and differences in forecasts often account for the availability of a counterparty to directional trades. But it is worth noting that there may be traders to whom their counterparties' forecasts are irrelevant—traders who are quite unconcerned whether their counterparties are informed or otherwise. Dorsey (2007) points out that

> ... some relative value strategies are perpetual in nature, where it is not so much the spread in valuation between securities that is being captured on a completed basis as it is the volatility of the spread that is being captured through dynamic changes to the amount of exposure to the short or long portion of the securities involved in the trade. (53)

This situation is a product of the peculiar, not-quite-systematic relationships that obtain among many fixed-income instruments, but it suggests that fixed-income arbitrage desks may not even require an Over-the-Counter counterparty to structure a volatility generator. See Chapter 10 for more on the quasi-systematic correlation that underlies this phenomenon.

CHAPTER 3

Some Features of the Quantitative Toolkit

The material in this chapter covers ground that is probably familiar to many readers, but the intent here is to point up some of the peculiarities of the quantitative tools used in finance that, at least in some cases, do not often receive as much comment as they probably deserve. An earlier draft of this book scattered this discussion throughout the text, making it more difficult for those who would prefer to skip over such matters (either because of excessive familiarity or because they are repelled by them) to do so. By grouping it all together, I hope to serve the needs of both those who prefer to remain innocent of quantitative matters as well as the needs of those who are quantitatively sophisticated and who are unlikely to learn much from anything that is covered here. The result is a somewhat scattershot chapter, dealing with a number of topics that are only loosely related by their connection with mathematics.

I announced in the Introduction my intent to accomplish my objectives in this volume without using equations, and I will keep to that promise. My own aesthetic preferences regarding mathematical notation have much to do with this. Is there any reason, other than a desire to impress, that authors in financial economics glory in such ugly and needlessly complex mathematical notation? There is *never* a justification for "$\Phi^{rc}_{t=2}$" or similar Rococo embellishment when plain vanilla "Φ" would do, and in fact there is rarely a justification for resorting to Greek at all. This tendency seems traceable to statisticians, whose notation embraces such mysteries as the Romanization of Greek through raising it to a power:

thus ρ (the coefficient of correlation) somehow metamorphoses into R^2 (the coefficient of determination) simply through being multiplied by itself: either $\rho \times \rho$ should equal ρ^2, or $\rho \times \rho$ should equal R. Where did the superscript in R^2 come from?

The deliberate disservice to readers begins with a refusal to define variables (is it really such a burden to tell us what "D" means rather than requiring the reader to guess?) and extends to such notational solecisms as superscripts that are not intended to indicate that something is raised to that power (R^2 as an example) and complex subscripts where simply making use of a different symbol for the variable would be clearer. A case might be made that Georg Cantor really did need Hebrew for his treatment of transfinite numbers, but I do not believe that any of the concepts of financial economics are sufficiently arcane to demand anything more than good old Roman letters. At this stage it would be confusing to substitute new symbols for the Greek that is widely recognized—for example "σ" is far too well established as the symbol for standard deviation to make replacing it sensible. For all that the concepts are frequently misused, "α" and "β" are similarly entrenched in the notation of finance. This is yet another instance in which bad nomenclatural practice seems to have become permanently enshrined, and surely there is nothing I can do to correct the situation, but at least I will avoid contributing to it. All the more reason, then, to avoid using mathematical formulae, because many would probably object that my preferred style of notation is insufficiently confusing.

Compounding and Volatility

Since time imposes a risk on investments, it also can provide a return. I assume that all my readers are quite familiar with the "magic" of compound interest: time is investors' friend in successful cash flow strategies, such that they, like the Dukes of Westminster or the Mars family, may never wish to exit from them. As previously noted, over very short time periods cash flow trades are impossible. Over perpetuity, cash flow trades are the *only* permanent investment possibilities, and investors with that time horizon (and whose operations are unaffected by marks-to-market) can be blithely indifferent to volatility. But for the rest of us, time is at its friendliest when the volatility of portfolio returns is low, because average returns are not equivalent to compounded returns.

This peculiarity of compounding provides the fundamental explanation for why investors should seek to avoid volatility of returns in the first place, and thus the basic principle that underlies the doctrine of portfolio diversification. Investment advisors are occasionally confronted with the question, "Why should an investor be concerned about the volatility of returns?" The simple arithmetic of percentages provides the explanation. The effect of volatility on compounded returns also crops up frequently in the consideration of alternative investments because of its consequences for leverage and hedge ratios. A brief illustration will make the point better than an examination of the arithmetic.

Figure 3.1 shows two hypothetical assets that produced identical cumulative returns of 500 percent over twenty periods. Asset B, with zero volatility, requires a *per*-period return of 9.34 percent to achieve its return, while the volatile asset (which despite its volatility never experiences a one-period return of less than +1 percent) requires an average return 9.80 percent—46 basis points more. Average per-period returns are not the same thing as compound returns, and it is in reaching for higher per-period returns that portfolio risk is increased, so investors are well advised to pay attention to both measures. The arithmetic of percentages requires the volatile asset to "work harder" when its returns are strong to compensate for its periods of comparatively weak

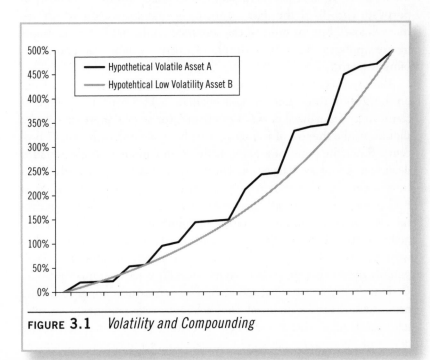

FIGURE **3.1** *Volatility and Compounding*

performance, in order to achieve an increase in wealth equivalent to that produced by the non-volatile one. Because its returns are unchanging, the non-volatile asset's average returns are identical to its compound return, but whenever there is any variation between period-to-period returns, a difference between the two measures begins to insinuate itself. To the extent that portfolio volatility can be reduced, curtailing this variation insofar as possible, compound returns increase—making the reason why investors should have an aversion to volatility rather obvious.

Statistical Significance

There is a general prejudice that three years of returns are needed to establish a performance track record for an investment vehicle. This prejudice is sufficiently widespread among consultants and other centers of influence that three years has become a sacred cow that has taken on very great commercial importance to the sponsors of newly launched investment products. Most such sponsors are advised not even to bother investing much in the marketing of their new product until it has have reached the three-year mark. The figure has been pulled out of thin air. Textbooks advise us that a series of thirty-six monthly return data points qualifies as a "large" sample for statistical purposes (provided the data is normally distributed, on which see more below), but for most of the statistical tools that investors might like to apply to this data, a sample of thirty-six entails an enormous sampling error.

For example, the standard error of a standard deviation, calculated on the basis of three years of monthly data, is 11.8 percent. The proud claim that "annualized $\sigma = 6.49$ percent" for such a short time series should, in the interest of full disclosure, be appended with "±0.77 percent." Since the point of making such a claim about a fund's standard deviation is to draw a favorable comparison with some similarly short time series—say, one for which its annualized standard deviation is 8.12 percent, with a standard error of ±0.96 percent—it is worth noting that, within the bounds of statistical significance, there may in fact be no contrast between the series at all. For many statistical tools that we would probably like to use to assist our investment thinking, most notably the coefficient of correlation, these error terms compound.

Practitioners of the natural sciences are routinely appalled by the promiscuous use in financial circles of statistical analyses with such tenuous claims to significance. Few statistical results in finance have the degree of significance that would be regarded as a minimal requirement for, say, a drug trial—let alone an attempt to measure a physical constant. There is not much that financial theorists can do to repair this situation: the available history of accurate financial time series is in almost every case simply too short. While this should not discourage us from applying statistical concepts to investment problems, it should give us pause before we rely on them too heavily. The lack of long time series is clearly a constraint on our ability to obtain robust significance for many of the analyses we would like to perform, but it is disingenuous to ignore the problem. Their error terms should always be appended to such analyses. However, this is a tiresomely repetitive exercise, and I (like other financial authors) will forego it in what follows.

Correlation

No statistical concept features more prominently in discussions of investment allocation than correlation, so it is disappointing that some of the peculiarities of this calculation are not more frequently highlighted in the literature of investing. I will begin with the calculation itself. Finance textbooks rarely refer to a geometric explanation of the coefficient of correlation, but for many people, this treatment is likely to be more informative than its algebraic expression.

Figures 3.2 and **3.3** pair the daily returns of different financial time series, plotting the return for one on the vertical axis and the other

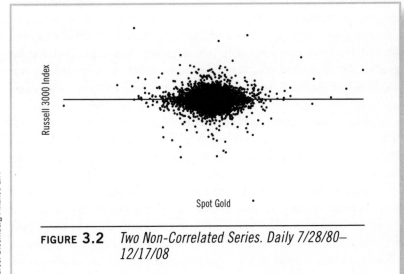

FIGURE 3.2 *Two Non-Correlated Series. Daily 7/28/80– 12/17/08*

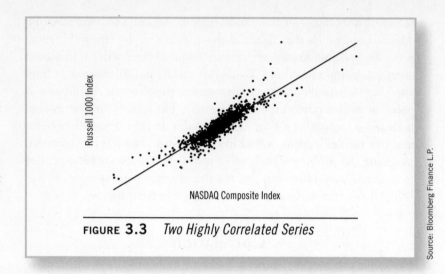

FIGURE 3.3 *Two Highly Correlated Series*

Source: Bloomberg Finance L.P.

on the horizontal axis. Each data point represents one day's relative performance for both of them: for example, on May 21, 2001, spot gold rose 6.46 percent while the Russell 3000 Index rose by 1.78 percent. The trendlines inserted into the scattergrams, which are obtained by linear regression, tell the correlation story. A perfectly horizontal line indicates zero correlation, and the degree of correlation or counter-correlation is indicated by the extent to which the trendline departs from the horizontal. A regression line at a 45° angle would indicate perfect correlation (1.0000) if it angles up and to the right, and perfect negative correlation (−1.0000) if it angles down and to the right. In fact, the correlation statistic is nothing other than the slope of that line, which permits various geometric/trigonometric demonstrations that are graphically interesting and may be of some value to those who are less algebraically-inclined. See Zerolis (1998) and Singer (1999), who demonstrate some interesting applications of these geometric properties.

It has become fashionable in financial circles to use R^2 (the coefficient of determination) rather than the coefficient of correlation (ρ) for many discussions of this type. But in one respect, use of R^2 detracts from the information that is conveyed. Because R^2 is simply the square of the coefficient of correlation, and because a figure squared is necessarily positive, R^2 tells us how closely two series are related but neglects to tell us whether the relationship between them is one of correlation or counter-correlation. R^2 is more properly used as a measure of the closeness with which a linear regression trendline fits the underlying data—a concept that is intuitively related to correlation, but one for which negative values would be meaningless. Its use should, for the most part, be restricted to that purpose.

However, R^2 has the advantage over the coefficient of correlation that, in a different respect, it has greater intuitive meaning: an R^2 of 0.4720 indicates that 47.2 percent of the price movement of the dependent variable is determined by the price movement of the independent variable. So its use as a substitute for the coefficient of correlation is by no means wholly inappropriate and will probably continue. However, in that case, investors have to determine for themselves what the sign of the coefficient of correlation is for any given example. Note that one price series can "determine" opposite as well as congruent changes in another, and that in this context, as in all statistical contexts, "determination" is something quite different from causation.

What should we consider to be weak or strong correlation? Statistics itself cannot provide an answer to this question, which depends substantially on the context in which the measurement of correlation is used. For example, what is regarded as a strong correlation for the purposes of zoological research might not much impress a physical chemist. However, the relationship between the coefficient of correlation and R^2 at least gives us the basis for making an intuitive judgment for ourselves.

Table 3.1 shows, for example, that a correlation of ±0.4000 indicates that the price movement of one instrument determines 16 percent of the price behavior of the other—a noticeable but hardly a very strong relationship. My rule of thumb is that correlations below that level can be

TABLE 3.1 *The Coefficient of Correlation and R^2*

COEFFICIENT OF CORRELATION	DEGREE OF DETERMINATION	COEFFICIENT OF CORRELATION	DEGREE OF DETERMINATION
±0.1000	1%	±0.6000	36%
±0.2000	4%	±0.7000	49%
±0.3000	9%	±0.8000	64%
±0.4000	16%	±0.9000	81%
±0.5000	25%	±1.0000	100%

considered weak and correlations higher than ±0.7072 (R^2 = 50.01 percent) can be considered strong, with correlations in the regions in between qualifying as moderate. Readers must decide for themselves.

Counter-correlation is the *sine qua non* of a hedge. This is hardly controversial, as the whole point of a hedge is to offset at least some if not all of the price variation of the instrument that is being hedged. In general, the more counterintuitive peculiarities of correlation calculations tend to stand out most strongly when speaking of negative correlation, so I will turn to that specific aspect of correlation calculations for a moment. As mentioned, negatively correlated series would slant the opposite way to the one shown in Figure 3.3 (as in fact the trendline shown in Figure 3.2 does, although so slightly that its negative slope is not easily discernable).

A glance at **Figure 3.4** is enough to convince most casual observers that A and C counter-correlate, while B is some other series entirely. In fact all three are derived from the same data. Series A chain-links 2000 daily returns of a familiar equity index, Series B multiplies the same daily returns by negative one then chain-links them, while Series C multiplies the chain-linked returns of Series A by negative one. What is illustrated here is another aspect of the magic of compounding mentioned above: Series A and C are compounded return

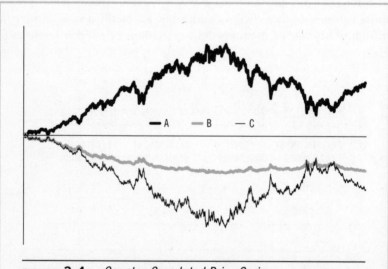

FIGURE 3.4 *Counter-Correlated Price Series*

series while Series B is not. Series A and C have a perfect counter-correlation of −1.0000 with respect to each other, while Series A and B have −0.9017 correlation, despite the fact that, before chain-linking, the daily data from which A and B derive have a fully systematic, mathematically precise correlation of −1.0000. That is, B hedges A with complete precision on a day-to-day basis but not over longer periods of time. As might be expected from the comments above, the degree of hedging inaccuracy is a function of both the volatility of the instrument that is being hedged and of the number of compounding periods involved. That is, the accuracy of a point-to-point hedge will decrease as volatility between the points increases and also as the number of periods increases. This accounts, for example, for the otherwise inexplicable tracking error exhibited by some Exchange-Traded Funds.

All of which is no doubt entertaining, but of what relevance? Correlation of −0.9017 would seem more than adequate for most hedging purposes, yet B is clearly a very imperfect hedge for A over any significant period of time. But more importantly, it is not always possible to obtain a compounding hedge, and in almost all hedging activities that make use of derivatives, expiry and the consequent need to roll over the position bring in exactly the same compounding issues. While rolling such a hedge is unlikely to be necessary on a daily basis, so the effects of rolling may be *de minimis* in much actual practice where the roll must be executed only once a quarter or once a year, over long periods of time this consequence of compounding effects will inevitably make its presence felt. If the trade is leveraged, even these minor hedging discrepancies can be the difference between profit and loss if the period under consideration is sufficiently protracted and/or the instruments involved are sufficiently volatile.

Another often overlooked aspect of the coefficient of correlation is that it weights coincidence or contrast in the *direction* of relative price movements far more highly than it weights differences in the *magnitude* of those price movements. Thus, for example, if in order to obtain Series C we had multiplied the observations in Series A by −0.5 rather than by negative one, the coefficient of correlation between the two series would remain 1.0000, even though the recalculated series would obviously be only half as effective as a hedge against the price movements exhibited by Series A as the version of Series C actually shown in Figure 3.4. Remember that even a perfect correlation of 1.0000 between two instruments does not ensure that one of them is adequate to serve as a hedge for the other, at least on the basis of a one-to-one hedge ratio.

Many believe that calculation of hedge ratios is necessary only where options—with their systematically variable relationships to the price of the underlying as described by the various option "Greeks"—are employed as the hedging instrument. But this clearly is not the case. There is, potentially, optionality built into every hedging transaction, if we assume variable levels of correlation or standard deviation. Optionality implies asymmetry of returns, which is clearly an important concern for any would-be hedger, given that a countervailing symmetry of returns is precisely what a hedge attempts to achieve. As can readily be observed from the numerous correlation histories illustrated in this volume, most relationships of correlation between financial assets are in fact quite variable over time, implying that this option-like feature is pervasive throughout the realm of hedged trades.

Thus, when considering correlations—as investment policymakers frequently must—it is important to be aware of the time period over which the statistic was calculated, and be careful to assess the relevance of that period to the future period with which the investment allocator is actually concerned. The near-zero correlation shown over the long period illustrated in Figure 3.2 was not experienced over shorter time frames, as can be seen from **Figure 3.5**. For analytical purposes, the

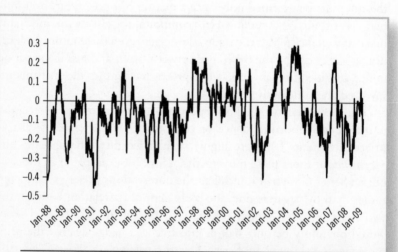

FIGURE 3.5 *Spot Gold and the Russell® 3000 Index: 90-Day Trailing Coefficient of Correlation*

Source: Bloomberg Finance L.P.

correct correlation period must be chosen with reference to the anticipated holding period. There is no point in pretending that forecasting correlation is a simple matter, but if the holding period is expected to be significantly shorter than the twenty-eight years illustrated in Figure 3.2, a correlation derived from twenty-eight years of data is probably of little relevance and in fact is likely to be quite deceptive.

Correlation and the Efficient Frontier

Taken on its own, the almost precise non-correlation between physical gold and the broad U.S. equity market would seem to suggest that physical gold has been a pretty nearly ideal diversifier of broad U.S. equity exposure over the last twenty-eight years. However, correlation is not the only factor that determines whether one asset or investment technique is an attractive diversifier of another. The data in **Table 3.2** indicate that gold provided a miserable return at higher volatility than stocks displayed during that twenty-eight-year period. Adding anything more than a very small allocation of gold to an equity portfolio increased volatility while reducing return—hardly the result for which investors might have hoped from a diversifying investment.

In terms of the efficient frontier shown in **Figure 3.6**, adding increments of gold exposure to an equity portfolio had the effect of moving the portfolio from the top of the chart toward the bottom along the heavy black curve indicating zero correlation. Each increment of gold exposure decreased return, but initially the tradeoff in reduced volatility was marginally favorable. Based on data for the time period shown and at current interest rates, the tradeoff ceases to be favorable at approximately 9 percent exposure to physical gold in a two-asset portfolio.

TABLE **3.2** *Statistical Characteristics of Gold and Equities*

	SPOT GOLD	RUSSELL 3000 INDEX
Compound Annual Return	1.01 percent	10.18 percent
Annualized Standard Deviation	18.60 percent	17.49 percent
Coefficient of Correlation to Spot Gold	1.0000	−0.0083

Source: Bloomberg Finance L.P.

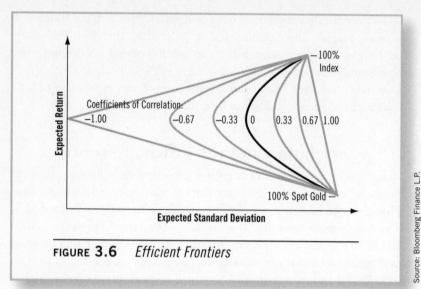

FIGURE **3.6** *Efficient Frontiers*

Source: Bloomberg Finance L.P.

If gold had a significantly more negative correlation with the broad equity market, say −0.6667, increasing the portfolio's holdings in gold to as much as 40 percent of the total would have provided a favorable tradeoff between risk and return. If the correlation of gold with the broad equity market were +0.6667 or higher, then there would be no favorable tradeoff at any level of exposure to gold, and zero exposure to it would be optimal. In that case, each incremental addition of gold to the portfolio would have increased volatility more than it reduced returns—the worst of both worlds. **Figure 3.7** illustrates the more frequently encountered situation where the asset with the lower return also has the lower standard deviation. Here the favorable tradeoff between volatility and returns that is central to the quest for investment diversification can be much more clearly seen, because allocating between assets with such a relationship can achieve considerably more noticeable diversification benefits.

Note that the efficient frontier for a 1.0000 correlation is linear—a one-for-one tradeoff as would be expected—while the −1.0000 frontier is discontinuous at zero. The intersection of the −1.0000 efficient frontier with the vertical axis defines the hedge ratio between the two instruments. It is worth noting that the calculation is sensitive to the expected standard deviations of the instruments involved, *not* the expected returns. For assets with identical standard deviations, the most accurate hedge will always hold 50 percent of each, regardless of the

Erratum

p. 71

Figure 3.6 was erroneously reproduced in **Figure 3.7.**
Figure 3.7 should appear as follows:

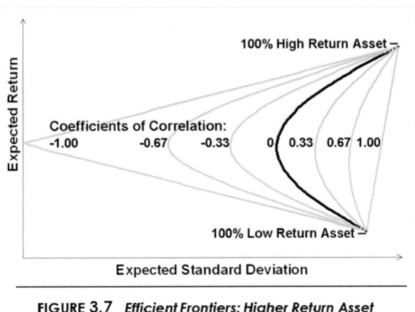

FIGURE 3.7 *Efficient Frontiers: Higher Return Asset has Higher Standard Deviation*

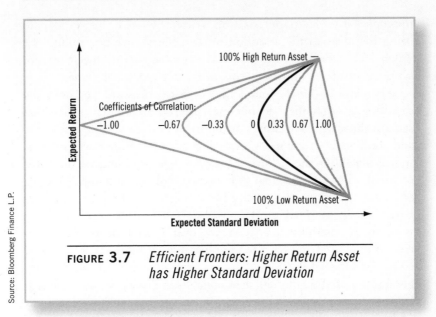

Source: Bloomberg Finance L.P.

FIGURE 3.7   *Efficient Frontiers: Higher Return Asset has Higher Standard Deviation*

returns they offer. Referring back to the discussion of Figure 3.4, this accounts for how assets with −1.0000 correlations can be imperfect hedges of each other. A perfectly hedged position is *not* an optimal one, since it offers zero return. In the thought experiment we performed there, Series A and C had identical standard deviations, while the version of Series A multiplied by −0.5 had half the standard deviation of Series A, and consequently the zero volatility portfolio—i.e., the perfectly hedged one—would be comprised of one-third of the asset represented by Series A and two-thirds of the asset that exhibits half of Series A's standard deviation.

Non-Normality

According to standard, Gaussian statistics, the universe is nowhere near old enough to make a one-day event of greater than 20 standard deviations likely, yet one occurred on October 19, 1987. Was it just phenomenally bad luck that several trillion more years had not passed before the Crash occurred? The breathtaking improbability of Black Monday sent finance theorists scurrying back to their models, and eventually led them to a finding that Benoit Mandelbrot—a respected mathematician, but not an economist—had published in 1962. Although Mandelbrot has consistently (if intermittently) revisited the topic,[1] it took a popularization written by one of his students to bring his ideas to the attention of the general investing public (see Taleb 2007). Fat tails, black swans, and various other metaphors for statistical exotica are now well ensconced in investors' thinking.

Mandelbrot (1962) found that cotton prices are not normally distributed—that they do not meet the requirements of Gaussian statistical analysis. He chose cotton prices because an unusually long and good quality time series, extending back to before the Civil War, was available for them. Such a long series lessens some of the issues of statistical significance that were discussed above, although even that series was not long enough to alleviate them entirely. Empirical evidence has gradually mounted, until it now seems that *no* financial time series is normally distributed, at least not over most time periods. This recondite observation has deep implications. It means that the entire edifice of Modern Portfolio Theory—from Harry Markowitz's inaugural paper of 1952 through the Capital Asset Pricing Model, Arbitrage Pricing Theory, and all three option pricing models—systematically underestimates risk.

Financial theorists had until then simply assumed that financial series are normally distributed. This was not an arbitrary or unexpected assumption—Gaussian distributions are called "normal" for good reason, and are found throughout science and nature. Mandelbrot seems to suspect a conspiracy to suppress his finding, but I doubt that anything other than statistical normality even occurred to financial economics' leading lights until the events of 1987 rubbed their noses in the inescapable fact of non-normality. Economists with the mathematical sophistication to deal with non-normality were until recently quite few and far between (if there were any at all), so the significance of Mandelbrot's finding is unlikely to have been clear to those whom it most concerned, even though they were almost certainly aware of it.

Normal distributions are fully described for mathematical purposes by a specification of just two "moments"—their mean and the variance of their distributions. The importance of the assumption of normal distributions to Modern Portfolio Theory is obvious when it is recalled that the foundation of the theory is known as "mean-variance

---

1. Most recently, Mandelbrot and Hudson, (2004). There is little in this book that Mandelbrot had not written elsewhere, many years earlier, but it indicates how slowly his ideas gained traction with the investing public that this title won an award as "the most innovative book in business and finance" for 2004—forty-two years after its central insight appeared in print.

optimization."[2] Mathematical descriptions of non-normal distributions require the specification of additional moments and are truly daunting to all but the most quantitatively sophisticated. The higher moments of financial time series distributions that have received most attention consist of their moments of kurtosis and in many cases their skewness. Exploration of still higher moments of these distributions has not, to my knowledge, attracted very much of finance theorists' attention to date.

Kurtosis—or more accurately, high positive kurtosis—is what has come to be referred to in the investment community by the unflattering term "fat tails" (surely "steatopygia" would be more consistent with statisticians' fondness for Greek). In positively kurtotic distributions, high standard deviation price movements occur more frequently than a normal distribution would suggest, as do low standard deviation movements that approximate to the mean, while price movements between these extremes are underrepresented (see **Figure 3.8**). For investors, positive kurtosis means that extreme price changes are more frequent than they would be if financial time series were normally distributed, but that price changes close to the average are also more frequent than under a normal distribution. In other words, returns cluster around the average except when they *definitely* do not, with comparatively little room for shades of gray in between.

Based on empirical research, it seems that all or almost all financial price series are positively kurtotic, at least most of the time, but not all are skewed, or at least not significantly so. Skewed distributions are asymmetric: the number of data points to the right of the mean or average

---

2. This has not gone unnoticed, and there have been various efforts to incorporate the higher statistical moments into an optimization framework. Perhaps the most promising are proposals to substitute a Bayes factor (see Harvey et al. 2004) or the Ω-function (see Keating and Shadwick 2002) for variance, since neither abstracts from the higher moments of distributions. In conjunction with non-standard utility functions, these have been adopted enthusiastically by some (see Bacmann and Pache 2004), but I suspect that solving the estimation problem for the third and fourth moments of time series distributions simply pushes the problem to higher moments, as Keating and Shadwick themselves seem to recognize (12). While considerably more research is needed in this area, I am not sanguine that the problems associated with non-normality can be solved with such (comparative) ease and elegance—in particular, I suspect that the utility functions used reintroduce many of the problems that substitution for variance is designed to solve, and that in any case they may not reflect investors' actual utility functions. See Page (2006) for an approach using brute-force, trial-and-error optimization that I believe illustrates this point. The instability of correlations over time is a further complicating factor.

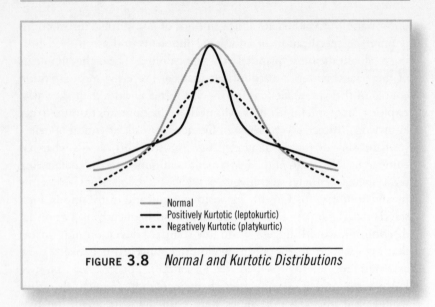

— Normal
— Positively Kurtotic (leptokurtic)
---- Negatively Kurtotic (platykurtic)

FIGURE **3.8** *Normal and Kurtotic Distributions*

value for the distribution is greater than to the left, or vice versa. In the former case, the skewness is said to be negative, and in the latter case, skewness is said to be positive. Note, by the way, the peculiar nomenclature of skewness: negativeness or positiveness are in terms of the tails rather than the bulk of the distribution, so that a negative distribution has the bulk of its observations on the positive side of its mean return. Negatively and positively skewed distributions are also sometimes called left-skewed and right-skewed, respectively—preserving this terminological peculiarity.

Because the number of data points on one side of the mean of the distribution is greater than the number on the other side, the average standard deviation of the data points on the underpopulated side must be greater: in other words, the mean must differ from the median. An investment vehicle with negatively skewed returns (as shown in **Figure 3.9**) will more consistently produce above-median than below median returns. But when it does post a below-median return, that return is likely to be further from the median than an above median return is likely to exceed the median. That is, in negatively skewed distributions, more returns are favorable than not, but the unfavorable ones can be expected to be noticeably more unpleasant than the favorable ones are desirable. For financial series that are negatively skewed, this usually means that the most extreme negative returns are more negative than the most extreme positive returns are positive, but that the rest of the data points pair off

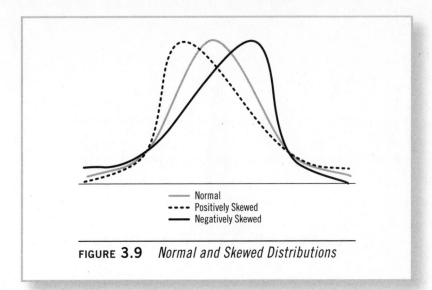

Normal
Positively Skewed
Negatively Skewed

FIGURE **3.9** *Normal and Skewed Distributions*

with each other to produce a sum that approximates pretty closely to the average level of return for the whole series. That is, while kurtotic distributions have "fat" tails (disproportionately many outliers) skewed distributions have "long" ones (disproportionately extreme outliers on one side of the distribution).

Taking a look at the distribution of an actual financial time series in **Figure 3.10**, a glance should suffice to convince anyone that it is not Gaussian—it is too tall and thin to be a normal, "bell-shaped" curve. Whereas a normal distribution would have 68.3 percent of its observed data points in the interval between one and minus one standard deviations, Figure 3.10 shows 79.1 percent. The scale of the illustration does not allow the most extreme data points at -21.6σ and $+12.2\sigma$ to be very easily visible, but such data would not be expected to appear at all in a normal distribution of only 14,838 observations. However, the scale of the illustration is just large enough that it is plain from a little close inspection of it that the distribution is negatively skewed. Rehearsing for the Standard & Poor's 500 Index what has already said about non-normal distributions generally,

❑ on average, the Index rose 0.029 percent daily: compounding explains its 7.45 percent *per annum* gain over a little more than fifty-nine years;

❑ it was comparatively rare for the Index's daily change to deviate much from its average value—it clustered closely around it;

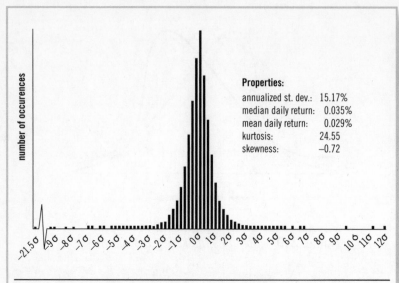

Properties:
annualized st. dev.: 15.17%
median daily return: 0.035%
mean daily return: 0.029%
kurtosis: 24.55
skewness: −0.72

Source: Bloomberg Finance L.P.

FIGURE 3.10 *Standard & Poor's 500 Index: Distribution of Returns Daily 12/26/1950 to 3/12/2009*

❑ but large one-day price moves—more than 2.82 percent down (−3σ) or 2.85 percent up (+3σ)—were more common than a normal distribution would lead us to expect;

❑ *much* more common: in a normal distribution, one-day price movements of that magnitude should have occurred forty times in the period shown: there were 527 in this sample;

❑ more days exhibited above-average performance than below-average performance, but this was almost completely offset (recall the 0.029 percent mean) by the fact that below-average days tended to be weaker than above-median days were favorable; and

❑ positive price changes of greater than 3σ occurred more than negative price changes of less than −3σ, but when big drops did occur, they tended to be more extreme than the gains experienced in very strong markets.

It is illustrative of the high kurtosis and positive skewness of most financial time series that there has been a near-regular occurrence of crisis events of 10σ or greater in some financial market or other since the 1980s, while positive 10σ events were extremely rare. **Table 3.3** rehearses this tale of woe.

TABLE 3.3 *A Chronicle of Crises*

1981	Collapse of gold and oil prices
1984	Dollar reversal
1987	Equity market crash
1990	Collapse of Japanese equity and high-yield markets
1991	Oil crisis
1992	European currency crisis
1994	Mexican peso crisis
1997	Asian crisis
1998	Russian crisis
1999	Brazilian crisis
2000	Collapse of technology bubble
2001	Collapse of high-yield market
2004	Volatility drought
2005	Collapse of convertible bond market
2007	Credit crunch

However, these statistical properties of financial time series require another important comment that is far too frequently ignored: as with standard deviations and correlations between data series, kurtosis and skewness may vary considerably over time. Measured over different time periods, the same price series may exhibit negative, positive, or zero skewness, and shift—sometimes violently—between various degrees of kurtosis or skewness, as shown in **Figures 3.11** and **3.12**.

While this vulnerability to a single data point is arguably an artifact of the relatively short sample periods available for most financial data series (although the series shown in Figures 3.11 and 3.12 derive from 14,878 daily observations, the calculation from which each data point in them is based on only ninety observations), those series, however imperfect, are all that investment practitioners have to work with.

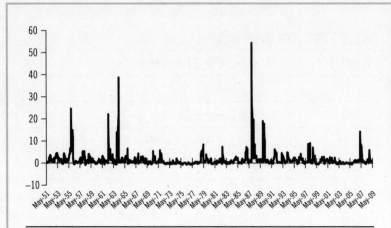

FIGURE 3.11   *Standard & Poor's 500 Index: 90-Day Trailing Kurtosis*

Source: Bloomberg Finance L.P.

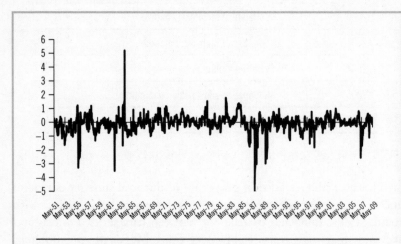

FIGURE 3.12   *Standard & Poor's 500 Index: 90-Day Trailing Skewness*

Source: Bloomberg Finance L.P.

Average figures for the full period shown in the figures—kurtosis of 24.5 and skewness of −0.72—tell only a very small part of the story. For some of the sample periods in Figures 3.11 and 3.12, the Standard & Poor's 500 Index's returns were even normally distributed. As will be stressed throughout this volume, it is important for investment policymakers to select time series that are comparable to their expected investment horizons, and to examine the behavior of the time series that is relevant to their considerations over the accumulation of all those time horizons for which data are available.

Having belatedly come to appreciate the importance of the higher moments of statistical distributions to the problems of investment, there is a tendency now for commentators to focus exclusively on them—or at least on the third and fourth moments: there are higher moments still, which, as mentioned, finance theory has to date tended to ignore. This is almost equally distorting, since without referring to the first and second moments—mean and variance—the higher moments are in fact almost meaningless. Generalizations such as "positive skewness good/ negative skewness bad" are naïve to the point of dangerousness. After all, a positively skewed distribution with a negative mean will enjoy a few strongly positive returns scattered among overwhelmingly many more negative ones. For example, the returns from a lottery have very strong positive skewness, although they are also very highly kurtotic, and in general positive skewness is typical of the distribution of returns from gambling. One of the attractions that accounts for the persistence of the noble anachronism of horse racing is that its bettors can choose among a wide range of return distributions, from lottery-like wagers on long-shots to combination bets with comparatively low positive skewness and negative kurtosis. Steeplechasing, where favorites can be expected to win more than a third of the time, is particularly amenable to the latter sort of betting strategy.

Investors must look beyond statistics to the nature of the data that give rise to them, and to stress-test conclusions based on statistical analyses of any sort. Blind acceptance of this, that, or the other statistical generalization about investments' return series without such "background checks" can be ruinous, and the worst of it is that its victims may not only fail to see it coming, but be unable to isolate the source of ruin even after it has materialized. Perhaps the simplest way to express the importance of non-normality in an investment context is that a proper appreciation of it encourages investors to expect the unexpected.

The Sensitivity of Statistical Calculations to Outliers

Given the very real suffering that crashes and financial panics leave in their wakes, it probably seems insensitive or even churlish to complain about the damage that they do to financial time series. But concern about this statistical consequence of market turmoil is not merely pedantic carping, because high standard deviation events that, as many do, involve sharp increases in correlation, tamper with the market's signposts, leaving market participants at a loss for guidance in their wake. It was common for some years in the aftermath of 1987 for analysts simply to omit the observation for October 19, 1987, from their data series. This is certainly not a satisfactory solution: for all that the Crash was anomalous, it will hardly do to pretend that it simply did not occur.

On the other hand, a data point with such a high standard deviation and its accompanying rise in correlation has a substantial effect on the statistical characteristics of the whole time series, and finding a way to accommodate it is not easy. For example, if we remove just the single data point for October 19 from the 14,838 daily observations included in the illustration of the Standard & Poor's 500 Index's return characteristics in Figure 3.10 above, then the kurtosis for the entire distribution falls from 24.55 to 16.16 while its skewness changes from an appreciably negative −0.72 to a more modest level of −0.40. Those who have suffered catastrophic losses as a result of such market drama may not be much impressed with these examples of statistical sleight-of-hand, but the efforts of those who are tasked with rebuilding the wealth that was destroyed in those episodes are hampered by them.

CHAPTER 4

Risk Estimation

T he problems with fitting alternative investments into a conventional investment allocation framework begin with the fact that many of them have no prices that can be analyzed with the tools—optimizers, multi-factor models, and so on—that are normally used to build such a framework. Mean-variance optimization, for example, is rather beside the point if neither the mean nor the variance of returns can be obtained. Investments that lack a public market such as private equity, some forms of direct lending, and real estate cannot be marked to a market that does not exist or exists only intermittently. Estimated values for these assets both attract considerable skepticism in their own right[1] and at any rate cannot reproduce the minute-to-minute vagaries of supply and demand that are among the primary source of price volatility in listed instruments. As risk analytics and thus investment allocation

---

1. As well they should. Fraser-Sampson (2007, 143) tells of a private equity investment whose "fair market value" was variously judged by accountants to be a positive figure, twice that figure and zero. Even more disturbingly, two of the estimates were produced by the same accounting firm. Although it is understood that many investors require periodic return data on which to base their actuarial, tax and other calculations, they should consider whether data of this quality is of even the slightest value to their deliberations. Nor are private equity funds the only vehicles guilty of "interesting" approaches to valuation: see Rahl (2001) on hedge funds' valuation practices. Standards for valuation in private market lending are somewhat better established, but there is still room for differences of opinion there, too.

models rely on volatility as their proxy for risk, this constitutes a very significant problem for investment policymakers.

Even assuming that plausible estimates of this data can be created to feed into the hoppers of the standard models, there is the question whether these models are adequate to the task. Alternative investments involve statistical characteristics, degrees of optionality, and time horizons (as well as severe contrasts in time horizons) that push the standard toolkit to its limits—and arguably well beyond. Compound this with the situation that many of the more common varieties of hedge funds may exercise real options in adjusting their long/short bias within a wide range and may pursue different strategies or even different asset classes as market conditions change, and there are grounds for despair. Given that some private market investment vehicles are similarly catholic in their disciplines, the magnitude of the problems facing investment policymakers begins to become clear. In fact, they are insuperable: if investment policymakers are rigidly tied to the use of traditional investment allocation models based on sound and objective data, then they have no choice but completely to avoid all but a very few types of alternative investments. The institutional popularity of long-only commodity exposure in recent years is probably not least due to the fact that it is one of the few alternative investment categories readily amenable to analysis within a traditional mean variance framework.

All of which are challenges to any project of analyzing alternative investments on a continuum with conventional ones, and indicates in advance that this volume will not be able to offer an elegant new mathematical model for doing so. This should be neither surprising nor disappointing. Any such model would of necessity entail simplifying assumptions that would be so sweeping that they would throw out numerous babies with the bathwater, rendering such a model nearly—if not completely—useless in practice. As we shall see in Part IV, even the models that are used to drive allocation decisions between just conventional, long-only stocks and bonds lack nuance and are not terribly robust. It would be unreasonable to expect more rigor here, where the complexity of the problem in hand is significantly greater.

Estimating Volatility

Virtually every hedge fund's or fund of fund's marketing materials include a reference to the fund's Sharpe ratio, but it is an extremely rare pitchbook (has any reader in fact encountered one? I have not) that appends a cautionary footnote. Yet many such funds are heavily exposed to non-marketable securities. There has been a steady tendency for the illiquid holdings of hedge funds to increase, and quite a few of them hold 30 percent of their assets or even more in direct loans, venture investments, and similar instruments that have no public market to mark to, as well as assets purchased in a market that subsequently saw its liquidity and thus its ability to provide meaningful marks vanish. Because these assets have no measurable volatility and because the denominator of the Sharpe ratio is volatility, the marketers' little oversight is, in fact, a significant misrepresentation. The effective Sharpe ratio on these funds is considerably lower than what they report. While there is no neat solution to this problem, funds should at least, in good conscience, alert their audiences to it.

There is no neat solution to this because, on the one hand, estimating volatility is not by any stretch of the imagination an exact science, especially for assets without a natural public market proxy, and, on the other hand, simply reporting the volatility of that portion of the portfolio that does enjoy public market pricing causes distortions of similar magnitude, which, as we saw in the previous chapter, can be extremely deceptive. And recall that everything said here about volatility goes for correlation as well—volatility is in fact a term in the equation for virtually all the statistical measures, ranging from correlations and factor loadings to value at risk, that an investment policymaker might have an interest in studying.

There cannot be a science of volatility estimation for the simple but profound reason that counterfactual statements are neither true nor false. There is no way to verify a claim such as "If it were publicly-traded, Bechtel Corp.'s share price would have an annualized standard deviation in the high 40 percent range," although the figure feels about right. This fact of logic ensures endless entertainment for those who enjoy speculating on topics such as "What if Lee had won the Battle of Gettysburg?" but it offers little comfort to investors who are seeking firm ground for their decision-making.

There is a further impediment to estimating volatility for many of the investments for which estimates are needed. Private equity and real estate offerings are blind pools: the investments they will purchase are generally unknown at the time that investors are invited to subscribe to them. While in many cases a rough idea of the General Partner's intentions is explicit in the offering material—many funds will indicate that they intend to concentrate their investments on biotech venture capital or hotel properties—in others it is not. Investors who subscribed to leveraged buyout funds early in the 2007 vintage are finding that they are not getting anything that resembles the exposure they anticipated at the time they made their commitments. If access to these investments is through purchase of partnership interests in the secondary market, it is likely that at least some of their investment exposure can be known prior to purchase, but not if an investor subscribes to them during their initial offering period.

So volatility estimates are very approximate. Any confidence I might place in my guess about Bechtel derives from its source: I examined the volatility of comparable firms' shares, and found that price variation across the group is reasonably consistent. For large private firms in familiar industries, estimation by analogy is uncontroversial and widely practiced. However, it requires a couple of caveats. The balance sheet structure of private firms is unlikely to resemble that of their publicly traded brethren—venture firms will in almost all cases be less leveraged than their publicly traded counterparts, and firms that have experienced leveraged buyouts will be much more deeply in debt. Financial condition should undoubtedly be reflected in share price volatility, so by rights my Bechtel figure should be adjusted for data to which outsiders to the firm do not in fact have access. There is little science in how such an adjustment should be made, but then, given the amount of approximation that has already gone into this exercise, a little more guesswork will not greatly increase its error term. It may also be appropriate to adjust for size and the post-issuance price behavior of recent initial public offerings (IPOs).

The second caveat is simply to warn against index illusion. We tend to think of indices as averages, and that is what they are—averages of prices. However, it does not follow from this that they are averages of the *properties* of prices, such as volatility. As **Table 4.1** shows, most individual components of an index have higher volatility than the index itself (in this case, 16 percent higher on average). This is to be expected, given the diversifying effect of different correlations among index components (note that the average β of these stocks is only 0.7701 and none is greater than one), but it is surprising how easily this fact is forgotten. Any subset of an index is by definition less diversified than the index itself, and unless a deliberate effort is made to select the defensive components of the index, a subset of it can almost always be expected to be more volatile than the index as a whole. Private market investment vehicles are unavoidably much less diversified than a broad metric such as the Standard & Poor's 500 Index. Private equity people are occasionally horrified with my rule of thumb that their asset class has effective volatility of two to four times the volatility of the S&P 500. But when

TABLE 4.1 *Annualized Daily Standard Deviation of the Standard & Poor's 500 Total Return Index and its Largest Components Ranked 3/17/2009, data 3/18/2008 to 3/17/2009*

	STANDARD DEVIATION	β	INDEX WEIGHT
Standard & Poor's 500 Index	**43.72%**	**1.0000**	**100.00%**
Exxon Mobil	52.79	0.8268	5.19
AT&T	46.44	0.8451	2.21
Procter & Gamble	32.75	0.7924	2.11
Johnson & Johnson	31.22	0.8045	2.08
Chevron	57.56	0.8524	1.96
Microsoft	52.61	0.8116	1.91
International Business Machines	38.99	0.8283	1.84
Wal-Mart Stores	35.67	0.6810	1.65
General Electric	68.47	0.7180	1.55
Pfizer	42.89	0.8018	1.42
Cisco Systems	52.33	0.8838	1.40
JPMorgan Chase	99.07	0.7376	1.39
Apple	57.95	0.7295	1.31
Verizon Communications	44.95	0.7878	1.25
Intel	54.18	0.8396	1.22
Coca-Cola	37.65	0.6737	1.22
Google	56.27	0.7439	1.18
Philip Morris International	41.13	0.7188	1.15
PepsiCo	33.17	0.7139	1.13
Abbott Laboratories	33.04	0.6729	1.13
Hewlett-Packard	49.22	0.7447	1.08
Wells Fargo & Co.	108.93	0.6831	0.91
Qualcomm	56.19	0.7480	0.91
Oracle	49.97	0.8450	0.89
McDonald's	34.06	0.7677	0.88

nearly a quarter of that index's components (accounting for a bit more than 40 percent of its total weighting) exhibit volatility that is at least 25 percent higher than the index's (and in two instances considerably more than twice as high), mine do not strike me as especially remarkable figures, although they are higher than some others' estimates.

Lerner (2007) reports that, at least at the time that he was writing, the Yale University Investments Office estimated the volatility of private equity to be 29.1 percent versus 20.0 percent for "U.S. equities" (benchmark unspecified) (5). Assuming volatility for highly leveraged or start-up companies that is comparable to that of AT&T, Hewlett-Packard, General Electric, or ConocoPhillips seems rather low to me. However, vintage diversification will tend to reduce volatility. Singer et al. (2003) offer a vintage-diversified private equity simulation by diversifying "purchases" of the Standard & Poor's 500 Index over five years (103). They arrive at the conclusion that the volatility of such a portfolio is "on the order of two times" that of the Index. While the volatility of private equity funds is reducible through diversification, those authors note that a sufficiently diversified holding will acquire greater correlation to equities, which of course reduces its portfolio benefits. Using nine years of Danish pension fund return data (regulation requires that this data be publicized), Nielsen (2005), Table 4, finds that the standard deviation of the private equity portions of their portfolios is 2.8 times that of their conventional portfolios.

Similar estimates for real estate can be drawn by analogy to real estate investment trusts (REITs), publicly traded Master Limited Partnerships may prove to be usefully similar to certain other assets, and the traded fixed-income markets provide a wealth of comparators for privately placed debt instruments. However, this raises the question whether such estimates should be adjusted to allow for the public market β that attaches to all such instruments, and, if so, how this is best accomplished. The coefficient of correlation between REITs and stocks over the period shown in **Figure 4.1** (prior to April 1, 2009, the index shown there was known as the Dow Jones Wilshire REIT Total Return Index) is moderate at 0.2376, but clearly the aggregate statistic tells only a very small part of the story. Disentangling the market β component of REITs' returns from the return component specific to the assets that underlie those instruments for the purpose of constructing an estimate of private market real estate volatility is not at all straightforward. It seems to me that it is also methodologically debatable. If the market in which private real estate is transacted were a continuous auction, who is to say what that market's correlation to equities might be?

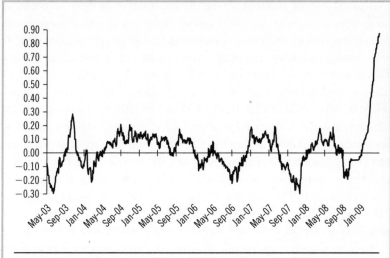

Source: Bloomberg Finance L.P.

FIGURE 4.1   *Dow Jones Select REIT and Russell 3000 Indices: 90-Day Trailing Coefficient of Correlation*

To assume that it would have none is at least as arbitrary an assumption as the assumption that it would have the same correlation as REITs, if not even more arbitrary.[2]

There are non-marketable investments for which it is much harder to find analogues, and here we may find ourselves on even shakier ground in our attempt to craft volatility estimates. What, for example, is an appropriate market-traded comparison for life insurance settlements? In this case, at least we have the possibility of consulting actuarial tables, and by stretching our imaginations in ways that are more familiar to insurance underwriters than to security investors, we might find ways of conceptualizing them as bond-like. But what of artworks?

---

2. DiBartolomeo et al. (2005) propose an intriguing alternative methodology for estimating the volatility of real estate that employs multi-factor analysis. DiBartolomeo has communicated to me that the technique "works well," at least in a commercial real estate context. However, it is very demanding of data and preparatory research, and I suspect that it is unlikely to attract much favor from investment policymakers at any but the largest, most real estate–intensive institutions. But there are at least some factor analytic considerations that certainly should contribute to any institution's real estate investment decision-making process, if not perhaps ones as detailed as those required to feed DiBartolomeo's model: see Chapter 23.

Discussions of investments in the broadest sense tend to mention collectibles in passing and then ignore them, for the very good reason that such questions are virtually unanswerable. Mamarbachi et al. (2008) is a notable exception in giving serious attention to collectables at all. This chapter has no choice but to follow precedent in this matter. But a painting by Vermeer is unquestionably an investable asset with a realizable price that is subject to change. Consulting auction histories for Old Masters, the Mei Moses Old Masters Index, or one of the two Art Market Research Dutch Old Masters indices may provide starting points for constructing such an estimate, but given the unique nature of artworks and their infrequent transaction histories (particularly Vermeers, of which only thirty-five are reliably attributed: the most recent sale was in 2004 and the next most recent was in the 1920s), index illusion is probably even greater for this sort of asset than for others. The only recourse in these situations is to consult the experts, but on the evidence of the distance between auction houses' pre-sale estimates and the prices actually realized for such assets (Sotheby's estimate for the Vermeer sold in 2004 was only 18 percent of the price it actually commanded), there are considerable grounds for caution in relying upon them. Unique or near-unique assets pose insoluble problems to investment allocators, which account for the general conspiracy to skirt around the topic.

Many investments are hedged opportunistically, and many hedge funds are opportunistically long- or short-biased, creating an additional challenge to volatility estimation. Those that are systematically hedged or that, like high-frequency traders, are sequentially long and short, will eventually produce time series that are susceptible of statistical analysis, but a decision to hedge substantial portions of a portfolio that had not previously been hedged breaks the continuity of its return history dramatically. For example, most international equity managers do not hedge their currency exposure, arguing variously that actively managed non-U.S. equities are to some extent self-hedging against the dollar, that currencies are a zero-sum game in the long run so not worth the trouble of hedging, or simply that currency management is not their area of expertise.[3] Yet the temptation to make currency

---

3. An additional, less frequently mentioned reason is that hedging results usually show up in a portfolio's cash account. No manager looks forward to explaining how a loss was made on cash if a hedge turns out to be inopportune. For that matter, the hedge itself, as a short position, shows up in the account as a negative asset, which also can be interesting for a portfolio manager to have to explain to those who are unfamiliar with this accounting presentation.

forecasts and to act on them is always present for portfolio managers who are engaged with foreign exchange on a daily basis. So it is not at all uncommon for an international fund that had eschewed hedging abruptly to succumb to temptation and hedge its currency exposures aggressively.

During the market dramas of 2008, not a few conventional portfolio managers who would not previously have dreamed of hedging their market exposure convinced themselves to do so, in the process spoiling the continuity of their time series. While it would be ungrateful of investors who benefited from this departure from custom to complain, that does not change the fact that the managers' opportunism subsequently confronted investment policymakers with a difficult problem. If there were a guarantee that the departure would not be repeated, they could probably ignore its occurrence. But this is to fly in the face of human nature: having once hedged opportunistically with excellent results, the likelihood that a manager will do so again is clearly increased.

Volatility is itself volatile (see Jones and Wilson 2004). So, as with every other statistical property of financial time series, estimates of volatility need to be re-examined regularly and critically—in effect, stress-tested. Over the extended time horizons encompassed in strategic, investment policy-driven investment allocations, volatility might reasonably be expected to revert to its long-term mean, although this is an assumption that ought to be examined with a high degree of skepticism. It certainly bears close examination and stress-testing in any particular case.

But for the purposes of tactical allocation, prevailing volatility conditions have to be monitored closely. Investors who believed that changes in market structure accounted for the long trough in volatility from 2004 to 2007 (shown in **Figure 4.2**: note here and elsewhere that the Barclays Capital fixed-income indices were formerly known as the Lehman Brothers indices) or who for other reasons expected it to continue indefinitely were rudely surprised when market conditions changed. Shifts in the volatility environment are often event-driven, and consequently very difficult if not essentially impossible to anticipate. While most investors benefited from this two-and-a-half year period of comparative calm, to market-makers and others whose trading strategies are heavily dependent on volatility for their returns, the "Volatility Drought" (which also affected equities) was a disaster that forced many of them into different trading strategies or retirement.

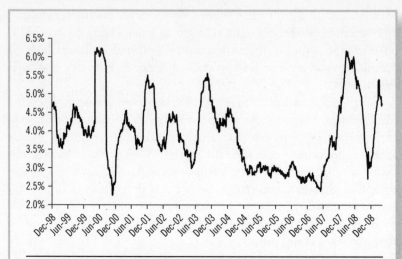

Source: Barclays Capital

FIGURE 4.2   *Barclays Capital U.S. Aggregate Bond Index:*
90-Day Trailing Standard Deviation

Autocorrelation

As elementary as the features of compounding discussed in the previous chapter are for finance, it is worth calling attention to a related matter. The time series of many alternative investment vehicles are autocorrelated (that is, serially correlated, so that previous readings influence subsequent ones), because the values of all or a significant portion of their assets are estimated, and the estimates do not incorporate the volatility of market pricing. This can have a surprising and substantial effect on various statistical measures of their behavior. A thought experiment offered by Merton (2008, 9–10) that simulates this situation indicates the extent of the problem. If a hypothetical fund, whose sole asset is some index, only prices every second week, its β relative to the same index priced weekly may be less than half what it would have been if the fund had also been priced weekly. Consequently, the α of an index fund can be higher than that of the index and thus its Sharpe ratio can be higher. This is absurd: the fund tracks the index, and its reported returns will be identical to those of the index over time. The effects of stale prices matter a great deal to the basic statistical tools employed in investment allocation.

Much has been written recently about the autocorrelation of hedge fund returns—that is, their rather puzzling lack of volatility—and Lo (2008) argues that the lion's share of this arises from the illiquidity of their positions, although he notes other causes including deliberate smoothing to make their reported returns more attractive to potential investors (64 *ff*). While this lack of liquidity pales before that exhibited by assets such as Old Masters, it is insidious because it is largely unexpected. Lo offers a means of adjusting hedge fund returns for their autocorrelation. To provide an illustration of the magnitude of the smoothing he believes his method eliminates from reported returns, he compares raw and adjusted Sharpe ratios for various hedge fund style indices. He compares these to raw and adjusted Sharpe ratios for several mutual funds, where autocorrelation is virtually absent, and his analysis produces some startling results. Autocorrelation among mutual fund returns is minimal, and thus the difference between their raw and adjusted Sharpe ratios is minimal as well. In the most extreme case for the hedge fund indices, the raw calculation was 68 percent higher than the recalculated ratio, and the average for all the indices was 30 percent higher. There are many reasons to be skeptical of the use of Sharpe ratios as measures of hedge fund risk, but stale pricing that results in autocorrelation is certainly one of them.

Investment Allocation Models and Alternative Investments

As though the problems of obtaining data to feed into familiar risk and allocation models were not daunting enough, the models themselves are challenged when they are confronted by alternative investments. The challenges are not unique to the attempt to apply them to such investments—they are the problems addressed in the previous chapter's discussion of non-normality. They derive from problems that are inherent in the models and known to adversely affect the quality of the results achieved when they are applied to conventional investments as well. However, various aspects of the return characteristics of alternative investments—most noticeably their optionality, their widespread use of hedging, but also their use of leverage—magnify the models' resulting error terms even further. Here again, alternative investments resemble conventional ones, "only more so."

The point in bringing all this up is not to launch into a rehearsal of the myriad joys of non-Gaussian statistics, but to underline the extent to which alternative investments add to the difficulty of allocating among investments. As applied to conventional investment techniques, Modern Portfolio Theory already encounters significant underestimation of risk due to the kurtosis and skewness of financial time series. One of the features that recommends alternative investments to many investors (whether wisely or not) is precisely that their skewness and kurtosis may be very different from those of conventional investments. However, magnified third and fourth moments of return distributions increase the error term in estimating alternative investments' risk compared to the error term that arises from application of standard models to conventional investment techniques. And because the characteristics of all assets' and investment techniques' price series distributions change over time, estimates of their risk and how it compares to that of other investments are subject to continual revision.

Are We Theoretically Rudderless?

So between the lack of good volatility data for many alternative investments and flaws in the standard analytic models that alternatives only tend to exaggerate, are we left without theoretical grounds for asset allocation? I think not. And at the end of the day, none of these problems should come as a tremendous surprise. There is a return to investment allocation, whether strategic or tactical, and therefore an attendant risk. Where there is risk, there is uncertainty, and that is precisely what we have encountered in stumbling across higher-than-expected and changeable error terms for these models.

The advocates of Modern Portfolio Theory dominate academia, and since the 1970s the theory has become investment orthodoxy, if not precisely dogma. However, the fact that the theory is not as unassailable as its proponents have been wont to imply does not require that we adopt the contrary view that it is built on loose sand. "Working hypothesis" or "heuristic tool" hardly seem appropriate descriptors of the status that most of us have been taught to ascribe to one of the monuments of twentieth-century economics. But that is probably how Modern Portfolio Theory should be regarded. An analogy might be helpful here. We know that Newtonian physics gives only an approximate description of the behavior of bodies in motion, but for most purposes (including getting safely to the moon and back) the approximation suffices. We can use Modern Portfolio Theory without accepting it as received Writ, just as we can use Newtonian physics for many purposes, provided that we keep the shortcomings of both firmly in mind.

The key to successful heuristic use of Modern Portfolio Theory or any other working hypothesis is to know where its limits lie, so that if we approach them, as is likely with alternative investments, we know that it is appropriate to reduce or at least apply increased caution to our reliance upon it. But as most practitioners have always at least intuitively understood, such caution is required even when dealing with portfolios restricted solely to conventional investments. What this means in real-world application is that we must stress-test those of our conclusions that rely on statistical reasoning—for the quality of the data that are used to obtain the statistics, for the error terms that attach to our limited sample sizes, and for the more imponderable error that non-normality entails for their conclusions. To draw once again on the analogy with classical physics, we can happily calculate our orbit using seventeenth-century methods most of the time, but when we approach very massive bodies, measure to a degree of precision where quantum effects become meaningful, reach relativistic velocities, or when we are in orbit long enough for miniscule errors to accumulate into large ones, we must expect our calculations to diverge from what we actually experience. In my view, proposals such as substituting the Ω-function for variance in portfolio optimizations (mentioned in the preceding chapter) have the ad hoc and approximate character of the orbital adjustments that are required to keep satellites in position.

This comes most to the fore in any investment discussion involving correlation. These range from the most general considerations of investment policy to the specifics of calculating hedge ratios for a particular paired transaction, from which it is clear that the need for caution pervades the whole gamut of investment thinking. This includes not only the obviously affected areas of hedging and diversification, but also any analysis that, through various implementations of Arbitrage Pricing Theory, involves isolation and analysis of the factors that drive returns. A second area of particular stress is in the analysis of any trade that involves optionality, and the stress mounts the longer the time horizon of the trade, and mounts again as expiry becomes imminent. Much of the optionality of various alternative investment strategies is inherent in the trades they pursue, suggesting permanent options without expiry dates (see Chapter 13) and thus error terms that may be impossible to estimate but that could conceivably be quite large. Because many trades that exploit optionality are hedged transactions, the first points mentioned also apply. All these considerations, combined with the lack of volatility data for many alternative investments, should be more than sufficient to recommend caution about the application of traditional modes of statistically grounded analysis to pretty much the entire universe of such investment vehicles.

Will there be an Einsteinian revision to Modern Portfolio Theory's Newtonian approximation? There is good reason to doubt it. Since the statistical characteristics of financial time series' distributions are inconstant, it is difficult to conceive of a static theory that could accommodate them through their changeable lives. This is at the root of the skepticism I expressed above and in the previous chapter about the proposal that the Ω-function might supplant standard deviation in the Theory's calculations. It might seem that this consideration is irrelevant to investment policymakers, as their deliberations are (or ought to be) "for the ages," but unless their conclusions are fixed and unchanging, their point of entry into their new allocation target will almost inevitably be at a time when correlations do not mirror the long-term averages they will exhibit over the future life of the allocation. The best we can probably hope for is something counterintuitive and mathematically daunting like quantum mechanics. Mandelbrot is, after all, the originator of "chaos" theory, and if his proposed solutions prove to be as pertinent to the problem of allocating investments as his criticisms have been, then any eventual revision of Modern Portfolio Theory along lines that he might suggest would certainly not be the stuff of "Investing 101." I suspect that even that much will not be forthcoming, and that progress beyond Modern Portfolio Theory will remain trade-specific, closely tied to a limited set of empirical circumstances and incapable of broad generalization. And most likely, any practical applications will remain largely proprietary, lurking in the quantitative research departments of investment banks and a handful of the most sophisticated and quantitatively oriented hedge funds.

This is where "postmodern" criticisms of Modern Portfolio Theory seem to me to come up disappointingly short. In addition to the objections to its statistical foundations that I have discussed, these include the criticisms offered by behavioral economists that dispute its assumption that investors are rational utility maximizers. As far as anyone has as yet been able to take them, both strands of criticism lead only to very general cautionary pronouncements rather than replacement theories. This is not to say that they are without value, only that they fail to offer solutions to the completely legitimate issues that they raise. Their recommendations resemble Polonius's "to thine own self be true"—universally acknowledged to be sound but ultimately not terribly helpful. While I have indicated that I am skeptical that the statistical critics will find a replacement for Modern Portfolio Theory, such a replacement is probably at least possible in principle. Ad hoc analyses that apply non-Gaussian statistical techniques to individual types of trades are in fact in use. This provides some reason to hope that a theoretical resolution of the problems with which non-normality confronts investors is not an entirely empty dream, despite my doubt that it will be achieved.

In the nature of the case, those critics who draw on arguments from behavioral finance cannot replace what they have spurned. This is an inherent drawback to any form of epistemological nihilism: in rejecting rationality it necessarily undermines its own claims to rationality, too. That is, if as an inalterable consequence of our cognitive psychology investors are irrational, then investors' response to this datum can only be . . . irrational. The driving assumptions behind the behavioral finance critique demand that those who aspire to exploit others' cognitive biases must necessarily be subject to those same biases. Proponents of behavioral analyses are, of course, aware of this—see, for example, Montier (2002): "I am subject to exactly the same emotional biases that confront each and every one of us. I am probably being both overly optimistic and over-confident in my assessment of just how valuable behavioural [*sic*] finance is likely to prove" (180). Wright et al. (2008) present evidence suggesting that behavioral considerations' contribution to investment performance is limited and that, as might be expected, it results in a value/contrarian bias to security selection. Behavioral analyses have important roles to play in investment thinking, particularly in helping investors to specify their utility functions, but not as the primary drivers of investment decision-making.

Applying Theory to Practice

It is all very well to urge caution, but what exactly does caution entail? If the advice is to be more valuable than Polonius's essentially contentless advice to Laërtes, it requires some elaboration. We cannot calculate a level of optimal exposure to the riskiest investment techniques and then simply trim it arbitrarily, because the uncertainty of our calculations affects all positions in the portfolio. Over long time horizons, carrying a larger cash reserve than our optimization programs would otherwise suggest is not a very satisfactory alternative. The statistical digression in the previous chapter indicates that outliers are less rare than Modern Portfolio Theory suspected, but they are still uncommon. For example, the negative tail (-3σ or greater) comprises 0.67 percent of the observations in Figure 3.10 (as opposed to the 0.27 percent that would be found in a normal distribution): substantially more, but still a rather small number. Most strategies that involve carrying a greater cash position (but one still small enough to allow for satisfactory returns) would provide only limited protection against these rare-ish events at a substantial cost to performance most of the time, as the negative skew of the Standard & Poor's 500 Index and most other financial time series indicates that they produce above-median returns more frequently than below-median ones.[4]

Another response is to diversify further: if four thousand positions previously seemed adequate diversification, tack on a few thousand more. This is certainly a possible solution, although taken to an extreme it would entail an unacceptable increase in transaction and management costs, sufficient to offset all of the diversification benefits that it offers. It also lands us in a *sorites* paradox, such that a satisfactory level of diversification is always just beyond reach and can never in fact be obtained. Increasing diversification without limit is consistent with Modern Portfolio Theory, which holds that the only truly optimal investment is the Market Portfolio—the aggregate of all possible investments. But the Market Portfolio is an abstraction that cannot in practice be replicated. For example we, like the modern Greeks, are unlikely ever to be able to obtain ownership exposure to the Elgin Marbles, which are included among the assets that comprise the Market Portfolio. From a purely theoretical standpoint, no level of diversification short of the Market Portfolio can ever be "enough."

In an earlier chapter, I drew a weak distinction between diversification and hedging that relied on the claim that diversification involves return-seeking while hedging is always risk-avoiding. The implication of this distinction is that diversified portfolios should seek investments that are weakly correlated rather than strongly counter-correlated. Counter-correlation reduces both risk and return, and perfect counter-correlation eliminates both entirely. Weak correlation (whether positive or negative) offers the possibility of enhanced return due to the effect of reduced volatility on compounded returns, without neutralizing exposure to another strategy and thus cutting too deeply into its return. The search for diversifying alternative investments should concentrate on those that carry low correlations to all other portfolio components. It is less important that they are positive or negative than that they are reasonably close

---

4. A possible exception is Nassim Taleb's own strategy, pursued by Universa Investments L.P., of which he is a principal and the senior scientific advisor. This involves carrying large cash positions and buying equity or index put options that are far out of the money—a strategy that was well rewarded during the numerous high standard deviation events of 2008. However, his much less successful experience with an earlier fund during the "Volatility Drought" indicates the risks of relying almost entirely on rare events to generate the bulk of returns: see Patterson (2008).

to zero. By constructing portfolios from weakly correlated investments, policymakers can approximate more closely to the Market Portfolio while restricting holdings to a cost-efficient and manageable number. Consideration of investments' comparative volatility is also valuable, insofar as that can be estimated.

To take an example, long-only commodity strategies have found their way into numerous portfolios because of their low historical correlation with stocks and bonds, combined with their attractive performance record. Although **Figure 4.3** indicates that the relationship between these three asset categories has been highly changeable over the period shown, commodities' low average coefficients of correlation (0.1317 to equities, −0.0512 to bonds) bear out the diversification benefits of introducing them into conventional portfolios. What is especially attractive about Figure 4.3 is that the shifting correlations between these assets seem to counterbalance each other with fairly reliable consistency: there is no appreciable period of the time that is shown in the chart during which all three correlation series moved in concert. It is no surprise that investors' interest in long-only commodities has mounted steadily over the last decade or so, and that they are often the first alternative investment category to which investment policymakers decide to allocate. It will be interesting to see whether this interest persists after the experience of 2008, when these favorable characteristics of these metrics were severely tested.

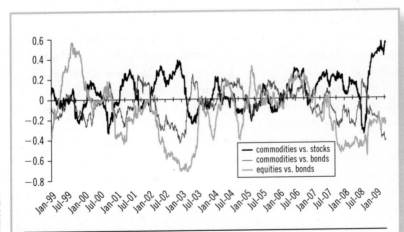

Source: Bloomberg Finance L.P.

FIGURE 4.3 *Stocks, Bonds, and Commodities*: 90-Day Trailing Coefficients of Correlation*

*Russell 3000, Barclays Capital U.S. Aggregate Bond and UBS Bloomberg Constant Maturity Commodity indices.

Volatility data are as readily available for commodities as they are for any traded investment vehicle, hedging is not involved in long-only exposure, liquidity in most cases is strong, and leverage, although amply available, need not be employed (investors can hold an offsetting cash or fixed-income portfolio) to make their returns attractive relative to equity or fixed income. It would be difficult to find an alternative investment that is easier for policymakers wedded to traditional investment allocation techniques to make an allocation case for. But in making the case, a glance at a chart is not sufficient. It is important to examine the causes of the relationships observed, to support our confidence that the observed correlations are not simply spurious statistical accidents. In the case of commodities, these include but are not limited to

❑ positive correlation with inflation, for systematic reasons that are intuitively clear and that encourage a low correlation to bonds; and
❑ positive event risk: shocks due to excess commodity supply are comparatively rare, and consequently commodity returns exhibit fewer negative outliers than equities. In fact, at least for the time period shown in Figure 4.3, commodity returns were positively skewed, consistent with the view that commodity shocks tend to come in the form of interruptions to supply rather than sudden increases in supply or abrupt, unpredictable disappearance of demand.

Detailed examination of such considerations is what was intended by my earlier comment about stress-testing conclusions that depend on statistical reasoning. Figure 4.3 amply illustrates the point that correlations among asset prices that are not systematically related are rarely stable, so decisions that are even partially based upon them must be examined very critically.

But policymakers' decision to include commodities within the scope of investment policy only leads to new questions: what should be the neutral allocation, how should the allocation be funded from the existing allocation, and what parameters should be placed around tactical decisions to depart from neutral exposure? These are more difficult to answer, and it is notable that proponents of a long-only commodity allocation differ very widely—by as much as 3,500 basis points that I am aware of—in their recommendations for the neutral allocation. However, for the moment at least, answering these questions can probably be dodged through obfuscating the issue. Precision becomes less and less possible the more investment categories our investment policy circumscribes. And, given the way that their investment vehicles are structured, if we include private equity or private real estate among them, any hope of precision in allocation levels departs quickly by the window. But I will return to these topics in Part IV, after examining some individual alternative investment categories in more detail.

SOME EXAMPLES

CHAPTER 5

Long/Short Equity

The previous chapters have been long on generalization and anecdote, but it is time to address the concrete problems that confront investment policymakers who have an interest in allocating to alternative investment vehicles. I will begin Part II of this book, which is devoted to case study–like chapters, with what is arguably the most "classic" and probably the most widely pursued hedge fund strategy—the launch of which is credited to Alfred Jones in 1949—because it highlights many of the issues that were raised in Part I. "Classic" and long-lived, too: a lineal descendent of Jones' original partnership is still in operation. The first use of the term "hedge fund" seems to have been in an article about Jones: see Loomis (1966).

Not the least of the problems that confront investment policymakers is that we are immediately thrown into the sort of terminological morass I discussed in my Introduction. Investment techniques that can reasonably be described as long/short include those that are consistently biased toward the long side, those that are consistently biased toward the short side, those that shift opportunistically between long or short biases, and those that attempt to be rigorously market-neutral. Most of them can be further differentiated based on whether the hedge side of the book uses instruments that are systematically linked to those on the long side of the book or instruments that more or less weakly correlate relative to the long positions through statistical arbitrage relationships. From this it is already clear that "classical" turns out to be rather confusingly baroque. While index providers and others are at pains to distinguish among them, for the purposes of my discussion here it is useful to lump them together and to construe the term "long/short" as encompassing all of these techniques.

In any case, some of the differences between them are obvious from **Figure 5.1**, and the handful of calculations shown in **Table 5.1** making use of the data shown there underlines the point. The types of investments

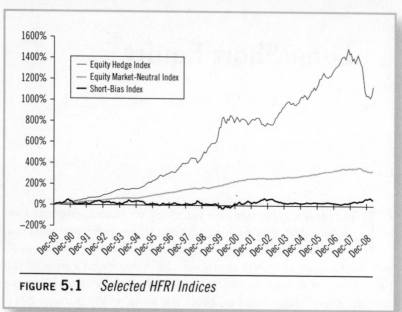

FIGURE 5.1   *Selected HFRI Indices*

Source: Hedge Fund Research.

TABLE 5.1   *HFRI Long/Short Indices*

	EQUITY HEDGE INDEX	EQUITY MARKET-NEUTRAL INDEX	SHORT-BIAS INDEX
Compound Annual Return	13.83%	7.87%	2.31%
Median Monthly Return	1.29%	0.61%	−0.13%
Annualized Standard Deviation	9.23%	3.27%	19.56%
Correlation to Russell 3000 Index	0.7514	0.2203	−0.7415
Kurtosis	1.84	1.37	2.07
Skewness	−0.17	−0.23	0.14

Source: Hedge Fund Research, Bloomberg Finance L.P.

measured by two of these indices are self-explanatory. The Equity Hedge Index is a broad measure that includes market-neutral and short-bias as well as several other strategies.

Treating techniques with such wildly varied return characteristics together is not likely to result in excessive confusion between them, although it will require some irritating circumlocution. Doing so makes discussion somewhat unwieldy, but it facilitates an examination of the hedged nature of the trade that is at the core of this approach to investing; that is, the significant differences between them should be mutually illuminating.

Long/Short as an Investment Technique

Long/short investment techniques, of whatever variety, are first and foremost directional trades. The bulk of their returns derive from price movements. Long positions in dividend-paying equities are likely to generate a certain amount of income, and short positions will have their borrowing costs (whether explicit in security borrowing or implicit in derivative pricing) as well as dividends on the underlying that the investor may be required to pay if security loans are employed. So there is some admixture of cash flow strategy in the trade. And as we have seen, hedging is arbitrage-related. Thus long/short incorporates elements of all three investment strategies, although it is fundamentally the directional returns that it produces that motivate investment policymakers to incorporate any of its various techniques into an institution's investable universe.

Many—but by no means all—long/short hedge funds seek returns from both the long and the short sides of their books. This may seem to fly in the face of the distinction I attempted to draw in Chapter 2 between hedging and diversification, but for those funds that seek returns from both sides of their books, the short positions perform both functions. On the one hand they are straightforward directional trades— the manager forecasts that the price of the stock will decline and sells exposure to it accordingly. In this respect, the manager has not hedged but has diversified, because the security sold short is not elsewhere held long and the intention behind the trade is return-seeking. On the other hand, all equities have β—correlation to the general market[1]—so selling

---

1. In strict accordance with Modern Portfolio Theory, β is a security's correlation with the Market Portfolio, and therefore an unknowable quantity. Whether in ignorance of this nicety (and some authors' understanding of the Market Portfolio is rather surprising) or simply to obtain some value from theory, market practitioners generally use correlation relative to a broad market indicator such as the Standard & Poor's 500 or Russell 3000 indices.

one short hedges (within the sense of my distinction) the β of another that is held long to a greater or lesser degree, depending on the correlations and βs of the securities involved. Long/short managers who seek return from their short books hope that they have found a way to have their cake and eat it, too, as far as the dangers of equivocation between hedges and return-seeking positions are concerned.

But a fund's short book need not be return-seeking. Selling exposure to the broad market through the options or futures markets provides a fairly accurate hedge against β, leaving only the α of the long book plus any residual β exposure as the producers of the technique's returns. Most of the return differential between market-neutral techniques and long/short techniques in general that is shown in Figure 5.1 derives from market-neutral investors' strategic decision to forgo most of the returns to β—"most" because, as we shall see, they rarely succeed in eliminating exposure to β entirely. But a market-neutral investor need not have recourse to the derivatives markets. Maintaining a balance of short and long exposure through individual security positions can hedge away the bulk of a portfolio's β exposure and allows the short book to be return-seeking if the manager so desires. However, maintaining the relevant balance between long and short exposures is not so easily achieved: there are numerous factors that must be attended to, not least the relative βs of the long and short books, as well as sector exposure, and so forth. Few of these factors are stationary.

The haplessness of short-bias managers in the context of the solid returns posted by conventional long-only equities is predictable, so it should come as no surprise that dedicated short sellers and short-bias long/short strategies have had limited success in asset gathering—which raises the question why these managers persist in the attempt. There are clearly easier ways to earn a living within the hedge fund world. While individual short sales have on occasion performed heroically, a market that is generally rising (recall the implications of the broad market's negative skew around a positive mean return from Chapter 3) provides considerably less than ideal conditions for strategies that fly in the face of the prevailing price trend. As would be expected and as **Figure 5.2** clearly indicates, short bias counter-correlates with the market—the correlation coefficient for the period shown is significantly negative at -0.7415. This provides commercial salvation to the rather limited number of short bias managers that remain in operation at any given time: their products are primarily used by funds of funds to provide a hedge against market exposure. Market-neutral funds clearly do not provide such a directional hedge, but their positive sensitivity to volatility, given that

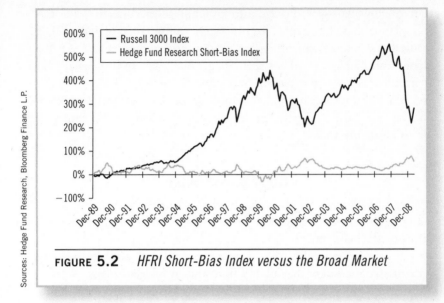

Sources: Hedge Fund Research, Bloomberg Finance L.P.

FIGURE 5.2 *HFRI Short-Bias Index versus the Broad Market*

volatility generally accompanies declining markets, gives them marginal hedging characteristics on the downside, which is an attractive property. We will encounter such optionality frequently in what follows.

But of course, there are periods when a short-bias leads to out-performance—for example, in the two years after February 2000, the Short-Bias Index gained an eye-catching 17,155 basis points relative to the Russell 3000 Index, and relative performance after the credit crisis began to take hold in mid-2007 was also quite strong. Episodes of market-wide movements are an invitation to opportunistic adjustment of a fund's long/short bias for market timing purposes or, for funds of funds, to reallocate to one or another bias. Funds of funds and opportunistically long/short managers who take a view on general market direction will increase their exposure on one side of their book or the other accordingly. Tactical allocation of this kind is a sort of directional overlay on the underlying long/short strategy, although changes in bias at some funds may be dictated by bottom-up idea generation rather than top-down calls from a market-timer-in-chief.

It is worth noting that, as virtually everywhere in the hedge fund world, there is little pretense to style purity among long/short managers. While some funds stick rigorously to a circumscribed and articulated discipline, most are more or less free-wheeling. For example, the temptations of a bond market in extraordinary turmoil after mid-2007 proved irresistible (and in some cases highly profitable) to many purportedly equity-only managers. Forays into commodity speculation were also popular with self-described equity funds during that period. A less radical and more frequent departure from accustomed behavior is for long/short managers with a specific target bias—say, to be generally 20 percent net long—to depart from it while remaining net long. For the purposes of this discussion it is useful to ignore all these forms of eclecticism, but those who perform due diligence on hedge fund managers must be alert to them.

Long/Short Risk

As with any directional trade, the fundamental risk to the performance of long/short investment techniques is the failure of their price forecasts. Because the main return driver is change in the market prices of its positions, price action other than that anticipated will produce negative returns. To the extent that a long/short strategy hedges its β exposure—its degree of bias or elimination of bias through neutrality—it is more, less, or almost entirely reliant on α for its returns. Hedging reduces or, in principle, eliminates the possibility that β will come to the rescue of unfortunate security selection, although a tactical overlay of opportunistic shifts in long/short bias will bring back this driver of returns in very highly magnified form. Managers who do not practice such opportunism have in effect deliberately rejected the exploitation of tactical allocation as a potential contributor to their returns. To the extent that they are consistently long-biased, they accept at least that much β exposure, and to the extent they are consistently net short, they are short β to that extent.

These vehicles' long book will tend to produce a certain amount of income, and the short book will carry interest costs in one form or another and pay dividends on some positions. The extent to which one offsets the other will depend largely on the amount of short interest these funds carry, although interest earned on Treasuries employed as futures margin may boost income for those funds that employ them. The cash flow element of long/short equity techniques is not typically important to their returns, although occasionally it may be. The costs and potential risks entailed by carrying short positions are not so trivial that managers can treat them with insouciance.

Beyond their cost of carry (including, where dividend-paying stocks are borrowed, being short the dividend) and the pressure for them to perform as expected that their carrying cost highlights, short positions involve other risks. Borrowed securities can be called, putting paid to a carefully crafted trade structure at what may be (and in fact frequently is) the most inopportune moment. Option expiry dates impose trading deadlines that, for all that they are known at the time the trade structure was created, may turn out to be inconvenient given the way the market has developed since the trade was put on. The factor relationships between positions held long and those in the short book require constant monitoring. To offer a trivial example, to which a naïve implementation of long/short techniques might nevertheless fall prey, the market may ignore the operational exposures of airlines and oil producers to the oil price during extended periods of relative oil price stability. A manager may then be tempted to short one against the other as a β hedge, based on the apparent neutrality of the two equities' price behavior relative to that factor, when in fact it is not a case of neutrality at all but the result of temporary stability in the factor. This mistake would have obvious, unattractive results when the market again attends to these issues' exposure to this factor, likely as a result of the return of oil price volatility. It is the sort of mistake that trade discovery based on short correlation histories and lacking common sense human oversight might make—a typical, if caricatured, error of a naïve implementation of quantitative techniques.

But probably the most important risk factor regarding short positions is their return asymmetry compared to long positions. When a long position works out badly, its subsequent contribution to portfolio performance is reduced—it shrinks relative to the total value of holdings, offering the manager automatic risk reduction for that position and the opportunity to commit new funds to it if its poor performance is thought to enhance the attractions of the position. The situation for short positions is the mirror opposite. If a position proves unfortunate, its size relative to the portfolio increases, magnifying risk. If the manager retains conviction in the position, risk controls or the need to match the short exposure against the position it hedges may nevertheless require that the short exposure be reduced. It is more difficult to recover from a failed short trade than a failed long one, and short positions that go awry offer long/short managers less opportunity to manage their exposure.

The need ultimately to cover short positions[2]—whether of borrowed securities or naked puts—exposes every short seller to the risk of a short squeeze. It is my impression—unsupported by research—that the sort

---

2. Oft-quoted but irresistible: "He that sells what isn't his'n, buys it back or goes to prison"—attributed to the "Great Bear," Daniel Drew. On predatory trading in general (of which Drew was a master—he was one of the main protagonists in the "Erie Wars" and is believed to have originated the term "watered stock"), see Brunnermeier and Pedersen (2005).

of bare-knuckle trading environment that fosters such transactional aggression is experiencing something of a Golden Age. It seems to me and some other commentators that predation is on the rise in securities markets worldwide, and short sellers can be extremely vulnerable to it because of the way their risk increases as their short positions deteriorate. Furthermore, the publication of short interest per security acts as virtually an engraved invitation to predators. But perhaps I am simply naïve, and these commentators and I have taken far too long to become aware of the fact that trading morality has always been as compromised as it appears to be today. Of course, short sellers are hardly immune to the charge of abusive trading practices—whether deserved or not, they have over time acquired sufficient notoriety for such practices that their plight is unlikely to attract a great deal of sympathy. To add to these woes, in recent years quantitatively driven long/short investors seem to have acquired a previously unobserved talent for cornering themselves.

As hedging relies on positive correlation between the long position and the security that is sold short against it, it entails arbitrage risk. Specious correlations are rife, and even relative price behavior that is solidly grounded in economic fundamentals can change as the fundamentals do or even in anticipation of such a change. Because the hedges must be imperfect if the strategy using them is to be productive of returns, long/short traders deliberately expose themselves to this risk, which is difficult if not impossible to quantify, and mistakes in this area are easy to make. The indices that are combined in the pair trade shown in **Figure 5.3** had a 0.9698 coefficient of correlation for the period shown, and their annualized standard deviations were 26.59 percent and 30.01 percent—about as close to a perfect hedge as instruments that are not systematically related to each other are likely to exhibit. And fundamentals certainly support the idea that two widely used benchmarks of U.S. small capitalization stock performance should move in fairly tight lockstep. Yet an investor who shorted the Standard & Poor's SmallCap 600 Index against a long position in the Russell 2000 Index would have posted a 1207 basis points loss that year, before borrowing and transaction costs. As discussed in Chapter 3, the differences between the two series' volatilities contributed to their failure to hedge each other more effectively, but in this case the composition of the indices played a more decisive role: see Soe and Dash (2009).

It is vernacular wisdom in hedge fund circles that "quants can't short." This is usually no more than just the kind of off-the-cuff disparagement that is characteristic of hyper-competitive personality types, although

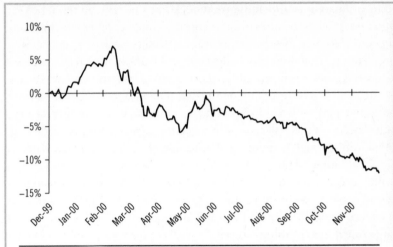

FIGURE 5.3 *Long the Russell 2000 Index, Short the Standard & Poor's SmallCap 600 Index, Excluding Transaction and Borrowing Costs*

it also probably reveals some latent animosity toward alleged eggheads, but there is a kernel of truth in it. As discussed in Chapter 2, the primary difference between a hedge and a return-seeking position is the portfolio function the trader envisages for the position—there is nothing inherent in a security that qualifies shorting it against some other security as either one or the other. A return-seeking trade should be unwound when it either has produced all the return that can be expected of it or when it is no longer likely to produce the required return, while a hedge should be unwound when the insurance it offers is either no longer necessary or no longer provided by the instrument that has been sold short. The difference may seem subtle, but it is real. Computer-based models have difficulty making distinctions based on intentions that they do not have, and consequently cannot apply this rather basic rule of hedging.

I am not strongly persuaded by arguments that quantitative long/short strategies are more information-efficient than those driven by bottom-up fundamental analysis, because timing risk means that just the perception of over-valuation (regardless of how that perception has been obtained) is often insufficient grounds for putting on a short position. Given their cost and the other risks associated with short sales of individual securities that I have mentioned, they require stronger conviction than long trades, even if their portfolio function is solely as hedges. Costs are easy to incorporate into a quantitative model, but call risk and several of the other unattractive features of short selling, such as the potential for being squeezed, are not. Neither are sentiment factors, which, given the timing issues surrounding short sales, can make all the difference between a successful and an unsuccessful short position, regardless of whether it is intended as return-seeking or a hedge. The ideal candidate for a short position comes with a near-term catalyst, such as a disappointing earnings announcement that will cause its price to drop. Such catalysts are difficult to identify through computerized screening of publicly available data.

While none of this is likely sufficient to argue strongly in favor of a prejudice against quantitative long/short vehicles, it gives pause for thought when performing due diligence on a technique where such qualitative peculiarities of the individual equities employed play such a large role in determining returns. As we have seen, many low-frequency quantitative funds tend to employ the same securities, so they may in effect corner themselves. Insofar as these sorts of managers permit prospective investors to lift the lids on their black boxes (which is not generally very far), due diligence should concentrate on determining whether their processes are sufficiently unique that they will tend to avoid such risk. If the factor model employed is not proprietary, if the proceeds of short sales are used to leverage the long book, if data feeds are nothing out of the ordinary and no quality control or fundamental analysis is applied to them, the vehicle is very likely to fall into the "can't short" category. Put another way, quantitative methods for identifying the α, which is the bread and butter of long/short techniques, are not dime-a-dozen and are unlikely to be present where considerable, value-added quantitative research has not been devoted to finding them.

Note that my reservations about shorting in quantitatively-driven portfolios only apply to those that short individual equities and only to low-frequency approaches to quantitative security selection. None of those reservations are relevant to trades in index derivatives or other instruments with fewer idiosyncratic or specific risks than individual equities. Nor do they apply to high-frequency trading models, most of which rely primarily on proprietary, non-fundamental transaction signals to guide their investment activity rather than factor analysis of publicly available data.

Nor is it true that quants are unique in being challenged by the management of their short books. As we have discussed, return-seeking short sales entail significant timing risk. This risk is mitigated for a purely hedging approach to the short book, provided that the fund uses index instruments. But it is not eliminated completely. And even if short positions are employed solely as a β hedge, if individual securities are used to craft the hedge, timing risk can affect returns in a very noticeable way, potentially causing the fund to have significant β exposure or unanticipated factor loadings until the hedge performs as desired.

It is logical that the correlation between a long/short investment technique and the broad equity market should be a function of its bias: the more short-biased, the greater the counter-correlation, and the more long-biased, the higher the positive correlation. For example, the coefficient of correlation of the Russell 3000 Index with the indices and period shown in Figure 5.1 was 0.7474 for the long-biased index, –0.7385 for the short-biased one, and 0.2236 for the market-neutral index. For funds that actively manage their long/short bias, tilting net long or net short opportunistically as timing signals or the trade discovery process dictate, a correlation measurement is unlikely to be very meaningful and may be quite deceptive.

I have referred to Hedge Fund Research's HFRI indices because they offer a nearly twenty-year history. However, they only price monthly, providing too few data points to construct the sort of rolling correlation study that I think can be valuable. However, the same index provider has introduced a second set of indices—its HFRX series—some of which feature daily pricing from March 31, 2003. A rolling correlation study for the HFRX Market Neutral Index is shown in **Figure 5.4**. There is no HFRX index for short-bias, and Hedge Fund Research's broad indices—whether HFRI or HFRX—remain too broad to make such a study very useful, although their daily pricing at least makes one possible

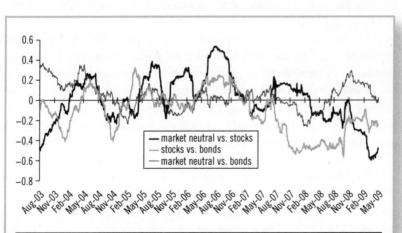

Source: Bloomberg, Barclays Capital, Hedge Fund Research.

FIGURE 5.4   *Stocks, Bonds, and Market-Neutral:* 90-Day Trailing Coefficients of Correlation*

*Russell 3000, Barclays Capital U.S. Aggregate Bond and HFRX Market Neutral Indices.

in principle. Because the broad indices include vehicles that more or less systematically counter-correlate with each other as well as opportunistic long/short funds, they can reveal little about how any individual investment vehicle might be expected to perform.

For the entire period shown in Figure 5.4, the HRFX Market-Neutral Index had very low coefficients of correlation of −0.1004 to stocks and 0.0456 to the Barclays Capital U.S. Aggregate Bond Index—notably lower than the twenty-year history of monthly readings for the corresponding HFRI index. But for shorter periods, market-neutral does not appear to be quite so "neutral": transient correlation levels of ±0.40 strike me as being on the borderline between weakly and moderately significant (see Chapter 3). Although none of these periods of comparatively high correlation or counter-correlation was especially protracted, they raise a question about just how effective these funds' β-hedging is. When combined with the higher-than-expected returns mentioned above, the fact that these periods tend to be on the side of positive correlation indicates that that their removal of β exposure is by no means precise.

The challenge confronting market-neutral managers is that market correlations (and thus the managers' β estimates), as well as all the other factor loadings that their positions may carry, change over time and are difficult to predict. Although a great deal of intellectual capital has been put into finding ways to make reliable predictions of these series, in my view the results of all this effort have been less than satisfactory. Consequently, the correct hedging ratio at any given moment is uncertain. For managers who use index derivatives to hedge, the uncertainty only affects their long book, but if individual securities are used, the uncertainties triple. These managers must hope that their estimates of their long books' β, their short books' β and the correlation between their long and short books are as sound as possible.

Mathematical precision in market-neutrality is not achievable except through a perfect hedge (being short exactly what the long book holds), which is a trade that generates zero directional return. So the hedging inaccuracy inherent even in using index derivatives in the short book will allow some (positive or negative) exposure to β to seep into a market-neutral manager's returns, at least briefly, until the hedges are adjusted. The performance of market-neutral indices suggests that these managers underestimate the appropriate hedge ratio fairly frequently, but not always consistently. Overestimation (resulting in counter-correlation) seems on the evidence of Figure 5.4 to be less common, but the low average correlation figures for the entire period shown there might instead suggest that, as a group, these managers' estimation errors offset each other. Alternatively, the low figures may be a symptom of mean reversion for βs, although the time period shown is insufficient to lend statistical support to such a hypothesis. Mean reversion of βs will come in for some further examination in Chapter 17.

There is a growing armory of instruments that, held long, provide effective short exposure. Inverse Exchange Traded Funds are proliferating, some of them leveraged, and other products of this sort will no doubt be created. Most of them have fairly high tracking error, making their use in long/short portfolios somewhat problematic. However, I am aware of managers who use long positions in VIX Index[3] futures or call options on those futures in this way. Although it is commonly referred to as a "fear indicator"—I believe rather inaccurately—the VIX has actually been a moderately effective hedge against Standard & Poor's 500 Index β, as **Figure 5.5** suggests. Although it, too, has exhibited significant

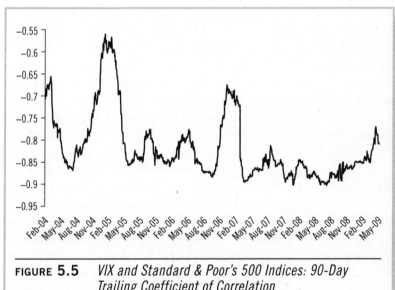

Source: Bloomberg Finance L.P.

FIGURE 5.5   *VIX and Standard & Poor's 500 Indices: 90-Day Trailing Coefficient of Correlation*

3. The Chicago Board Options Exchange Volatility Index provides the implied volatility of a synthetic 30-day index option long straddle, based on an analysis of the implied volatilities of actual index options traded on the CBOE. VIX futures and options on those futures are traded. Originally calculated for the Standard & Poor's 100 Index, in September 2003 the "new VIX" was launched, with an improved calculation methodology based on the Standard & Poor's 500 Index. See CBOE (2003).

tracking error—and its use as a hedge must adjust for the fact that it has nearly five times the volatility of the underlying Standard & Poor's 500 Index—it is interesting that its negative correlation seems to have stabilized at a high level over the last few years, despite its recent decline. The VIX offers its users the advantage that, as a market-derived instrument, it reflects the aggregate of option market participants' volatility estimates.

Long/Short in the Context of Conventional Portfolio Holdings

Taken all together, my discussion of long/short makes it fairly plain that there are not many useful generalizations to be made about it, given the fairly broad definition adopted in this chapter. This may argue against so all-inclusive a definition, but given many managers' discretion over whether they are net long or net short, over the extent of bias adopted by directionally specific vehicles and the choice of instruments they may use to implement the short leg of the trade, a more restrictive definition would be unlikely to permit a very substantially greater number of valuable general observations.

Investment policymakers must look beyond a broad-brush treatment of long/short equity that discusses it as though it were a monolithic investment category and recognize that it is a trading technique with a wide range of performance characteristics determined by the amount of long/short discretion that its various managers permit themselves and the intentions behind their hedging. Where enough managers impose similar disciplines on themselves—as is the case with market-neutral managers—generalization and analysis of aggregate performance data may add some real value. Otherwise, apples-and-oranges comparisons abound, and are likely to be more deceptive than revealing.

Regarding market-neutrality in particular, it is difficult to make a compelling case for its inclusion in an investment policy. Assuming that an institution's policy starts from a point that already includes actively managed long-only equities within its investable universe, a market-neutral approach can be synthetically recreated at very low cost simply by hedging all or a portion of long-only exposure in the futures markets. Although this excludes the possibility of return-seeking short exposure, market-neutral vehicles are probably not the best place to pursue that source of return in any case. Candidates to perform such a role among market-neutral managers would be required to make their short books serve the twin masters of β hedging as well as return-seeking—which is possible, but far from easy, because adjustments to the short book that are needed to maintain a neutral hedge ratio would inevitably interfere with return-seeking. If they desire exposure to a return-seeking short book, those who control investment policy are probably better-served to consider hiring short-bias managers or dedicated short-sellers instead.

Similarly, exposure to long-biased long/short management that seeks only to hedge β rather than to pursue returns with its short exposure should probably be replicated at low cost rather than purchased expensively through a hedge fund. As in the case of market-neutral techniques, provided that an institution already has exposure to long-only actively managed equities, investment policymakers who are attracted to this approach can spare themselves the not inconsiderable inconvenience and expense of hiring a hedge fund manager to carry it out. In fact, replicating this technique is even easier than replicating a market-neutral one, since less precision in the hedge is required and the structure can be essentially passive.

However, Figure 5.2 makes clear why short-bias and dedicated short-selling are nowhere very substantial investment policy allocations. While the tactical attractions of this investment approach in a cyclical downturn are obvious, like distressed debt (which is to some extent its economic cousin), it is a trade with a finite opportunity set. When conditions improve, the opportunities available to these funds decrease and their economics deteriorate. While all market and economic circumstances offer equities that are troubled or overvalued, the timing risks of shorting them are substantial, and in a favorable economic environment the distress or overvaluation must be severe enough to offset the stock's β to a market that is biased toward appreciation. During the leveraged buyout boom of 2005 to 2007, the risks were magnified further, as many of these acquirers actively sought out troubled firms upon which to exercise their turnaround skills. Unlike distressed debt, opportunities for return enhancement of short equity trades through activism are limited: holders of short positions cannot vote, and market manipulation that would attract regulators' attention is not a recommended commercial strategy. Short-bias is an investment opportunity that is best-suited to tactical allocators, and investment policy that is intrigued with its potential should probably seek access to it through funds of funds, multi-strategy funds, or opportunistically biased long/short vehicles. By extension of this reasoning, any fund that is return-seeking in its short exposure and attempts to maintain a fixed level of net exposure will experience difficulty finding suitable shorts in many periods.

The most attractive of the long/short equity investment techniques from an investment policy perspective are those that are long-biased with discretion to adjust the extent of their exposure and those that are opportunistically net long or net short. Inevitably, these are the strategies that are most difficult to analyze for the purposes of portfolio allocation. Their correlation with respect to long-only benchmarks is, given the flexibility of their net exposures, likely to be highly variable over time. Long-term average correlation figures for such funds reveal little about their portfolio function. While statistics about their volatility will give some indication of their riskiness, they are unlikely to have much predictive value. Aggregate figures for indices of these products reveal essentially nothing about the likely return characteristics of any particular vehicle and are of little or no use to analysis.

Confronted with this situation for a candidate investment, investment policymakers would typically just throw up their hands and look no further. But long/short equity is *not* an asset class. The task that confronts investment policy is the same that it encounters when it chooses to allocate among active equity managers, for the very simple reason that equity long/short is at bottom an active equity management style. The principal challenges to applying familiar manager selection techniques and processes to the problem of selecting an equity long/short manager is that any given hedge fund's investment discipline is likely to be less strict and less clearly articulated than is typical of conventional institutional equity managers. This, and leverage, cause the dispersion of returns among long/short managers to be much higher than for long-only managers.[4] Whereas Brinson et al. (1986) argue that manager selection is a considerably less important contributor to portfolio variance than policy allocation decisions (although this is a matter of considerable dispute: see Chapter 22), if long/short funds are treated as a component of the equity allocation rather than regarded as a new allocation category, then the importance of manager selection to the performance that will be achieved becomes more clearly the paramount consideration. That is, in choosing to group long/short managers with conventional equity managers, we lose the ability to treat them as radically different, and this underscores the importance of manager selection.

---

4. Reddy et al. (2007) find that the dispersion of long/short equity returns, measured by the difference between 25th and 75th percentile performance over the period March 2002 to March 2007, was nearly three times that of large-cap value managers and 2½ times that of large-cap growth managers. They drew on the CSFB Tremont and Morningstar databases. As would be expected, the dispersion among market-neutral managers was considerably less.

Some funds of hedge funds explicitly classify the long/short vehicles in which they invest along familiar "Style Box" lines as growth or value managers, further distinguishing among them as practicing "relative value," "growth-at-the-right-price," and other security selection techniques commonly used to describe and foster diversification among conventional equity managers. As with conventional managers, long/short hedge funds may often also differentiate themselves as U.S.-oriented, "international," "global," or "emerging market" investors. Interestingly, in most cases funds of funds seem to use these classifications solely for risk control purposes, to ensure that the funds' portfolios are diversified in their security selection techniques. Many funds of funds tend to maintain constant weightings to each of the categories they identify, suggesting that they eschew tilting their allocations among them for the purposes of exploiting return-generating tactical opportunities. A potential investor might well ponder over what it is that earns these funds of funds managers their performance fees.

Although these characterizations no doubt give funds of funds managers some picture of the processes and the investment universe that their underlying managers employ in the construction of their long books, it is questionable whether they can capture what exactly goes into their selection of securities that they sell short. Given the timing risk involved in short sales, the short book discipline is likely to incorporate considerations of investor sentiment, perhaps through use of technical analysis or other momentum indicators, and the search for catalysts to price activity such as corporate actions or announcements, in addition to or perhaps even to the exclusion of the Style Box considerations that determine the composition of its long book. As already indicated, if an underlying manager relies primarily on quantitative techniques to drive its security selection, due diligence should pay especially careful attention to how the short book is constructed.

As either a long-biased or an opportunistically net long fund is fairly certain to exhibit meaningful positive correlation to equities (and a net short one, counter-correlation), allocation to such funds should primarily be at the expense of the conventional equity allocation. However, because the correlation with equities is not likely to be extremely high, it is tempting to think that diversification effects can allow the aggregate equity allocation (including the fund) to be larger than it might otherwise have been, while retaining the portfolio's previous risk characteristics. Most of the time this is probably true, but for periods when it is not, the portfolio consequences may be dramatically unfavorable. The kurtosis of long/short is substantially higher than for long-only equities, while its return distribution is considerably less skewed.[5] This indicates that

❑ long/short returns tend to cluster more tightly around their average than long-only equity returns; and

❑ high standard deviation returns from long/short are much more common than from conventional equity management, but the less negative skewness of the long/short distribution suggests that imbalance between how negative the most negative outliers are *versus* how positive the most positive ones are is less disadvantageous to investors.

In other words, long/short can be a wild ride, and only limited comfort can be drawn from the second point about its skewness. While the distribution of high standard deviation returns is tilted less to the negative for long/short than for long-only, it is still tilted somewhat in that direction, and the number of high standard deviation returns (both negative and positive) is much higher.

Leverage contributes strongly to long/short's magnified kurtosis. Investment policymakers must pay close attention to leverage in determining the size of their allocation to long/short. A rule of thumb that is fairly widespread among long/short managers is that a leverage ratio of 2:1 (67 percent debt to capital) is ample for most of the trades into which they enter, and it is not generally advisable to invest where the ratio is significantly higher. Sometimes a General Partner who has uncovered an opportunity for which a substantial increase in leverage is required will consult with Limited Partners before making a commitment to it, particularly if it involves a significant departure from the manager's past

---

5. Using the Lipper TASS database for 1995 through 2003, Malkiel and Saha (2005) find the kurtosis of long/short equity to be 15.5 × that of the Standard & Poor's 500 Index, and its skewness to be only modestly negative at 10 percent of the Index's (81). Stefanini (2006), using the same database for the period 1994 through 2004, arrives at comparable figures (66). Anson (2002), using Hedge Fund Research data for 1990 through 2000, arrives at quite different values: his kurtosis is only 1.5 × the S&P 500's, and he finds positive skew. This is consistent with the data drawn from Figure 4.1 above. While the differences may largely be an artifact of the data series chosen, they nevertheless provide a *very important reminder* to investment policymakers that, quite apart from differences in sources, differences in the periods examined can produce contrasting conclusions about the statistical characteristics of return distributions. Although some financial time series are more stable in the moments of their distributions over time than others, all seem to be variable and some highly so.

practice. For example, I am informed that at least one fund did so in 2007, before building a very large short position in mortgage-backed securities that made its subsequent returns the sorts of positive outliers that investors are happy to experience. But this is unusual: note that the trade involved not only a substantial increase in leverage but also substantial exposure to something other than equity. On the rare occasion that a Limited Partner is afforded such an opportunity to pass judgment on a proposed trade, it should be taken as encouragement to engage in intensive research into the trade's fundamentals.

All of which argues that investment policy should approach long/short manager selection in a manner consistent with its approach to selecting individual equity managers rather than with its approach to setting policy for its equity allocation generally. Diversification by security selection style, capitalization category and geographic exposure should be pursued in a parallel manner. Having found a group of attractive long/short manager candidates, the investment policymakers' determination of the appropriate size of the allocation to them should, in my view, be strongly influenced by each specific fund's typical leverage and short exposure levels.

CHAPTER 6

Direct Lending

I f Part II of this volume were intended to be a comprehensive introduction to alternative investments, direct lending would hardly be the most natural topic to follow immediately after the chapter on long/short equity, and if direct lending appeared at all, it would probably be toward the end in a chapter on "all the others." But as indicated in the Introduction, my intention for these strategy-specific chapters is to illustrate rather than to assemble an exhaustive catalog of alternative investment practice. In its economics, its risk profile, and its likely role in an investment policy allocation, direct lending is sufficiently different from long/short equity that the contrast between them should be interesting. This is the sort of consideration that accounts for the peculiar ordering of these chapters.

Direct lending has taken an increasingly prominent place in the alternative investment landscape, to the point that it would be something of a challenge these days to find an "absolute return"–oriented fund of hedge funds that completely lacked exposure to it. This is a comparatively recent development. Although there have always been numerous firms engaged in these types of activities, and some of them may have had Limited Partnership or other fund-like structures and an active program of seeking capital from outsiders, they did not attract widespread attention as candidates for institutional investment until the end of the 1990s. Previously, most direct lending vehicles were private agreements among like-minded investors, most of whom were active in the business as principals and who capitalized it themselves, with limited or no recourse to the capital contributions of inactive Limited Partners.

Institutional interest was largely stimulated by the paucity of yield available in conventional fixed-income markets, as yields continued to slide and issuance in the high-yield segment dried up following the collapse of that market segment late in the 1980s. Concurrently, banks' commercial decisions to de-emphasize many of the loan categories in which direct lenders are active increased opportunities for direct lenders to deploy capital. In some cases, banks went so far as to decrease their lending to small- and medium-sized businesses across the board. Finally, the creeping institutionalization of the alternative investment arena increased demand for the stability of returns that successful implementations of this investment technique can offer. Although data are hard to come by, direct lenders now provide a greater portion of the credit available to small- and medium-size businesses than many people realize, and their market share in this borrowing segment has almost certainly increased further as a result of the predicament in which banks have found themselves since 2007.

Although few individual funds dedicated solely to direct lending are large, their numbers have multiplied, and opportunistic exposure to direct lending by funds of hedge funds has become fairly common. Further, a number of multi-strategy hedge funds that are not devoted solely to the strategy participate in it as one among several sorts of investments that they pursue as a matter of policy. Without much restraint on their choice of investment activities—either from regulators or from their own private placement memoranda—any hedge fund may choose to accept whatever lending proposals come its way. Some of them regard lending as central to their investment activity, while others are opportunists who may lend on occasion.

I have spoken of hedge funds as direct lenders, but mezzanine, resource development, and private market real estate lending are usually structured the way that private equity vehicles are, rather than as perpetual vehicles like a hedge fund. That is, many if not most such funds have long lockup periods, draw down capital for deployment to specific investments as the opportunities arise, return capital to investors as specific investments are retired over the life of the fund, and more or less regularly distribute their loan income (net of expenses and performance fees). Further, their private placement memoranda are in most cases comparatively specific about the activities in which the funds permit themselves to engage. Hedge funds typically have shorter lockups of a year or two, require up-front commitment of their Limited Partners' entire investment, return no capital except at redemption, and have quite few if any restrictions on the investment activities that they may pursue. But direct lending has given rise to some hybrid structures as well—hedge fund–like vehicles that nevertheless make income distributions to investors and private equity-like vehicles with lockups that do not distribute and that may have considerably shorter lifespans than the typical ten years.

Direct Lending as an Investment Technique

Direct lending is fundamentally a cash flow trade, and in many of its instantiations it is a completely pure one, without admixture of any other investment strategy. That is, many funds, particularly those that are short-term lenders, make loans directly to borrowers and hold them to maturity. However, there are various ways—apart from borrower default—that directionality can insinuate itself into the trade. Although mezzanine funds also tend to hold their loans to maturity, their lending terms are generally sweetened with a grant of equity warrants, and the returns on this equity component of their loans (which in some but by no means all cases may account for as much as half the funds' returns) are directional. This is true even though the warrants may exercise into cash: the warrants' value may be determined by formula (say, the higher of some multiple of cash flow, "fair market value" or appraised value), and in the absence of a public market price for the equity, the lenders may have put rights to ensure that they are able to obtain that value. Oil and gas and private real estate lending may have similar, although differently structured, debtholder equity participation rights. Some funds, particularly those that invest in distressed debt—whether by lending directly to the debtor or purchasing its debt from the original lender after it has become distressed—may subsequently sell their investment for a directional gain if the credit quality of the borrower improves, because they perceive a better opportunity or simply because a tempting bid is received. Arguably, vehicles that engage in purchasing existing debt are not "direct" lenders at all, but they are generally lumped together with loan originators under the category. And even funds that are able to source all their loans through their own efforts may opportunistically purchase some that were originated by others.

Use of leverage varies widely among direct lenders: many are not leveraged, many are, and opportunistic lenders are very likely to be. Opportunists may or may not be explicitly leveraged—that is, some would and some would typically not borrow in order to lend—but leverage in any part of a fund's portfolio in effect leverages every trade in which it participates to some extent. Although for analytic purposes it may often be useful to assign leverage to the specific trades for which it was incurred, it is also useful for analysis to regard any leverage that is taken up as leveraging an entire fund. Leverage introduces an element of arbitrage into the strategy, because in effect such a fund's returns are derived from the difference between the cost of borrowing (a short credit position that may be at a fixed or a variable rate) and the rate of interest received (the long position, which may also be fixed or variable). Leverage involving fixed rates introduces the potential risk of asset/liability mismatch. But this is a subsidiary matter of how leverage is obtained and managed rather than something inherent to the trading strategy: leveraged or not, direct lending remains a fairly pure cash flow strategy.

Generalizations about direct lending are, in fact, mostly futile: about the only thing that is common to all these strategies is that the debt in which they invest is not registered with the SEC and thus is not, technically, in the form of a security. I will try to impose some order on all this by distinguishing between funds based on the terms of the loans they typically offer, and then further distinguish among them based on the kind of security they accept against their loans. While these distinctions are not hard and fast, they are reasonably firm, and they even have an economic basis of sorts: ignoring loans to private individuals, with few exceptions long-term lenders generally finance investment and development while short-term lenders provide working capital to their customers. So I group together those that take on comparatively long-term exposures (significantly more than a year) from those who offer shorter-term financing. The lists in **Table 6.1** are illustrative rather than exhaustive.

Note that the lists are restricted to commercial loans. There are opportunities for direct lending to consumers as well—long-term examples include loans made against structured legal settlements and lottery proceeds, while short-term loans include residential mortgage bridges. Some direct lenders also enter into standby equity distribution agreements with public companies, which technically are not loans, although they have some similarities to short-term collateralized lending.

There are also numerous opportunities for funds to purchase consumer debt, particularly from issuers of credit cards, and recently there has been a growing business in buying distressed auto loans. Conceivably, a fund could structure itself as a pawnbroker, too: although I am unaware of any that are available to outside investors that have done so, there are

TABLE 6.1 *Some Direct Lending Techniques*

LONG-TERM LENDING PROGRAMS	SHORT-TERM LENDING PROGRAMS
Mezzanine debt	Factoring
Oil and gas development loans	Trade finance
Mortgages	Inventory finance
Distressed lending	Equipment leasing
Loans against long-term receivables: Royalty streams, structured legal settlements, etc.	Forfaiting

several listed corporations that engage in this activity. An unusual form of consumer lending that probably demands a category of its own is the purchase of life insurance settlements. It is unique because the purchaser incurs the obligation to pay the premiums on the policies acquired as well as because of the actuarial nature of the loan security. See Dorsey (2007, 261–63) on the mechanics of this unusual trade; indications of its return characteristics are offered by Hodson (2009). I will concentrate my discussion on commercial lending, although much that I have to say applies to consumer lending, too.

The loans featured in short-term varieties of direct lending are typically senior claims on identifiable collateral. Mortgages, of course, are secured by the property mortgaged. Mezzanine debt and most private lending in support of energy development are exceptions, both as to creditor ranking (they are typically second lien credits, whereas mortgages may be more or less senior) and lack of collateral. The equity or equity-like "kickers" that are usually attached to these latter types of loans might be regarded as proxies for loan security, in that the put provisions that attach to them are powerful inducements to the debtors to meet their obligations, but they are not technically collateral since they become equity rather than a more senior claim on assets if the borrower fails. While this may not offer much protection to the lender if the borrower is in deep trouble, in most cases it is fairly substantial security. Virtual ownership through warrants also confers some measure of influence on management, and unlike senior lenders or those who obtain more tangible loan security through mortgages, inventory claims, or equipment liens, mezzanine lenders typically obtain at least board observer status if not actual board representation.

Where loans are truly "direct"—where the fund originates the transaction—the General Partner of a direct lending fund is in effect running a financing business, employing the Limited Partners' capital contributions as equity and paying them the profits from the business less the fees and incentive payments that cover the General Partner's expenses and constitute its profit. Although the transaction is not legally structured that way, investors in a direct lending fund should in certain respects regard their investment as a private equity holding in a financing business, and due diligence should be careful to take this into consideration.

Like any business, a truly "direct" lender faces the challenge of customer acquisition in a competitive environment. Even in the credit crisis of 2007 to 2009, direct lenders were not most borrowers' sole possible sources of finance. All the potential customers for a fund's lending facilities already have ample business dealings with banks and other potential lenders. The commercial and managerial challenges of direct lending militate against gigantism, and I would be skeptical of the ability of a dedicated vehicle with much in excess of, say, $400 million in assets to generate acceptable returns.[1] Successful direct lending is, in virtually all cases, a niche strategy. But such operational constraints do not apply in quite the same way to funds that purchase existing debts, and some truly enormous funds designed to purchase distressed debt were raised in 2008. It remains to be seen whether the opportunities for purchasing bad debt were in fact as close to unlimited as that fund-raising frenzy would imply. I am inclined to think that this cycle's distressed debt trade

---

1. This figure is arbitrary, and intended only to suggest an order of magnitude. Throughout the investment management industry, the question of optimal fund size is pressing and, to my mind under-studied, although the topic has attracted a limited amount of academic attention: see Shawky and Li (2006), who mention this rather surprising academic neglect. Kahn (2006) argues that appropriate size is some function of the information ratio and costs, but it seems to me that many factors are trade- and asset-class specific. Kovacs and Turner (2004), who manage small capitalization U.S. equity funds, offer a formula based on the characteristics of their funds and the trading characteristics of the universe in which they invest. In the case of direct lending in particular, optimal size must at least partially be determined by the challenges of loan acquisition and analysis. The conclusions that different firms reach, even regarding quite comparable vehicles, vary widely and, as near as I can see, unsystematically.

will ultimately prove to be woefully overcrowded and that returns will consequently be disappointing to investors.

The size of the loans a direct lending vehicle offers is roughly proportional to their maturity terms: long-term loans are generally larger than short-term ones. This is consistent with the commercial imperatives of acquiring customers and getting funds invested. Loans without tangible collateral and that involve long repayment periods are more demanding of the lender than shorter-term exposures. They are likely to be much more highly customized to the specific lending situation and require a degree of due diligence that goes well beyond evaluation of collateral and certification that the borrower has title to it. Given the associated higher acquisition costs, and the fact that the same borrower is not likely to be a frequent repeat customer, the loans must be larger to justify the extra effort. Mezzanine loans are typically in seven or eight figures, and resource development loans in roughly the same size range,[2] while private real estate loans may be much larger. As a consequence, the credit exposure of these types of lenders is likely to be considerably less diversified than for lenders at shorter terms. There is no formal syndication process for these long-term loans, but mezzanine lenders, as part of the private equity community, are highly clubbable, and the same is true of energy lenders. Cooperation among long-term lending vehicles to form consortia for loans that are larger than any one fund would individually contemplate is fairly routine. While the conclusions that Ljungqvist et al. (2005) reach regarding the importance of their networks of contacts to venture capitalists' returns apply specifically to practitioners of that investment technique, I think it is fair to extend their findings to most investors in long-term private market assets, including these sorts of lenders.

Shorter-term lenders may actually create revolving facilities for their customers, but in general their types of loans give rise to repeat business, so much of the due diligence portion of the cost of loan acquisition is spread over exposures repeated through time rather than a single, large borrowing. Lending terms and contracts are more stereotyped—often completely so—providing significant savings on legal and administrative costs. Loan security is more tangible and usually exceeds the value of the loan. So—provided the lenders understand

---

2. Figures quoted by Kirschner et al. (2006) imply an average loan size of $15.4 million in the oil patch, but it is unclear whether this is the total that individual borrowers require or whether it represents individual funds' contribution to consortia (219).

the collateral and the market for disposing of it should they be forced to take possession—board representation or observer status are less necessary. In fact, they may be impossible: these sorts of funds are very likely to lend to firms that compete with each other, so board service would create unacceptable conflicts of interest and interfere with customer acquisition. In the interest of diversification, mezzanine and real estate lenders avoid this situation by restricting their loans to firms or projects that do not compete with each other, while energy lenders to a greater or lesser extent simply have to accept the risk that lack of industrial diversity entails.

Among short-term strategies, factoring and forfaiting require special mention because of the peculiarities of their credit exposures. Both involve purchase of receivables from the debtor, so in effect their economic exposure is to the debtors' debtor rather than to the debtor itself. In most cases, lenders in these areas will not accept receivables from low quality credits, so in general they are purchasing relatively high quality paper at a significant discount. Some of the largest debtors whose paper is likely to be factored, such as government entities and some major retailers, are notoriously slow to pay—a strong encouragement to demand for factoring services in the first place—but nevertheless represent excellent credit risks. The typical payment cycle on receivables is ninety days, so direct lenders who engage in these strategies need a wide range of borrowers, ideally with different seasonal loan demand patterns, to keep their capital gainfully employed.

Direct lenders are approached for the same reasons that corporations take out loans of any type: to bridge cash flow shortfalls. These can result from virtually every aspect of commercial activity, ranging from financing sales to bridging inventory turnover times to funding expansion. There are various special cases, however. If a borrower is controlled by a private equity fund, the search for mezzanine finance is often initiated, and the terms of the loan ultimately negotiated, not so much by the borrower as by its equity owners. Where the primary reason for using a mezzanine loan is to bridge the period before an IPO without unduly diluting the venture capitalists' interests, their concern about the terms of the warrants attached to the loan is obviously crucial. While the lender's economic exposure is to the firm in which the venture capitalists are invested, the demand for the loan and its terms are heavily influenced, if not completely determined, by the venture capitalists rather than the by borrower itself. However, the bulk of such loans are actually made by investment banks seeking the mandate for the borrower's IPO: mezzanine lenders outside of investment banks concentrate more on middle-market lending situations, which may or may not be venture-backed, where an IPO is not imminent.

Factoring, forfaiting, and export/import lending programs may attract borrowers at least as much because the loans outsource various operational tasks as because the borrower actually requires the financing. Specialists in these lending areas are typically dedicated to the efficient execution of these tasks, which are crucial but at the same time only incidental to the businesses of the customers to which they lend. Offering such solutions may have a value to the borrower that goes well beyond its temporary funding requirements. Obviously, the loan would not be sought in the first place if there were no cash flow gap to bridge, but the form of finance employed (and the potential providers approached) may well be strongly influenced if not determined by issues other than the financial situation of the borrower. As a symptom of the inexorable decline of credit morality, many large purchasers have found that a conveniently devious way to delay payment to small suppliers is to make the paperwork necessary for collection as daunting to their creditors as possible. By no means the least important attraction of factoring is that the collection problem is shifted to the factor.

As indicated in the preceding, some of the activities that are lumped under the rubric "direct lending" may not be "direct" at all. There are always opportunities to purchase loans, especially at the bottom of a credit cycle, when distressed loans account for an increasing portion of lenders' assets and their need to free up liquidity may become pressing. Direct lenders typically seek to purchase such loans at a significant discount. At other points in the credit cycle direct lenders (whether buyers of loans or strictly self-originators) may seek to sell loans for investment reasons unrelated to any pressing need to raise liquidity, but motivated instead by a perception that better opportunities exist elsewhere. These, of course, are directional trades, which for the purposes of discussion I am ignoring here.

Direct Lending Risk

As with any cash flow strategy other than investment in U.S. Treasuries, the overriding risk to direct lending is the risk that the source of the cash flows may fail to deliver them—in the case of lending, through failure to service the loan and ultimately default. To protect themselves from this risk, direct lenders fortify their loans with all the protections that their legal counsel can devise and that their borrowers will tolerate. In particular, where tangible loan security is obtainable, they tend to demand significant over-collateralization—120 percent is fairly typical. Their credit work-ups must be thorough, and those that have industry specializations can usually be expected to understand the credit risks to which they expose themselves more fully than, for instance, banks' lending or credit review officers, most of whom are generalists who have limited familiarity with any particular borrower's industry. None of this amounts to ironclad protection, but even in the worst cases, complete write-offs are unlikely unless deliberate fraud on the part of the borrower is involved. However, defaults do occur, and they are costly. Recourse to collateral is never a lender's favored outcome, as disposal is time-consuming and will inevitably add to costs. Over-collateralization may seem like a gift to these lenders, but measured against liquidation costs and the loss of interest income, 20 percent is not exceedingly generous.

Most direct lenders' relationships with their loan customers are at arm's length, providing the lenders limited warning of developments that might affect their loan or its security and no opportunity to intervene in the management of their borrowers to prevent such problems from arising. Where this is not the situation, as may be the case in mezzanine finance, the lender's participation in the oversight of the borrower can be regarded as a form of investor activism. While it is arguable whether this is activism in the cause of return enhancement, as discussed in Chapter 2, activism in the interest of risk avoidance is clearly an enhancement on write-downs, and I would regard activism in the interest of risk-adjusted returns as much the same thing as activism in pursuit of absolute returns.

Pricing in direct lending markets is not transparent. Few borrowers have credit ratings, and if they do, the ratings are unlikely to be very relevant to the specific type of credit facility the borrower contemplates. The nature of the loan security can be as important as the borrower's repayment history to a lender's willingness to grant a loan and to the loan's pricing. The value of loan security can deteriorate precipitously, and a direct lender's familiarity with the security it accepts is essential to the success of its lending program. Not only is knowledge of the collateral essential to judging its adequacy, but if the lender is forced to take possession, it must understand how to dispose of it. Perishable items are obviously risky loan collateral, but the value of many non-perishable items can be time-sensitive, too—for example, seasonal fashion items. I am aware of a direct lender that was approached by a borrower with which it had good experience to finance purchase of ships for breakup in the Far East on the security of the ships themselves. In this case the collateral was explicitly intended to be rendered into an indistinguishable pile of scrap on the other side of the world before the asset could possibly generate any revenue to service the loan.[3]

Direct lending is a return-enhanced trade: the strategy would not be particularly attractive to investors if it were unable to capture the liquidity premium relative to publicly traded securities that private market lending can demand. The loans involved are generally not of a size to make registration and all the associated costs of issuing even privately placed bonds economical for the borrowers, and the terms of the loans are, in many cases, too short to make such paper attractive to potential purchasers. Further, the credit exposure of many of these loans is idiosyncratic by bond market standards. I have mentioned the peculiarities of factoring and forfaiting, but outside of structured products (collateralized debt obligations), equipment loans, inventory loans, and so forth, are not the typical fodder of the traded fixed-income markets either. Estimating liquidity premia is not an exact science, which creates pricing risk. But more importantly, lack of liquidity confronts direct lenders with redemption risk, because funds are in most cases unable to forecast an increase in their Limited Partners' demands for redemption unless they already have encountered the sorts of problems with the quality of their loan assets that are likely to stimulate them.

While there are informal markets for direct loans, they are illiquid, providing no guarantee that a buyer even for sound loans will be available should a direct lender require one. Keeping leverage low or avoiding it entirely mitigate liquidity risk significantly, but even without leverage, direct lenders cannot avoid the consequences of having taken liquidity risk if they are confronted with investor redemptions. Notice periods for redemptions from direct lending vehicles tend as a result to be longer than is typical for many hedge funds, providing their managers some extra breathing room to seek buyers for their loans if liquidity is not available from other sources. Where notice periods are not longer than is usual for hedge funds, due diligence should be especially careful in its analysis of loan terms and portfolio turnover. If a forced sale becomes necessary, it would be difficult for the manager of a direct lending vehicle lacking the protection of an appropriately lengthy notice period to escape having to sell positions at a discount, perhaps a substantial one. Of course, such sales spell opportunity for the fund's counterparty.

---

3. I am indebted for this example to a friend who tells me that, remarkably, the principals of the fund actually considered granting the loan, until he pointed out what seems to me the rather glaring shortcoming in its proposed security.

Recalling my analogy between direct lending and a private equity interest in a financing company, there are a number of risks to the activity that are essentially business or operational risks. Direct lenders are subject to the lending cycle, business competition, challenges to customer acquisition, and so on. Due diligence should be alive to the implications of all this, and in fact business considerations of this kind should in many cases be its most important focus. While all investors can be said, in a sense, to compete with each other for investment opportunities, the sense in which direct lenders are in a competitive marketplace is quite different from managers of publicly traded investments.

Unlike many other investments, direct loans are generally not acquired in a competitive auction: they are in fact sold to the business customers who contract the debt. Put another way, direct lenders' trade discovery and execution processes are quite different from those of investors who can call an agent to execute a transaction in an instrument that already exists. While price indications are clearly the most important determinant of borrowers' ultimate choice of credit provider, any number of other factors may influence their decisions. Many of these are not financial in nature, such as loan turnaround times, the availability of ancillary services, the bureaucratic encumbrances the lender attaches to the loan application process, and even just the knowledge that a direct lending alternative is available to them. Direct lenders do not operate in a public marketplace that more or less naturally aggregates potential counterparties: they must seek them out and persuade them to do business with the fund rather than with other willing providers. Some of these competitors are multi-service firms with which the potential borrower is almost certain to be doing some sort of business already. While providing credit where none might otherwise be available is probably a direct lender's strongest selling point, if it is its only selling point then its business model should probably be regarded as badly flawed. Consequently, most direct lenders specialize in one way or another—by industry, by geographic region, by loan type, or by any combination of the same—to maximize their visibility to potential borrowers.

As with much of my discussion, mezzanine finance and much other long-term, "virtually-secured" lending are the exceptions here: banks and other non-specialists generally do not compete for this business. While senior lenders may crowd out mezzanine providers and private lenders to real estate and oil and gas developers in "frothy" credit markets, in more disciplined credit environments they are largely content to leave second lien financing to the alternative investment community. The exception is where banks participate in the Small Business Administration's Small

Business Investment Company (SBIC) program, in which case they may compete directly with mezzanine lenders for second lien opportunities. To all intents and purposes these bank-affiliated SBICs can be regarded as mezzanine funds, too, so in normal credit market environments the competition in this category is with other, similar funds. All face most of the same customer acquisition challenges, although affiliation with a bank clearly gives bank-sponsored SBICs a marketing channel that is not available to the unaffiliated funds with which it competes. Identifying borrowers for mezzanine, private real estate, and oil and gas lenders is in most cases word-of-mouth, through a known network of equity investors and centers of influence such as law and accounting firms. This is what I meant in referring to these lenders as "clubbable," and attention to these lenders' networks is crucial to forming a judgment of their ability to acquire customers.

Like all businesses, credit provision is subject to cycles of activity and profitability. Some of these are determined by macroeconomic developments, but others are due to changes in commercial behavior that are seemingly random. Banks that did not previously pursue the small- and medium-sized business segment aggressively may unexpectedly awaken to the opportunity, and firms that had not previously offered one or another form of financing may decide that it is attractive to do so. Or competitors may decide to withdraw from the market, either by degrees or all at once. Even apart from the oceanic movements of the economic and credit cycles, business conditions for direct lenders are in constant flux, and conditions in their particular local or industrial environment are likely to be highly significant to them if they specialize in that way. If conditions become too difficult, one or all of lending margins, credit quality or the ability to attract borrowers at all (that is, from a Limited Partner's perspective, to get invested) will suffer, with obvious consequences for returns and possibly for the fund's risk levels as well.

For short-term lenders with ample opportunities to re-lend the funds that are paid back to them, the risk that their borrowers will pre-pay the loans is not very significant, as the loans are short-term in any case and they can readily find other ways to deploy that capital. But pre-payment risk can be a significant problem for longer-term lenders, which generally cannot find new borrowers so quickly, and which often are required by their partnership agreements to distribute returned funds to their investors. Pre-payments eat into the fund's ability to generate its required returns over its lifespan, particularly if the fund must continue to pay down leverage. This encourages longer-term lenders to include significant pre-payment penalties in their loan documents, but such penalties are forbidden under SBIC status. While this risk is not easily managed, it may be partially compensated by the warrants that are often attached to these loans: the equity value of a borrower that is in a financial condition to pre-pay its debt is likely to be fairly high.

Loans are carried on direct lenders' books according to various valuation methods (GAAP, FAS 157, etc.) and the fund may or may not choose to reserve against them. Consequently, the sources of volatility in such funds' asset values vary depending on how valuation is performed and whether reserves are employed. Absent write-downs and exercise of warrants (which are generally carried at zero value until realized), what little volatility of returns the funds do exhibit is the result of changing loan margins and fluctuations in the amount of business they are able to capture. Default risk and to some extent the amount of business transacted can be mitigated through diversification, and even a small direct lender is likely to have at least twenty borrowers in its portfolio.

Hence customer acquisition is essential not only to a direct lending fund's returns but also to its risk control efforts. Direct lenders that are effective at finding borrowers will usually make a point of touting the fact to prospective Limited Partners: the percentage of loan exposure that is internally sourced is an important measure of fund quality for those that originate loans. For those structured as hedge funds, with permanent capital, the turnaround time for redeployment of investors' capital when a loan is paid down is a key factor in returns, and an ability to source borrowers internally lends their potential investors some comfort that the turnaround time will be short. As a corollary, not only ample availability of potential new borrowers, but staggered borrowing schedules that permit capital to be more or less continuously employed are important factors in maximizing these funds' direct lending returns. For those vehicles that are structured more like private equity funds, the demands of diversification require that the fund have ample and diverse sources of borrowers.

Direct Lending in the Context of Conventional Portfolio Holdings

Direct lending funds are unusual among semi-liquid alternative investment vehicles (i.e., those not structured like private equity or private real estate funds) in that many (but not all) of them distribute a significant portion of their income to Limited Partners. This may be in the form of regular, even payments—say, 0.75 percent a month—or in annual and variable distributions. Hedge funds that engage in other fixed-income strategies generally do not distribute income, which instead they credit to Limited Partners' capital accounts. This is only recoverable upon redemption, although in the meantime their taxable investors are liable for the taxes incurred on this "phantom income." Note, however, that funds of funds with exposure to direct lending do not distribute income from it even if the underlying fund they hold does. So the portfolio role of direct lending is rather different from the typical hedge fund's, and in its income characteristics resembles that of fixed income in the case of short-term lenders that do distribute and private equity or real estate in the case of longer-term lenders.

Of all forms of alternative investment, direct lending is probably the easiest to relate to a conventional asset category. From an investment policy perspective, it is clearly an alternative to conventional fixed income, in many cases even featuring a coupon-like return element. Unlike conventional fixed income, duration management is not a potential source of return, but credit exposure clearly is. From the standpoint of portfolio function, direct lending is most comparable to an allocation to high yield.

Since it does not mark-to-market, direct lending lacks the volatility data that would permit direct comparison with publicly traded instruments. I discussed volatility estimation in Chapter 3, and suggested that there is nothing to prevent investment policymakers from deciding that a particular direct lending program is comparable in credit quality to bonds with this or that credit rating. On that basis they can assign a level of virtual volatility to it for analytic purposes. While I think it is important to repeat the caution I offered there about the need to be careful to avoid index illusion in making such estimates, I do not think there is much that is controversial about using high-yield instruments as an analogue for direct loans. The task is not simple, because the loans are not completely comparable to registered securities, but I think it is possible in principle. However, pre-payment risk must be modeled into some of these analogies, and that complicates matters considerably.

Direct lenders who make such loans argue with some justice that senior secured claims are superior credits to most publicly traded high-yield corporate bonds. But the small size, local nature, and likely the weaker controls and audit standards of direct lending's borrowers probably offset this. And whether the credits are of quality comparable to Standard & Poor's B- or CC high-yield ratings may be largely beside the point, given the substantial illiquidity premium that attaches to them. Even where a direct lender offers no credit facility that is longer-dated than ninety days and its total portfolio turns over between four and five times a year, its holdings cannot be liquidated instantaneously and acquiring new ones is not a matter of just sending a purchase order to a market maker. Similarly for factors and forfaiters, even though their effective credit exposures will typically be of significantly higher quality than those of other direct lenders and in most cases are likely to be investment grade.

Hence a direct lender must, in theory, demand a return on its loans that is higher than that available in public markets for instruments of comparable credit quality (whatever that may be). However, the liquidity of bonds, and therefore the illiquidity premium to be demanded of seldom-traded ones, is poorly understood. Although a paper that, in my opinion, represents substantial progress on the topic of illiquidity premia in corporate bond markets has recently been published, it is still only a first step. Given the behavior of fixed-income markets in 2007 and 2008, it seems likely that more research in this area will be forthcoming. One of that paper's observations is that the liquidity of even publicly traded corporate bonds is extremely limited: the median time between transactions for corporate bonds in the extensive universe that its author examined was two months (Chacko 2008, 159). This suggests that, in terms of liquidity as well as credit exposure, the similarity between bonds and most forms of direct lending is strong enough that the lessons that are eventually learned from analyzing the liquidity of publicly traded debt can safely be applied with only minor adjustments to at least the shorter-term varieties of direct loans.

The performance of a representative index of high-yield bonds is illustrated in **Figure 6.1**. Unfortunately, there is no index of direct lenders available for comparison, so a debate over the justice of comparing them with high-yield instruments is not resolvable (the same index provider does track loans, but its time series is rather short). However, ignoring the compound annual return of 4.29 percent and the annualized standard deviation of 5.21 percent exhibited by the index, its other statistical characteristics are suggestive for direct lenders. Kurtosis of 33.40 is quite high, indicating that returns cluster closely around the median, but that outliers tend to be quite extreme. This is what one would expect for direct lenders as well. Skewness is noticeably negative at −1.94, which indicates that the values that cluster around the median tend to be higher than it, while the outliers tend to be strongly negative. This also seems a likely description of direct lending.

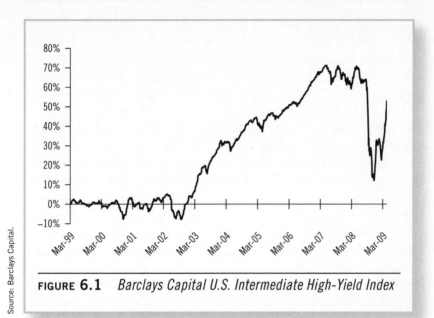

FIGURE 6.1 *Barclays Capital U.S. Intermediate High-Yield Index*

Despite the considerably more stable return streams that most direct lenders in my experience are able to report, this comparison with market-traded instruments does not strike me as egregious. Much of the volatility shown for the high-yield index results from swings in market sentiment, which do not apply to the direct lender's return stream. Sentiment is, of course, a function of the perception of default risk rather than actual defaults. This factor certainly exaggerates the contrast between the two types of instruments, and a direct lender's returns would no doubt be considerably more volatile if there were a way to adjust them daily for market perceptions of corporate default risk. Actual defaults are reflected to some extent in direct lenders' returns, although those that use provisioning smooth their default experience in ways that also affect comparison with traded instruments—this is, in effect, to pile autocorrelation on top of the autocorrelation resulting from the lack of a market to which to mark. In performing due diligence on a direct lender, institutions must consider the precise nature of the loans, accounting standards, and provisioning involved in order to form an estimate of this "virtual volatility."

But default experience for a well-managed direct lending program is in any case less extreme than for high-yield bonds, if only due to recovery of collateral (or, in the case of mezzanine debt, the "nuclear option" of converting warrants that have put provisions attached to them). On the other hand, diversification is relatively easy for a high-yield manager, and no direct lender is likely to be as diversified as, say, the Vanguard High-Yield Corporate Fund with its 249 positions (on a recent count). The insertion of "well-managed" in the previous sentence was not accidental: collateral is only part of the story here, which also includes superior due diligence and, in the case of short-term lending, a shorter exposure period.

Once again, the situation is different for long-term lenders. Although they expect to achieve high current income, too, mezzanine, private real estate, and resource development lenders are at least theoretically compensated for the credit and liquidity risk components of their loans by their equity or equity-like "kickers," and real estate lenders by their ability to take equity possession of the property in the event of default. This is a directional component of their strategies that is quite different from a risk-compensating increment in yield, and something that is completely absent from other forms of direct lending and most forms of fixed-income investment. It is also something that is completely un-analyzable: meaningful valuation of a warrant on equity in an asset that is not publicly traded and which by definition therefore has no volatility history, is impossible. Mezzanine lenders generally avoid this problem by carrying warrants at zero value unless the borrower ultimately achieves an IPO, in which case they carry them at a value determined by option formulae. As a value is only achieved for the warrant by an IPO or by its actual exercise into cash, this component of returns can be expected to be quite "lumpy." Having been forced repeatedly to call attention to the exceptionalism of the various forms of long-term private market lending in this chapter, it may seem odd that I have included it here at all. But because this type of debt frequently appears under the 'direct lending' rubric, I felt obliged to do so, if only to forestall confusion at the cost of complication. And in any case, I hope that the contrast between these forms of finance and other sorts of direct lending activities may sometimes have been revealing.

All of which means that investment policy should probably demand levels of return from direct lending that are roughly comparable to those on analogous high-yield bonds. My experience suggests direct lending achieves these, and that, even after heroic adjustments for imputed volatility, the return distributions are statistically less unattractive than those of high yield. While more data specific to any fund that is actually under consideration would be necessary to justify such a claim, it seems likely that, in many cases that are relevant to the purposes of investment policy, direct lending should be regarded not just as an alternative to high-yield corporate bonds, but as a more attractive replacement for them.

CHAPTER 7

Merger Arbitrage

Merger arbitrage, which is also often called risk arbitrage, has a reputation as an aggressive, no-holds-barred trade, and its practitioners have acquired a fair amount of notoriety as financial buccaneers. This is largely undeserved, although this claim should not be taken imply the reverse, that it is really a pedestrian activity pursued by colorless, green-eyeshade-and-sleeve-garter types. The reputation probably stems from the insider trading scandals of the late 1980s, which brought attention and eventually a prison sentence to Ivan Boesky, an arbitrageur who was far from colorless. The paraphrase of his thoughts on greed that contributed the only memorable line from the film *Wall Street* probably ensured that merger arbitrage would henceforth carry a whiff of sulfur. In my experience, most merger arbitrageurs do not fit the stereotype. As we shall see, merger arbitrage requires an unusual combination of analytic and trading skills that leave participants in the activity little time to cultivate a more benign image.

Nevertheless, merger arbitrage is not wholly lacking in bare-knuckled elements. Some practitioners are highly vocal activists, whose presence on shareholder registries is rarely welcomed by management and whose exploits at shareholder meetings and in the press make them magnets for media attention. But even for these investors, the core of the trade they pursue is the analysis of relative values and of the legal or regulatory considerations that can affect the outcome of a proposed acquisition—interesting to some, but hardly the stuff of pot-boilers. While practitioners may find that flamboyance furthers their interests in particular situations, the trade is grounded in thorough knowledge of the investment banking complexities of the acquisition process.

Although merger arbitrage is a "classic" hedge fund strategy, the number of pure merger arbitrage vehicles has declined over time. At the end of 2008, assets under the management of firms included in the HFRI Merger Arbitrage Index amounted to only $16 billion: see Vaughan (2009). This suggests that total assets under management by dedicated merger arbitrage funds were probably in the region of $30 billion. Recurrent droughts in the availability of arbitrage opportunities—about which more below—probably account for most of this. But I suspect that over-exploitation of the trade during periods when opportunities were plentiful has also contributed to the scarcity of vehicles now devoted exclusively to it.[1] One way that merger arbitrageurs have responded to this situation is that most of them have become fully global in their search for trading opportunities. Restricting their funds to just the U.S. investment universe has increasingly become an unsustainable business strategy, so dedicated merger arbitrageurs are active wherever there is takeover activity to provide them with the opportunity to pursue their trade. The sharp increase in cross-border merger activity in the last few decades—both foreign acquisitions of U.S. companies and U.S. acquisition activity overseas—has offered further encouragement to this trend. Once familiarity with overseas corporate governance and merger practices has been acquired in connection with one transaction, it would be wasteful of the intellectual capital the manager so acquired—with some effort and at a cost—not to take advantage of whatever additional opportunities to exploit it that may present themselves.

The bulk of merger arbitrage is now carried out by vehicles that label themselves as "event-driven" and engage in a variety of other trades along side it. "Event-driven" is yet another amorphous hedge fund category, largely but by no means exclusively involving various equity trades. These include trades that exploit buy-backs and spin-offs, various forms of distressed and bankruptcy investing, investment in firms that are experiencing proxy contests, shareholder or other forms of litigation,

---

1. See Jetley and Ji 2010. Kirschner et al. (2006, 99) offer a third explanation—that rapid dissemination of acquisition information has robbed merger specialists of their information advantage—which I find less persuasive. Rapid dissemination does little to speed comprehension, and dedicated merger arbitrageurs retain the advantage of experience and contacts that can provide legal and other analysis. In any case, the basic information relating to acquisition announcements has been more or less instantaneously available to tape-watchers since the 1960s.

and a variety of other so-called "special situations." Returns on most of these trades can also be enhanced through activism, and frequently are. Event-driven investment is discussed in more detail in Chapter 11.

Event-driven managers' exposure to merger arbitrage is likely to be variable and opportunistic, with the other trading strategies that they pursue providing return-seeking opportunities when merger-related trades are not available or insufficiently attractive to exploit. This is not to imply that event-driven managers are arbitrageurs by preference and resort unenthusiastically to other trades only in the absence of merger activity. This is certainly not true in most cases, and if anything, merger-related trades probably now take a back seat to the many other "event" opportunities that these managers can find to exploit. This seems to be true even of those event-driven funds that started life as purely merger arbitrage vehicles. The discussion in this chapter will restrict itself to the pure merger arbitrage trade.

Merger Arbitrage as an Investment Technique

In principle, merger arbitrage is exclusively an arbitrage strategy, but in fact both directional and cash flow strategies are intermixed with it. Directional strategies generally appear only in individual trades, depending on how a particular acquisition is structured, but cash flow elements are always present because of the need to leverage the trade. Returns from merger arbitrage would be unattractive without leverage, so leverage must be regarded as inherent to the activity.

Without further analysis of the indices shown there, **Figure 7.1** and **Table 7.1** are sufficient to suggest the attractions of merger arbitrage. Compared to directional exposure to equities, it is a trade that exhibits significantly reduced volatility, sufficient non-correlation to the underlying equities to provide diversification, and a history of solid returns. Kurtosis is substantially higher, and returns are more negatively skewed, which results from the binary nature of trade failures when a proposed merger collapses. Lo (2008, 95) finds modest but nevertheless significant negative autocorrelation among monthly merger arbitrage returns—that is, a pattern that suggests that the trade's sequential monthly returns are at least partially determined by price reversal effects. As a consequence, if his method for adjusting for autocorrelation, discussed in Chapter 4, is applied to a merger arbitrage index, adjusted volatilities are *less* than raw, unadjusted ones, so that its Sharpe ratio, when calculated using unadjusted data, is on Lo's accounting under-reported by 12 to 15 percent.

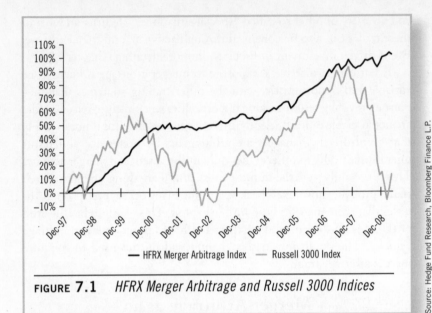

FIGURE 7.1 *HFRX Merger Arbitrage and Russell 3000 Indices*

TABLE 7.1 *Merger Arbitrage and the Broad U.S. Equity Market*

	HRFX MERGER ARBITRAGE INDEX	RUSSELL 3000 INDEX
Compound Annual Return	6.40%	1.08%
Median Monthly Return	0.67%	1.01%
Annualized Standard Deviation	3.85%	16.96%
Correlation with the Russell 3000 Index	0.4054	1.0000
Kurtosis	3.46	1.11
Skewness	−1.21	−0.75

However, it is also quite plain from Figure 7.1 that merger arbitrage can experience extended fallow periods. For example, in the two-year period from mid-2001 to mid-2003, the Index produced essentially no return. The reason for this is clear from **Figure 7.2**. Merger activity follows a long

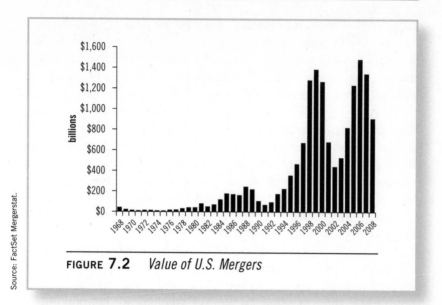

FIGURE 7.2 *Value of U.S. Mergers*

cycle, and when conditions for acquisitions are not favorable, there are few opportunities for merger arbitrageurs to exploit. Hence the imperative of a globe-spanning trade discovery discipline. While the merger cycle is global, too, so that a slowdown in the United States will generally be accompanied by a slowdown elsewhere, the cycles do not move in precise lock-step, and at least by expanding their horizons to embrace all the opportunities available, merger arbitrageurs have better hopes of finding trading opportunities to tide them over periods of merger drought. The factors that govern the merger cycle are varied, but most of them are closely related to the same factors that determine the economic environment for equity market investment generally. This, and the fact that when conditions for mergers are favorable, merger activity can itself sometimes play a significant role in equity market returns, account for what might otherwise seem to be surprisingly high correlation between a trade that is, as an arbitrage, at all times fully hedged, and metrics for the broad equity market. In addition, failures of mergers, which may result in large losses for arbitrage practitioners, often occur when equity markets experience a crisis, which further contributes to the correlation between them. So the correlation, although moderate (its R^2 is 18.6 percent), is higher than might otherwise be expected of a non-directional trade.

The prototypical merger arbitrage situation is one in which a firm seeks to buy another, using a new issue of its own stock as the sole consideration it offers. This deal structure provides a pure arbitrage, because no additional valuation factors other than the prices of the two firms involved come into play. **Figure 7.3** illustrates the history of such a merger. It traces the value of XM Satellite Radio shares in terms of the price of the 4.6 shares of Sirius Satellite Radio that were offered for it on February 19, 2007, from five days before the merger announcement through the much-delayed completion of the transaction on July 29, 2008. Based on the two firms' average closing prices for the week before the deal was announced, the Sirius bid priced XM at a 25.2 percent premium. This is reflected in the closing of the valuation gap at the beginning of the history, which occurred despite the fact that the market greeted the deal favorably and the shares of both XM and Sirius rose in the wake of the announcement of the agreement.

The subsequent performance of XM in terms of the 4.6 Sirius shares offered for it reflects the regulatory complexity of the deal. The merger required multiple approvals in both the United States and Canada, and became something of a political football, accompanied by vocal public lobbying of the Federal Communications Commission in particular. As Figure 7.3 indicates, the fate of the deal was in question up to the Commission's approval (which required significant concessions from

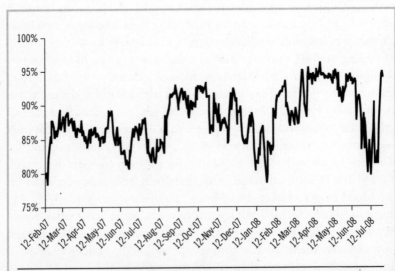

FIGURE 7.3   *XM Satellite Radio Price versus the Price of 4.6 Sirius Satellite Radio Shares*

Source: Bloomberg Finance, L.P.

the combined group) four days before it finally closed. Although the resulting delays would have eaten significantly into the profitability of the arbitrage if a trader had held the position from announcement to completion, its volatility provided numerous opportunities for active and well-informed traders to profit from exiting and re-entering the trade over its 530 calendar-day life. Merger arbitrageurs have frequent recourse to market timing, informed by their assessment of the shifting probability that the transaction will be brought to completion, in an effort to enhance their returns. The negative autocorrelation exhibited by merger arbitrage provides fertile ground for "trading around" positions, although it is not clear to me whether this feature of merger arbitrage returns is a cause or a symptom of this behavior. Conceivably, it could be both—that is, a tendency for the arbitrage spread to oscillate randomly around "fair value" may encourage trading that in turn amplifies these swings in the relative pricing of the deal's constituents.

Neglecting these opportunities for investors to drink repeatedly from this deal's well, what exactly was the profitability of the arbitrage it offered? Any answer to this question requires too many more-or-less arbitrary assumptions to permit an exemplary calculation that would offer any real value, but it is useful to give some detail as to what those assumptions would be:

❑ trade timing at entry and exit (assuming the arbitrageur did not anticipate the announcement, whether or not based on illegal inside information, the entry trade would have to have been subsequent to the deal's announcement);

❑ transaction costs (note that the short position required 4.6 sales of borrowed shares for every share of the long leg of the trade purchased);

❑ security borrowing costs, the level of collateralization required over the life of the stock loan (which is typically a negotiated figure in excess of the value of the short position and is marked to market daily) and net interest earnings on the collateral;

❑ dividends received on the long leg of the trade and payable to the security's lender on the short leg (in this case this was not an issue, since neither firm was dividend-paying); and leverage costs.

There are a large number of component parts in such a trade, so that the announcement of a bid at, say, a 25.2 percent premium does not imply that an unleveraged return of that magnitude can be extracted from it. Any arbitrageur will know in advance what the costs associated with its trading will be. But security borrowing conditions are trade-specific and changeable, and interest earnings on collateral are variable, while the total interest received on collateral, the interest paid on leverage, and the net dividends paid or received will be a function of how long the position is carried as well as various shifting market factors during that period. So the potential returns of a merger arbitrage may be known in broad outline before a manager enters into the trade, but they can be known with complete precision only after the transaction has closed.

Figure 7.4 provides an illustration of the hedge characteristics of merger arbitrage. The period between the deal's announcement and its closing coincided with a period of considerable drama in world equity and credit markets. The stocks of both the acquirer and its target suffered more than the broad market as a result of concerns about their commercial prospects in a deteriorating consumer environment as well as concern about the conditions regulators might impose on the proposed combination (or whether they would even permit it to occur at all). But because the bid caused the correlation between the two stocks to be high for the period, at 0.8248, shorting one against the other hedged away the much lesser correlation that the two stocks had relative to the broad market (Sirius and XM had correlations of 0.3677 and 0.3412 with the Russell 2000 Index, respectively).

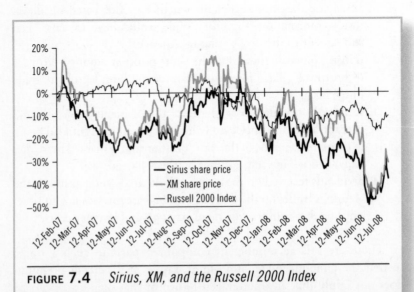

FIGURE 7.4 *Sirius, XM, and the Russell 2000 Index*

The transactions exploited by merger arbitrage are not restricted to all-stock bids. Because the need to borrow large sums to carry out an all-cash transaction affects a would-be acquirer's balance sheet and thus its stock price, hedged pair trades of the sort that are the obvious arbitrage response to an all-share transaction are also frequently the appropriate trading response to all-cash transactions. **Figure 7.5** illustrates such an all-cash transaction. On June 11, 2008, the Belgian brewer Inbev offered $65, entirely in cash, for all the shares of Anheuser-Busch outstanding. The bid was rejected by Anheuser-Busch on July 1, but the two firms reached agreement on an all-cash price of $70 two weeks later. Unlike many such transactions, the acquirer had little trouble securing pre-approval for most of the financing that the deal required, and regulatory considerations played a comparatively limited role in the way that the bid unfolded, since neither firm had substantial activities in the other's markets that might have raised antitrust concerns, and brewing is not subject to a special regulatory regime similar to that governing broadcasting in the United States and most other countries.

This accounts for the low volatility of Anheuser-Busch's share price for a month and a half after it accepted the enhanced bid. But the drama in world equity and credit markets mentioned in connection with the previous example became even more extreme in the autumn of 2008, as a result of which Inbev's lead bank was partially nationalized on September

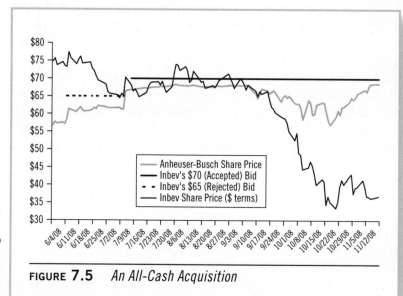

FIGURE 7.5   *An All-Cash Acquisition*

29, and the Belgian government attempted to break it up and sell off pieces of it. Ivbev's plummeting stock price caused it to postpone the equity issue it had intended to help finance the transaction on October 14. The resulting concern about the continued availability of financing for the deal accounts for the behavior of both companies' share prices from the end September. Anheuser's shares fell because of uncertainty that the $70 offer would remain good, but Inbev's fell further, as failure to complete the bid would have exposed it to a write-off of considerable legal and investment banking costs, uncertainty over its future strategic direction, and might have exposed it to liability to Anheuser-Busch. Market crises that affect the availability of credit can be very dangerous for all-cash bids, and a number of high profile transactions were scuppered by recent market developments, as also occurred after the 1987 Crash. However, with some well-publicized difficulties that are reflected in the development of its share price as shown in Figure 7.5, Inbev ultimately succeeded in obtaining the necessary financing and the deal—at $60.8 billion, the largest all-cash acquisition on record—was completed on November 18, ninety-one days after Inbev's initial, rejected offer.

Note that, in keeping with my comment in Chapter 1, neither of the firms acquired in these transactions had completely converged on the indicated transaction price at the time that the deals closed. Traders did not "arbitrage away" the discrepancy between market prices and transaction prices—a 2.07 percent premium remained in the case of Anheuser-Busch and a more substantial 5.85 percent in the case of XM Satellite Radio. In the Anheuser-Busch/Inbev transaction, the final market price approached fairly closely to a predetermined cash price that was known to be fully funded. In the case of XM Satellite Radio/Sirius Satellite Radio, traders could never be certain of the final transaction price until trading in XM was suspended. Further, the fundamental outlook for the satellite radio industry was poor in an environment of weak advertising sales, and the commercial implications of the concessions extracted from the combined entity by the Federal Communications Commission as a condition of its approval of the transaction were not entirely clear. Amid all this uncertainty, and given the shares' relatively restricted liquidity (the combined group had a market capitalization of $4.9 billion on its first day of trading), arbitrageurs left more "on the table" than they might otherwise have. This measure of caution was amply justified by the renamed Sirius XM Radio's subsequent share price performance.

If the acquirer is not public, there may be no way that an arbitrage can be constructed around a proposed transaction. However, the skills involved in analyzing such deals are essentially the same as those applied to transactions in which the acquirer is public, and many arbitrageurs are tempted to make long-only directional speculations on these situations. The temptation became especially strong during the buyout boom of 2005 to 2007, when private market purchasers virtually drove trade purchasers from the acquisition playing field. Clearly, this type of trade is not an arbitrage at all, since it is not a hedged convergence trade.

But if the target has debt outstanding, a form of arbitrage can be fashioned around such an acquisition, as purchase by a leveraged buyout fund will usually result in downgrading of the target's credit rating. Long the target's equity and short its debt is a hedged convergence trade that involves additional considerations to those employed in "classic" merger arbitrage. In other cases, the target's credit rating might be expected to improve upon its acquisition, and in still others its debt covenants may contain a change-of-control provision that requires the debt to be retired at par, which may offer opportunity if the debt had traded at a discount prior to the announcement of the deal. In both these latter two cases, long the target's debt and short its equity provides a hedged position. But where such trades are not possible, an arbitrageur who succumbs to the temptation to engage in unhedged directional trades on acquisition targets delivers risks to its Limited Partners that are not, in most cases, what they signed up for. Assuming that, in performing a search for a merger arbitrageur, investment policymakers are seeking arbitrage exposure and not directional speculation, due diligence should attend carefully to the trades in which candidate managers have actually engaged, with special attention to those in which the acquirer was not public.

Because they are, of professional necessity, closely in touch with the merger and acquisition scene, if any investors are likely to be able to anticipate a merger transaction, they are likely to be part of the arbitrage community. Such activity has inherent dangers: even if it is carried out entirely above-board and innocent of any inside information, it could easily attract unwelcome attention from security regulators if it is successful in anticipating an announcement, and it will usually result in a failed directional trade if it is unsuccessful. Where conditions are appropriate, merger arbitrageurs may take long positions in a potential target and pursue activist initiatives to put it "in play." Just the presence of certain investors in a company's share registry is enough to encourage speculation over its imminent sale, and if they become vocal proponents of a change in ownership, their efforts may be able to bring it about. But this stratagem is not infallible, and its likelihood of success is dependent on many of the same factors—the psychology of the potential target's management, the shareholders' rights as determined by the firm's articles of incorporation or corporate governance statutes, the financial logic of such a transaction, and so forth—that determine the success or failure of any deal. Here again, the trader has taken only one side of a potential arbitrage, and consequently is unhedged and thus directionally exposed, at least until a potential purchaser for the target can be identified. This is not arbitrage. Those investors who pursue this sort of activism merit a reputation for bare-knuckled scrapping and buccaneering opportunism more than the merger arbitrage fraternity generally.

Merger Arbitrage Risk

As with any arbitrage, the primary risk of merger arbitrage is that the relationship of correlation between prices that it seeks to exploit can disappear. The announcement of a deal creates contingent fungibility between the shares of the acquirer and its target. The degree of contingency is determined by market participants' and other interested parties' acceptance of the deal's rationale and the regulatory complexity and financing challenges that are implied if the transaction is to come to completion. Occasionally other factors, such as union approval or conditions attached to commercial contracts to which the target is a party may also come into play. The degree of contingency changes over the course of the deal as market perception of these factors and of the positions of both the acquirer's and the target's managements change. The dynamics of agreed transactions, such as the two examples given above, can be quite different from those of hostile deals. Then there is always the possibility that, once an acquirer's actions have placed a target "in play," it may attract a competing bid—a possibility that increases proportionately to the degree of hostility of the initial offer. Agreed transactions may occasionally attract a competing bidder, but conditions attached to the agreement generally discourage the target from cooperating with the competing bidder.

The regulatory environment in which a deal takes place varies by country, by industry, and over time. The course of Sirius's bid for XM was very strongly affected by the involvement of the Federal Communications Commission in the regulation of both firms, and as mentioned, the Canadian government also had an interest in the matter. Other highly regulated businesses, such as financial services, railroads, or utilities, face similar regulatory hurdles to the successful completion of merger transactions. Every transaction faces at least cursory review by competition authorities, and the regulatory landscape is constantly shifting.

Perhaps the most notable instance of this is the way that regulatory activism by the European Union has created a wildcard for transactions among multinational firms, even if neither the acquirer nor the target is headquartered within its jurisdiction. General Electric scrapped its proposed acquisition of Honeywell in 2001 largely as a result of restrictions that the European Union placed on the scope of that proposed deal, despite the fact that neither firm is an E.U.-domiciled entity. Microsoft has been in more or less continuous litigation with the European Union for many years, at least partially as a result of acquisitions it has made of various U.S.-based firms. Assessing the degree of regulatory contingency that accompanies a transaction proposal requires deep knowledge of the regulatory background to any transaction, including attention to its political sensitivity, as this can make approvals that appear on the surface to be routine to become considerably less so—note, for example, the political hue and cry over the proposed acquisition of various U.S. port operators by the Dubai Port Authority, which ultimately was sufficient to stymie that transaction.

By way of contrast, Inbev's agreement to acquire Anheuser-Busch was comparatively straightforward. Yet there were complications there, too. Anheuser-Busch's unions used the occasion to extract management concessions in a new contract, and Grupo Modelo, a Mexican brewer with which Anheuser-Busch was in discussions in the run up to acceptance of Inbev's revised offer, also attempted to have a say in how the transaction ultimately played out. Parties with an interest in a transaction may extend well beyond the more obvious regulators, so merger arbitrageurs must be alive to the possibility of unforeseen entrants into the transaction process and possess the ability to analyze the strength of their claims to have an influence on its outcome.

Even where the financing for a transaction seems to be completely assured at the time of its announcement, the arbitrageur faces the risk that the arrangements could fall through. The Inbev/Anheuser-Busch merger was hardly the first to encounter difficulties deriving from completely exogenous financial market developments. And an acquirer's shareholders, if they oppose a deal, can in some cases block a transaction even if financing is available, by preventing the acquirer from tapping it. Successful merger arbitrage requires careful attention to the changeable conditions under which financing is available as well as the specific details of and costs involved in each particular transaction's financial structure. It also requires familiarity with both firms' articles of incorporation and the corporate governance statutes that determine shareholders' power to block a proposed deal. As more and more mergers are cross-border transactions, this necessitates that arbitrageurs have access to international legal and regulatory expertise. It is unlikely, for instance, that many U.S. arbitrageurs had personal and intimate knowledge of Belgian corporate governance practices before Inbev launched its offer for Anheuser-Busch.

There is also a certain amount of armchair psychology involved in analyzing merger transactions. Chief executives are, more or less by definition, highly competitive personalities, and having publicly embarked on a course of action, they often find it difficult to reverse course even if changing circumstances recommend against continuing along the path they had chosen. But other times they can surprise the market with their willingness to abandon what was apparently a cherished goal. Steven Ballmer, the CEO of Microsoft—unquestionably a competitive personality—was widely expected to pursue a proposed acquisition of Yahoo! more or less regardless of price and the target's opposition. No doubt he disappointed numerous traders when he thought better of pursuing such a transaction in 2008. And it is not only the psyches of the two CEOs involved that concern arbitrageurs. Where a deal is not favored by the acquirer's shareholders, unions, or other stakeholders, sound judgment of the depth and resourcefulness of these parties' opposition to the transaction is very useful to traders.

While merger arbitrage is not a directional trade, a portion of the analysis that underpins success in merger arbitrage is a sort of second-order directional calculation. One unavoidable component of an arbitrageur's thinking has to be a calculation of the value of the target to its would-be acquirer. For all that psychology and other factors come into play in any acquisition, a sound understanding of the economic fundamentals of both the firms involved in a transaction provides the most important component of the analysis needed to judge whether a proposed transaction will be consummated. A firm grasp of the valuation background to the deal provides a standard against which the psychological factors can be weighed, as well as providing grounds for determining the likelihood that financing for it will be obtainable, and the likeliest outcome if a second bidder for the target company emerges.

If an acquisition proposal ignites a competitive contest for the target, the task of a merger arbitrage analyst becomes a far more difficult triangulation. An elaborate system of regulatory provisions governing such situations comes into play, and the competing bidders are likely to become activists with respect to regulators, potential political allies, the target's management, and its shareholders in an attempt to sway the outcome of the competition. No body of law or regulation can foresee all contingencies, and novel situations can arise, such as Grupo Modelo's intervention in the Inbev/Anheuser-Busch transaction, about which legal opinion on the merits of the interloper's claims may be divided. As with the physics of the multi-body problem, the dynamics of a three-way acquisition contest can be highly complex, with all the forces in operation interacting in ways that are very difficult to predict.

Occasionally, the complexity of a transaction drives merger arbitrageurs nearly to despair. For example, the contested bid for ABN AMRO Bank involved competing consortia, each consisting of several firms from several different countries, all of them outside the target bank's home jurisdiction. The acquisition target they contested was a highly diversified multinational that was itself subject to numerous regulatory regimes, and the transaction occurred in the context of untested takeover and corporate governance codes in ABN AMRO's country of domicile and an unpredictably activist governing competition authority at the transnational level. Precedent was not a great deal of help to arbitrageurs in this instance, and many of them would have had difficulty obtaining advice, due to a significant shortage of experienced securities lawyers in the Netherlands. As cross-border transactions become more frequent and competition authorities in much of the world take a more inclusive, border-crossing view of their regulatory remits, the breadth and depth of knowledge that arbitrageurs require to negotiate the merger landscape successfully has ballooned. Although merger arbitrageurs may not merit their reputations as financial buccaneers, a reputation for polymathy is increasingly deserved. This is not to say that merger arbitrageurs must be smarter than other sorts of investors, only that the range of things that can affect their trades and of which they must be aware is more extensive. As in every endeavor, in investment management, too, there is a place for both "Renaissance men" and specialists—and not only in merger arbitrage. Distressed investors with an interest in the Lehman Brothers bankruptcy were confronted with seventy-six separate insolvency procedures involving three thousand legal entities (see Cairns 2009).

Clearly, the task of a merger arbitrageur embraces considerations that go well beyond security valuation. Despite the fact that this chapter has devoted considerable attention to the regulatory, investment banking, and other considerations that can delay a deal, developments that may affect the progress of an acquisition toward its completion can arise quite suddenly. Situations that may require a trading response will not wait patiently. While they may not require exactly a snap response, they are unlikely to allow time for in-depth research and detailed consultation with outside experts. Consequently, successful arbitrageurs need to have a considerable amount of the necessary analytic expertise in-house, and to have access on short order to any necessary expertise that they do not themselves possess. Of course, much advice can be purchased, but reliance on outside sources for core competencies is very risky to any business endeavor, and transaction speeds require merger arbitrageurs to have a substantial portion of what they need to know at their finger-tips in any given situation. Hence, the skepticism about the suggestion of Kirschner et al.—that exploitable merger information has become a commodity available to essentially all market participants—that I expressed earlier in this chapter.

Then there are the many risks that attach to any arbitrage trade. The high levels of leverage that are generally deployed in the activity—typically 4:1 or 80 percent of capital employed—are, as in any leveraged trade, a double-edged sword, and impose a cost of carry that becomes progressively more difficult to bear if the period between a transaction's announcement and its closing turns out to be lengthy. The collapse of a merger arbitrage is in many cases sudden, forcing traders to scramble to unwind in conditions where virtually all their competitors are doing the same: this is not an ideal situation in which to trade. Managing the short leg of the trade is subject to all the risks that attach to any form of short selling, as described in Chapter 5, and since there are likely to be a fair number of traders simultaneously pursuing the short sale that is one leg of the arbitrage, borrowing costs are often high. The risk from market-timing is largely one of potential opportunity cost—that is, from being unexposed to the trade when something transpires that encourages the arbitrage gap to narrow. Given the intermittent availability of merger arbitrage opportunities, missing all or any significant part of the returns generated by a transaction while engaged in market-timing can have serious consequences for fund performance.

Horwitz (2004) remarks on the fact that merger arbitrage seems to be almost exclusively a directional speculation on the success of trans-actions, rather than a "true" relative value trade, in which the manager would logically be equally willing to speculate against completion. I am not convinced that merger arbitrageurs do not in fact occasion-ally express a trading view that a transaction will fail, but to do so by employing a mirror image of their normal trade structure—that is, by leveraging a pair trade that is short the target and long the acquirer—would be highly risky. The failure of many deals is greeted with relief by the owners of the acquirer, and many targets that escape one firm's approach quickly become another acquiring firm's prey. Such trades would in effect be a form of reverse arbitrage.

Merger Arbitrage in the Context of Conventional Portfolio Holdings

Merger arbitrage is, at least in principle, a form of market-neutral investing, and much of what was said regarding that investment approach in Chapter 5 applies to merger arbitrage as well. In theory, it should in fact be more purely market-neutral than most such investment approaches, because of the fungibility of the acquirer's and the target's shares and thus the high correlation between them that is established upon announcement of a bid. Further, the discussion in this chapter has stressed that the fungibility created by a bid is contingent on a wide range of influences that demand considerable analytic effort. Merger arbitrage is more binary than most market-neutral approaches to investing. The trade either works out, or, when a transaction collapses and fungibility disappears, it decidedly does not. Merger arbitrage offers little room for partial successes since the correlation at its heart is likely to collapse suddenly rather than fade away like an old soldier. The relationship between the merger cycle and the stock market cycle, as well as the sensitivity of many proposed transactions to market crises and the influence of merger activity on the returns of the broader market, ensure that merger arbitrage retains meaningful β exposure.

The binary nature of the trade would typically argue in favor of maintaining broad diversification among merger arbitrage managers. However, given the limited number of transactions that are under way at any given time, diversification among managers provides variety only in the attitudes toward particular merger situations, rather than exposure to a significantly different universe of merger transactions. Although scarcity of opportunity is not always the rule in the merger arena, and there are occasionally periods of "merger mania" when the exposures of different managers may vary widely, much of the time merger arbitrageurs compete with each other to extract maximum returns from the same set of deals.

Extracting this maximum is to a substantial extent a product of successful market-timing, and this in turn is a function of superior understanding of, or more rapid reaction to, information as it becomes publicly available. As merger arbitrage is a finite or bounded trade, the success of some managers in capturing that maximum is necessarily at the expense of other managers. Lhabitant and Learned (2002, 30f) find that diversification across event-driven strategies increases kurtosis and the negative value of skewness, which is consistent with this comment. Although their analysis is based on an event-driven index, I suspect that it is the merger arbitrage component of the returns of the managers included in that index that is the dominant influence on their findings. This discussion has stressed the intellectual/informational requirements of merger arbitrage because most of any edge in the trade is to be found in successful market-timing that anticipates the moves of regulators, managers, shareholders, and competitors, but that should not detract from the importance of trading prowess to a manager's success in this technique. The negative autocorrelation among merger arbitrage returns that Lo finds gives emphasis to this point.

Given that, in most merger market conditions, the bulk of any diversification that is achievable among managers consists of exposure to different market-timing signals rather than to different transactions, seeking only a limited amount of diversification among merger arbitrage managers themselves is the appropriate response of investment policy. Rather than expending effort on identifying a wide range of managers, policymakers should concentrate on finding one or two extremely capable ones. Although performance track records provide some indication of capability, examination of them must make due allowance for the number and richness of the trading opportunities available during the period that the managers have been in operation. Due diligence will probably benefit manager selection most if it is able to provide a detailed investigation of the manager's trading behavior and the considerations that motivated it over the course of specific transactions. This will reveal whether a merger arbitrageur possesses the knowledge and information contacts that are necessary to underwrite consistent outperformance. Before meeting with a merger arbitrageur, it is useful to become familiar with deals in which it has been involved and to ask the manager to walk through its thinking over the course of those transactions. This is an atypical approach to due diligence, but I have found it to be fruitful.

Given the opportunity constraints from which merger arbitrage can suffer, is it appropriate for investment policymakers to seek pure practitioners of the trade at all? Because much of this activity has migrated into event-driven vehicles, it is becoming increasingly difficult to identify many purists in any case—raising the question whether the discussion in this chapter has been a largely academic digression. I do not think so, because the comparative market-neutrality of merger arbitrage sets it apart as an identifiably different trade than some others that event-driven managers pursue. While many of the analytic requirements of merger arbitrage are also necessary to the successful pursuit of other event-driven opportunities, and while event-driven trades generally have fairly low correlation to equity markets, many of them are nevertheless directional in nature. Taking advantage of the opportunities for putting on hedged, market-neutral trades that are offered by mergers is a fundamentally different type of strategy from say, trades that exploit equity spin-offs or corporate distress. This by no means implies that event-driven managers are less capable of exploiting the strategy than purists (I strongly doubt that this is true). Rather, it is only to emphasize that their promiscuous blends of arbitrage and directional trading offer their investors a significantly different sort of aggregate investment exposure, and consequently a different pattern of returns, than would merger arbitrage on its own.

I wish to stress that I am in no way raising an objection to event-driven investment vehicles—they can offer quite an attractive form of equity market-correlated exposure, as will be discussed in Chapter 11. However, from the standpoint of pedantic tidiness, I cannot help feeling that it is unfortunate that merger arbitrage has migrated toward that territory rather than toward the market-neutral environment. The reason that it has gone in the direction that it has rather than toward the market-neutral segment is clear: the commonality of analytic disciplines between it and event-driven investment makes sharing resources a very valuable source of economies of scale, particularly given the cost of obtaining and nurturing that expertise. Exploiting many types of "event" requires exactly the same sorts of information and investment banking expertise that exploiting mergers does.

But the result is the creation of hedge funds that, from a risk perspective, are neither fish nor fowl. Admixture with directional trades dilutes the market-neutrality of the arbitrage: note from Table 11.1 that the market correlation of event-driven techniques is two-thirds higher than that of merger arbitrage. While trade diversification may improve upon the return characteristics of stand-alone merger arbitrage because it offers a more consistent opportunity set, it does nothing to improve upon its risk characteristics. The risk reduction that results from mixing these trades is the less powerful form that results from multiplying correlated exposures, rather than the stronger form in which exposures are partially offsetting. If merger arbitrage had instead migrated toward market-neutral funds, it would have created products with a more consistent risk profile, while introducing an element of investment value added that, as Chapter 5 suggested, is otherwise missing from many vehicles of that type.

If investment policymakers are unable to identify suitable merger arbitrage purists, then they should recognize that their exposure to the strategy via event-driven vehicles does not provide like-for-like replacement. Given the fallow periods that merger arbitrage cyclically experiences, a multi-strategy solution that offers occasional exposure to it when attractive opportunities to exploit the trade are available is probably the best institutional investment solution. This is most likely to be found among event-driven managers, for the reasons discussed. And merger arbitrage improves the risk characteristics of the event-driven funds in which it plays a part by reducing their aggregate equity market correlation. The resulting hybrids have an unusual return profile, with significant attractions of their own, as we will see.

CHAPTER **8**

High-Frequency Trading

T he reader may well wonder whether adoption of a very short time horizon is, in and of itself, a sufficiently distinguishing feature of an investment technique to qualify it for separate discussion. Restricting itself to a short-term time horizon will clearly determine some aspects of an investment approach and the sources of its returns—for example, its trades will necessarily be directional or arbitrages, because a short period offers insufficient opportunity for any appreciable amount of cash flow to be earned, even from very high-yielding instruments. But does hyperactivity in pursuit of it really differentiate a return stream in any fundamental way? And if so, where do we draw the line—at holding periods of seconds, minutes, hours, days, or weeks? The convolutions in the discussion that follows indicate that these are not straightforward questions, and in fact I have deferred a satisfactory resolution of them to Chapters 13 and 18.

There is some reason to believe that asset price time series are fractal. Establishing that they are fractal has been the nearly lifelong project of Benoit Mandelbrot: see, for example, Mandelbrot and Hudson (2004). The task is not simple: it is quite common for things to appear to be fractal without actually exhibiting fractal ordering, so that the phenomenon of quasi self-similarity must be admitted by the theory of fractals. I am not persuaded one way or another about whether financial time series are in fact fractal or only appear as though they might be, and I suspect that a definitive answer to the question will not in fact be forthcoming. But if they are, that raises a formal objection to the idea that short time horizons, in and of themselves, create a fundamentally different environment in which to pursue directional or arbitrage trades. Fractals have the peculiarity that they are self-similar: when viewed over a range of coarser or finer levels of detail, their geometry appears much the same (but they need not exhibit invariance under scaling at *all* levels of detail). For example, **Figure 8.1** depicts the annualized period-to-period percentage change in the Standard & Poor's 500 Index over two 100-period time frames. They are for all practical purposes indistinguishable, although one illustrates more than eight years of monthly changes and the other an hour and forty minutes of minute-to-minute ones. The series have been re-scaled, as the absolute magnitude of the changes experienced over these time horizons are quite different (and would reveal which series is which), but their geometry is much the same. This price series is certainly self-similar, at least in the portions of it that are illustrated here.

Fractal self-similarity implies consistency of mathematical description across a range of levels of detail—in the case of a time series, across various time horizons. So if price series are self-similar, as the preceding thought experiment suggests, the factors driving them are unchanging whether the time period under consideration spans seconds or much longer periods. This conclusion has the powerful virtue of being with common sense—regardless of time scale, the driver of financial prices is the shifting balance between supply and demand. This would seem to argue

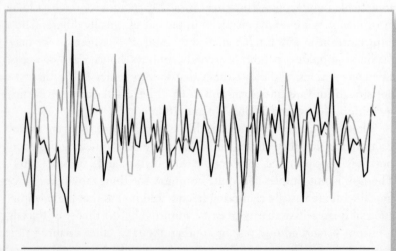

FIGURE 8.1   *A Price Series at Two Levels of "Magnification"*

Source: Bloomberg Finance, L.P.

against any claim that short-term directional trading is a fundamentally different activity, with distinct return drivers, from trading over other time horizons.

Given that changes in supply and demand are the cause of all financial price activity, the question, then, is whether there is a difference in the behavior of these factors over different time horizons. Price changes are seemingly random over short time horizons, while over time horizons that make such influence meaningful, supply and demand are determined by asset-specific and global macroeconomic fundamentals. That is, there is an economic rationale for longer-term price movements, while short-term price change is merely the result of the accidents of order entry.[1] The existence of the financial industry's enormous infrastructure of economists, strategists, and research analysts is predicated on the belief that supply and demand are derived quantities over longer periods. Over short time horizons, the influence of those fundamentals on the behavior of prices is negligible, and academics have long struggled to explain why prices nevertheless change so frequently over these short periods. Those of us brought up to worship at the shrine of fundamental investing routinely dismiss short-term price variability as "anarchy amidst the noise," to borrow from Milton. This "noise" is golden to high-frequency traders.

Volatility may be measured statistically using variance or standard deviation, and once measured in this way it can be included as a term in equations of any desired degree of complexity, and manipulated algebraically for our amusement or enlightenment. But at bottom, it is nothing other than price change, and at the coalface of price formation—among market makers, for instance—it is more frequently measured in pennies, ticks, or pips than with the aid of statistical constructs. Regardless of how the market microstructure for an instrument is designed or how liquid the participants in that market cause the instrument to be, momentary differences in the amounts of an instrument available for purchase or sale inevitably result in "noise-like" price movement.

---

1. See, for example, Fabozzi et al. (2006): "From an economic point of view, the long-run behavior of stock prices is influenced by factors different from those that influence their short-term behavior. At time horizons of days or weeks, trading practices and the way traders react to news are primarily responsible for asset price predictability; in the long run, the price of an individual asset is determined not only by the financial performance of the company but also by the quantity of money in the market and the global performance of the economy" (46). Engle and Rangel (2008) confirm this view with a comparison of low- and high-frequency volatility relative to macroeconomic data.

While market microstructure can be crafted to keep this "noise" to the minimum possible—the New York Stock Exchange has long argued that it excels in this regard, although there are some who would beg to differ—it cannot be completely eliminated in any market structure. Volatility poses execution risk to any trade: market orders may be filled at undesirable prices and limit orders may fail to be executed at all. Where there is risk there is potential for return, and high-frequency traders exploit as their source of return what to longer-term investors is only an unavoidable, non-diversifiable risk.

As with the traders who employ volatility generators, mentioned at the end of Chapter 2, high-frequency traders are largely indifferent to what it is that they trade, provided that it is sufficiently liquid to facilitate their trades and sufficiently volatile to produce the risks that they exploit. Naturally, their trading practices will vary somewhat, depending on the microstructure of the market(s) in which they are active, but most traders are readily adaptable.[2] In an important respect, they trade volatility itself, and the asset that exhibits it, its fundamentals, and the return drivers that motivate longer-term investment in it are essentially beside the point as far as they are concerned. There is much current discussion in derivatives circles about whether volatility is an asset class—this despite the fact that the "asset" in question is virtual, as volatility is always a quantity derived from the price behavior of some other, actual asset. Even the Chicago Board Options Exchange Volatility Index (VIX) future, which would appear to offer traders direct investment access to volatility, is at bottom a synthetic straddle on Standard & Poor's 500 Index options, and relies on that Index as its volatility generator.

Although high-frequency trading may not be fundamentally different in kind from other, longer-horizon forms of directional and arbitrage trades, it exploits volatility rather than suffering from it. Continuous trading in the market, sequentially on the long and short side of numerous instruments, exposes these managers' trading books

---

2. This claim was put to the test in the period (roughly the decade beginning in the mid-1990s) when many exchanges migrated from floor trading to off-floor, screen-based trading. Although some traders went on to other pursuits as a direct result of the floors and pits closing, in my experience they were quite capable of working with the new systems, but they simply did not enjoy it. The camaraderie of an exchange floor is a valuable asset that finance has virtually abandoned. One consequence is a high rate of attrition among screen traders due to burnout. Life in front of a trading screen is brutal and short, if not necessarily nasty. It was not at all infrequent for floor traders to remain active well beyond the normal age of retirement, but few electronic traders last much into their forties.

to volatility as a potential generator of return rather than just a risk. It is this observation—that what high-frequency traders primarily seek to exploit is the volatility of the underlying—that must support any claim that short time horizons are a distinguishing characteristic of a directional or arbitrage trading activity. In the case of arbitrages, the connection is clear—it is volatility that creates the divergences of related prices in the first place. In the case of directional trades, however, making this case requires introduction of a factor not considered so far, because price changes over any longer time horizon are ultimately just the aggregation of shorter-term changes, so no strong claim for distinctiveness can be made for high-frequency trading without bringing in an additional consideration. I will postpone discussion of this additional factor until Chapter 13, which discusses optionality, and the real options available to the practitioners of various investment techniques in particular. But to preview, the aggregate exposure of a directional high-frequency trading book resembles the option payoff diagram for a buy straddle that was illustrated in Figure 2.1, based on the aggregate of real options that the traders at the firm possess and the nature of the trading disciplines that they apply to them.

Yet, apart from my analysis, there is some published evidence of a difference in kind between high-frequency and longer-horizon trading activities, based purely on the duration of the trades involved, and quite likely considerably more evidence that remains proprietary.[3] Apart from this, the distinctiveness of high-frequency traders is somewhat muddied by that fact that many longer-term investors engage in something not so dissimilar to high-frequency trading when they "trade around" their long-term holdings.

---

3. I will not pursue this further, however, precisely because all or almost all of the best work in this area is outside the public domain. This represents a real loss for academia, but keeping this research within the firm that generated it is unavoidable, for the obvious reason that it creates an opportunity for market participants to trade with a legal information advantage relative to their trade competitors. See Engle (1996). I am quite certain that a great deal more work has been done to extend the conclusions obtained by Engle and others. Academics who pursue research in this area tend to be hired by investment banks or hedge funds, and the working papers and published articles on such topics that they previously made available to the public are removed from the Internet shortly thereafter. Bookstaber (2007, 251), estimates that the half-life of investment techniques built around such discoveries is three to four years, giving firms a strong incentive to maintain confidentiality. However, due diligence should take careful note of the risk that this state of affairs entails: the departure of key personnel can destroy a firm's investment "edge" virtually over night.

High-Frequency Trading as an Investment Technique

High-frequency trading can be pursued in any market that permits a significant amount of dealing desk hyperactivity. That obviously eliminates private equity and private real estate, and the reference to median times between corporate bond transactions in Chapter 5 indicates that most of those instruments offer limited opportunities to such traders, too. Financial futures, with their very high liquidity, embedded leverage, and efficient clearing infrastructure offer especially happy hunting grounds to volatility traders, attracting many CTAs to the activity. Equities, options, and actively traded markets in Treasuries, Agencies, and some other bonds, many commodity futures and a few physical commodities also provide grist for their return-generating mills.

But liquidity is not these traders' sole requirement. The comparative short-term price stability of the major currency crosses or of short-term Treasury bills, for example, offers essentially no opportunity to most traders, despite the ample liquidity available in these instruments, unless they can obtain large amounts of leverage at very low cost.[4] Consequently, high-frequency trading in low volatility instruments such as Treasury bills is the all-but exclusive domain of financial intermediaries, which have access to large amounts of essentially interest-free funding through their clearing accounts. Some hedge funds register as broker-dealers and obtain exchange memberships to gain access to clearing finance and the lower transaction costs that attach to exchange membership, which provide them a cost structure that allows them to exploit some of the less rich trading opportunities in equities, options, and futures. But I am unaware of any who make it their business to trade in short-term interest rate markets other than through the use of futures or options. Conversely, financial intermediaries that restrict their business to market-making and similar principal trading activities are, to all intents

---

4. Lo et al. (2004) explore in detail the fixed cost constraints on active traders, concluding that "Investors follow an optimal policy of not trading until their risk exposure reaches either a lower or upper boundary, at which point they incur the fixed cost and trade back to an optimal level of risk exposure" (1085). In other words, fixed costs not only affect the returns on trades executed but place a constraint on the number of trades that can profitably be entered into in the first place. Environments where the return productivity of individual trades is low cause traders who suffer those constraints to search for more lucrative opportunities elsewhere.

and purposes, high-frequency hedge funds—although only a handful of them are explicitly structured as such. Adoption of such practices is most common in the futures, options, and some physical commodities arenas, but there have been examples in equities as well. Market design militates against such a structure for fixed-income traders.

Apart from volatility arbitrageurs—about which more below—other high-frequency traders cannot access volatility so directly as their derivatives-trading brethren, and their trading is less a matter of forecasting increases or decreases in volatility than of positioning themselves to take advantage of whatever volatility the market chooses to deliver to them. Theirs are, in most cases, sequentially rather than simultaneously long/short trades, which have directional exposure to volatility over time that derives from the relationship between their returns and volatility levels. In general, assuming constant levels of traded value, more volatility will permit them to produce higher returns. Chapter 4 mentioned that the "Volatility Drought" of 2004 to 2007 was an extended fallow period for many (but by no means all) trades of this type. But increased volatility is beneficial to high-frequency traders only up to a point. The extremes of volatility experienced during high standard-deviation events can be at least as challenging for these traders to negotiate as they are for all other market participants, if not more so. While it may be possible for them to post good returns in such times of crisis, there is certainly no guarantee that they will be able to do so.

Directional high-frequency traders are sequentially long and short: their trades are not generally hedged, but their frenetic activity may find them on either side of an individual instrument's longer-term directional trend at any given moment. Consequently, although minute-to-minute returns on their trading book in any individual security will closely track with (or be exactly opposite to) those generated by that instrument, when measured over the long-term, directional high-frequency traders' returns do not correlate highly (or counter-correlate strongly) with those of the individual instruments they trade. Because they are active in numerous instruments at any particular time, in the aggregate their total market exposure is likely to be roughly neutral over any appreciable period. Although transitory periods of net long or short bias will inevitably occur, they will be extremely short. High-frequency traders who engage in arbitrage, for instance along the Treasury yield curve or in the short-term exploitation of merger situations, are at all times directionally hedged.

Unfortunately, there are no indices available for high-frequency trading other than volatility arbitrage (see below). My investigations of individual equity-oriented funds suggest standard deviations of about a third of those exhibited by broad market indices and correlations in the area of 0.25 to 0.35 relative to them. The skewness of their return distributions is generally less negative than that of the indices, but kurtosis is quite high, indicating that returns cluster closely around the mean, and that gains and losses are fairly evenly distributed. This is more or less what would be expected from vehicles that are serially long and short over periods that do not permit the large gains or losses that arise from attempts to exploit price trends. I suspect it is a rather different pattern of returns from what most conventional investors might expect.

With regard to high-frequency techniques applied to fixed-income instruments, my investigations find a somewhat different picture. Correlations tend to be close to zero relative to fixed-income benchmarks, which is consistent with trades that are often arbitrages or at least arbitrage-like. However, volatility is puzzlingly high relative to benchmarks. I am not certain why this should be so, but I suspect it results from the high levels of leverage that these vehicles typically employ, and the discontinuous nature of the trades (since, unlike directional trading, arbitrages can only be put on when conditions permit), which causes them to experience fallow periods as well as highly productive ones. Skewness seems generally to be similar to that of the benchmark, while kurtosis is noticeably lower, suggesting a greater dispersion of returns that is consistent with these traders' opportunism.

Precisely how frequent is high frequency? That depends on a variety of factors, including transaction costs, the volatility of the underlying instruments that the traders exploit, the trading signals that motivate their transactions, and so on. Some trading strategies are so hyperactive that they can only be executed by computerized trading algorithms— human reaction times are simply inadequate to the task—while others are almost leisurely by comparison. As a broad generalization, subject to numerous caveats and exceptions, high-frequency strategies are day-trading strategies, not out of any strong conviction that a market session is an optimal time horizon, but to avoid the cost of financing positions overnight. A further incentive to bringing exposure to neutral at the end of the trading day is that traders who do not trust their position books to machines are often reluctant to risk exposure to news developments during periods when local markets are closed and they are unable to react to them. Arbitrageurs, who are by definition hedged, and generally need to finance only their residual net rather than their gross exposure, are under less pressure to close out their positions at the end of each session. While the rise of twenty-four-hour markets would seem to offer the prospect that at least computer-assisted algorithmic trading could become a continuous activity, liquidity outside the hours of traditional market sessions is uneven and often poor, resulting in price action that is too unpredictable for most algorithms to exploit successfully. There are algorithms specifically designed to identify and exploit such periods of illiquidity, but they are different from those that are likely to trade successfully during periods when markets are active. A fund that does not automate its trade submission may, of course, operate a night shift.

A more systematic answer to the question of appropriate time horizon would refer back to the distinction suggested above between "noise" and trend—that is, between time horizons where changes in supply and demand are explainable in terms of economic fundamentals and those where they are not. This is a difficult distinction to draw, since it involves another *sorites* paradox: the long-term is, after all, nothing other than an accumulation of the short-term. However, a familiar trading-desk discipline provides a clue. Head traders frequently admonish their staff to banish all thought of where an instrument's price "ought" to be, and to pay attention solely to where its price currently is and where currently visible trading interest is likely to lead it. So the short-term might be defined as the period over which active trading interest is visible. This is rarely much longer than a couple of days, and usually shorter. A day-trading discipline is consistent with this.

Given time horizons that cause them to cruise beneath consideration of economic fundamentals, directional high-frequency traders must look elsewhere for their trading signals. Virtually all high-frequency directional traders rely on signals derived from readings of momentum and reversal indicators, and beliefs about mean reversion, whether they are incorporated into algorithmic trading models or a matter of instinct and heuristic rules of thumb. This is disturbing to conventionally trained market participants who have been thoroughly inculcated with the prejudice that "noise" is just that—a pattern-less consequence of traded assets' Random Walk that is completely resistant to further analysis.

Sources of trading signals other than asset fundamentals are held in such low esteem among those educated in academic finance that practitioners of technical analysis and similar skills are at best accused of apophenia (the obsession with finding patterns where there are none to be found) and not infrequently of intentional fraud.[5] Traders who, in the absence of fundamental indicators, seemingly grope after transaction signals in the analysis of past price behavior are condescended to, and the persistence of these practices on trading desks despite what academia purports to know is regarded as just that much more ammunition for behavioral economists' skepticism regarding investors' rationality. Yet the practices stubbornly persist—completely without apology in currency and commodity trading circles, where finance theory has hardly penetrated, and with the practical person's universal response to theorists ("I don't care—it works for me") just about everywhere else.

I have no desire to enter the debate over market efficiency and the Random Walk hypothesis. This ground has been gone over so many times that it resembles Ypres circa November 1917—with similar amounts of mud and lives wasted. However, I believe that there is ample evidence that the price series of traded assets have a certain amount of fine structure. This also would be consistent with Mandelbrot's view that price series are fractal. If there is order embedded in short-term asset price developments then it seems reasonable to me that traders (who are—notoriously—monomaniacally focused on the matter at hand) should be able to detect and exploit it, at least consistently enough to make the activity of trading worth the effort expended upon it. Those who do not share these views—probably as a result of a traditional education in financial theory—are unlikely to have the remotest interest in making an allocation to directional high-frequency trading, although there is no reason in principle that they should object to high-frequency arbitrage. However, the persistence of investment in high-frequency directional trades—by investment banks as well as hedge funds and others—should

---

5. However, despite the weight of academic disapproval, finance theorists are here and there are beginning to find something other than complete moonshine in technical analysis: see Lo et al. (2000) and Lo and Hasanhodzie (2009). For an even more exotic analysis involving multi-valued logic (a discipline to which I have made a very minor contribution, of which I am nevertheless inordinately proud), see Zhou and Dong (2004). I am unaware of anyone who has noticed that the Fundamental Law of Active Management (see Grinold and Kahn (2000), Chapter 6) is of considerable relevance here: a low information coefficient may result in a high information ratio given the number of independent trading decisions involved in high-frequency techniques. Material from this volume is used with the permission of the McGraw-Hill Companies, which have requested a full citation as follows: Richard Grinold et al., *Active Portfolio Management* (New York, NY: McGraw-Hill Companies, second edition, 2000).

cause them to reflect that if the returns on this activity net to zero, it is unlikely that so much capital and overhead would be devoted to it.

Volatility Arbitrage

As **Figure 8.2** and the data in **Table 8.1** suggest, only a portion of what goes under the name "volatility arbitrage" is in fact arbitrage. A correlation of 0.4000 to the broad equity market indicates that some of it is clearly directional in nature. Although all such trades are structured using pairs or greater numbers of derivatives and their underlyings, some of them are motivated by a perception that the implied volatility embedded in options incorrectly forecasts the actual volatility outcome that the underlying will exhibit over the option's life, an observation (like all such forecasts) that motivates a directional trade. Option structures can be created employing puts or calls and the underlying that permit traders to create long or short exposure to this forecasting error, so returns on the trade depend on the accuracy of their forecasts rather than convergence of related prices as in a true arbitrage. Their payoff is thus not symmetrical regardless of developments in the actual volatility of the underlying, and therefore such trades are not truly arbitrages.

Volatility arbitrage trades may in fact have fairly long duration—in principle, over the entire life of an option or a future—but they qualify

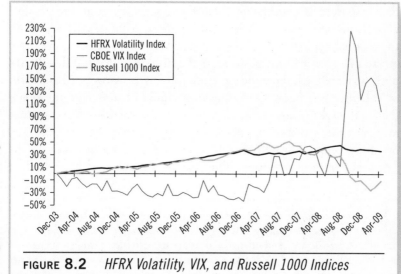

Source: Hedge Fund Research, Bloomberg Finance L.P.

FIGURE 8.2 *HFRX Volatility, VIX, and Russell 1000 Indices*

TABLE 8.1 *HFRX Volatility Arbitrage Index versus Market Indicators*

	HFRX VOLATILITY INDEX	RUSSELL 1000 INDEX	CBOE VIX INDEX
Compound Annual Return	5.98%	−2.17%	13.77%
Median Monthly Return	0.84%	1.12%	−2.77
Annualized Standard Deviation	4.17%	15.26%	71.33%
Correlation to the Russell 1000 Index	0.2992	1.0000	−0.6539
Correlation to the CBOE VIX Index	−0.4909	−0.6539	1.0000
Kurtosis	2.65	3.55	4.68
Skewness	−1.53	−1.26	1.81

Note that the calculations are based on only sixty-four observations, leaving their statistical significance open to question.

as high-frequency trading because the Δ-hedging required to maintain their exposure is continuous. Trades of longer duration are possible because, in derivative markets, clearing finance charges only accrue on the residual net exposure of the combined positions rather than on the gross value of each of the positions in the structured trade. When derivatives are employed, the trade structure can in fact be regarded as a form of volatility generator. Operating over time horizons that are longer than is typical for high-frequency trading, the volatility forecasts that motivate those trades may have an at least partial basis in the sort of fundamental research that is otherwise absent from most high-frequency trading activities.[6] These sorts of trades may be embodied

---

6. Enormous energy has been expended on the mathematical foundations of volatility forecasting—see, for example, Javaheri (2005)—but again, much of the work in this area is proprietary. And often, forecasts are based on less formidable analyses, such as keeping an eye on the date that a merger offer expires, that restricted securities become freely tradable, or that a pharmaceutical compound is expected to receive Food and Drug Administration approval.

in variance swaps on a range of underlyings, in which case it is the bank that serves as counterparty to the swap purchaser that is using them as volatility generators in the way described in Chapter 2, rather than the purchaser of the swap. Banks with large exposures of this kind may lay off some of it by entering swap agreements with hedge funds: this is fairly widespread practice in Asia, where retail customers are enthusiastic users of structured products that give their banks unmanageably large volatility exposures.

The index shown in Figure 8.2 has a somewhat longer history than the textbooks would require of a "large" sample, but caution should be applied to the statistical observations given in Table 8.1: their significance is not really satisfactorily high. Despite the limitations of the data set, it is clear that volatility arbitrage has substantially different—and noticeably less attractive—return characteristics than those of the directional high-frequency strategies discussed above. The kurtosis of the index is considerably higher than indicated above, around a noticeably lower median return, and its skewness also contrasts sharply at −1.87. The low level of the median return is somewhat puzzling, and suggests either that at least a portion of volatility arbitrageurs' trades are less than perfectly hedged, that directional trades based on volatility forecasting may have inherent β exposure, or both. I am inclined to think that both are the case.

However, high-frequency volatility arbitrage is a diverse group of trades, and the value of the index as an indicator or benchmark for any particular technique is probably low. Trading techniques that employ futures only are likely to exhibit considerably less negative skewness than techniques employing options only. Trades employing options that do not involve volatility forecasts probably also exhibit reduced negative skewness.

Figure 8.2 clearly shows that many of the funds included in the HFRX Volatility Index suffered noticeably from the market conditions of 2007 to 2009. The other indices included in the accompanying table do not add greatly to our understanding, and are included only for purposes of illustration: volatility arbitrage seems to have some, but not terribly strong correlation with equities and consequently, negative correlation with the VIX Index. A mathematically punctilious reader may object to chain-linking VIX Index values to form a time series of this sort, and I share some doubts about the procedure. However, if as some argue, volatility is an "asset class," then there must be some way to measure its performance over time, and this is what is readily available. At any rate, negative correlation with the VIX Index is not an indictment of the trade: insofar as volatility arbitrages are based on forecasts of volatility that differ from those embedded in traded options, they *should* be expected to behave differently from a measure of that embedded volatility. And, at least based on my own investigations, the VIX in fact turns out to be a rather poor indicator for actual volatility outcomes.

Other option trades that exploit the volatility smile are true arbitrages. These do not rely on a forecast of volatility but instead on an analysis of the relative implied volatilities of options on the same underlying. Again, this is an area where some formidable mathematics comes into play, and the analysis is heavily dependent on computer-assisted modeling. These arbitrages are systematic: they exploit discrepancies in option pricing for which standard option-pricing models do not allow and that have expiry as a catalyst for their convergence. They arise because the standard models assume Gaussian distributions for the return behavior of the underlying, an assumption that is not borne out in actual option pricing. This is an area that has received some of the most intensive work toward extending modern financial theory into non-Gaussian domains, and it has produced some of the most sophisticated of these analyses. Consistent with comments made in Chapter 4, most of them do not seem to be capable of generalization. For example, models such as SABR (Stochastic Alpha, Beta, Rho: see Hagan et al. 2002) that seem to work well in trading interest rate options, do not appear to be equally successful when applied to currency or equity options. Considerable proprietary empirical research underlies each of these applications, so their details are not in the public domain, although the general, formal structure of most of these models has been widely discussed—insofar as such mathematically challenging ideas can be said to receive "wide" attention at all.

Commodity Trading Advisors

Not all CTAs are high-frequency traders, but many are, and many more combine high-frequency with longer-horizon trading approaches, not only as a matter of "trading around" long-term positions but in a separate, dedicated trading account that structures its exposures independently of their long-horizon book(s). As mentioned, futures are especially well-suited to hyperactive trading, and they afford opportunities for a variety of arbitrages both within the futures arena and physical against futures, as well as directional trades. Apart from physical-against-futures trades, arbitrages may be locational (NYMEX aluminum against London), calendar trades (front month *versus* later months), or within a commodity complex (soybeans against meal). In addition to calendar and physical-against-futures trades, financial futures offer a number of arbitrage opportunities among bond tenors and between currencies. Some, but not all, of these trading structures can be exploited over short time horizons.

All of these arbitrages are more or less systematic, at least over the time horizons that high-frequency traders are likely to have exposure to them—"more or less" because over longer time horizons some of the correlations upon which they rely may be considerably less than exact, as will be discussed in more detail, although in a different context, in Chapter 10. For example, there is a seasonal trade between hard red winter wheat traded in Kansas City and soft red winter wheat traded in Chicago, because of the greater uncertainty of weather conditions in areas where the former is grown, but over short horizons these discrepancies can usually be ignored, and traders may engage in an arbitrage that, while not quite systematic, has a certain, perhaps indefinable logic to the convergence upon which it depends. Yet because the correlations they rely upon are not exact, these arbitrages tend to be richer than those found among systematically related financial products such as options against their underlying. Even physical-against-futures trades in physical commodities are richer than systematic arbitrages among financial instruments, largely because of the operational challenges they present to traders who engage in them. The low liquidity of the markets for commodity futures compared to those for financial futures may contribute to this: it is noticeable, for instance, that arbitrages within the oil complex, which is the most actively traded group of physical commodity futures, are generally less rich than those among agricultural complexes that are similarly closely related.

High-Frequency Trading Risk

Trading is a risky activity, and multiplying trades multiplies risks. These include the execution risks mentioned above as well as operational risks that result from trade failures and incomplete fills. Neither can be reduced through diversification, as each trade is statistically independent of the next: every additional trade implies an additional risk. Consequently, trading risk must be managed, and traders do this through continuous quality improvement. Although 6σ Black Belts are relatively uncommon in the trading community, the concept and the disciplines that such quality programs involve have long been quite familiar to trading operations. In an activity whose participants have been known to worry about things like whether their distance from the exchange disadvantages them in the competition to trade (bearing in mind that telecommunication signals propagate at relativistic speeds), technology and back office audits are crucial to identifying funds that will outperform.

These traders also worry about transaction costs. High-cost high-frequency trading is an oxymoron, or at least a recipe for a disastrous investment. It is probably apocryphal, but it is a good story nonetheless: a representative of the UK Department of Trade and Industry is said to have claimed that, although British Leyland lost money on every automobile it produced, it "made it back on volumes." High frequency will simply multiply high costs, to the obvious detriment of returns—there are no economies of scale to be captured. Transaction costs dictate the opportunities a trader can exploit and the expected volatility required to make a trade profitable: higher costs translate into fewer opportunities accompanied by greater levels of risk. The importance of trading infrastructure and rigorous control of transaction costs in the context of this investment approach cannot be underestimated, and in examining these activities due diligence should concentrate on this set of issues, unfamiliar as they are to most institutional investors, above all else. Although transaction efficiency raises issues for any investment technique, its importance to high-frequency traders is crucial. It is not stretching the point too far to regard high-frequency trading funds as a private equity interest in a trading operation: the imperative for thorough inspection of operational quality should be abundantly clear.

The fundamental investment risk to any directional trading is poor forecasting. Regardless of the transaction signals to which a trader attends, if the signals are misinterpreted or the thinking behind them proves to be incorrect, losses will result. These are likely to be magnified by leverage, as the returns from short-term trading would generally not be worth pursuing without it. This argues in favor of trade automation, to reduce the scope for human error. While few if any high-frequency traders eschew automation entirely, the extent to which it is allowed to insinuate itself into the trading process is largely a matter of the individual manager's taste. Fear of the subjective element in interpreting transaction signals will bias a firm toward building systems that receive and analyze data, as well as generate trading instructions and transmit them to the point of execution without human intervention. Fear of enshrining poor decision rules in unthinking computer code will bias a firm toward insisting upon some measure of human oversight. For every manager who completely automates the input-to-execution chain there is another who refuses as a matter of principle to "let a computer manage my trade blotter."

Most managers of directional high-frequency products rely more or less heavily on computerized analytics to track data and provide them with trading signals, if only because of the enormous amount of data involved and the speed with which it can change. These are invariably proprietary "black boxes," and it is rare for due diligence to be allowed even the briefest glimpse of their inner workings. In some cases this secretiveness protects true, even profound innovations in the application of mathematical analysis to financial data that provide the fund an edge that its competitors' research may take years to erode. For a detailed discussion of what some of these might look like, see Dacorogna et al. (2001). One of the particular pleasures of Derman (2004) is his ability to convey the excitement of breaking new ground in this area. But more frequently it is because their decision rules are founded upon rules of thumb or simple empirical observations that could readily be exploited by others if only they were aware of them. Whether connected directly to the point of execution or not, these programs will suffer from any subjectivity, misconception, or lack of foresight that their authors embed in their code. A computer can be no freer of bias than the person who instructed it. And while artificial intelligence programs can be created that learn from their mistakes, first they must make them. Unlike flesh-and-blood traders, even the most sophisticated programs are incapable of innovation on the fly.

In place of mean reversion and similar momentum factors as the drivers of their trades, high-frequency arbitrage traders rely on departures from correlation as their trading signal. Mean reversion may be what drives the discrepancy to narrow, but it does not drive the identification of it. Because their trades have a basis in systematic (or near-systematic) correlations, they are generally not very exposed to the risk that the correlations that underlie their trade will collapse. Insofar as they are exposed to the risk that the correlation might disappear, it is to a lesser degree than their longer-horizon colleagues, simply because their exposure times are shorter. Should an unexpected news announcement that affects the trade occur, as traders rather than analysts they are likely to be able to react to it very quickly. The temptation to automate here is even greater than for their directional brethren.

Although the analysis that underlies most volatility arbitrage employs some rather daunting mathematics, the activity of forecasting volatility is by no means itself a science. Everything that relates to option pricing is subject to magnified error terms of the sort discussed in Chapter 3, compounded by the number of instruments involved in the option structure employed by the specific trade that the manager pursues. This is the reason that non-Gaussian statistical analysis has made greater inroads in options than elsewhere in finance. And these trades are generally leveraged. So volatility arbitrage can be quite risky despite the systematic nature of the arbitrage relationships among options that make direct directional speculation on volatility possible, as reflected by the high kurtosis and fairly strong negative skew of the index shown in Figure 8.2. The option structures that the trader creates may provide perfect hedges to directional movements in the underlying, but that offers no protection against incorrect forecasts of the direction of volatility, to which their structures are leveraged.

The approximation to market-neutrality that the hyperactivity of directional high-frequency traders creates defends them against general market movements. However, those that take on market-making responsibilities, generally in the interest of lowering their transaction costs, may have obligations to accept trades under circumstances that would ordinarily recommend against trading or would recommend taking the opposite side of the trade that their obligations require of them. This can result in losses, especially during periods of high volatility when the pressure of orders reaching the market tends to be all in one direction ("phase locking," "correlations go to one"). Although no exchange requires of its market-makers Canute-like opposition to the incoming tide, some have requirements that are sufficient to guarantee losses in the face of extraordinary price action. For example, all New York Stock Exchange (NYSE) specialists posted very substantial losses in the fourth quarter of 1987. For arbitrage traders, the situation is reversed: high volatility may make it impossible to enter safely into their trades. While their hedges protect their existing positions against the market's directional movement, initiating new positions in periods of high volatility is excessively risky, and these traders will consequently tend to stay on the sidelines. The result, of course, is low return productivity for high-frequency arbitrageurs during periods of extreme volatility.

On the other hand, directional high-frequency traders are vulnerable to prolonged secular declines in market volatility. However, the experience of individual funds seems to vary widely, probably because of differing admixtures of arbitrage and trading in instruments other than equities. While some vehicles escaped the worst effects of the Volatility Drought of 2004 to 2007, many others did not. My own, admittedly rather limited research into the matter has uncovered at best only very weak evidence that volatility is mean-reverting. If in fact it is not, then there is little comfort to offer to these traders during periods when volatility is depressed.

High-Frequency Trading in the Context of Conventional Portfolio Holdings

The foregoing suggests that high-frequency trading and volatility arbitrage share certain crucial return characteristics with market-neutral investment approaches, while in other respects they resemble private investment in a market-making business. These implications are not mutually exclusive, and are suggestive for due diligence. The importance of thoroughly examining a fund's operating capabilities—digging deeper than the routine back office audit that should be part of any manager review—is what might be expected of the due diligence required of a private investment. The extent of a directional fund's market-neutrality will be dictated largely by the breadth of its trading activities and the degree of opportunism it permits to or discipline it imposes upon its traders. A high-frequency arbitrageur's market-neutrality will be a function of the "purity" of the arbitrage techniques it employs.

As with merger arbitrage and in contrast to hedged rather than return-seeking market-neutral approaches, the market-neutrality that can be achieved by directional high-frequency trading cannot be replicated by an overlay of futures on a long-only conventional portfolio. From a return perspective, directional high-frequency trading is most closely analogous to return-seeking market-neutrality, although this result is achieved through sequential rather than simultaneous long and short exposure. The logic of this analogy is founded upon return-seeking in each individual position taken, while no position is held long enough to expose the fund to the compounding effects that produce directional trends. High-frequency arbitrage is most similar to purely systematic arbitrages.

Investment policymakers are likely to be uncomfortable with the idea of high-frequency trading. A grounding in academic finance, an aversion to transaction costs, and, often enough, an impression derived from press accounts of losses on banks' trading desks that the activity is fraught with risk all contribute to this. One or other of them is likely to mutter about "picking up nickels in front of steamrollers." Committee members are unlikely to appreciate the extent to which, in its focus on operations and infrastructure, due diligence on trading firms resembles private equity due diligence as opposed to the analysis of investment policy and research capabilities that is more typical of the manager selection process as applied to other liquid market investment techniques. They may well be concerned about the extent to which successful trading often seems to rely on individual traders' skills. And an activity that consists of endlessly repeated application of simple strategies is not likely to excite the imaginations of those who devote large amounts of intellectual firepower to thinking about the markets.

Putting it charitably, high-frequency traders are rarely their own best advocates. The part of the investment world that they inhabit is far removed from portfolio management and the various theoretical structures with which it surrounds itself. They are likely to share with investment policymakers a failure to appreciate the portfolio function of high-frequency activities relative to longer-term approaches to investment, since very few of them are accustomed to thinking in portfolio terms at all. I am reminded of a lengthy exercise in mutual incomprehension during a discussion of volatility that I had with a NYSE specialist. He was, as near as I could tell, completely innocent of the concept of standard deviation, which, from my somewhat more pedantic perspective, is the source of his livelihood. From his perspective, volatility is price change, measured in frequency and cents per tick. Neither perspective is superior, and it behooves academics to bear in mind the thoroughly reductionist understanding of a trader, as a touchstone against which they can test their thinking about volatility.

But while it is arguable whether the very short-term implies a separate marketplace with its own dynamics, trading over short time horizons undeniably generates patterns of return that are rather different from longer-term trading even in the same instruments. As the tenor of the discussion in this chapter is meant to suggest, high-frequency trading even in conventional assets can be a significant diversifier of conventional portfolios. While it requires an intellectual effort to gain comfort with it and unaccustomed approaches to due diligence to identify superior managers, high-frequency trading can be a preferable solution to market-neutral techniques that are return-seeking in their short books, from both return and risk perspectives. This is precisely because of its atheoretical, high-frequency characteristics and its optionality. On the one hand, it is not dependent on forecasts of correlation among assets to achieve its hedge. On the other, trading activity is likely to adjust more or less automatically to changing correlations, well in advance of the slow accumulation of data points that indicates to less active traders that the characteristics of a price series have changed. Paradoxically, traders do not time markets. This may sound odd, given the rapid back-and-forth of their long/short exposure and their frequent recourse to technical trading indicators, which in longer-horizon investment techniques are mostly used for timing purposes. But it follows from the fact that they do not allocate, but let the market dictate their positions. They seek an opportunity to trade given what the market is providing them: they do not seek a particular trade and wait for the market to provide them with the opportunity.

CHAPTER 9

Holding Private Assets for Their Cash Flows

A quick transition here from very short time horizons to long and potentially unlimited ones. Apart from the mezzanine and other long-term loans discussed in Chapter 5, there are numerous assets for which there is no liquid market that can also be held over long periods in order to enjoy the cash flows they generate, and many of these have no terms to them. These include, but are by no means limited to:

❑ commercial or residential real estate,
❑ operating companies,
❑ mines,
❑ timberland,
❑ intellectual property rights,
❑ farmland and agricultural operations,
❑ public infrastructure such as toll roads,
❑ private infrastructure such as pipelines,
❑ aquaculture, and
❑ ocean-going vessels.

Although any of these can be acquired with the intention of exploiting their anticipated price appreciation through a directional trade as well, if acquired with care they are eminently suited to income-generating investment. These assets may be held directly or through fund investments—although most such funds pursue directional investment strategies, some of them do not, particularly those that invest in assets such as timberland or public infrastructure that, in most circumstances, are less suited to directional strategies than many of the others. The Mars, S. C. Johnson, and Grosvenor families have already been mentioned as long-term holders of such assets, and thousands of other investors, ranging from Princess Gloria von Thurn und Taxis to the Bass family, could be added to these to form a very long list. There is in fact an enormous amount of private wealth held in the form of private assets, and there has been since time immemorial. But numerous institutional investors have considerable historical experience with long-term ownership of cash flow–generating private assets as well, and their interest in the associated investment techniques seems to be reviving.

While real estate and, more recently, private equity are probably the illiquid investment categories that are most familiar to institutions, it is likely that an institution somewhere is happily exposed to each of the categories of investments cited above. The land grant universities were originally financed by deeds to undeveloped lands granted them under the Morrill Act of 1862, and bequests of land were also used to underwrite the creation of most of the ancient European universities. A great many older institutions, including the Yale University Endowment, have a history with direct exposure to private equity, for all that their experience has frequently been a mixed one (see Swensen 2000, 62*f* and 2009, 59*f*). But in its modern incarnation as a diversified investment with professional management, usually through the medium of funds, this investment category has become important to the investment practice of many more of them. Further, quite a number of universities have long operated publishing companies on a not-for-profit basis, regarding them as part of their contribution to scholarship, but in the 1970s it began to become apparent to them that at least some of these activities could actually generate attractive returns.[1] Extensive timber acreage is held in trust on behalf of Mississippi schools, and portfolio investment in timber and also in farmland has become important to a substantial number of insurers and other institutions.

---

1. University presses frankly surprised themselves. Although some standard reference works, such as the *Oxford Shorter English Dictionary*, had always been reasonably good earners, an early and entirely unexpected commercial success was Yale University Press's multi-volume paperback translation of Ernst Cassirer's *Philosophie der symbolischen Formen* in the 1960s. Perhaps the first university press "bestseller" was the equally unlikely 1977 biography of the lexicographer J. A. H. Murphy, *Caught in the Web of Words*, which was published jointly by the Oxford and Yale presses.

Quite a few hydrocarbon-producing properties are in institutional hands, and in the last decade or two many universities and a few hospital endowments have taken an active investment interest in the intellectual property generated by their staff members' research in technical disciplines. In the same period, public infrastructure became an increasingly popular institutional investment category: a study produced by Rogerscasey reports that Australian superannuation funds have allocations of 4–9 percent to this asset category and Canadian pension funds 10–15 percent.[2]

Corporate investors may also participate in a buy-and-hold strategy of private market investment. For example, Intel Capital, with $1.1 billion in investable resources and a track record with 908 ventures (according to Dow Jones VentureSource, March 2009), is primarily a conventional venture capital investor, seeking directional returns from the eventual sale of its investments. But its parent corporation has an obvious interest in some of the assets in which its venture capital unit may participate that goes well beyond anticipation of the returns that their eventual liquidation might offer. It has on occasion sought full control and integration of companies in which its subsidiary originally held a minority interest strictly for investment purposes. Many other technology- and bioscience-based firms pursue similar hybrid investment activities that primarily seek directional investment returns but that keep an eye out for companies that may have long-term potential as subsidiaries of their parent corporations. Firms may also enter into long-term private equity investments to cement commercial relationships with firms that they have no desire to purchase outright. And some older, established technology firms such as Motorola make active efforts to identify and exploit the value of intellectual property that their scientists and engineers have created over the years, which might otherwise simply molder away in the U.S. Patent Office archives. The improbable appearance of Dennis Hopper as a spokesman on behalf of a provider of retirement products and services suggests that "personal brands" are also intangible assets that can be resurrected and exploited in similar ways.

Most private asset categories are suitable to directional investment as well. Historically, timber investment has been an exception that offered little or no directional return. Speculative interest in this investment category has raised timberland values considerably over the past decade

---

2. McDonald (2007, 4); Newell and Peng (2008) provide evidence that the return characteristics of infrastructure investment are quite distinct from those of real estate, but the time series they analyze is rather short.

or so, particularly in southern states where forest productivity is highest. But traditionally, timberland investors expected simply to maintain liquidation value through sound forestry practices rather than to capture appreciation, although sales for higher, better uses (such as second homes) occasionally offered some directional return. Farmland provided a consistently attractive directional trade up to about 1980 (see Conkin 2008, 133), but directional returns, although sometimes substantial, have since tended to be highly dependent on market-timing. Wasting assets such as mines or oil and gas production lend themselves to directional speculation only if supported by good long-term price forecasts for the commodities they produce and comparatively short time horizons—otherwise, the more "natural" way to exploit them is through the cash flows they generate while they are still productive.

Timberland, farmland, infrastructure, and wasting assets certainly benefit from good management and well-targeted investment, but they are less amenable to active management in the pursuit of directional returns than private equity or some of the more opportunistic varieties of real estate investment. Intellectual property may have either characteristic, depending on the nature of the property. While active management may increase the value of the investment and provide an attractive directional return, much intellectual property is a wasting asset. For example, Algemeen Burgerlijk Pensioenfonds, the Dutch pension giant, can expect to earn strong returns from its major investment in music publishing rights for some time to come, potentially selling them at a gain. But it is questionable whether, fifty years and numerous changes in musical taste down the road, these assets can retain anything approaching their current value. Historically, photo archives have been long-lived assets, but widespread Internet piracy has devalued much of this property, and only "prime" assets of this nature—usually those with historical significance, such as those owned by the Bettmann Archive—are likely to retain value over the long-term, and even then, they require active management (see Vara 2005).

Holding Private Assets for Their Cash Flow as an Investment Technique

A fundamental attraction of private market assets is that in many cases they can be structured to pay little or no corporation tax, removing a significant haircut on cash flow returns compared to conventional equities. This feature explains much of the interest of private individuals in this sort of investment. While tax-exempt institutions must take considerable care to guard against adverse tax consequences from taking advantage of these structures, and should be mindful that tax treatments can change, the advantage to them is also compelling. The ability of assets that are appropriately structured to pay out almost all of their entire cash flows, rather than just their after-tax income, clearly enhances their ability to provide income to their investors.

Active management is essential to successful long-term exploitation of private assets. All of the assets considered here depreciate over time, whether through depletion (in which changing fashions and technological obsolescence can be included) or simple wear and tear. Consequently, cash flow–oriented investment in private assets involves at least occasional negative cash flows in the form of investments to maintain the assets' positive cash flow characteristics. Even timberland, for which minimally assisted biology is overwhelmingly the dominant driver of returns, will generate attractive cash flows and maintain its liquidation value over the long run only if a program of scientific forest management in support of nature is actively pursued. The only—and partial—exception to this is farmland, which may not require improvement. But even here, the lease typically specifies investments or planting practices that are required of the user of the property to prevent erosion and to maintain its fertility. The cost of these to the farm's operator is reflected in the level of lease payments the landowner receives from it and thus reduces cash flow received from the investment rather than requiring periodic disbursements.

Apart from farm properties, timberland and in many cases intellectual property can usually pay for their essential upkeep from the current income they generate. In other cases, significant investment well in excess of the asset's annual returns may be required periodically to maintain the asset's value. Fortunately, many private assets are excellent loan security—real estate can be mortgaged, sound operating companies usually have little difficulty obtaining finance, and as discussed in Chapter 5, the oil patch has attracted its own sources of financing. But in cases where an asset will ultimately deplete, which pretty much guarantees a negative directional return over a purchased asset's complete lifecycle, maximization of return requires investment to front-load positive cash flows, the reinvestment of which in some other asset can offset the loss of value from the original investment's ultimate depletion. Alternatively, cash flows on a wasting asset can be sold forward and the proceeds redeployed. An example involving a non-purchased asset was David Bowie's 1997 sale of "Bowie Bonds" to Prudential Insurance, which allowed him to monetize future royalties from his song rights for redeployment to other investment opportunities, while maintaining ownership and some control over the assets he had created.

Thus, in most cases leverage plays a role in the economics of private assets held for cash flow, even if it is not employed in their initial acquisition and the asset is leveraged only occasionally over the duration of its holding period. However, leverage is likely to be considerably lower than if the same asset was purchased in a directional trade. Directional investors may achieve their required return without benefiting from any cash flow that the investment throws off, and may consequently be willing to forgo it or even to endure net negative cash flow for some period in order to maximize their return at exit. Since the point of a cash flow investment is to enjoy the asset's cash flow, the attraction of leverage to buy-and-hold investors is correspondingly much less. The breathtaking levels of borrowings that were injected into leveraged buyouts prior to the collapse of that market in 2007 are entirely inappropriate to a buy-and-hold investment program. For institutions that do not receive any benefit from the tax deductibility of debt payments, and especially if they may face issues of Unrelated Business Taxable Income liability as a result of employing leverage, its attractions are even less.

The degree to which leverage is tolerable is partly a function of the predictability of the investment's cash distributions. Nothing in investment is certain, which argues for conservative assumptions on this score, too. But in the nature of the case, cash flows from high-quality real estate on long-term lease are likely to be more predictable than those from, say, highly cyclical operating businesses. Investors in assets such as farmland that involve short leases, in assets with cash flows that are linked to commodity prices, and in private businesses that are volatile or highly cyclical must be willing to tolerate quite variable cash flows, including the possibility of periods in which no or negative cash flows are generated. The degree to which such investments can appropriately be leveraged requires careful consideration, for all that higher-than-prudent levels of debt may be readily available. I will mention a number of instances where the fact that something can be done does not argue in favor of doing it: this is one of them.

Although the discussion here has repeatedly referenced long time horizons, and they clearly account for the bulk of opportunity from private market cash flow strategies, long holding periods are not necessarily inherent to the opportunity. Some exposure period is of course required for any cash flow strategy, but in principle there could be private market opportunities of comparatively short duration—perhaps a year or two. Most of these would probably take the form of direct loans rather than ownership interests in productive assets, but opportunities for investors to provide what might be called "bridge equity" occasionally arise: some very lucrative ones can be found in financing the transfer and movement of physical commodities. And, of course, investors may take short-term directional advantage of what were originally intended as long-term cash flow investments if market conditions permit. One of the largest university endowments purchased timberland as a long-term, potentially perpetual investment, but sold it within a year when the properties attracted a bid that it regarded as too good to refuse, transforming the trade into a directional one before its owner had time to enjoy much of the cash flow it originally intended to capture from it.

The Risks of Holding Private Assets for Their Cash Flow

Ideally, the degree of investor activism in a private market investment should be proportional to its expertise in that investment area. In addition to his description of Yale's nineteenth-century misadventures in private equity to which I alluded above, Swensen also recounts those of Boston University nearly two centuries later (see Swensen 2000, 326*ff* and 2009, 324*f*), providing ample illustration of the dangers of inexperienced but excessively self-confident management. However, contracting out the management task lands the institution with agency risk, which is present in any decision to permit third parties authority over an institution's assets, but is in almost all cases more extreme in the case of private market assets than others. The opportunities for misalignment of interests are simply more numerous than in other investment categories, and barring such close operational oversight that the institution might as well be managing the asset itself, they are likely to be more difficult to detect than in public market investments.

Direct involvement in the management of private assets also poses some risks. An institution takes on liability under environmental, employment, and other regulation if it takes a legally recognized role as a director of the business in which it invests. Board observer status theoretically insulates an institution from this risk, but at a cost of reduced access to information and loss of any actual authority over operations. As a practical matter, an institution that takes such a role and is large enough to be an inviting target for litigation may find itself at least temporarily embroiled in plaintiff actions even if the legal theory for involving the institution in the action is weak. Although intelligent structuring of ownership makes the risk of such a plaintiff succeeding in obtaining recourse to the institution remote, the legal costs of disentangling the institution from creative theories of liability can easily become material, and the tort bar is aware of the negotiating value of threatening actions in the full knowledge of its inability ultimately to litigate them successfully.

Although institutions run reputational risks even if their involvement in an investment is through public markets and entirely driven by third-party security selection in which the institution plays no part, private market investment magnifies those risks. Private investment, simply because it is private, invites uncharitable speculation and even con-spiracy theorizing. The Carlyle Group, which has attracted extensive and not infrequently unhinged criticism because of its political connec-tions and its involvement in the manufacture of defense equipment, provides an extreme example: the fourth item that came up in a recent Google search for "Carlyle Group" was headlined "Exposed: The Carlyle Group. Shocking documentary uncovers the subversion of American democracy." Unfortunately, to suspicious minds "private" implies "secretive." On the principle that "Where there's smoke there's fire," secretiveness in turn implies that there is something sinister or shameful for an institution to be secretive about. Private investment in an asset that attracts controversy for whatever reason is likely to create worse publicity and greater risk to an institution's reputation than public market exposure to an identically controversial invest-ment, especially if the private investment involves complete control over the asset.

Legislators are hardly immune to conspiracy theory, which lends political attractiveness to the idea of raising revenues at the expense of private market investors. Although the tax treatment of private invest-ments has been fairly stable for more than a decade, it is a perennial subject of debate at both federal and state levels. Depreciation schedules, depletion allowances, and other inducements to investment are under more or less continuous re-examination, and these may be crucial com-ponents of these investments' returns even to non-taxable institutions. The 110th Congress's ultimately unproductive discussions surrounding the taxation of private equity were largely focused on the tax treat-ment of General Partners, but they could easily have metastasized into an effort to extract greater revenues from Limited Partners as well. It remains to be seen what will become of these proposals in subse-quent sessions of Congress. A particular risk to private investment comes from the U.S. Tax Court, since many aspects of private investors' tax treatment are matters of interpretation of the Tax Code rather than specific items of legislation. They are thus vulnerable to judicial reinterpretation without recourse to Congress. The legislative process at least offers those affected by a tax proposal the opportunity to lobby, as private equity General Partners did so effectively in 2007, to the benefit of many incumbents' campaign chests. The statutory nineteen members of the U.S. Tax Court are (or at least should be) immune to such blandishments.

Private investments' lack of market liquidity exacerbates these risks, because an investor that loses favorable tax treatment, that attracts unwelcome controversy because of some aspects of its private market exposure, or that becomes disenchanted with its third-party manager will find it difficult to extract itself from its investment. In most cases the investor will be forced to accept a significant discount to the investment's fair liquidation value in order to offload it—particularly if its reasons for divesting its holding are public knowledge, as they unavoidably will be in the first two instances. Sales that counterparties know to be forced sales or that are motivated by known dissatisfaction with the asset's manager are unlikely to attract favorable bids, assuming they can garner any purchasing interest at all.

Although at any given time the liquidation value of an asset that is intended as a long-term holding may be essentially irrelevant to its owner's satisfaction with the returns that the investment is generating, it may be extremely important from an accounting perspective if the asset must be marked to market. Fluctuations in asset values that are unrelated to the investment's cash flow productivity may have significant implications for measures of an institution's actuarial soundness and almost certainly for the investment staff's relationship with the institution's trustees. Chapter 4's discussion of the difficulties of estimating many assets' volatilities applies equally to the problem of estimating their value, and in addition to being inexact, valuation estimates can be costly and inconvenient to obtain. At the very least, valuation questions regarding private assets can be a nuisance for institutions, and for many, a considerably more serious problem than just that. For assets that require significant periodic investment in their renewal, such as commercial real estate, valuations may affect the cost or even the availability of financing for that purpose.

Neither tax nor reputational risks are diversifiable. An adverse tax interpretation could easily affect all of an institution's investments in a given category of private assets, and in some cases could even have wider tax implications for the institution's entire portfolio. This is an extremely strong inducement to investment staffs to be certain of all the implications of the way that the institution's ownership of an investment is structured. The damage to an institution's reputation from owning a controversial investment is unlikely to be mitigated by the fact that the exposure is small relative to the institution's wide range of other investments. Recall, for example, that in the furor over investment in South Africa before the end of apartheid, few if any of the "offending" institutions carried anything approaching substantial exposure.

Agency risk can be mitigated through diversification only in the weak, "eggs in one basket," sense that it can be diluted through exposure to more than one manager. That is, good manager selections do not provide a hedge against bad ones—they only dilute them. Use of multiple managers can reduce the portfolio consequences of selecting an excessively self-interested one, but cannot offset them.

The risk peculiar to each individual private investment can be reduced through diversification. But given the large size of most individual private market commitments relative to most institutions' total assets under management, only the very largest institutions are likely to be able to take full advantage of this opportunity for their private investment exposures. Most institutions that invest in private assets—whether they are motivated by a desire to capture their cash flows or as a directional strategy—are forced to accept that they will not be able to achieve optimal diversification of the risks entailed by those positions. The alternative of taking numerous but small exposures is not realistic: the costs and continuing burdens of due diligence are too high to be justified by tiny exposures, even where the investment vehicle under consideration permits small investments.

Even with the use of multiple funds, institutions' exposure to the risks specific to individual investments is almost inevitably concentrated compared to the diversification that they can achieve in the conventional stock and bond portions of their portfolios. If investments are made directly rather than through funds, their portfolio concentration in private assets is likely to be even greater, as the full burden of due diligence and continued monitoring of the investment then falls on the institution's staff. The degree of concentration of a private asset fund is only partly a function of its size and is in most cases dictated more by the nature of the assets in which it invests and the burdens of acquiring and managing them. If a typical manager of active equity portfolios is likely to carry some forty to seventy-five positions, the manager of a diversified private asset vehicle is unlikely to carry even a third as many and often significantly fewer. Except for the very largest ones, private real estate vehicles tend to be especially concentrated.

However, position size in private assets can be difficult to determine. While it might seem clear that a marine transport fund that owns eight vessels has eight positions, concluding this may not be quite so cut and dried if they are all time-chartered to the same operator for the same time period. An investor may regard three parcels of timber-producing acreage as one, three, or even ten positions, depending on their locations relative to each other, the species and maturity of their standing timber, and so on. From a functional standpoint, a position should probably be regarded as a unit of factor exposure, so what should be regarded as a position varies depending on the type of exposure that is under consideration. To continue with the example of timberland, adjacent properties share a more or less identical risk of tornado damage, and so constitute one position from that perspective, but if the timber on one is largely softwood and on the other it is predominantly hardwood, their risks from insect infestation may be quite different, and in that respect they constitute distinct positions. Two non-adjacent parcels of farmland are in an important respect only one position if they are leased to the same farmer. Measures of concentration are asset-specific, and may be quite idiosyncratic to different types of private assets. Investment policymakers must be alive to these peculiarities, not least because, in thinking about them, they can improve their understanding of the risks that they are taking.

Private Asset Cash Flows in the Context of Conventional Portfolio Holdings

Private investments of the sort discussed in this chapter are clearly not debt instruments, although their portfolio function as more or less reliable generators of cash distributions resembles the role that buy-and-hold fixed-income techniques can play in portfolios. They have the advantage over debt that they are real rather than financial assets, and consequently to a greater or lesser extent, depending on the underlying asset, are insulated from the effects of inflation. Many of them also have the advantage over fixed income that they can be perpetual investments. Scarcity suggests that it would probably be difficult if not impossible to build much of a portfolio using perpetual bonds, and in any case almost all perpetual bond issues are callable (including the British Treasury's famous "consols," which date to 1752, although their terms have been modified repeatedly).

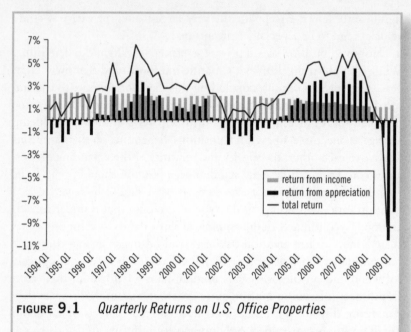

FIGURE 9.1   *Quarterly Returns on U.S. Office Properties*

On the other hand, in many cases private assets' cash flows are less predictable than bonds', and ownership of them is legally structured as an equity interest, so they have lower credit ranking than debt in the event of bankruptcy.

However, in their risk profiles, private assets more closely resemble equities, again to a greater or lesser extent, depending on the underlying asset. Yields on timberland, farmland, and prime office buildings on long-term lease are somewhat bond-like (see **Figure 9.1**: the annualized standard deviation of income was 0.69 percent, while that of appreciation was 5.43 percent and the σ of total return was 5.02 percent), and in the past many institutions have regarded their real estate holdings as essentially a part of their fixed-income allocation. But since the 1970s, farmland and office prices have been considerably more volatile than those of fixed-income instruments (at least in normal bond market conditions), and timberland has become more volatile in the last decade. As a contrasting example, dry bulk carriers in the voyage-charter market are and always have been very much operating assets with high volatility of both yields and asset values, although the increase in vessels' yield volatility over the last decade has been truly remarkable, as illustrated by the charter index in **Figure 9.2**.

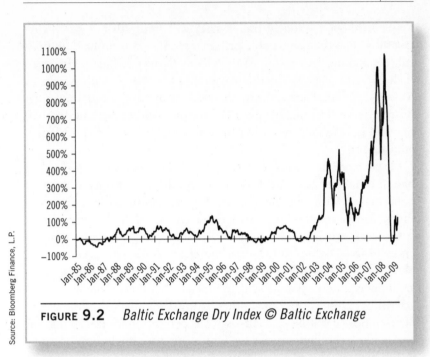

Source: Bloomberg Finance, L.P.

FIGURE 9.2 *Baltic Exchange Dry Index © Baltic Exchange*

Annualized standard deviation in voyage charter rates prior to August 2002 was an equity-like 11.4 percent, but subsequently it climbed to 30.5 percent. Note that this is simply the volatility of vessels' revenue yield, and does not incorporate changes in their asset value, which raise the volatility of this investment category's total returns even higher. The volatility of the asset prices and income generated by the other investment categories discussed in this chapter range themselves between these extremes.

But the sizes of their cash flow distributions, significantly abetted by their freedom from corporation tax if the investment is properly structured, set private assets' return characteristics apart from those of listed equities, even where the underlying assets exhibit quite volatile earnings and distribution patterns. Although many of these investments' payouts are fairly certain to vary considerably from one year to the next, even for the very highest quality commercial real estate, average yields over a relatively few years on attractive private market assets are multiples of those usually achievable on listed equities. Meanwhile, the costs and uncertainties of transacting in such liquid investment categories are avoided.

If investment policymakers seek to draw analogies from public markets to make volatility estimates for such assets, in most cases the lower yield on a publicly traded-asset will imply that it has higher volatility than the comparable private asset. There is no hard and fast rule for making such an adjustment to a volatility estimate. However, if the best-fit analogy for the private market asset is with REITs or Master Limited Partnerships, their tax treatments (and thus their distribution yields) roughly parallel those of private assets, and the analogy will be stronger, requiring little (inevitably somewhat arbitrary) adjustment.

Even more than with high-yield bonds or direct lending, the dual nature of private assets held for their cash flows confronts investment policymakers with a problem in deciding how to fund an allocation to them. Careful attention to the risk characteristics of the underlying asset is obviously crucial, which implies that attempting to craft a volatility estimate for it is probably worth the effort, for all that the estimate obtained cannot be relied upon very heavily. While some of these assets are more equity- or bond-like than others, all of them share both characteristics to some degree or another. If any determination of the degree of resemblance can be reached—say, 30 percent bond-like/70 percent equity-like—the implications for how a purchase might appropriately be funded from the existing allocation would be fairly clear. But in most cases it is unlikely that such a degree of clarity can be achieved. Nevertheless, at the very least the exercise is likely to have heuristic value. And where they are relevant to the institution, any such funding decisions should be significantly influenced by mark-to-market considerations. It is tempting, given this situation, to apply the rule of thumb, "When it doubt, regard it as equity." But in many cases this would be a distortion. The problem deserves the effort it requires to come to as nuanced a resolution of it as possible.

The decision between direct investment and use of third-party managers to access private assets is also a difficult one. In some cases, policymakers can avoid it by taking both routes: co-investment alongside private equity funds in which an institution participates is an established practice that seems to be on the rise in commercial real estate circles as well. At least in theory, co-investment provides the best of both worlds—the opportunity to piggy-back on professional management as well as the opportunity for improved information flow and direct participation in the investment's governance. Co-investment also solves a problem that the use of most fund investments entails for investors who seek long-term cash flow rather than directional gains. Almost all private equity and real estate funds are vehicles with finite lives and are thus to a greater or lesser extent oriented primarily toward capturing directional rather than cash flow returns,[3] but co-investment affords the opportunity for an investor to hold the underlying assets over longer time periods than such funds are designed to do.

Otherwise, investment policymakers cannot escape the uncomfortable choice between accepting management responsibilities and their accompanying liabilities or running agency risk. The examples that Swensen provides of Yale University's and Boston University's mishaps with direct ownership furnish ample grounds for institutions to be cautious about taking the self-management route, and in most cases the instinct for self-preservation is enough to prevent investment policymakers from pursuing it. Where that is not sufficient, some thorough and frank self-examination on the part of investment staff who propose to manage what may be quite exotic business enterprises is certainly called for. Yet tales of self-interested mismanagement by third-party agents are too numerous to require elaboration here, and the cost to staff (let alone the institution) of making a poor choice of manager is not likely to be immaterial. When dealing with private market assets more than virtually anywhere else in the realm of investments, the burden of due diligence—whether on the investment itself or on the agent proposed for the selection and management of it—falls very heavily on those who are tasked with implementing investment policy.

Best practice in private equity investment argues strongly against market-timing and urges strict adherence to a discipline of vintage diversification over a period of at least five and preferably ten years. Similar thinking seems to be gaining acceptance in real estate circles. These are considerations that do *not* apply, or apply only in a much attenuated way, to private market investment in pursuit of cash flow. The near-universal advice to take care to diversify by vintage diversification is largely dictated by the directional nature of most of those trades, as both entry and exit prices are instrumental in determining the success of the strategy. Although there is always some uncertainty that valuations at entry are attractive, there is complete uncertainty about what conditions will be at the time of exit, and this urges risk avoidance through diversification. Opportunism dictated by perceived undervaluation, unaffected by considerations of diversification over time, is much

---

3. The venture community is highly critical of open-ended funds on the continental European model, which are not designed to self-liquidate, precisely because the structure provides a disincentive to managers to realize and distribute directional gains, since this would reduce their assets under management and thus their fee capture. See Fraser-Sampson 2007, 12.

more appropriate where capturing cash flow returns over an indefinite and conceivably perpetual time period is the institution's investment goal. It also offers some protection from adverse marks-to-market.

This places a timing burden on investment policymakers that many of them may be quite justifiably reluctant to accept—in which case they are well advised to avoid embarking on such a trade. Given the increased level of due diligence that is required by this form of investment in any case, if it is insufficient to provide the investment committee with reasonable certainty that the timing of the trade is opportune, then it is insufficient to support policymakers in embarking on such an investment program at all. Institutions that do not have a staff or access to advisors that are prepared on comparatively short notice to judge the timeliness of investment in, say, Tasmanian toll bridges or Ukrainian farmland, should almost certainly avoid participation in them. Their employment of private assets for the purposes of cash flow generation, if they are to employ them at all, should be restricted to those opportunities that they feel most competent to judge.

CHAPTER 10

Fixed-Income Arbitrage

The enormous variety of fixed-income instruments available in numerous currencies and the many relationships among them, ranging from systematic to mathematically pleasing to economic to temporary and perhaps spurious, offer myriad opportunities to arbitrageurs. While the highly intermittent liquidity of many of these instruments can present a major impediment to high-frequency trading of them, illiquidity itself is also a rich source of mispricing, which is the bread and butter of all arbitrage activities. And many arbitrageurs resort to the much more liquid futures and swap markets to craft most if not all of their trades, so in many cases the liquidity of the underlying presents less severe obstacles to their activities than might be imagined. This chapter addresses itself to longer-term trades than those typically pursued by high-frequency traders, although, as we have seen, hyperactive traders are frequently involved in various forms of fixed-income arbitrage, too.

Otherwise, this chapter will address most of the return-seeking things that hedge funds do in the fixed-income markets—yield-curve arbitrage, spread and basis trades, mortgage trades, and capital structure arbitrage. But it will also skirt around unhedged trades in emerging market, distressed, and high-yield debt, which are not arbitrages at all, although they are frequently lumped together with them. And it will neglect convertible arbitrage, a true arbitrage trade between convertible bonds and related equity or equity options. Convertible arbitrage is in several respects quite a different investment technique from the other fixed-income arbitrages because of its equity component and because of its explicit optionality, which can be used to construct trades of quite different types, such as volatility arbitrages. However, convertible arbitrage is in fact a "purer" arbitrage than many of the others that are discussed here, if not purely a fixed-income technique, because there is a firm systematic link between such a bond and the equity of its issuer, and a catalyst incorporated into its term structure that will cause that connection to be realized. Over the last few years, the virtual evaporation of convertible bond issuance, accompanied by excessive exploitation of the hedge trades that make use of these instruments, has reduced this once very popular strategy to a comparatively minor sideline, although its performance recovered significantly in the first quarter of 2009.[1]

Referring back to the caricature of cognitive styles mentioned in the Introduction, most fixed-income market participants are decidedly "lumpers," meaning that they seek to find commonality among the instruments in their markets. Given the amount of effort put into this project, it should not be surprising that they succeed. The most basic element in bond investors' toolkit—the concept of yield to maturity—is used to make instruments with different coupons, payment schedules, and maturities comparable to one another. And the further elaborations of that concept such as duration, convexity, and so on, provide even more detailed ways in which the relationships among various fixed-income instruments can be analyzed. These tools allow bond market participants to abstract from the differences between bonds in pursuit of common treatment with respect to their pricing and behavior in different bond market circumstances. Credit ratings, while they have recently shown themselves to be considerably less than perfect, are intended to

---

1. The extent of convertible arbitrage's decline in popularity is illustrated by its weighting in the Credit Suisse/Tremont Hedge Fund Index—an asset-weighted benchmark as opposed to the unweighted Hedge Fund Research indices used elsewhere in this volume. From a peak of 8.40 percent in May 2003, its weighting had fallen as low as 1.70 percent by October 2008, although this was certainly abetted by miserable performance relative to other hedge fund categories in 2008. In addition to overcrowding and a shortage of opportunities to exploit, some high profile failures of hedge funds that specialized in convertible arbitrage no doubt contributed to its loss of popularity: see Swedroe and Kizer 2008, 195. However, in imitation of merger arbitrage, the trade has begun to migrate into multi-strategy vehicles, with the result that, if opportunities for exploiting the trade improve, funds dedicated exclusively to convertible arbitrage may still be somewhat thin on the ground. The cycle of convertible issuance is slow moving, but having shrunk by a third in 2008, issuance seems to be in process of recovering.

serve a similar purpose, although investors have, for reasons that are no doubt painfully clear to the reader, come to rely on them considerably less since 2007 than they had in the past. These tools are used to make different fixed-income instruments fungible in the eyes of the market, and imperfect pricing of fungible instruments is the source from which all arbitrage opportunities derives—in fact, this could almost serve as a definition of "arbitrage opportunity."

Consequently, many of the core activities of even conventional, long-only fixed-income management have the character of relative value arbitrages. For example, in the context of a benchmarked portfolio, a neutral exposure to the benchmark can be regarded as taking zero risk relative to it or, on a correlation-adjusted basis, effectively as no net investment at all. If we embark on such a thought experiment, then duration trades involve "borrowing" from one portion of the benchmark's yield curve to finance positions at one or more other points along the curve. They come to be seen, in the context of this thought experiment, as long/short positions. Similarly, relative to a benchmark, credit trades are founded on the observation that an instrument is trading at a discount to where its valuation relative to other bonds (whether with the same or different ratings) suggests it ought to trade, and also can be characterized as involving "loans" from one portion of the benchmark to fund overweighting of another portion.

In terms of the distinction offered in the Introduction, traditional (as opposed to quantitatively driven) equity-market participants tend to be "splitters," seeking to exploit the characteristics and risks specific to individual instruments. Conventional fixed-income investors whose discipline places a heavy emphasis on credit analysis tend to pay more attention to similar specific risks than other fixed-income investors, adopting techniques that resemble the practice of their non-quantitative equity brethren, and much of the research that drives their trades is rather similar to equity research. In periods where credit quality is under strain, bonds' specific risk can take center stage in their valuation, provided that the fixed-income markets are not so severely strained that credit considerations are simply abandoned as "correlations go to one" amid a flight to the safety of Treasury paper, as occurred in 2008. On the other hand, there is a noticeable contingent of "lumpers" among both conventional and alternative equity investors. Quantitative equity managers employ Arbitrage Pricing Theory as an analytical tool that abstracts from specific risk, to a greater or lesser extent transforming equities into fungible "counters" and consequently making them manageable in ways more similar to those employed by participants in fixed-income markets. In such a quantitative equity context, β may take on a role closely analogous to that of duration in fixed-income management.

Fixed-Income Arbitrage as an Investment Technique

The wild abundance of fixed-income instruments and of mathematically specifiable relationships between them give rise to a correspondingly diverse profusion of arbitrage opportunities. The trades that are addressed in this chapter include but are by no means restricted to

- ❏ *yield-curve arbitrage*, which exploits changes in the shape of the yield curve;
- ❏ *swap-spread trading*, which trades the fixed and floating rates embedded in an interest rate swap against each other;
- ❏ *basis trades*, which exploit the difference between futures pricing and the prices of deliverable bonds;
- ❏ *credit-pair trading*, which trades the instruments of similarly rated issuers against each other;
- ❏ *capital-structure arbitrage*, which is a long/short trade in the obligations of a single issuer, although it may involve an issuer's equity or preferred equity as well as its debt;
- ❏ *inflation trades*, which trade Treasury Inflation Protected Securities against their conventional Treasury counterparts; and
- ❏ *mortgage trades*, which trade the convexity (pre-payment risk) of structured mortgage products (similar trades can be fashioned for Collateralized Debt Obligations and various other structured instruments).

There are many more such trades, but it would be tiresome to list them all, and many of them—especially those that entail currency risk—are even less "pure" arbitrages than these. Several of these trades can be exploited by high-frequency traders as well, but some that are more or less exclusive to high-frequency traders and thus will not be discussed here include

- ❏ *snap trades*, which exploit the price convergence between on-the-run Treasuries that are about to go off-the-run with earlier off-the-run instruments; and
- ❏ *TED spread trades*, which trade short-term Treasuries against comparable maturity Eurodollar contracts.

Even after eliminating a number of trades that are sometimes classified with fixed-income arbitrage, the list that remains makes it clear that this activity is a broad church. Although many of these trades are true arbitrages, arguably some of the hedged trades listed above are not arbitrages at all, and simply use long/short strategies and leverage to magnify exposures that may also be exploited by conventional long-only fixed-income managers. The question of whether they qualify as arbitrages comes down to a largely semantic debate over how systematic some of the characteristics of fixed-income markets that are exploited by these alleged arbitrages actually are. A skeptic might contend that many of these trades verge on statistical arbitrage, where the risk of spurious correlations is significant, but I think that is too strong. There is a degree of systematic relationship exploited by these trades that is in some sense less systematic than, say, the relationship between an option and its underlying, but that nevertheless has considerable persistence and can provide suitable fodder for arbitrageurs. This halfway house between systematic relationships and statistical arbitrage is what I alluded to in the first sentence of this chapter with my reference to "mathematically pleasing" relationships among fixed-income instruments. For all that the fixed-income markets are very intensively researched, the profusion of relationships among bonds—many of which involve options that result from call and prepayment features—provides ample scope for arbitrageurs' trade discovery processes to identify the pricing discrepancies that constitute their opportunities.

Consider a butterfly trade around a yield-curve discontinuity, as illustrated in **Figure 10.1**. In this instance the trading strategy would be implemented by taking a long position at B and shorting positions at A and C that have a combined value equivalent to that of the long position. The trade is productive whether the yield at B drops into line with the yield curve or the curve rises to bring itself into line with B's yield: the returns are symmetrical and thus the trade is directionally hedged, as any true arbitrage must be, by definition.

However, this is a situation that is in some ways reminiscent of the Italian savings shares example discussed in Chapter 1: there is nothing to force either occurrence other than the activities of arbitrageurs, and anomalies of this kind can persist for long periods, as students of the U.S. Treasury yield curve are aware. While aesthetics might suggest that the ugly bump on the yield curve "should" disappear, aesthetics rarely plays a causal role in security price developments. Unlike truly systematic arbitrages, for which there is a mechanism (typically expiry) that crystallizes any potential gain from exploiting the mis-pricing involved,

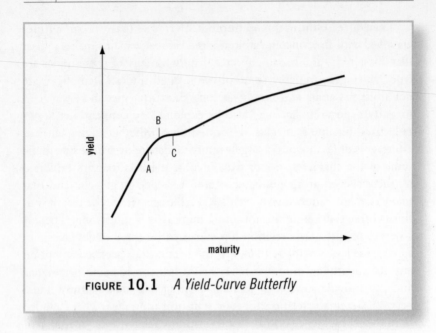

FIGURE 10.1 *A Yield-Curve Butterfly*

many fixed-income arbitrages exploit relationships of this nature, which are clearly anomalous but for which there is no systematic guarantee that the anomaly will disappear. The situation is similar but not identical to the Italian example, because a return to yield-curve normality is far more certain than the convergence of common and savings shares, but there is no mechanism that forces it to happen by any particular date. This is an example of the "mathematically pleasing." Note that the same butterfly structure, when implemented in futures rather than physical bonds, is still an only quasi-systematic trade: expiry does not force the "wings" of the trade to converge with the "body" of it, and the discontinuity may continue with the new nearby future. Other aspects of yield-curve arbitrage that call its "purity" as an arbitrage into question are discussed in the section on risk below. But it is worth noting here that such arbitrages are worth the attention of investors (unlike the Italian savings share arbitrage) because they can be financed economically, allowing traders considerably more latitude to wait for the market to "come to them."

This peculiar semi- or quasi-systematic character adheres in various ways to quite a number of fixed-income arbitrage trades, and while in the example of yield-curve arbitrage above it does not result in market risk, in other cases fixed-income arbitrage trades have greater market exposure than would generally be regarded as consistent with their classification as arbitrages. Yield-curve arbitrage trades are fully hedged against uniform changes in the *level* (what might be regarded as fixed income β, although analogies with the Capital Asset Pricing Model's use of this notion are far too profligate in writing about finance) but not to the *shape* of the yield curve. Exposure to change in the shape of the curve is, after all, what drives the trade's returns, and if hedged away would result in a trade with no returns other than the negative ones arising from leverage and transaction costs. Consequently, even yield-curve arbitrages can go awry, for example if the bump on the curve in Figure 10.1 becomes even more pronounced, either through an increase in B or a decrease in A and/or C.

A study of fixed-income arbitrage strategies (Duarte et al. 2007) finds that typical capital structure and mortgage arbitrage trades actually have fairly significant market correlation. In the case of capital-structure arbitrage, the authors' finding that a large number of the relationships that its trades seek to exploit fail to converge probably accounts for much of that technique's market correlation, as holders of these positions frequently discover that they do not actually hedge each other. In mortgage arbitrage it probably results from the reliance of many of these trades on mortgage pre-payment models, which provide yet another example of an inexact science that is employed in finance, and an arbitrage's dependence on them ensures that it cannot be entirely systematic. Quite apart from the empirical nature of any such model, pre-payments have optionality, and wherever a trade exhibits optionality there are inevitably some fairly intractable statistical problems with applications of linear models to it.

The paper by Duarte et al. merits more discussion because its methodology is both powerful and fairly unique. The authors' analysis is based on model trades in a way that probably has implications for actual investment practice only in the context of fixed-income arbitrage. For example, the authors survey a historical time series for yield-curve arbitrage opportunities, and then "trade" them retrospectively within parameters derived from actual experience (including transaction costs) and analyze the return distributions that result. This paper gives valuable insight into the return characteristics of specific trading opportunities in which a fund might participate, in a way that no other study of hedge funds (of which I am aware) has succeeded in doing. Although in principle such an analysis might be performed on a few other trades, such as those employed in merger arbitrage, the challenges to doing so are daunting. Unfortunately, a methodology that offers some valuable results when applied to certain fixed-income arbitrages simply cannot be extended to the trades employed by most other types of hedge funds,

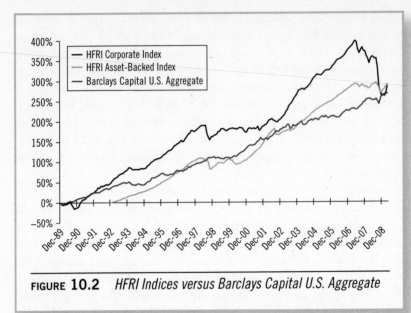

FIGURE 10.2   *HFRI Indices versus Barclays Capital U.S. Aggregate*

since screening would be unable to identify the trades or time the model's entry into and exit from them.

Figure 10.2 and **Table 10.1** illustrate the long-term return histories for the indices that Hedge Fund Research offers for fixed-income arbitrage trades (other than its Convertible Arbitrage Index). The Corporate Index aggregates the returns of various credit-related arbitrage vehicles, while the Asset-Backed Index (which was launched a couple of years later) primarily comprises funds that pursue convexity trades in mortgages, although it also includes traders in other forms of structured credits. The Barclays Capital U.S. Aggregate Index, indexed to the start date of the Corporate Index, is included for reference.

Few fixed-income arbitrage funds are in fact purists to the extent that the HFRI indices and Duarte et al. might be taken to imply. Although individual mortgage traders, for example, generally stick to their mortgage knitting, and similarly for credit traders, and so forth, most funds actually employ separate teams of traders to exploit several of these trade categories simultaneously, alongside but independent of each other. The individual traders involved will usually differ from trade to trade, with some staff pursuing trades on swap spreads, other traders on the Treasury yield curve, and so on. This provides such a fund risk reduction through diversification, but also a more consistent flow of productive trading opportunities. While some of these trades are perennials that can

TABLE **10.1**   *HFRI Fixed-Income Indices and the Barclays Capital U.S. Aggregate Index*

	HFRI CORPORATE INDEX	HFRI ASSET-BACKED INDEX	BARCLAYS CAPITAL U.S AGGREGATE INDEX
Compound Annual Return	7.23%	8.17%	6.97%
Median Monthly Return	0.81%	0.84%	0.66%
Annualized Standard Deviation	6.80%	4.23%	3.89%
Correlation to Barclays Capital U.S. Aggregate Index	0.1268	0.0546	1.0000
Kurtosis	8.09	24.82	0.65
Skewness	−1.37	−3.83	−0.27

be pursued fairly consistently over time, price discrepancies sufficient to exploit in some of the other trades may only arise occasionally. From my investigations, it appears that diversification seems to be successful both from a return-seeking and a risk-avoidance perspective relative to the characteristics exhibited by either of the HFRI indices that were shown in Figure 10.2 or the return streams implied by the model trades investigated by Duarte et al. However, it is worth noting that diversification within these vehicles often stretches well beyond employment of a variety of arbitrages to include directional trades in distressed debt. While distressed debt also offers arbitrage opportunities, in the form of capital-structure arbitrage, this is not necessarily either a purely fixed-income or a purely arbitrage trade.

Fixed-income arbitrage is invariably quite highly leveraged. For all that the relationships it exploits may not be completely systematic, they approach closely enough to being so that the trades are not rich, and for the most part would not be worth the trouble of pursuing without the return-enhancing benefit of leverage. Fixed-income arbitrage funds tend to be among the most highly leveraged investment vehicles of all, rivaled only by CTAs and leveraged buyout funds in their 2005 to 2007 heyday. The risk disclosure section of one fund's private placement memorandum that I recently encountered stated that the manager may leverage a single bond "up to 900 percent." This is a little on the high side even by the current standards of fixed-income arbitrage, but not extraordinarily so, and this manager is by no means unique in its appetite for leverage. Note also the document's use of "may." While the leveraged excesses of Long-Term Capital Management are no longer common among such traders, leverage of 6:1 to 7:1 is probably the norm. In this instance "may" was probably intended to cover the eventuality that the fund's trade discovery process could throw off proposals for specific trades where higher levels of leverage are appropriate. In contrast, the "norm" that I specify is for the entire fund, not for any individual trade.

Leverage clearly contributes to the riskiness of fixed-income arbitrage. The leverage used in some trades can be structured to have positive carry, but at a cost of interest rate or other risks that "pure" arbitrage is designed to avoid. For example, trades across yield curves in different currencies may have positive carry, but in many cases only if the foreign exchange exposure is left unhedged, since the hedge would reverse at least part of the carry and in some cases perhaps absorb more than all of it. The collapse of the "classic" currency carry trade in the autumn of 2008, as funding currencies such as the yen or the Swiss franc appreciated sharply against currencies such as the New Zealand or Australian dollar that typically constituted the long leg of the trade, provides a reminder of these risks. While such currency market occurrences are comparatively rare, they can be very costly to leveraged traders.

Fixed-Income Arbitrage Risk

The title that Duarte et al. give to their paper refers to the common accusation that some alternative investments, including fixed-income arbitrage, resemble the obviously risky sport of "picking up nickels in front of a steamroller," alluded to in Chapter 8. While the authors are at pains to argue that it need not do so in the case of all fixed-income arbitrage techniques, they recognize that some trades are considerably riskier than others, and this is without taking their degrees of leverage (or possible differences among their degrees of leverage) into account. But it would be a serious mistake to dismiss the accusation of extreme riskiness in the pursuit of limited rewards as a canard of the sort so routinely thrown about among hedge fund managers, who seem to delight in offhand disparagement.

The HFRI Asset-Backed Index provides a case in point. With extraordinarily high kurtosis around a monthly median return of only +0.84 percent and sharply negative skewness, the chance that there is a steamroller out there somewhere, lying in wait for unwary participants in this trade, is clearly quite high. The 193-month time series shown in Figure 10.2 exhibits two substantial outliers, one of which is an absurdly improbable negative 7.8σ of the median monthly return for the period. This is one month's performance that, if the returns were normally distributed, would be expected to occur once in something like three trillion years—more than two hundred times the age of the universe. If financial distributions were normally distributed, then we certainly would be living in interesting times! This one very unfortunate month eliminated an entire year's average return. Neither of the other two indices shown in the chart experienced anything remotely as extreme in the somewhat longer periods (229 months) for which data is available and shown for them there. The high leverage typically carried by funds that exploit arbitrages that are not rich gives further force to the accusation that participants in these trades my be taking extraordinary risks to achieve insufficient rewards.

At nearly a third again those generated by the broad fixed-income benchmark, it is tendentious to regard the returns exhibited by the HFRI Asset-Backed Index as mere "nickels," even allowing for the contribution of leverage to the index's returns. And its 10 percent higher standard deviation does not at first glance seem to be too great a price to pay for that increment of return. Due diligence that digs no deeper into the characteristics of a trade than an investment technique's Sharpe ratio would be likely to pounce on the opportunity to earn such returns. But the potential significance to investors of the higher moments of its return distribution amply illustrate what the fuss over the non-Gaussian nature of financial price series is all about. This alone need not be sufficient to convince investment policymakers that the HFRI Asset-Backed Index represents a risk that is too great to take—its lack of correlation with the broad bond-market index lends it some attractions that at least partially offset its risks—but it should certainly give them pause.

The leveraging of fixed-interest arbitrage trades should also bring thoughts of small change and construction equipment to mind, since there would be little need for high degrees of leverage if the trades involved were inherently richer. Investors are completely justified in questioning whether the quasi-systematic character of the relationships that some of its trades exploit can bear the weight of so much borrowing, and are well advised to explore the question in detail. It would be interesting, for example, to know how greatly the returns exhibited by the HFRI Asset-Backed Index rely on return enhancement. Especially in diversified funds, the leverage employed is likely to vary considerably over time and from one trading technique to another, so an average leverage figure over the fund's life or even just its recent history is not likely to provide a great deal of insight into its style of management. One feature of a candidate fund to which investment policymakers should pay particular attention is whether increases in leverage reflect the manager's perception of increased opportunities or just the reverse—that is, a paucity of rich opportunities for which the manager has compensated by piling additional leverage onto decreasingly rich trades. The same datum is likely to elicit diametrically opposite responses regarding a recommendation to invest, depending on the answer to that question.

Further, the fixed-income landscape is a minefield of potential liquidity traps. Given the lack of richness in the underlying trade, leverage makes fixed-income arbitrage especially vulnerable to situations where a trade is easy to enter but difficult to unwind, because the leverage clock ticks louder the greater the leverage that is applied to a trade. Most fixed-income products trade in dealer markets where there is no obligation on the brokerage firms that provide liquidity actually to do so, even in instruments they were happy to sell to an investor the day before. In particular, techniques that exploit corporate bonds encounter numerous liquidity challenges. For trades that exploit relationships between different issuers, this has tended to encourage the use of swaps rather than individual securities, but that facility is unavailable to capital structure arbitrageurs, since the swaps are generally issuer- rather than issue-specific. The consequences of risking frozen positions in leveraged trades that fail to converge because there is essentially no other trading activity in the instruments involved probably accounts for the high correlation to corporate bonds and even to equities that Duarte et al. ascribe to the relevant disciplines of fixed-income arbitrage.

Also related to the liquidity challenges that many of these trades face is a high level of operational risk. The infrastructure for executing trades with two or more legs efficiently is far less well developed in fixed-income markets than it is in equity and derivative markets, and the risk of trade failures is correspondingly much greater. Failure on one side of a two-legged trade results in a highly leveraged directional position for which the liquidity needed to unwind the trade may not be available. Although funds can mitigate some of these risks by executing all legs of a trade as a basket transaction with a single counterparty, it remains the case that most fixed-income trading is primitive by the standards of other instruments—as is the pricing data on which it necessarily relies. Poor pricing in a context where the price differentials being exploited are very narrow may raise questions about whether there is in fact a discrepancy to exploit at all. As a broad generalization, it is fair to say that liquidity, trading infrastructure, and the quality of price data are at their most dire in the municipal markets and least bad for Treasuries, with other instruments occupying various points of territory in between. However, futures and options are generally more liquid than their underylings.

The trade discovery process is a source of considerable risk if it is not supported by in-depth research before a trade that is suggested by it is actually put on. On the other hand, price discrepancies may be of fairly short duration, requiring prompt action. These opposing considerations, together with the fact that fixed-income markets throw off a bewildering amount of quantitative information, create a virtual invitation to computer-assisted data mining, even though it might be thought that the poor quality of much of this data would curb enthusiasm for mindless screening. The fixed-income markets offer an abundance of perceived anomalies due to specious correlations or discrepancies that are readily explained by market circumstances that numerical data themselves may not reveal. Where a portfolio manager contemplates leveraging a trade in a bond by as much as nine times, one should expect, for instance, that it would examine the bond's indenture to check that there is no fundamental explanation for an apparent pricing anomaly. These reasons can be subtle, such as a difference in the applicable legal jurisdiction between an issuer's various obligations. The debacle in mortgage markets that began in 2007 suggests that managers of conventional investment vehicles are not as attentive to such niceties as their investors have every right to expect them to be, and there is little reason to assume that, just because they are leveraged, hedge fund managers are always more assiduous. At diversified funds, product specialization among trading teams is in part intended to foster appropriate respect for the idiosyncratic risks that are specific to a product category or even to individual bonds within one.

The research methodology employed by Duarte et al. indicates why it would be comparatively simple to automate the trade discovery process in many fixed-income arbitrages, and virtually all fixed-income arbitrageurs use price-aggregating screening techniques to a greater or lesser extent. By this point in the book, the reader can probably anticipate my criticism of funds that do not at least apply human oversight to their machines. Too many anomalies occur for reasons that are well grounded in market dynamics, such as changes in the cheapest-to-deliver Treasury for use in futures settlement, which often cannot be filtered out by simple machine algorithms. The presence of an old hand or two on the trading desk can save a fund from numerous apparent opportunities that offer little actual prospect of returns but may entail substantial risks. It should be axiomatic that, the further the trade is from the exploitation of strictly systematic relationships, the greater the value of experience and judgment in screening apparent opportunities to trade. Where credit instruments are involved and issues regarding the availability to borrow loom large, informed judgment is critical not only to success but possibly to survival.

Figure 10.3 takes the example from Figure 10.1 and assumes a shift to a more upwardly sloping yield curve that retains the anomaly at point B at the new point E. It illustrates another source of risk in fixed-income arbitrage, due to dynamic hedging requirements. Because a trade of this type involves three positions, a changeable yield curve causes the hedging relationship between them to change in non-linear fashion, and the combined positions will experience directional exposure during the shift and retain that exposure after the shift until it is rebalanced. In contrast to a merger arbitrage trade, where the announced terms of the transaction establish and fix the hedging ratio reasonably firmly, hedges of this type must constantly be adjusted to changing bond market conditions. While

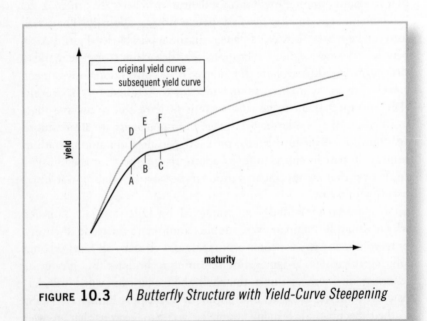

FIGURE 10.3   *A Butterfly Structure with Yield-Curve Steepening*

the same can be said of various derivative-against-physical arbitrages in options and futures markets, the dynamic hedges employed in those trades change with more precision relative to the prices of the instruments involved. Changes in the shape of the yield curve are not linear (hence the need for at least three positions), and are consequently more difficult to hedge. Trades that exploit convexity—such as many of those exploited by traders in mortgages—can pose even greater hedging problems.

Most arbitrageurs "trade around" the positions that they have put on, and fixed-income practitioners can be expected to do so as well. This can transform the nature of the trade if it involves taking directional risks alongside arbitrage ones, and the risk of this is increased by the constantly changing hedging ratios required for many fixed-income arbitrage trades. The more complex the trade—in terms of the number of positions required to craft the arbitrage—the greater the risk that may be created through "trading around" the structure. As we saw in our discussion of merger arbitrage, it is quite possible over the life of a long-term trading opportunity to remain a pure arbitrageur yet exploit partial convergence, taking the trade off if the prices of the relevant instruments are expected to diverge in the short-term, then putting the same trade on again when its richness has improved. However, it is often more difficult in fixed-income markets to defy Herakleitos and step in the same river twice in the same way that merger arbitrageurs can, because of the restricted liquidity of most of the debt instruments involved and the more changeable nature of the hedge ratios that characterize many fixed-income trades. Consequently, "trading around" a fixed-income position runs greater risk of creating inadvertent directional exposure, and to a significant extent each trade should be regarded as a new position, supported by fresh analysis, rather than a repeat of a previous one. That is, merger arbitrageurs can "trade around" their positions more cleanly and with less additional expenditure of analytic effort than fixed-income arbitrageurs can.

Many fixed-income arbitrageurs make substantial use of swaps and other OTC derivatives. Recent experience underlines the fact that derivative markets without a central counterparty structure are highly vulnerable to crises in the banking system. The failure of Lehman Brothers left numerous traders highly exposed, while freezing the positions of others during a period of extraordinary market volatility. The result was some very substantial losses for firms exposed to the London branch of Lehman Brothers in particular. This risk can to some extent be reduced through diversification among multiple prime brokers, but it cannot be reduced beyond a fairly large residual risk for any trader who chooses to use instruments that lack sound infrastructural support. It will be of considerable benefit to fixed-income arbitrageurs, if not perhaps to other users of swaps, if a sound market infrastructure for swaps and similar instruments, perhaps under the aegis of the Depository Trust & Clearing Corporation, is eventually put in place.

Fixed-Income Arbitrage in the Context of Conventional Portfolio Holdings

The return data for the indices given above argue for funding an allocation to fixed-income arbitrage from the conventional fixed-income portion of portfolios—both return and volatility characteristics are broadly comparable. The low correlation between these trades and conventional fixed-income reinforces the case—investment policymakers should be attracted by an investment that provides diversification to a segment of their portfolios for which it is otherwise difficult to obtain much effective diversification. The components of a "core/satellite" approach to bond investing that embraces non-U.S. debt, high-yield and other long-only strategies are neither so exotic nor are their returns so uncorrelated that they escape being slaved to U.S. Treasury market developments to a greater or lesser but never immaterial extent. As a group, bonds afford the numerous arbitrage opportunities that they do precisely because of this high degree of interrelation among their various individual instruments and their broader categories. Fixed-income arbitrage introduces a more truly heterogeneous return generator into the fixed-income allocation than most of the long-only fixed-income categories that are generally employed as "satellites" in these fixed-income portfolio structures. For the increasing numbers of institutions that adopt such a structure, this constitutes a strong recommendation for the inclusion of fixed-income arbitrage within their investment universes.

As we have seen, however, the higher moments of fixed-income arbitrageurs' return distributions should cause investment policymakers to think twice before rushing into the category. The dispersion of returns among fixed-income arbitrageurs is wider than among most long-only bond managers (emerging-market and high-yield debt providing partial exceptions), and although the higher moments of individual funds' return series are also broadly dispersed, kurtosis is in virtually all cases noticeably higher than for long-only bonds. Low correlation is not such an enticing proposition if it is caused by a few very negative outliers, and due diligence should examine the time series with outliers removed to see if, most of the time, correlation is in fact much higher than when calculated with outliers included. Once again, the dynamic nature of security return distributions must be borne in mind: a return distribution that is not negatively skewed or at any rate tolerably so can become strongly negative with a few or even one sufficiently large single high standard deviation outlier, as was shown earlier with reference to the Standard & Poor's 500 Index and the Crash of 1987. In the case of the two indices shown in Figure 10.2, removal of their highest standard-deviation data points does increase their correlation relative to the benchmark, but not dramatically.

Which returns us to nickels and steamrollers. Duarte et al. actually find *positive* skewness for four of the five trades they analyze—that is, outliers tend to be to the right rather than to the left of the median. But this does not seem to be the experience of actual fixed-income arbitrage funds. Even where a fund has a lengthy return history that includes no negative high standard deviation event, investment policymakers are probably well advised, in the interest of conservativeness, to assume that there is road-building equipment lying in wait out there somewhere in the underbrush. A diversified fund can obtain only a weak form of diversification resulting from the dilution of high standard deviation returns across numerous trading strategies. That is, different arbitrages do not hedge each other—exposure to several of them only waters down the effects on aggregate returns of those that go wrong, rather than offsetting them. An allocation to fixed-income arbitrage should probably be made on the understanding that a short-term loss equivalent to an entire year's average return is always a possibility, and be sized accordingly. This reinforces the suggestion that a role as one among other "satellites" of a core fixed-income portfolio is probably the best use for this investment category, although an aggressively return-seeking institution might decide that it is appropriate to make it a larger "satellite" than at least some of the others it employs.

CHAPTER 11

Event-Driven Investment

Event-driven investing achieves its objectives if the manager of a fund correctly anticipates a particular corporate action—an issuer announcing its intention to repurchase securities, regulators blocking an acquisition, a firm entering or being discharged from bankruptcy, a credit rating raised, a drug trial abandoned, and so on. Although most of its trades are clearly directional in nature, it contrasts with traditional investment approaches that rely on the realization of value over time, in that its returns, or at least the bulk of them, derive from binary and in some instances virtually momentary occurrences. The line between it and various conventional, long-only investment approaches is not sharp—conventional investors' returns may also be affected by these incidents, and some of them may actively seek them out. For most of their trades, managers of event-driven vehicles can be expected to carry at least some market β exposure, however temporary, while awaiting "events." But event-driven investors derive *most* of their returns from exploiting these one-off occurrences, rather than benefiting or suffering from them more or less by accident while pursuing returns that derive from the realization of perceived value over longer periods. Although not all the trades listed below are directional, a reasonably comprehensive catalog of event-driven opportunities would include trades that exploit:

❑ proxy contests;
❑ spin-offs;

- [ ] management change;
- [ ] buybacks;
- [ ] major litigation;
- [ ] bankruptcy and distress;
- [ ] restructuring; and
- [ ] mergers and acquisitions (as already discussed).

Note that the "events" these trades exploit are not necessarily to an investor's advantage and may be best exploited through short exposure. As with any trade that depends on forecasting price movements, incorrect "event" forecasts produce unacceptable returns, and where expectation of an "event" that does not subsequently occur is already built into security prices, its failure to materialize will inevitably lead to losses for those who carry exposure to it. There are medium- to long-term trends affecting some categories of "event"—merger activity waxes and wanes, and regulatory policies change over time at institutions such as the Federal Railroad Administration or the Food and Drug Administration, whose decisions can be decisive for the industries under their supervision—but these cycles have limited (in the case of the merger cycle) or essentially no (in the case of regulatory policy) correlation to market movements generally. The ready availability to investors of "events," such as mergers and bankruptcies, is favored or otherwise by macroeconomic developments. Some types of "events," such as litigation outcomes or management changes, exhibit little obvious relationship to each other or to trends in the broad market or economy, whereas the frequency of some such as buybacks seems to be at least partially subject to the dictates of fashion.

Although event-driven investment is primarily a technique applied to equities, there are also fixed-income "events" that can be exploited, notably when an issuer is in distress or bankruptcy, and other asset categories offer "events" as well—consider a commodity speculator who correctly anticipates a supply interruption or a real estate investor who accurately predicts the path of a new freeway. The voting rights that attach to equity, permitting activists to influence management, are absent from debt instruments except by analogy in bankruptcy situations and completely lacking in other assets. As might be expected, the ability to influence "events" is widely exploited by event-driven practitioners. But in some circumstances fixed-income provides a partial hedge for event-driven trades whose returns are driven by equity exposure. Consequently, event-driven funds are predominantly but seldom purely equity vehicles.

"Events" are binary: they either happen or they fail to. In many cases, the return on an individual "event" is fairly predictable, and the risk that provides managers with a return comes from uncertainty about whether it will in fact occur and how long they will have to wait for it to do so. Again, this is a spur to activism, but given the directionality of these trades, also an inducement to diversification. Their binary character makes returns on event-driven trades "lumpy": the security involved usually moves roughly in line with its market until the "event" causes its price to lurch in the desired direction. Often this is a two-stage process, in which the security makes an initial move when it becomes apparent to the market that an "event" might be in the offing, and then another when the "event" actually occurs. Once an "event" is complete, there is little benefit and some risk to these investors from holding onto the position, so event-driven investors tend to be fairly active traders. Positions are seldom held much longer than a year, implying at least 100 percent annual portfolio turnover. Producing a stable return stream requires diversification across numerous "events," and given the need for diversification and the limited shelf-life of "events," it also requires a steady stream of new opportunities to exploit. Consequently, the appetite of event-driven managers for new trading ideas is relentless.

Event-Driven Investing
as an Investment Technique

On the face of it, event-driven investing might be expected to have low correlation to equities. "Events" bear limited correlation to each other or to broader market movements—a large measure of what makes them "eventful" is precisely their departure from normal market influences. This characteristic is, as might be expected, stressed in these funds' marketing materials. Extreme market conditions may affect them (for example, the 1987 Crash forced several mergers to be scrapped and no doubt various spin-offs and other planned "events" were also abandoned). In panic conditions, the prospect of a buyback may lose some its luster to potential investors, the IPO market for spin-offs dries up, and merger financing may also disappear. While general market weakness may not affect these transactions, extremes of volatility can be expected to do so. But even market drama that temporarily causes all securities to correlate highly, thereby cancelling some "events," is likely in the aftermath to generate a substantial new crop of them. And apart from periods of high volatility in the markets, "events" are essentially discrete: one firm's buyback, for example, has little to do with another's spin-off or still a third firm's slide into distress. Further, "events" may also be exploited on the short side, some of the trades in which these managers participate are market-neutral arbitrages, and others can be partially hedged. All this argues against a high equity market β for event-driven vehicles.

So the picture given by **Figure 11.1** and **Table 11.1** may come as something of a surprise. The correlation shown is comparable to the 0.7234 figure posted by the HFRI Equity Hedge Index, a broadly based long/short index illustrated in Figure 5.1, and certainly cannot be regarded as "low"—by my lights (see Chapter 3) it qualifies as high. Short sales and participation in arbitrage and other hedged trades no more suffice to eliminate the β from event-driven vehicles than their more consistent (if still, in most cases, not predominantly) short exposure does from most long/short ones.

The reason for this correlation is the market exposure these traders must carry while awaiting "events," coupled with the fact that the returns from "events" are also reflected in broad market metrics. Event-driven managers are even less likely to be net short than their long/short brethren—although several of them were very aggressively short the mortgage-backed securities market in 2007, and their funds may well have been net short for the full year. Event-driven managers react quickly to eliminate their exposure to the "event" situation once the returns it proffers have been captured, as the securities involved are likely to revert sharply to a higher level of market correlation. But in the run-up to most

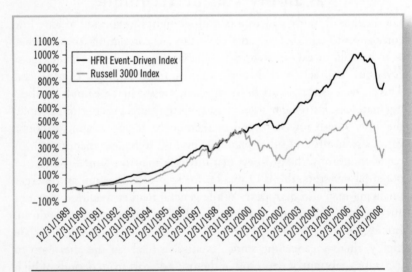

Source: Bloomberg Finance L.P.

FIGURE 11.1   *HFRI Event-Driven and Russell 3000 Indices*

TABLE 11.1 *HFRI Event-Driven Index versus the Broad U.S. Equity Market*

	HFRI EVENT-DRIVEN INDEX	RUSSELL 3000 INDEX
Compound Annual Return	11.88%	7.19%
Median Monthly Return	1.29%	1.35%
Annualized Standard Deviation	6.99%	15.29%
Correlation to Russell 3000 Index	0.7267	1.000
Kurtosis	4.39	1.51
Skewness	−1.39	−0.75

types of "event" these traders necessarily carry market exposure. Quick exit may eliminate the risk of experiencing the full brunt of any reversion to market β, but assuming that the proceeds realized from the previous trade are re-allocated to another "event-in-process," the exploitation of which also requires that the fund carry market exposure, rapid exits from trades that have run their course cannot eliminate the β exposure that attaches to these trades (unless the new trade is an arbitrage).

However, close examination of Figure 11.1 reveals something very interesting—and highly attractive—about the market β of event-driven vehicles. Although correlation tends to be high in rising markets, it appears to tail off fairly consistently in declining ones. This is even more dramatically illustrated by **Figure 11.2**, for which, unfortunately, the history of the 2000 to 2003 and earlier bear markets is unavailable, but which offers daily index values for the period for which the index has been in existence. Correlation with rising markets but non- or counter-correlation with falling markets is something of an ideal for investment practitioners, so it is worth delving into whether there are strong and systematic reasons to believe that event-driven managers have in fact stumbled upon it. In particular, it will be interesting to see if there is something inherent in their practice, rather than just an overlay of tactical allocation, that accounts for this return pattern.

I believe that there may be. While we have already seen that there are good reasons why their funds will tend to correlate with markets

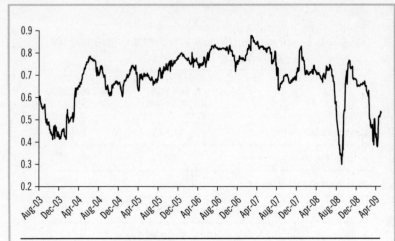

FIGURE 11.2 *HFRX Event-Driven and Russell 3000 Indices: 90-Day Trailing Coefficient of Correlation*

most of the time, the defensive characteristics of "events," which by definition imply a security's departure from normal market influences, provide them with a measure of downside protection in a bear market. That is, "events" provide opportunities to profit directionally from special situations even in a context where most prices are dropping across the board. Further, the appropriate trading response to some of the "events" may involve taking short or fully hedged positions, and these managers' ability to exploit distressed situations is made more opportune and may experience improved returns during periods that are suffering the economic conditions that generally accompany bear markets. It is interesting to note that long/short vehicles do not share this characteristic. This scenario, at any rate, is my take on the peculiar index behavior exhibited in Figure 11.2. However, there is at least one alternative explanation for this return behavior, which is noted in the final section of this chapter.

In this context, the peculiar downward spike and sharp rebound in Figure 11.2 illustrate a scenario that deserves special attention. The HFRX Index was carrying about its average level of correlation to the Russell 3000 Index up to the end of June 2008, when its correlation dropped sharply to a trough on September 8. In the following month it rebounded equally sharply to its previous, accustomed levels. As market conditions deteriorated in the summer of 2008, the defensive qualities of event-driven investment resulted in significantly reduced correlation to the broader market. However, as conditions degenerated into the sort of panic in which "correlations go to one," market participants swept aside much consideration of the defensive characteristics of "event" situations in their scramble to find an exit. Event-driven vehicles were probably saved from gaining an even higher level of correlation to these disastrous market conditions by their hedged and distressed exposure, but they suffered a measure of what everyone else did. So, unlike Galahad, event-driven managers have not quite found the Holy Grail—they are still vulnerable to market chaos—but they seem to have found a valuable measure of downside protection in more normal bear market conditions compared to conventional, long-only investors or even to long-biased long/short vehicles, because their trades are not entirely reliant on the process of value realization, which is best-supported by favorable economic conditions.

When market conditions are less extreme, "events" can be staged. Through proxies, participation on creditor committees, public grandstanding, or just plain jaw-boning, investment managers may be able to cause a firm's management to embark on a desired action. Large numbers of spin-offs have resulted from corporate activism by such investors, as have many share buyback programs, other investor-friendly corporate initiatives and even the occasional merger. Activism may accelerate returns from "events" that are already under way, or it may create opportunities where they did not previously exist. Note, however, that these practices are not exclusive to vehicles that would generally be regarded as alternative investments: even mutual fund managers can play.

Event-Driven Investment Risk

The individual "events" that these investors seek to exploit offer more attractive returns than most arbitrage trades, as well as entailing directional risk, so most event-driven funds are less leveraged than many other categories of alternative investment. Arbitrage is the more highly leveraged exception, and event-driven traders may run a segregated arbitrage book to isolate its leverage for the purposes of analysis.[1] But some

---

1. Note the rider "for the purposes of analysis." In marketing themselves, hedge funds frequently wish to minimize the risks that result from their leverage by giving separate ratios for the different parts of their trading books. This is useful to their internal risk management and to potential investors' attempts to understand their trading techniques, but leverage in any part of a portfolio affects the entire portfolio, creating the risk of forced sales if leverage is called by its providers. A fund's aggregate leverage level is at least as important to due diligence as its trade-specific levels, and unless its exposure levels to different types of trades are disclosed, separate ratios for different parts of its trading book may conceal more than they reveal.

leverage—usually less than 3:1 (debt = ¾ of capital employed) for the vehicle as a whole—is necessary to achieve returns that are sufficiently attractive compared to those expected from conventional equity investment to justify potential investors' interest. This level may in fact be on the high side for event-driven funds that do not participate in risk arbitrage, where 2:1 is probably more appropriate and more typical.

Figure 11.1 and the table accompanying it indicate why: event-driven investment is significantly correlated to equity markets, and the attractions of its comparatively low standard deviation are offset to a significant extent by its lower median return and the higher probability that it will produce negative outliers. Without enhancement of its returns through leveraging the trade, its standard deviation would approach Treasury market levels, but its returns would drop below those of conventional equities and resemble those of corporate bonds. Although corporate bond returns in exchange for only Treasury-like risk might sound like an attractive proposition, it is not so attractive in the context of high-ish negative skewness. It is noticeable that the returns, standard deviations, and skewness of the two indices shown in the table are all roughly half or twice each other—that is, almost certainly related to the amount of leverage typically employed in these trades.

In this context, the incentive for a manager to seek an acceleration of "events" through activism is clear, but activism also contributes a measure of risk reduction to event-driven techniques. The sooner "events" transpire, the sooner the manager can eliminate the directional exposure to the market that it requires in order to exploit them. This is not to say that these traders can avoid equity market β, other than through participation in arbitrage. As mentioned, assuming that they wish to remain fully invested, proceeds from an "event" are reallocated to the next "event-in-process," and thus acquire a measure of β again. But the new β exposure acquired is somewhat mitigated by the impending "event," while insofar as securities "revert to β" once the "event" has transpired, the reversion avoided is likely to be greater than the β exposure acquired with the new "event-in-process."

As an example of the last point, examine **Figure 11.3**, which plots the daily price change in Altria up to its spinoff of Philip Morris International, and then the combined, capitalization-weighted price changes of both successor companies, against the Standard & Poor's 500 Index. Unfortunately, it is not possible to illustrate this in terms of the instruments' coefficients of correlation, since that would require calculation of the coefficient over a trailing period, which would obscure the point-change nature of the returns ascribable to the "event," but it is clear from the

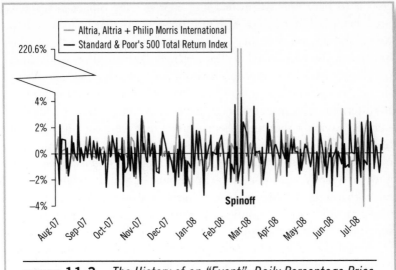

FIGURE 11.3   *The History of an "Event": Daily Percentage Price Changes, Stocks Market Value Weighted*

chart that the spinoff interrupted what had been a fairly stable correlation, which resumed immediately upon the occurrence of the "event."

Because "events" are *sui generis*—each with its own characteristics, driven by many factors specific to the issuer(s) involved—event-driven investing is research-intensive. While there are some firms that apply quantitative screens to the trade discovery process, event-driven trades vary so widely, and their attractiveness in almost all cases is so heavily determined by issuer-specific considerations, that there are few if any managers who would move directly from their screens to trade execution without further fundamental research. I am unaware of any who do, but if there are any, they take very considerable risks that are unlikely to be compensated by the transaction speed or portfolio diversification that automation of the trade discovery process might offer them.

I believe that it is a fairly accurate generalization that event-driven managers concentrate their trade discovery efforts on finding opportunities with six- to eighteen-month payoffs, in part to afford themselves the opportunity to carry out this research. Longer-tail opportunities stretch beyond the cost of carry, the range of easy economic visibility, and the managers' tolerance for β exposure, while "events" that are likely to occur in the short-term and have only belatedly been identified are almost certain to have been identified and exploited by others, leaving the fund that is late to the game with little opportunity to benefit from them. But exceptions are welcome: a near-term opportunity that the markets have somehow overlooked is clearly a highly valued prize, while an extraordinary long-term opportunity is unlikely to be rejected out of hand simply because it is a long way from realization. Long-term opportunities offer the additional advantage that the research preparation for them can be extremely thorough: hedge funds that were fortunate enough to be able fully to exploit the opportunity offered by short positions in mortgage-backed securities early in 2007 typically began their research into the trade at least six months in advance of building exposure to it. Firms that were considering taking on the contrary trade by purchasing whole loans late in 2008 indicated to me that their preparatory analysis would be at least as thorough.

Provided that an event-driven manager does not specialize too narrowly, there is usually a reasonably ample supply of "events" that arise spontaneously or that can be encouraged. But if a vehicle is too narrowly concentrated on one type of "event," it may find that sufficient opportunities are not available. Merger arbitrage has experienced such famines frequently enough, as discussed in Chapter 7, that its practitioners have felt it appropriate to ally themselves with more diversified vehicles, which accounts for that technique's near-disappearance as a stand-alone investment discipline. Distressed trades made a similar migration in the 1990s, and convertible arbitrage, as mentioned, seems to be undergoing one at present. Diversification among categories of "events" is sound strategy, to avoid fallow periods when assets cannot be profitably deployed. However, given the research-intensity of most of these trades, excessive diversification comes at a cost to event-driven managers who do not have access to large staffs of highly adaptable analysts.

A multitude of opportunities does not necessarily imply that event-driven portfolios are broadly diversified—while diversification is recommended by the β exposure inherent to many of their trades, as with conventional long-only equity managers, some event-driven investors prefer to concentrate their portfolios. This reflects the wisdom of "putting all your eggs in one basket and watching it like a hawk," as well as the research-intensity of many of these trades. It may also be influenced by a manager's activism, which can be time-consuming. Managers without the benefit of large research staffs may be forced to concentrate their exposures whether this reflects their preferences or not. But the amount of research devoted to many of these trades can to some extent compensate for their failure to achieve as much risk reduction through diversification as might otherwise be desirable—this is the benefit of being hawk-like. However, it is notable that the General Partners of event-driven funds tend to be among the most heavily staffed of hedge fund managers, suggesting significant investment in trade discovery and continued monitoring of the "events" to which their funds are exposed. The size of large event-driven firms is not measured solely in terms of their assets under management.

Once a range of opportunities has been uncovered, it is still a research-intensive task to discriminate among them, and this may also constrain managers' ability to diversify their portfolios extremely broadly. It is all very well for a firm to have fleets of analysts generating trading idea upon trading idea, but if a single Chief Investment Officer (CIO) has final decision-making authority over which trades are actually exploited, there is an obvious potential bottleneck on the way toward broad diversification. The successful CIO of an event-driven fund must be a polymath, at least as far as the very broad range of influences that can affect the fund's trades are concerned. But inevitably, there are limits to any one individual's range of experience and the time available to that person to devote to each of a large number of potential investment opportunities.

One technique that, at least in principle, may compensate for this problem is to split the portfolio among separate management teams with specialized expertise in, say, healthcare, energy, and so on, or alternatively among different categories of trades. Separate teams permit the portfolio to be built from the bottom up without centrally directed discrimination among proposed trades by a CIO who must otherwise perforce be a master of them all. Should due diligence encounter a fund that adopts such a management structure, it is important to obtain assurance that risk parameters, position and leverage limits, incentive structures, and so on, are in place that ensure that the resulting portfolio reflects the various teams' best thinking rather than the results of capital hoarding or other perverse and counterproductive behaviors. That is, a fund that adopts such a structure substitutes the risk of indiscriminate trading for the risk of a trade discrimination bottleneck, and must take care to put controls in place to avoid that risk. Neither risk can be diversified away, and a firm that relies on either approach must consequently address the one it chooses to take with structural measures and pay constant attention to the implications of taking on that risk. Optimal implementation of a structure that eschews the CIO bottleneck may still retain a CIO of sorts, but if it does, the CIO function is no longer one of final trade approval but of monitoring the teams' activities and perhaps performing research into new trades for which no team is currently in place.

Event-driven trades are often described as having optionality or asymmetric payoffs. This topic will be addressed in more detail in Chapter 13, where I will discuss the optionality of these trades alongside that of others. However, the comment is made frequently enough and inaccurately enough with respect to event-driven investment techniques that it is worth exploring what does *not* constitute their optionality here. A binary outcome is not in itself an indication of optionality: a coin toss offers a binary outcome but no optionality. Event-driven investors do not purchase an option on the return from the "events" that they exploit: they are fully exposed to whatever risks are entailed by seeking that return, less any hedging they may engage in, which reduces the return as well as those risks. That is, the asymmetry of their returns is not the result of an asymmetry in "events." If anything, the asymmetry of most of the returns achievable from "events" is unfavorable—implying greater losses if the "event" fails to occur than the gains achievable from the "event" if it does occur. This is certainly the case with merger arbitrage trades and is also characteristic of many other "event" exposures. This circumstance underlines the importance of research as a contributor to risk control as well as trade discovery.

However, it is possible to construct options synthetically through combining related long and short positions, and occasionally event-driven trades are structured this way. In some cases, these managers may also negotiate an appropriately structured swap with an investment bank (providing the bank with a complex and potentially attractive volatility generator). Particularly in distressed investing and capital structure arbitrage, it is possible through combinations of short and long positions in an issuer's debt and equity to craft trades that have many of the characteristics of collars—that is, defined upside potential with hedged risk exposure through the use of long put and short call option structures. However, one of the characteristics they do not share is exact hedging: the arbitrage relationships embedded in these trades are not systematic, and under stress may break down, with calamitous results if they are excessively leveraged.

Event-Driven Investing in the Context of Conventional Portfolio Holdings

Even in the fairly rare instance where an event-driven vehicle invests primarily in fixed-income markets, the return profile of its fund is likely to be more equity- than bond-like. On the one hand, credit events—which would probably constitute the bulk of such a fund's trading fodder—have high correlation to equity-market developments, as might be expected given the relationship between an issuer's credit standing and its equity fundamentals. And in any case, the binary nature of "events" creates a "lumpy" return stream that is not typical of fixed-income investments generally. Although Modern Portfolio Theory employs the volatility of assets' returns as a proxy for their riskiness, investment policymakers should not regard an investment with fluctuating returns that are caused by variable employment of capital as inherently more risky than another with a more stable return stream. From an actuarial or distribution-budgeting perspective, there may not in fact be that much difference between the risks involved, but from the perspective of investment risk there certainly is.

Investment policymakers whose thinking is dominated by the conventional asset categories may choose to regard event-driven fixed-income funds, if they can identify any, as fixed-income from a risk perspective while still allocating to them from the equity side of the portfolio on liquidity-budgeting grounds. But this is probably not advisable, and is likely to occur only if policymakers are fixated on asset allocation "buckets," about which more in later chapters. Event-driven fixed-income is largely driven by credit opportunities, which are, as might be expected, quite equity-like. Event-driven vehicles of all types have high correlation to equity markets, so it would be a very unusual product that such investment policymakers should put in anything other than its more aggressive risk-budgeting category.

While this chapter has made a rather bold suggestion in comparing the returns achievable by event-driven vehicles to finding the Holy Grail, in the case of any specific candidate for investment, investment policymakers should dig deeply to determine whether the vehicle invests in a way that is likely to achieve those highly desirable return characteristics. A feature of these funds that has been the focus of attention in this chapter is their research-intensity, and the cost of research encourages gigantism. Size militates against the flexibility and rapidity of response which may be an alternative explanation to the one that I already offered above for these funds' ability to be non-correlated in bear markets. In examining a prospective candidate in this investment category, it is useful to discuss the fund's activities in such markets: if performance was achieved by a timely shift in investment focus, the fund's subsequent growth into a large entity may argue against similar dexterity the next time market conditions deteriorate. Or such a success may distort the firm's subsequent behavior. I am aware of one large event-driven manager who, after producing spectacular performance in 2007 as a result of a timely shift of this kind, apparently convinced himself that he had a talent for market-timing to which his subsequent performance by no means bore witness.

This is important because, as Figure 11.1 and Table 11.1 suggest, much of the incremental return and risk reduction offered by event-driven investment relative to conventional long-only equities is achieved in periods when equity markets in general are performing poorly. It is probably not putting the matter too strongly to insist that allocation to event-driven investing stands or falls on the fund's bear market performance. However, it is only fair to add the proviso that, in a market panic, even the best event-driven vehicles may not provide a safe haven, and high correlation to equity markets during those episodes, while it should not be held against a candidate fund, is nevertheless a factor to consider in making any allocation to event-driven investing.

A related point, which was not stressed above, is that most "events" can profitably accommodate only a certain amount of investment. This has been touched upon in various comments made about arbitrages and other trades in this book, but it applies to most "event" trades, too. This also presents a problem to vehicles that have grown very large, and highlights an issue for event-driven investment as a category. Because respectable returns in favorable markets accompanied by the ability to avoid the worst effects of unfavorable markets is among the most attractive features an investment product can offer, funds that demonstrate these characteristics through a market cycle are likely to attract enormous inflows unless the manager has the self-discipline to close them to new investment. Thus there is both a fairly strong incentive for these firms to gather assets, related to their need to achieve economies of scale, and a ready supply of capital to invest in successful event-driven firms that is motivated by return-chasing. Note that the HFRI indices are not "investable," which means that at least some of their constituent funds are "soft closed" (closed to all but existing investors) while others are "hard closed" (closed to any new investment). It is by no means guaranteed that the funds actually available to an institution for its use will have characteristics as attractive as those of the index.

Event-driven investment funds are often regarded as "absolute return" vehicles and may be marketed as such. Because this is yet another term that has been stretched to the point of near-meaninglessness, a charitable interpretation may find this claim to be forgivable, but even so, it bears close examination. On the face of it, a correlation to equities in excess of 0.70 (i.e., R^2 implying that equity index behavior determines more than 50 percent of the return behavior of event-driven funds) does not seem terribly "absolute" to me. While an annualized standard deviation north of 6 percent is low compared to equities, it is not exactly bond-like. High kurtosis and fairly high negative skewness should also give pause to those who perform due diligence. The peculiarities of event-driven vehicles' correlation to the equity market that have been discussed here might argue for the "absolute return" designation, but they might as easily be regarded as evidence of their managers' ability to make the best of bad situations. Disentangling the influence of skill on returns from the influence of the basic strategy and the assets to which it is applied is a daunting task in connection with any investing technique. But the importance of pursuing the maximum achievable clarity in this regard in the case of event-driven investing is probably even greater than in other cases, precisely because of its unusually attractive correlation characteristics. Extra effort will be amply rewarded if a vehicle that in fact offers those characteristics can be identified.

To the extent that skill plays an important role in generating event-driven investments' return characteristics, then at least one of the most relevant skills should be familiar to investment policymakers, since it is their own. Whether there is something inherent to event-driven trades that accounts for these funds' peculiar return characteristics or not, allocation among those trades cannot help but play a significant role in producing those characteristics. So it is important to consider whether the allocation is a matter of strategy or tactics, and this can at least partially be determined by tracing the fund's allocation over time and relating it to developments in the underlying markets. For example: distress is always with us, and it is not unreasonable that a manager would maintain permanent exposure to trades that exploit it as a matter of strategy. On the other hand, a fund may be opportunistic in its exploitation of distress, based on its judgment of the outlook for the economy and/or the valuation of the opportunities available in the relevant trades compared to other opportunities. Evidence of a tactical approach to allocation may argue for the role of skill in creating event-driven investments' return characteristics. But evidence of a strategic approach to allocation does not argue the contrary view, since (as one would hope is quite clear to investment policymakers) there is skill involved in strategic allocation, too.

There is, however, some external evidence that has a bearing on this question. If the attractive, autocorrelated, and (compared to long-only equity) low β aspect of event-driven managers' return streams is largely the consequence of tactical trade allocation, then what is wrong with their long/short counterparts? Most long-biased managers' trading mandates permit them ample flexibility to shift their exposure to near-neutral or even to a short-bias, and many of them make full use of this freedom. And **Figure 11.4** (which plots the data from Figure 11.2 against similar data for the broad HFRX long/short index, the return history on which was illustrated in Figure 5.1) strongly suggests some successful tactical reallocation on the part of long/short managers when equity market conditions deteriorate. But if event-driven funds' correlation characteristics were driven primarily by similar tactical maneuvers, then they were quite noticeably more successful with them. This is implausible, particularly given that a move toward short-bias on the part of long/short managers should have *at the very least* the same non- or counter-correlating consequences for their returns as an increased allocation to distressed investments and other low β trades on the part of event-driven managers—nothing, after all, is more counter-correlating than a short. Unless we grant the dubious proposition that event-driven managers' market forecasting skills are on average considerably superior to those of their long/short brethren, then there must either be something inherent to "events" or to the way that managers allocate to them strategically that accounts for a significant portion of event-driven funds' unique return characteristics.

Having absorbed much of the hedge fund world's activities in distressed investing and risk arbitrage (although dedicated distressed funds have recently experienced a revival), with convertible arbitrage possibly soon to come, event-driven investing is an increasingly amorphous category with an over-abundance of trades its managers can allocate among.

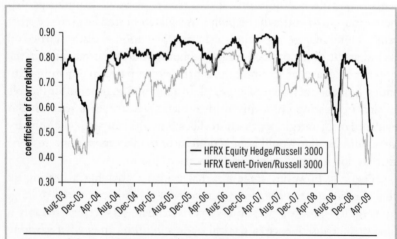

FIGURE 11.4 *HFRX and Russell 3000 Indices: 90-Day Trailing Coefficients of Correlation*

Source: Hedge Fund Research, Bloomberg Finance, L.P.

As investment policymakers are all too aware, having a great many choices does not make the process of choosing one in particular any easier. The dangers of excessive diversification are real, as are its costs, and the size of many funds may push them in that direction. Should this occur to an event-driven fund, it is questionable whether it could retain its attractive return characteristics. On the one hand, greater diversification could be beneficial, but on the other it could mire CIOs in confusion and their firms in spiraling research costs. To date, event-driven investors seem to have handled these challenges with a certain aplomb, but investment policymakers should remain vigilant to such risks.

The cliché that "trees do not grow to the sky" applies to firms as well as individual securities. No alternative investment firm approaches the gargantuan size of Blackstone, the Capital Group, Vanguard, or the conventional investment world's other leviathans, and no individual alternative investment vehicle is in imminent danger of exceeding $100 billion under management, as several conventional mutual funds already do. But the size of some alternative investment management firms and some individual funds is becoming large enough that it should cause some concern among investors, and (apart from the real estate and leveraged buyout behemoths) event-driven firms seem to be toward the front of those that are leading the charge. We have touched on issues of optimal fund size, and various trades' capacity to absorb capital will receive more attention shortly. But due diligence should be alive to the implications of size to the management of firms as well as the management of funds. I do not think that it is too much of an affront to the industry's *amour-propre* to suggest that the quality of management in the transactional finance sector—whether on the "buy-" or "sell-sides"—is not for the most part impressive. Whether talented investment managers will prove to be talented managers of enormous enterprises is something that investors in their funds might wish to ponder. Although fund sizes are shrinking rapidly as I write this, perhaps making this a concern that can be safely deferred to some other day, it is an issue that is not likely to disappear. In Chapter 7 I argued against broad diversification among merger arbitrageurs, but use of multiple event-driven managers is probably an advisable solution to this problem and those mentioned in the previous paragraph.

PART III

POSITION MANAGEMENT

CHAPTER 12

Investment Strategies in Practice

A s threatened in the Introduction and amply borne out in the event, the chapters in Part II addressed a disparate hodge-podge of investment approaches—three directional examples and two each involving cash flow and arbitrage trading techniques. Their time horizons varied from the ephemeral to the perpetual, market exposures were fully hedged, partially hedged, or naked; leverage was high, minimal, or none; and tactical choices and the ability to exercise real options were in some cases available to their managers and in others not. The examples, various as they were, were chosen to cover as wide a swathe of the range of investment management possibility as the limitations of my investment experience permit.

Many more illustrations could have been added to those included there, and omissions such as a discussion of directional private equity, Commodity Trading Advisors (although their activities were touched upon several times) or "macro" hedge funds might raise an eyebrow or two among those who were seeking from my discussions either comprehensiveness or even just due attention to the order of priorities. At the same time, some of the topics included in Part II were very peculiar to say the least—are many institutional investors really likely in practice to purchase oceangoing vessels solely in order to receive their charter income? Are they really much concerned about the trading activities of investment banks' structured products desks? Although it would be possible to iterate such examples nearly endlessly, the point in offering this eccentric collection of them was to generate interesting observations that apply to all investments, so an important selection criterion was variety, deliberately at the cost of representativeness. It is now time to begin to extract those observations.

Strategic Promiscuity

The analytic framework involving three investment strategies outlined in Chapter 1 was offered with the warning that those strategies are rarely encountered in their purity—that it is in fact unusual for an investment technique to contain no admixture of at least two of those three sources of return. On the one hand, most of the assets an investor might want to exploit bring more than one such source of return with them: many equities distribute cash flows in the form of dividends, the prices of bonds with fixed coupons are subject to directional change as a consequence of market-wide changes in interest rates, commodity futures involve positive or negative roll yield, and so on. On the other hand, the return-enhancing techniques that investors apply to these strategies may be the source of the admixture: as mentioned in Chapter 2, hedging incorporates aspects of arbitrage, there is an obvious cash flow element involved in leveraging a trade, tactical allocation among investment techniques involves directional considerations, and so on. Most investments that offer strategic purity, such as unleveraged hoarding of physical commodities, are in fact so far from the norm that academic discussions have often struggled to find ways to categorize them as investments at all.

The application of return enhancement techniques to investments needs no elucidation: investors quite naturally wish to maximize their returns and are seldom if ever much concerned with questions of strategic purity. But the hybridization that occurs in the investable assets themselves is a different matter. Here the analysis is often fraught, because these questions touch on some of the fundamental assumptions of economics.

Both academia and practitioners have long puzzled, for example, over the economic function of equity dividend payments.[1] The role of dividends in compensating investors for their indefinite capital commitments to private corporations is clear—there would otherwise be

---

1. Academic attention seems to have been drawn to this topic by Feldstein and Green (1983), but the issue is fundamental to the theory of corporate finance, as the founders of that theory recognized a generation earlier, in a paper produced shortly after their initial, groundbreaking work—see Miller and Modigliani (1961).

little incentive for them to maintain their capital commitments to them beyond the uncertain prospect of a gain on sale or employment with them. Investors such as the Mars or S. C. Johnson families would no doubt have long since lost patience. But analysts have had difficulty explaining why publicly traded corporations would imitate the practice of private entities, as their public listings allow investors a natural source of directional returns. The attractions of a stable base of shareholders are not so great as to justify the purchase of one so dearly, and when times became tough in 2008 and 2009, corporations that presumably still desired such a base showed little compunction about cutting their dividends. The contention surrounding backwardation and contango in futures markets has been similarly intractable. Although it dates back at least as far as a newspaper article written by Keynes in 1923, my earlier discussion of Metallgesellschaft indicates that it is not appreciably closer to resolution today. The directional element in the prices of fixed coupon bonds is a somewhat different matter. It is not at all clear to me why many investors would risk directional loss simply to achieve a fixed coupon returns, or for that matter, why investors with a desire for current income would be satisfied with an embedded capital gain to offset a portion of income forgone.

All of which may be enjoyably mysterious for those who relish such puzzles, but this is not the place to attempt to offer yet another proposed solution to any of these quandaries, which may not admit of one in any case. The point in raising them is to indicate that, while the hybrid nature of familiar investments does not appear to be truly inherent in them—plenty of publicly traded equities do not pay dividends (even those of issuers that are well past their high growth phases), futures may offer no roll yield at all, and it is quite possible to borrow and lend at floating rates—from whatever cause, they seem to be stubbornly resistant to analysis or to a change in investors' accustomed behavior. This raises a question about the validity of my distinction between investment strategies in the first place: if assets do not cooperate by falling cleanly into one category or another, how valuable can that distinction be?

However, the distinction is not intended to apply to assets but to investment techniques. The fact that assets appear to slop over the boundaries of the categories that the distinction delineates is not material, as the point of making the distinction is not to categorize assets. Investment techniques are something applied to assets: they are not the assets themselves. Thus an equity portfolio manager can pursue capital gains—directional returns—to the exclusion of all else, yet still receive cash flow returns. If we neglect arguments that their dividend payments merely detract from the potential of the underlying equities to generate directional returns, then whatever dividends such an investor receives are compensation. Receipt of them does not dilute the single-mindedness of the manager's pursuit of capital gains—it is an unintended consequence of its pursuit that contributes to the returns its activities generate without affecting the investment considerations that are embodied in its security selection techniques. Similarly, chefs may produce extra stock while preparing bouillabaisse, without detracting from the stock, the soup, or their status as chefs.

In other words, the term "strategy" applies to the activities of investors, not to their investments. A similar point can be made about investment "styles": they describe a security selection technique, not a security. There is nothing inherent in a security that makes it a "value": its value or lack thereof is an exogenous matter of how the market chooses to price it. I have already described how directional, cash flow, and arbitrage strategies can all be applied to the same investment, even simultaneously— by different managers or even by the same manager pursuing a multi-strategy approach. There is nothing to prevent equity managers from finding both "growth" and "value" in the same equity issue, and in fact some of the components of different equity "style indices" reliably overlap. Although I do not believe that Morningstar has ever lost sight of this, many consultants and others who regard its Style Box as virtually sacrosanct seem to slip into this error both easily and frequently.

Directional Investing

The feature that is common to all directional investing, regardless of the often hybrid nature of the instrument concerned, is price discovery through transactions that have been executed. Where a transaction in an instrument that is fungible into the one in question does not occur, pricing has a counterfactual (i.e., unfalsifiable) character and is derived from observation of transactions in other instruments that are as similar to the one that concerns us as we are able to identify. These may be based on estimates of cash flow generation, but they rely crucially on comparison with the value that the market has visibly placed on other, apparently similar cash flow streams, because the comparability that is relevant is a matter of the certainty and not just the size or timing of the cash flows.

Where no transaction in an analogous investment has occurred and no cash flow is observable, as may be the case for rare artworks, pricing is a matter of very rough guesswork, as discussed in Chapter 4. If there has been no recent transaction in a Vermeer, then recent experience with the paintings of Gerard Dou or Paulus Potter might provide some basis for an estimate, but definitely not for any degree of certainty. Where an asset is truly unique, pricing is impossible. For example, who can put a value on the Great Pyramid of Cheops? One might refer to the tourist revenues it is thought to attract, but how would those revenues be distinguished from the contributions that the Great Sphinx and the other pyramids make to tourism at the same site? Here again, it is difficult to determine what precisely constitutes an individual position in this asset. Despite the grumblings of cynics, there are plenty of real world examples of pricelessness, wherever no remotely comparable transaction is available for comparison.

Thus, pricing is always relative to some market metric, so β or something like it would appear to be inseparable from the concept of directionality. While the concept of β was introduced in connection with the analysis of equities, as I have suggested, I do not believe that it is stretching things too far to regard the interest rate sensitivity of fixed-income securities as a corresponding idea. The prices displayed by core real estate holdings and numerous other investments also exhibit similar explanatory relationships among themselves. Although investments with a high degree of idiosyncratic risk, such as opportunistic real estate or venture capital do not, this is readily explainable, and in any case it helps account for the difficulty in pricing them. Things become somewhat less clear in the case of commodities—while pricing within a commodity complex can clearly be specified in relative terms, it is not at all clear what, for example, sugar prices might relate to. It is this lack of a referent—in particular, their lack of a cash flow metric—that has caused some commentators to dispute whether commodities (or for that matter, currencies) can be regarded as investments at all; thus, as mentioned earlier, Black (1976). In particular, attempts to understand commodity pricing within the context of the Capital Asset Pricing Model seem to be doomed to failure: see Dusak (1973), Bodie and Rosansky (1980), and Erb and Harvey (2006). Why this should come as a surprise to anyone is rather surprising to me. I think that academic astonishment at this difficulty derives from a species of theoretical fundamentalism that accounts for why practitioners often pay such scant attention to finance theorists.

Yet commodities and currencies are clearly assets that may be purchased for directional gain, and to consign them to the realm of gambling as Black does is invidious. The Capital Asset Pricing Model derives an asset's expected return from the market risk premium and the asset's β, both of which are defined in terms of the Market Portfolio. Because the Market Portfolio is unobservable, both theoreticians and practitioners slip as unobtrusively as possible into treating β as though it referred to some broad equity market proxy. That is, the model, as it is applied, derives an equity's price behavior from the price behavior of equities. This has some explanatory value for individual equities but is an empty tautology when applied to equities as an asset category. Similarly, explaining corporate bond behavior in terms of Treasuries plus some form of credit-related risk adjustment does nothing to explain the source of Treasury prices. As Keynes amply demonstrated, the explanation for why interest is paid at all (rather than why one rate is higher than another) involves some amazing intellectual contortions. These stratagems are unavailable to commodity investors, because over long periods commodities display little correlation to each other, so the universe of commodities appears to be irrelevant to their pricing. The theory behind commodity futures' return drivers has been contentious at least since Keynes—one solution, to regard essentially all the determinants of commodity pricing that have been proposed from Keynes on as operating differentially at different times (Greer 2005), is little more than just a counsel of despair. Price relationships among currencies are at least as opaque. While explaining currency and commodity prices presents special challenges to theory, it seems to me that much discussion of the pricing of other assets merely sweeps not dissimilar challenges under the rug.

The Fama-French three-factor model (1993) is even more explicitly equity-centric, but multi-factor analysis can be applied to any asset category with useful explanatory results, provided that appropriate factors are isolated. Multi-factor models also have the extremely valuable characteristic that they can be applied to portfolios and used to model investment techniques, not just asset categories. This is not to say that I am an uncritical advocate of factor models, and although I think their use in modeling investment techniques can produce valuable analyses, claims that they can be used to replicate them are, to my mind, somewhat reckless (see Chapter 24). Factor models are highly vulnerable to the magnified error terms that result from assuming the normality of financial time series distributions, and they struggle with the optionality of many investment techniques. I repeatedly mention "naïve" approaches to quantitative investment management in these pages, and the hallmark of such approaches is the uncritical application of unmodified, off-the-shelf multi-factor models to the problems of investment. Many successful approaches to investment management have been destroyed by "insights" gathered in this way. Like all powerful tools, multi-factor analysis must be handled gingerly, and in particular its users must guard against falling prey to the illusion of science and accuracy that numerical results can so easily foster. But if we are to obtain any firm sense of what it is that all assets and investment techniques price relative to, it is likely that it will be through this and related analytical techniques. My prejudice is to proceed—but very cautiously.

All of which underlines the peculiarity of the emphasis that the marketing materials for most directional alternative investment vehicles place on their products' low β, and the implication they draw from this that the level and characteristics of the products' returns indicate a high contribution to their returns from α. This is arrant nonsense, as a simple thought experiment will demonstrate. Allow me to define an explanatory model for equity prices employing a novel single factor—call it "ζ" (zeta), because it is such an attractive symbol—and replace the β term in the Capital Asset Pricing model with it. The expected return of an asset or investment technique is then explained in terms of its ζ relative to the Market Portfolio plus the residual component of its returns, which I will follow convention in labeling "α." My research finds that high-frequency investing, for example, displays a ζ, of 0.27 and quite high α, while merger arbitrage exhibits a ζ of 0.80 and a correspondingly lower α.

If we lazily allow ourselves to fall into thinking "α good, correlation to Market Portfolio bad," then the choice between the two investment techniques is rather clear. But before grasping at the straw that ζ is a powerful new investment tool, it might be appropriate to ask how it is defined. It is the number of letters that the name of the investment technique shares in common with the term "Market Portfolio" (double-counting permitted), relative to the fifteen letters in that term. The point of this digression is that β, if defined relative to a broad equity market indicator, is not much more appropriate as an explanatory factor for most alternative investments' returns than ζ. Of course, alleged α is high where the purported explanatory factor is not appropriate to the investment under consideration in the first place. While measures of alternative investments' correlation to long-only asset benchmarks are of considerable relevance to the investment allocation process, as line items in a correlation matrix, they are *definitely not* appropriate measures of the value-added or any other supposedly compelling characteristic of a fund. Investment policymakers should pay careful heed to the following:

> A low beta is a double-edged sword, because it also implies that we have not yet identified the return drivers of hedge funds. In this situation, how

can we trust the alpha? Remember that a low beta often refers to equity and interest rate sensitivities, but there are numerous other types of risk that one can accept, *e.g.*, liquidity risk, spread risk and commodity risk. The risk premiums associated with taking these risks would appear as alpha, while in fact they are just beta. Hence, the risk is high that many hedge funds are packaging some sort of beta and selling it at alpha prices. (Lhabitant 2004, 274)

While my pedantic nature bridles at the use of "β" here, divorced from its original context as the sole factor in the Capital Asset Pricing Model, Lhabitant's point is clear and extremely valuable. The returns from any asset or any investment technique that might be applied to it must be understood in terms of their factor exposures. In fact, the α of directional strategies is quite rare and in all cases truly a residual factor— *never* the primary driver of a directional strategy's returns. The problem, as Lhabitant suggests, lies in identifying those primary drivers.

Cash Flow Strategies

It is natural to regard alternative investments that generate cash flow as being "alternative" to conventional fixed income, but investment policy should proceed down this road very carefully. A more specific analogy with mortgage-backed instruments is a bit more accurate: issues related to multiple credit exposures within a single vehicle and the convexity of the instrument are present in most cash flow–generating alternative investments. But this does not capture all the nuances, because even the alternative investment category that is most comparable to conventional fixed income—equity interest in core real estate—has features that are completely alien to conventional fixed income. For example, it carries factor loadings such as positive correlation to inflation and may embed arbitrage characteristics in its financing structure. Most alternative sources of cash flow are even more distinctively different from the conventional source, notably in the unevenness of their cash generation.

Chapters 15 and 17 will discuss the investment role of liquidity in greater detail, but clearly, an important reason to invest in cash flow strategies is to obtain periodic injections of cash into the portfolio. Apart from the spending needs of the institution that are supported by distributions from the portfolio's returns, such liquidity can play an important function in the management of portfolios, since it can be used to fund periodic rebalancing. From a planning perspective, cash flows that are intermittent and/or arrive in unpredictable amounts fulfill this role less satisfactorily than those that are predictable as to timing and size. They may not arrive when rebalancing is appropriate, and when they do arrive they may be too little or too great for the institution's purposes. Compared to fixed income, most alternative cash flow strategies are less suitable for this function because of the irregularity of their returns.

Because they are unhelpful for most budgeting purposes and cannot offer the safe haven of Treasuries, the employment of most alternative investments that exploit cash flow strategies stands or falls on their superior total return characteristics over the lives of the investments. Even long-term lenders and fund investment in core real estate are likely to suffer from the J-curve effect before their relatively steady distributions begin to flow through to investors. So their use in portfolios that are sensitive to the timing of liquidity inflows requires budgeting around an estimate of the duration of the period between the start of drawdowns and the beginning of distributions. The only alternative investments truly comparable to conventional fixed income from a stable distribution perspective are those offered by some short-term direct lenders. But they cannot offer the safe haven and immediate liquidity of the capital invested in them that are available from Treasuries, although they may provide an interesting substitute for some credit exposures that also lack that safe-haven characteristic.

While a liquidity shortfall is potentially a very severe problem for institutional investors, an embarrassment of riches is not necessarily a good thing, either. A large distribution from an investment may arrive when there is a lack of attractive opportunities to reinvest it, particularly if the institution desires to maintain a stable level of allocation to the investment technique that was the source of that distribution. This desire may not conveniently coincide with the offering period for an appropriate fund that is available for a new commitment, so the distribution may reduce exposure when there is no readily available means to recapture it. This circumstance is especially disconcerting in the early years of a vintage diversification program, when distributions may make the goal of attaining some desired level of exposure seem to be an all but Sisyphean task.

There has been a certain amount of discussion in academic circles (for example, Cvitanić et al. 2004) of the advisability of substituting even equity-oriented hedge funds, including market-neutral and merger arbitrage vehicles, for most if not all of an institution's conventional fixed-income allocation. This in the context of having already proposed the replacement of all of the conventional equity allocation with hedge funds. All the more reason, then, to imagine that hedge funds that invest primarily or exclusively in fixed-income securities might serve as surrogates for holdings in conventional fixed income. This is extraordinarily dangerous advice. It is driven by

- ❑ failure to recognize that total return may not be the sole portfolio function of an allocation to conventional fixed income;
- ❑ use of a single-factor model that explicitly relies on β relative to an equity index as its risk measure; and
- ❑ lack of attention to the higher moments of the hedge funds' return distributions.

Regarding the first point in particular, the failure involves neglect of the income-generating and safe-haven aspects of a fixed-income allocation, as well as the practical point that the only periodic liquidity of hedge funds also restricts the liquidity of the holding. The advice is a typical product of what I have referred to as naïve quantitative analysis, and relies for even superficial plausibility on a failure to adjust reported standard deviations for the hedge funds proposed. It is more than a little disturbing that this sort of "analysis" can find its way into refereed journals, and does nothing to enhance the reputations of those who write such things in the eyes of those who would actually have real-world accountability for the consequences if they were sufficiently imprudent to follow such advice.

Arbitrage Strategies

The generally very stable returns generated by arbitrage strategies make them appropriate surrogates for a portion of a total return-oriented fixed-income allocation, provided that inflows of liquidity, access to capital on short notice, and the safe haven of Treasury exposure are not required. In other words, as with alternative cash flow strategies, the employment of arbitrage strategies stands or falls on their superior total return characteristics, as they cannot perform the other portfolio functions that conventional fixed-income investments can offer.

I have stressed that there is an arbitrage element to all hedging activity. If the hedge involves a short position, as most do, then the notional leverage entailed by short positions comes into play. This is exaggerated in arbitrage, not only because the demand to hedge positions as completely and as perfectly as possible is usually greater than for most other alternative investment techniques that employ hedges, but also because of the degree of the normal variety of leverage that is usually necessary to make arbitrage trades worth the trouble of pursuing at all. This accounts for the strongly negative skewness displayed by the return distributions of all arbitrage techniques of which I am aware. The return distribution of any trade that employs a hedge will exhibit significant non-linearity, but it is most marked for arbitrage trades because the returns from them derive entirely from the structure and "perfection" of the hedge itself.

One might expect that arbitrages would offer returns that are uncorrelated with those of virtually all other assets and investment techniques—but that is in principle rather than in fact. The factor loadings of arbitrage strategies are difficult to isolate through normal methods because most of them are the result of conditional changes in volatility and correlation statistics. Because these are essentially the core of the trade—they account for the creation of the trading opportunity in the first place, the nature and accuracy of the variable hedge ratios that most of these trades employ, and, if the trade fails, the sharp reversion to directionality that the components of its structure exhibit—factor modeling is virtually no help in uncovering the risks in arbitrage. Conditional changes of this kind are not susceptible to linear analyses. As I will discuss in the next chapter, analyses that model the non-linearity of arbitrage and other alternative investments' returns in terms of embedded options are, I believe, a more fruitful avenue for exploring these issues, but they are necessarily outside the scope of linear multi-factor models. Not the least of their advantages is that such analyses offer an intuitively clear economic interpretation; for all that they are, in most cases, unable to offer a means of pricing those embedded options.

Just as the Capital Asset Pricing Model is challenged by commodities and currencies, it cannot deal comfortably with arbitrage, which also does not qualify as a capital asset according to the definition that is relevant to that model. In particular, in the case of arbitrage the appropriate proxy to use for the Market Portfolio is the risk-free rate (or something very similar to it), so a bit of algebraic manipulation reduces the expected return on arbitrage to the risk-free rate plus the trade's specific risks, which is hardly very informative. Further, the linear form of the Model's equations cannot capture the non-linear nature of arbitrage in particular and alternative investments in general. Efforts (such as the proposals of Harvey and Siddique 2000) to decompose specific risk exposures along statistical lines that can embrace their non-linear characteristics, for instance in terms of co-kurtosis and co-skewness, strike me as somewhat ad hoc and unconvincing. And they are not noticeably more helpful in assigning a specific value to expected return—which is, after all, the function of the Capital Asset Pricing Model—than an analogy with options is in assigning a value to those options. Perhaps most importantly, they lack intuitive explanatory power: thinking in terms of the price that they might be willing to pay for this or that level of co-skewness is not a familiar concern to most investors. Most investors' preferences for levels of co-kurtosis are similarly unarticulated. Neither concept is particularly obvious to intuition.

These difficulties are significant for investment policymakers, because arbitrage trades are definitely not exogenous return-generators like gambling, no more than directional trades in commodities or currencies are, but familiar linear analytic methodologies tend to treat arbitrages almost as though they were. This may give rise to even more dangerous illusions than the idea that alternative investments are an appropriate replacement for a conventional fixed-income allocation. The peculiarities of arbitrage strategies' risk exposures encourage the leveraged profligacy that ended so disastrously for Long-Term Capital Management. Flying in the face of both the evidence and common sense, academic commentators who are uncritically wedded to the familiar analytic methodologies were quick to come to the defense of the managers of that fund. Yet it was clear to any dispassionate observer that its leverage was irresponsible, insupportable, and if not criminally then certainly morally negligent. The idea of morality in finance probably seems stuffy and old-fashioned to many people of my generation, but it is to be hoped that the experience of 2007 to 2009 will have changed attitudes in this regard.

Interaction among the Investment Strategies

Given the very restricted number of investment strategies that my analytic schema offers, the ways in which they can affect each other to make possible the wild profusion of investment techniques merits some discussion. Their application to different types of assets naturally accounts for a respectable portion of this enormous variety, but that is a rather trivial source of different return outcomes that requires no further investigation. Of greater interest is the way that these strategies can affect one another through different applications of them to a single type of asset. For purposes of illustration, in what follows I will restrict my discussion to publicly traded equities, which probably provide the richest vein to mine in this connection.

The overwhelming bulk of equity holders are directional investors, and while they are rarely so single-minded as to consider the dividends that they receive to be beneath their dignity, most tend to regard them as a peripheral matter that has limited influence on their ability to meet their targeted levels of return. **Figure 12.1** indicates why: the 20.34 percent incremental return due to dividends achieved over the period shown there amounted to 1.63 percent per annum compounded. While doubtless this contribution to their returns was very welcome, given the return requirements that equity investors should appropriately place upon their investment exposures, capturing dividend return was unlikely in most cases to be their overriding consideration. As discussed above, there is even considerable debate as to why issuers of equity choose to pay dividends at all.

However, even where equity investors make it quite explicit that the cash flows they receive from dividends are not of primary importance to them as contributors to their targeted returns, dividend yield may play an important role in their security selection, as an indicator of relative value. That is, the cash flows offered by equities may be less important to these investors as a source of return than as a valuation metric that influences their investment decision-making. On the other hand, for some equity investors, dividend yield provides a significant component of their returns, even though price appreciation remains their primary

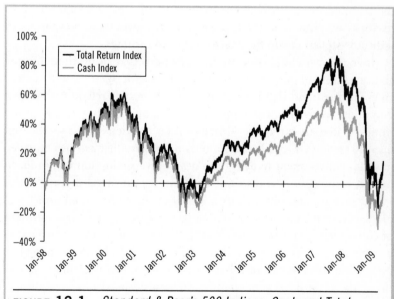

FIGURE 12.1 *Standard & Poor's 500 Indices: Cash and Total Return*

investment goal and the most important contributor to their returns. These investors may actively seek dividend yield as an element of their security selection discipline, regarding it as a valuable source of returns and downside protection rather than just treating it as a useful measure of relative value. Cash flows received from their investments may enter into equity investors' calculations in many ways that are subservient to, but nevertheless significant for, their primarily directional strategies.

Dividend yields may figure prominently among the supporting metrics used in reaching tactical allocation decisions, because of their ready comparability with yields on fixed-income instruments. The common practice of American and Asian issuers, which generally seek to maintain absolute dividend levels—in contrast to the European practice of seeking to maintain dividend payout ratios—increases the usefulness of dividend yields as indicators of relative values. By divorcing them to some extent from a strong relationship with the level of earnings, the American and Asian practice lends them stability over time and increases the reliability of estimates of future dividend streams. While earnings yields frequently play a similar role in tactical allocation as indicators of equity valuations relative to those of fixed-income instruments, they are far more vulnerable to estimation risk than yields on dividends that issuers determine in the American and Asian fashion. The variability of the absolute value of dividends that adjust to achieve a (more or less) fixed payout ratio, as in the European model, gives them no value as an indicator separate from their relationship to earnings.

Investors who hold concentrated positions that afford them limited ability to shift among equity exposures, for tax or other reasons such as an endowment gift that they cannot sell, are heavily reliant on the cash flows they receive from those positions to supply them with any utility from the investment at all. Although such positions can be—and frequently are—used as collateral to obtain liquidity that can be employed in seeking investment returns from other, diversifying sources, in many cases it is the cash flow distributions from the collateral that make this stratagem economically attractive, as they can be used to offset some or all of the cost of the borrowing. Alternative approaches to the management of concentrated positions, such as the use of swaps or other over-the-counter derivative structures, depend for their pricing on arbitrage-like calculations on the part of the investment bank that is counterparty to the trade. Cash flows generated by the concentrated positions may be equally important to the economics of these approaches, as they may be used to cover the premia that are inevitably embedded in the cost of such a hedge.

Arbitrage enters into directional equity investors' calculations most obviously when they embark upon a hedging program, but there is also an important respect in which all conventional, long-only active management of equities or fixed-income positions can be regarded as a form of arbitrage. As I mentioned earlier, overweighting a sector or individual security relative to a benchmark employed in a directional strategy is, in effect, a decision to carry a short position relative to some other portion of that benchmark. Such relationships are made quite explicit if a portfolio is submitted to multi-factor analysis, where negative factor loadings reveal that a long position is nevertheless an effective short relative to the factor that is underweighted by comparison to the benchmark.

Directional hedges may be protective or, if an equity is carried long against a short position in a relevant index or even against a commodity derivative, designed to isolate the equity's directional exposure relative to that factor or benchmark. Used in this way, arbitrage calculations allow investors to customize exposures—in effect, isolating those portions of the underlying equity's return stream that are of particular value to them—although at a cost of some risk if the arbitrage relationship breaks down. Arbitrages whose convergence is dictated by cash flow rather than directional considerations may also be constructed between common and preferred equities, between common equity and options on that equity or between options on the same equity that have different strikes or different dates of expiry.

The enormous creativity that has been applied to the equity universe would allow me to go on indefinitely with a catalog of this sort, but I think this is sufficient to make the point that three strategies provide ample flexibility in application, even to just a single asset class. Although equities may offer more extensive opportunities of this sort than most other asset categories, the quantity of trade structures that can be applied to fixed income and commodities should not be underestimated, simply because it is less familiar to most investors. And this is just within the sphere of publicly traded assets: as we have already seen in passing, and will shortly see in more detail, private market assets offer numerous opportunities to apply these strategies as well.

CHAPTER 13

Optionality

These days, the marketing materials for virtually every alternative investment vehicle lay claim to an option-like asymmetric pattern of returns, which marketers, at least, seem to regard as providing a sharp contrast with the return patterns that are generated by long-only investment techniques. In Chapter 11, I commented on the tendency to mistake the binary character of some trades' return patterns for optionality, but in many cases, alleged optionality is often erroneously credited to the fund's research efforts. There is much to say about optionality in this chapter, but these purported instances of optionality in which it is not in fact in play require demolition.

This form of alleged optionality is really nothing more than the increased confidence in their positions that research-based security selection can foster in investment managers. That confidence is equally available to any investor who is willing to expend the time and resources that are necessary to obtain it. While high fees certainly enhance their ability to carry out intensive research, in fact many alternative investment managers who base their security selection on such analysis previously applied precisely the same disciplines and essentially the same resources to long-only portfolios. If there is any basis to the use of analysis as a guide to investing—and the type of analysis involved is irrelevant, provided that it offers the manager increased confidence—then this form of so-called optionality is in fact nearly universal among investors. Having reasons for choosing one investment over another is a distinguishing feature of an investment technique or firm only in relation to "investors" who select positions entirely at random. Mistaking the confidence (or even the investment success) engendered by the firm's research efforts for optionality is a perversion of terminology.

I stress this point because optionality is a key concept in alternative investments, and the terminological waters of the alternative investment arena are muddy enough already. Optionality is a slippery concept, but that does not excuse the misuse of it. Difficulty in pinning down the precise meaning of a concept should in fact encourage careful circumspection in its use. The reason for this slipperiness is that the term embodies an equivocation between two related but nevertheless distinct properties. One is the power to determine outcomes through exercising a right of choice between different courses of action that are expected to lead to those outcomes. The other is an asymmetric return profile, often related to a trade's factor sensitivity to the volatility of the assets traded, in which positive and negative outcomes are incommensurate with each other. The first is related to real options, and the latter is a characteristic that is familiar from traded options that can be structured (sometimes unwittingly) into certain trades.

Real options are a matter of active control over investments subsequent to entering into them—including, of course, the options available to tactical allocators. Real options are *ex post* in the sense that the trade is structured in a way that leaves open the possibility to exercise them or not after the investor has entered the trade. Structured asymmetric return is a matter of *ex ante* trade design, where no such choice is available to the investor after it has embarked on the trade and "exercise" is effected by the market rather than through a decision by the portfolio manager. To a large extent, the difference between them is one of buying versus selling (writing) options: with real options, the investor purchases one or more rights to decide on matters that may affect its ultimate returns, while with trades that have optionality structured into them, the investor enjoys the premium for having granted that right to "the market."

Diversification and Concentration

When a friend of mine began his medical internship, his initial assignment was to a pathology department. The head of the unit felt it would be helpful to explain the medical hierarchy to him, which he outlined as follows: "General practitioners know nothing but do everything, specialists and surgeons know something but do less, and pathologists know everything, but they are too late." Because investment can only be pursued in an environment of uncertainty—everything about an opportunity can ultimately be known, but only "too late"—investors cannot know everything. So, like doctors, they face the choice between knowing nothing and doing everything or knowing something and doing less. That is, they can diversify broadly, perhaps on a completely passive basis that requires no familiarity with the individual components of their portfolio at all, or they can concentrate their investments in a few heavily researched and closely monitored positions. The investment techniques discussed in Part II range from the highly concentrated to the highly diversified. Diversification is (or should be) at its greatest where research offers the least value added—a high-frequency directional trader that engaged in fewer than (at a guess) two hundred more or less simultaneous trades would almost certainly offer unattractively volatile returns, and the fund probably would not be long for this world. On the other hand, we repeatedly encountered the constraint that research-intensity imposes on some managers' ability to diversify.

Finance theory is abundantly clear about which of the alternatives between concentration and diversification it prefers; in its view, concentrated positions entail large amounts of specific risk, which it regards as simply irrational not to diversify away. While theoreticians with a foot in the world of actual investments will allow that there are practical limitations to the extent of the diversification that can be achieved without transaction costs overwhelming its risk reduction benefits,[1] they are adamant that specific risk must always be reduced to the extent that is practically possible. If the objection is raised that there are investments that it is difficult if not impossible for a finite portfolio to diversify (for example, what portfolio size would be required to prevent 100 percent ownership of the Itaipu dam from constituting concentrated, exposure-distorting positions?), this would probably be regarded as an argument against allocating to them, or in favor of leveraging them in order to make diversifying investments elsewhere. Although theory recognizes that this asset, too, is a constituent of the Market Portfolio, the high degree of specific risk that, as a practical matter, full ownership of it would entail would probably be regarded as a conclusive argument against investment in it on theoretical grounds. It is, after all, noticeable that projects of that magnitude are not generally private sector initiatives.

---

1. See Statman (1987, 354*f*), whose analysis is built upon that of Elton and Gruber (1977), which took no account of transaction costs. Statman's results are illustrated in Figure 20.2.

Yet many investors willingly, even eagerly, expose themselves to concentrated positions, and while they recognize the riskiness of this approach, they are not usually accused of irrationality. Warren Buffett and numerous others whose opinions can hardly be rejected out of hand have espoused the virtues of concentration, not *despite* the specific risk that it entails but to a large extent *because* of it.[2] Risk implies the potential for return, and these investors reject finance theory's implied (but, to my knowledge, never conclusively demonstrated) contention that the returns to specific risk are necessarily incommensurate with it.[3]

These investors would be the first to admit that not just any old specific risk is worth taking. Containing the risk of concentrated positions involves two crucial features:

❑ Exhaustive research before entering the trade, encompassing to the extent possible (and in the time permitted) every aspect of the investment and every identifiable influence on its expected returns. This is not just required at entry but implies a continuing commitment to a degree of monitoring of the investment and its prospects that amounts to ongoing participation in its management, or at least its non-executive oversight; and not unrelated,

❑ Exercising control over the asset. While complete control—that is, 100 percent ownership of an unleveraged vehicle—may not be possible or in many cases even remotely desirable, significant influence over the management of the asset certainly is.

Most such investors would regard their research as their primary form of risk control, and the costs and time required to produce research of the quality and exhaustiveness of detail that lends confidence to their investment decisions militate against broad diversification in the first place. The continued burden of monitoring the investment in ways

---

2. In other cases, concentration may be less a matter of rational investment policy: Swensen (2009) notes that "Of the fifteen largest foundations in the United States, two (the Lilly Endowment and the Starr Foundation) hold nearly all assets in a single stock, another (the Robert Wood Johnson Foundation) holds well over half of assets in a single stock, and yet another (the Annie E. Casey Foundation) holds over a quarter of assets in a singe stock." He goes on to note, "Unfortunately, many single-stock foundations ultimately experience the costs of holding radically undiversified portfolios" (60).

3. Of course, there are strong dissenters—see, for example, Moskowitz and Vissing-Jørgensen (2002).

that are consistent with the research carried out prior to entry reinforces this constraint on the diversity of holdings. Concentrated investment is a matter of selecting the eggs and the basket extremely carefully, and "watching them like a hawk."

Real Options

Control can in many respects be regarded as a backstop for, rather than a necessary requirement of, risk management, but in other cases, particularly where diversity is low, it can be crucially important to investors from both risk and return perspectives. While few investment committees can or would want to exercise day-to-day management control over an operating asset, the amount of information available to active, involved owners gives monitoring of their investments depth, nuance, and a degree of foreknowledge that is completely alien to those accustomed only to the publicly available information that security issuers provide to non-insiders. This is all the more true since the passage of Regulation Full Disclosure. In the case of mezzanine lending, for example, we saw how the ownership of virtual equity confers rights to information that are unavailable even to higher-ranking, first lien lenders in their borrowers' capital structure, and how virtual equity provides indirect influence over management. While access to such information and the advance warning of adverse developments that it can provide is valuable in itself, influence over strategy, senior management appointments, major investment and financing decisions, and various other matters, all informed by that knowledge, are far more significant advantages of control.

The ability to dictate or at least to have strong influence, perhaps to the extent of effective veto power, over management decisions, can be considered a real option. Investment theory, grounded as it is in the consideration of investment in assets over which the investor has no effective influence, tends to neglect these options. At bottom, this accounts for theory's inability to find a place in portfolios for concentration and the resulting specific risk. Options have value, and where control can be acquired without paying an excessive premium for those options, the position should be regarded from an investment policy perspective as having a value in excess of its mark-to-market valuation—a concept that is completely alien to Modern Portfolio Theory but that is quite familiar to corporate finance professionals. However, institutions should not deceive themselves regarding the value of control: it is first and foremost founded upon the knowledge gathered in due diligence and continued monitoring of the investment. Without thorough understanding of the investment, control is at best worthless and is potentially a dangerous source of temptation or false comfort that can lead investors astray. The first Viscount St. Albans may or may not have been correct in equating knowledge with power, but power by no means implies the possession of the appropriate knowledge or an understanding of what to do with it, as our political leaders regularly and convincingly demonstrate. Thorough understanding of the investment is crucial to determining whether in fact the premium paid was appropriate in the first place, and it is this understanding of the investment that allows real options, if the institution succeeds in obtaining them, to have any material value to the institution.

Pursuit of opportunities involving real options, whether derived from concentrated investments or tactical allocation, requires a high level and quality of staffing, a willingness to expend significant resources on researching investment opportunities (the vast majority of which will be rejected rather than finding their way into the portfolio), and not merely a tolerance for creativity but active encouragement of it. Use of agents to purchase and manage concentrated positions may relieve some of this burden, but only by displacing it with the burden of performing comparably thorough due diligence on and continued monitoring of the agent. In most cases this is likely to offer less transparency than direct involvement with the underlying investment. Institutions with the resources and stomach for either of these burdens—which of necessity require a highly contrarian approach and closely involved, well informed trustees—should be able to buy real options at attractive prices. This is a potentially compelling proposition, which the received thinking about the necessity for reducing specific risk through diversification neglects. Use of agents to allocate tactically among liquid securities exposures is less controversial, although similarly unsupported by theory. Monitoring of their activities deserves similar thoroughness, although less effort, because the ability of such agents to exploit their role to the detriment of the institution is considerably less than it is with concentrated private market investments.

This theoretical neglect is not merely an oversight: it is grounded in the fundamental assumption of Modern Portfolio Theory that markets are efficient, which in turn assumes—without really examining the assumption—an essentially passive role on the part of the investor. While the assumption of market efficiency is arguable (yet another near-theological debate that I am desperate to avoid, recalling the question of how many angels can fit on the head of a pin), it is more or less true and an occasionally valuable working assumption with regard to liquid markets in equities, most actively traded commodities for which futures are available and some bonds—under "normal" conditions (see Chapter 14). That is, assuming no inside information, no influence over management, and no crisis of confidence in the markets. It is certainly not true of control investing, where such information is readily and legally available to investors and empowers them to have a significant say over the disposition of their investment. Unless the would-be control investor is spectacularly foolish—and there have admittedly been more than a few examples of this, including many who clearly should have known better—a passive approach to its concentrated private market investments is the last thing on its mind.

The number of such decisions an investor has—the number of real options available to it—varies with the investment. Those available to a manager of private equity investments are so numerous as to defy analysis, while in direct lending or commercial real estate the number, although still large, may be somewhat more manageable. Take timberland as providing an example on the relatively less complex end of this spectrum. A passive investor in a timber-owning Master Limited Partnership or other commingled vehicle takes what the General Partner who controls the real options chooses to offer—for example, maximizing near-term returns at a cost to future returns if the manager so decides. A direct investor in timberland can, at the extreme, choose which individual trees to harvest. But more realistically, it can advise its Timber Investment Management Organization on its preferences in choosing between harvesting young trees now for sale as lower per-ton value pulp or postponing revenue capture to some later date, in order to cut mature lumber and capture both the value of its increased tonnage due to growth as well as its significantly higher value *per* ton. Modern Portfolio Theory neglects options of this sort, and thus fails to assign values to them.

But real options do not have just an inherent value: in a portfolio context, they can provide investment policymakers with an enormously powerful tactical asset allocation tool quite apart from how the options may help maximize return. Taking the straightforward example of the logging/no logging option offered by control over timber assets, institutions can choose to exercise their option to harvest (or not) in the knowledge of the performance of their fixed-income portfolio, distributions received from their venture capital investments, equity market returns, and so on—as well as their current and anticipated liability position. That is, the harvest decision need not (and should not) be made in isolation from developments elsewhere both in the portfolio and in the institution's obligations. The trees will continue to grow if their current value is not realized ("storage on the stump," as it is known in the trade), increasing tonnage and, depending on their age, moving into new stages of maturity with higher inherent values per ton. Although prices for forest commodities are variable and there are substantial increases in the per ton value of trees at two maturity inflection points, biologically induced rates of increase in the tonnage owned are otherwise fairly constant and provide a basis for forecasting, since, as a base case, any tree can be sold as low-value pulp once it is past about seven years of age. Note that timber management is not without its share of idiosyncratic complexities, and management decisions are not so simple as this caricatured discussion makes them sound. In particular, this example neglects all the other real options that timberland offers its owner, relating to exploitation of softwood versus hardwood, the seasonal ability to exploit certain properties, and so forth. But from just this stripped-down example, it begins to become clear why institutional interest in timberland has grown rapidly in the last decade or so.

While there is purportedly such a thing as "real options theory," I am unaware of many practically applicable results from it, and I believe this it is of greater heuristic than theoretical value. There is by no means a scientific way of assigning a value to the options discussed here. Academic discussion of the topic revels in complex simulation techniques, many of which can be specified in considerable detail using impressive-looking formulae. But the formulae are concepts without percepts—essentially, empty theology—if no empirical means of assigning probabilities or returns to the points on a probability tree are available. In my view, a theory of how to value options that cannot specify what means are to be used in determining the values of the variables that its formulae manipulate is of limited practical value. Further, given the problem of non-normality as it affects option models, even assuming that there were sound means of estimating those variables, the results of applying the formulae to them would have to be taken with very substantial grains of salt—particularly remembering that error terms compound rapidly in such simulations.

However, the heuristic value of real option theory should not be discounted. For example, Berk et al. (2004) offer a model for understanding the value of real options to the manager of an early-stage, research-and-development-based venture that provides what I suspect would be useful guidance to the General Partner funding such a project. The insight into managerial decision processes that it and similar studies offer should not be ignored. But when it comes to finding guidance on concrete, yes-or-no responses at actual decision points, I have yet to encounter an example that has demonstrated its usefulness in practice by offering a convincing price for the option(s) involved. Consequently, real option theory is no help to us in coming to an assessment of the value of control. However, it certainly suggests that there is such a value, in sharp contrast to Modern Portfolio Theory, to which such value is completely invisible.

Of course, it is questionable whether we needed theory to inform us of this. Everyone who has ever had the misfortune to be backed into a corner is abundantly aware that options have a value, for all that it may be difficult if not practically impossible to calculate what it is in any particular circumstance. However, there are ways of coming up with what are at best very rough estimates of the probabilities and potential returns at the nearby nodes of a probability tree, and rough as they are, they should receive some attention from investment policymakers. The exercise is, at the very least, a useful management discipline, and it can facilitate communication with trustees, provided that they are not lulled into the completely spurious impression that estimates founded upon one or two iterations of a Monte Carlo scenario simulation or similar statistical tool have any useful degree of accuracy.

At the end of the day, productive implementation of a concentration strategy and trustees' confidence in the venture or other private market investment must be founded on the quality of personnel, the available resources, and institutional commitment. But an exercise in investigating the nearby nodes of a probability tree may help reinforce the quality of personnel and facilitate consultation with trustees. Most institutions are no doubt troubled by the thought of concentration, yet many of them are rushing into private equity investments even as I write (although rather more gingerly than two years ago). There is a cognitive disconnect involved here, into which I have no desire to delve further. However, it might shed light on the assumptions behind these institutions' decision-making if they ask themselves what it is that they believe that their agents possess that the institutions themselves feel they lack. As they are retaining these agents at no small cost, this strikes me as a perfectly reasonable question to ask.

Embedded Optionality

Options in one form or another are so pervasive in the realm of alternative investments that a hedge fund manager of my acquaintance goes so far as to claim that the pursuit of low-cost options constitutes the core of his investment technique. On other occasions, he describes his practice as seeking to create bonds with equity warrants, which is, in the final analysis, a very similar claim. His investment technique embraces both modestly and opportunistically long- or short-biased long/short and event-driven techniques, indicating a wide range of different types of exposures, so his comment is worth pursuing a little further. He is not speaking of real options—although his investing mandate clearly allows him a certain amount of tactical flexibility, his fund is fairly disciplined by the standards of such vehicles and makes only restricted use of that flexibility—but of trade structures that provide asymmetric patterns of return.

My acquaintance was not talking about embedded short positions in put options, which are used to model the negative skewness of many financial time series. But identifying these in various trading structures has become something of a minor industry: a review of this literature can be found in Agarwal and Naik (2004). Analogies to short positions in put options have been used to model everything from corporate credits (Fridson 1994, 83, building upon the risk management work of Bookstaber and Jacob 1986) to convenience yields on commodity futures (see Kocagil 2004). Agarwal and Naik find short put structures relative to indices of their underlying instruments in modeling distressed, relative value, convertible arbitrage, and short-bias investment techniques. Mitchell and Pulvino (2001), find the same embedded options in merger arbitrage, although they missed the opportunity to demonstrate remarkable foresight by noting that this trade also has a short put-like relationship to widening credit spreads. This form of modeling using options is distinct from the treatment of corporate bonds with indentures that incorporate call features as involving a short position in a call on the bond itself. This is a feature that bond investors analyze using the concept of convexity, which is a special case of γ, one of the option "Greeks."

The point of modeling in this way is to indicate the tail-risk sensitivity of the investment technique under consideration to factors such as general market volatility or an issuer's creditworthiness (note, however, that the Fridson/Bookstaber analysis of corporate credits does not concern tail risk exclusively: it is meant to capture the risk profile of corporate bonds in all conditions). As most financial time series are negatively skewed, isolating such factor exposures is clearly very important, because these risks constitute the most damaging ones to which employment of an investment technique might expose its investors. Unfortunately, the linear regression methodology that underlies multi-factor analysis is inadequate to the task of identifying such risks, for all that they are the ones that probably most concern investment policymakers. Multi-factor models invariably consign these risks to the unanalyzable residuum, where they can easily be mistaken for α (see Chapter 21). Although it is essentially an empirical, trial-and-error process, analyzing these risks in terms of short put option positions is a valuable tool for identifying them. It is also intuitively pleasing. As we saw in Chapter 7, the completion of merger transactions is vulnerable to extremes of general market volatility: analysis of merger arbitrage in terms of a short position in a derivative, such as an out-of-the-money put option on the Russell 1000 Index, that only exercises only when downside volatility is sufficiently exaggerated, explains both the factor sensitivity and the reason it is not isolable through multi-factor analysis. Although Lhabitant (2004, 207f) demonstrates that non-linear regression can produce similar results, he recognizes that they offer little intuitive explanatory power.

Embedded short-put positions can be identified in many alternative investment techniques—they model the steamrollers in front of which nickels may be gathered. But in some cases, a short straddle may provide a better analogy. In many high-frequency arbitrages, excessive volatility either upward or downward can interfere with a trader's ability to structure such trades. The straddle reflects the more-or-less narrow window of volatility (depending on the individual trade) that is productive for these techniques' return-seeking.

Clearly, my acquaintance does not seek to structure such options, although his fund inevitably has them embedded in it. Rather, those he wishes to craft are long rather than short positions, although it may be put options to which he wishes to have long exposure, and writing options may figure in certain of his trades. Analysis of investment techniques in these terms is of even longer pedigree, dating to Merton (1981, 365) and Henriksson and Merton (1981), with their suggestion that market-timing can be modeled using a long position in an index and long put options against the index. A static analysis of conventional, long-only portfolio management, which was not concerned with the real options that tactical allocation involves, was offered by Glosten and Jagannathan (1994). This model works only where the option is bivalent, and consequently is rather crude: it is unlikely that many of the more complex options available to portfolio managers are amenable to such treatment.

However, the model has power, and real estate, for example, can be analyzed in similar terms. It has long been observed that in its characteristics and return patterns, real estate seems to fall somewhere between conventional fixed income and equity, and arguably real estate is, in effect, a convertible bond, and thus embeds options. Convertible bonds are equity-like when the underlying equity is trading close to conversion price or where the prospect of bankruptcy may turn the convertible into an equity-like claim. Otherwise these instruments are bond-like. Real estate that is fully let on long-term leases to good quality credits is bond-like, but if demand in the relevant region increases significantly, boosting the value of the building, then the "convertible" is in-the-money and appreciates. If, on the contrary, the quality of the lessors deteriorates and vacancies begin to rise, the investment takes on a more equity-like character similar to that of a bond that is approaching default, and the value of the "convertible" is determined by the residual value of the building. Ownership of a vacant building or a hotel (since hotels operate on very short-term leases) is essentially pure equity exposure. Farmland, given that leases are generally for a single growing season, also has a predominantly equity-like character, while I am inclined to think that timberland, with its variety of real options, is more similar to private equity and not amenable to this sort of analysis. Public infrastructure investments can probably be regarded as fairly purely bond-like, while private infrastructure, such as pipelines, can be regarded as having embedded exposure to the equity of its users.

It should probably not come as a surprise, however, that analyses along these lines, employing conventional options, generally have more explanatory power for non-directional strategies rather than directional ones: see Agarwal and Naik (2000, 7). But complexity and options are hardly strangers to each other, and so-called exotic options can also be employed in such analyses, for example, by Fung and Hsieh (2001). These authors recommend the use of a lookback straddle (a trade structure consisting of long positions in put options that exercise at the maximum price of the underlying over some period plus call options that exercise at the minimum price) to model trend-following investment techniques. Not surprisingly, lookback options are expensive, explaining the need for significant volatility—that is, a substantial spread between the maximum or minimum price of the underlying and its average price—for such trading techniques to generate attractive returns.

An essentially very similar analysis in terms of an option straddle can be applied to high-frequency traders, although it requires some further elucidation. An individual trader acting in a single security can create a rough asymmetry of returns by applying even quite simple asymmetrical trading rules—for example, the trader's classic standby, "ride the gains and cut the losses." The more frenetically the trader is long, then short, then flat, then short, then long, then flat…and so forth, the greater the resemblance of such a technique to an option straddle on the instrument being traded. Multiply one instrument by two hundred or more, and assume that the exposures in each of them are uncoordinated—that is, that the aggregate portfolio may have a minor but random and always only momentary long- or short-bias, but is generally approximately flat—and the optionality produced by such a fund relative to general market indices becomes quite clear. At its root are the real options that each of the individual traders possesses over each of the instruments in their trading books. Individually these produce directional trades, but because the trading disciplines applied to them produce asymmetric returns, when spread over numerous instruments managed by numerous traders operating independently, the aggregate produces an asymmetrical return structure that can be modeled as long exposure to the relevant indices' volatility without a directional component. The traders' real options are continuously exercised, but as with many real options, each exercise generates a new set of options, so that, in its entirety, the trading book of the fund has continuous optionality. The cost of the position is the cost of putting trading infrastructure in place (including compensating the traders—whose compensation is itself option-like) rather than an option premium. The straddle is continuous rather than continuously re-created and thus does not incur an option premium with each option undertaken (which would be prohibitively expensive, given the number of options this investment technique constantly has at its disposal). This is an unexpected example of the sort of low-cost option to which my acquaintance referred.

As useful as these analyses are, it is important to recall that a model is not identical with the thing that it models. While various investment techniques offer clear analogies to various option structures, they are not in fact those structures. Employment of the concept of optionality is an extremely valuable tool in attempting to isolate the risks of various investment techniques, but it is a heuristic: the analogue should not be mistaken for the real thing. As we will see in the discussion of hedge fund replication in Chapter 24, equivocation between the two can have unfortunate consequences.

Optionality and Diversification

Where optionality is a matter of trade design rather than the possession of real options, investment managers will continue to seek diversification to the extent to which their capacity to discover and monitor trades allows.

This applies equally to managers who structure series of real options, too, but their ability to do so is sharply constrained because real options are demanding of an ever-burgeoning set of new options analyses for each option that has been exercised, to the point that management of more than a few initial option situations quickly becomes an intolerable burden. The history of corporate conglomeration strongly suggests that the capacity to manage even a moderately diverse portfolio of real options is beyond the abilities of most management teams. Short positions in options that are built *ex ante* into trade structure of course require the continued monitoring that is appropriate to any position, but because these options are not exercisable by the manager, but inherent to the exposure taken on, it is not the case that one damned thing leads inexorably to another in the same way that it does for long positions in real options. Optionality that is structured into the trade places no practical constraint on the degree to which positions can be diversified, although in real-world circumstances it may be more or less demanding to identify and monitor.

The exceptions are event-driven investing and merger arbitrage, an exceptionalism that explains my earlier emphasis on the research-intensity of these investing techniques. Given the binary nature of their trades, these investors' options do in effect exercise. However, these managers lack the ability to choose the exercise—they are in many ways analogous to option writers, and the trading conditions are delivered by the market, even where activism allows managers some influence over them—so the imperative to diversify is high. Consequently, such managers are voracious consumers of research in the pursuit of opportunities to replace those that have spent themselves, as well as to protect themselves against the risks entailed by writing such options. The Altria/Philip Morris International example in Figure 11.3 indicates fairly clearly that there is little benefit, and the risk of a high degree of unwanted subsequent exposure to market β, from retaining such positions once the "event" has occurred. While Chapter 11 stressed that β exposure is unavoidable for event-driven investment techniques, there is no benefit to these managers in retaining that exposure when the excess return from exploitation of an "event" has been successfully captured. These managers can tolerate such exposure only in pursuit of that excess return.

This ability of managers to structure trades that exhibit optionality without recourse to real options causes me to prefer my account of the distinction between strategic and tactical allocation to that of Anson (2004), which was touched upon in Chapter 2. There is nothing in principle to prevent creation of passive vehicles that nevertheless exhibit optionality—in fact, the ability to do so in at least some cases underlies the results obtained by Duarte et al. (2007), which were discussed in Chapter 10. The technique that Duarte et al. used to construct representative trading situations employs simple algorithms to identify situations in which optionality can be exploited. While Anson's analysis is highly suggestive (and I will return to it once again in Part IV), I believe that regarding optionality as an exclusive characteristic of α-generation, and using this alleged feature to distinguish between strategic and tactical allocation, neglects some substantial evidence to the contrary. That is, I believe that the burden of proof is on Anson when he contends that optionality is unique to α-generating trades, and it seems to me that Duarte et al. provide convincing counter-examples.

This discussion has put the pursuit of diversity among portfolios exhibiting optionality in a pragmatic context. I would be the last to devalue practical considerations, and in this case I believe that they are compelling. However, it is of interest to examine whether there are any theoretical grounds, extending beyond practical considerations, that suggest that diversification for *ex post* real options is less inherently desirable than for *ex ante* structured ones, despite any extra difficulty that is entailed in obtaining and managing it.

It is difficult to see what they might be. Real options offer their owners diversifiable risks, and for all that information management, decision coordination and a myriad of other pragmatic obstacles militate against exploiting this opportunity to the extent that investment policy might prefer, where it can be attained, theory dictates that diversification should be implemented. That is, the difficulty of achieving diversification does not argue against the desirability of doing so: the problem with conglomeration is not with the theory but with its implementation. Investment policy related to private assets and other investment techniques that involve real options is unavoidably faced with a decision on the amount of such risk that it is willing to tolerate relative to the efforts it is willing to take to reduce it.

Optionality and "Alternativeness"

The Introduction groped unsuccessfully after a feature that distinguishes alternative from conventional investment techniques, and some might think that, with the concept of optionality, we have belatedly stumbled upon one. Granted, there are some alternative investment techniques that seem to exhibit little or none of it, but it is prevalent enough that, if not precisely a defining feature, might optionality at least be considered a fairly reliable touchstone for "alternativeness"—if not a *sine qua non*, then at least a fairly reliable canary in the mine of investment policy?

To hear hedge fund marketers talk, it would seem so. Discussion of asymmetric returns is all the rage in these circles, and while frequently what is being referred to is nothing other than confidence in their firms' proprietary research, as discussed and dismissed above, the strong implication is that optionality is something that benighted conventional investors sorely lack. This is nonsense. Option overlay techniques, such as writing covered calls or purchasing protective puts, are familiar to virtually every investor who is in touch with a broker, and may be offered to institutions as part of a conventional investment program or as a separately managed overlay discipline applied to existing, conventionally long-only accounts. Overlay products of this type are sufficiently "mainstream" that they are offered to private client customers as well. While most institutions with an interest in employing structured products use investment banks to customize them, off-the-shelf solutions of this kind are widely available to all investors, and wealthy private clients can obtain customization, too. And while "portable α" receives most attention in alternative investment circles, there is nothing inherently "alternative" about it: there is no reason that conventionally derived α cannot be ported onto another conventional investment. Nor are conventional investors without real options: any holder of an Individual Retirement Account or certain annuities is quite aware of the optionality that is defined by the Internal Revenue Service and/or by the annuity contract. After all, hedge fund managers did not invent shareholder activism, and long-only activist managers are equally keen to ensure that the asymmetry of transactions that they wish to encourage falls their, rather than the undesired, way. While conventional investments do not generally incorporate options on volatility the way that other techniques may—volatility in the underlying is in most cases enjoyed or suffered by conventional vehicles in linear, symmetric fashion—in some cases *ex ante* asymmetry of returns can be structured into conventional trades. And structured products that embed optionality in quite complex ways have long been known: the 7 percent Confederate States cotton loan of 1863 gave holders the right to payment of principal in currency or bales of cotton, and if they took physical delivery, they had a choice of four ports.

As already indicated, these observations are by no means new. Use of options to analyze market-timing as practiced by conventional long-only managers dates back nearly thirty years, and numerous similar analyses of other aspects of investments have followed. But because of the difficulty of assimilating various alternative investment techniques to analytic methods that rely on mean variance, much of the subsequent literature that has pursued this hint has concentrated on hedge funds in particular (as opposed to alternative investments in general). This is unfortunate, and relates most notably to the application of factor-based Value at Risk models to the analysis of portfolios, as they cannot easily incorporate the analysis of a trade's optionality. While there are numerous challenges to such an analysis—not least a problem in valuing these options, similar to what we already encountered with reference to real options—at the very least the idea has heuristic power, and I will revisit it in Part IV. Its power consists in its ability to deal, at least conceptually, with the non-linear behavior of the returns derived from many alternative investment techniques, which is difficult for linear calculations employing correlation—such as those employed in factor or Value at Risk modeling—to make much sense of.

CHAPTER 14

Trade Capacity

I have mentioned bounded or finite trades at several points in my discussions. These are trades that have a prescribed potential to produce returns, which is generally known in advance of a manager's decision to enter into them. This naturally implies a contrast with unbounded trades. With the exception of buy-and-indefinitely-hold approaches to assets that do not mature, such as perpetual bonds, equities, real estate, and various other non-depleting assets that can be held over unlimited periods for their cash flows, all apparently unbounded trades do in fact have a return boundary in one form or another. What I have referred to as trades with bounded returns are those, such as arbitrages, that are inherently bounded by their structure. But limitations on the aggregate returns that all interested market participants can extract from a trade may also be imposed by market liquidity, by considerations of value that ensure that "trees do not grow to the sky" and by various practicalities connected with the commercial and operational aspects of the business of portfolio management. Each of these points were touched upon here or there in Part II, but they merit separate consideration because they have significant implications for investment decision-making, which investment policymakers neglect to their cost. Investment programs that bump up against any of these constraints can be expected to produce inferior returns.

Only cash flow trades can be truly unbounded, and then only where the asset involved is perpetual: a maturity date of necessity imposes a boundary, as the asset will be redeemed at a specific value on that date.

In some cases, as for bonds, this value is predetermined, but that is not essential: the trade is bounded even if the terminal value of the asset is discovered only in the process of negotiating its liquidation. This group of unbounded assets includes listed equity. There are, for example, investors whose tax basis in Exxon Mobil is a fraction of a dollar, courtesy of inheritance from a relative whose firm was acquired by John D. Rockefeller, Sr., back in the glory days of Standard Oil. Although the valuation of those shares has varied dramatically in the intervening period, the thinking of a buy-and-hold investor is not much affected by those changes—and given the tax basis of the shares, any taxable holder of them has for many years now perforce been a buy-and-hold investor. It is only if an investor seeks a directional gain from a cash flow investment position that might otherwise have been held in perpetuity that these trades become bounded.

The capacity of an individual fund or of all the funds that pursue a particular trading technique to absorb capital must be among investment policymakers' primary concerns when considering a proposal to invest in a new trading technique. Unfortunately, this is not always an easy matter to determine. Fluctuations in the liquidity of the underlying assets; the availability (or otherwise) of leverage; the amount of capital competing for the same sources of return; the ability of new issuance, new construction, or other influences on supply to react promptly to increased demand; and a wide range of other factors make any such determination difficult.

Financial engineering, with its ability to create virtual assets essentially on demand, clouds the picture even further, although it cannot in fact increase supply, only smooth its transfer provided that counterparty relationships remain sound. That latter provision is important, as the experience of 2008 demonstrated: financial engineers withdraw from the marketplace when the underlying becomes scarce and the ability to replicate the underlying synthetically is impaired. I am aware, for instance, of long-term over-the-counter equity hedges that were cancelled because conditions in the securities lending market interfered with the investment bank's ability to offset its risk as counterparty to such transactions—this despite the fact that, according to Bridgewater Associates (2009), the supply of equity loans actually increased in 2008 (3).

Inherently Bounded Trades

It is less challenging to estimate what capacity limitations for trades with clear return boundaries might be than it is for the other sorts of trades mentioned above, but it is still an inexact science. For example, the aggregate of underlying returns available to the community of risk arbitrageurs can be roughly estimated as the product of the total volume of acquisition activity and the average premium that acquirers paid (weighted for transaction size). However, leaving aside the issue that the premium may actually be somewhat difficult to determine, the opportunity available to merger arbitrageurs is not equivalent to that product. This is because the trades can be enhanced through the use of leverage and "trading around" arbitrage positions over the course of a merger transaction. But in a world where unlimited leverage is not available and the opportunities to trade profitably "around" an arbitrage are themselves bounded, the dollar value of the premiums paid clearly provides a rough indicator of the size of the opportunity available to merger arbitrageurs.

Arbitrageurs cannot capture 100 percent of the acquisition premium—barring insider trading they are virtually certain to forgo at least part of the initial price convergence that occurs when a deal is announced. And as we saw in Chapters 1 and 7, arbitrage trades always leave a portion of the premium "on the table" when the transaction closes. I would estimate that these factors cause arbitrageurs to pass up on roughly 12 percentage points of announced acquisition premia. On the other hand, "trading around" positions may recapture all of that. So if we estimate that the average premium on the $865.7 billion in U.S. acquisitions completed in 2008 (FactSet Mergerstat, December 2009, https://www.mergerstat.com/newsite/free_reports_m_and_a_activity.asp) was 17 percent, and assume that a meager (by the standards of recent years) 10 percent of those acquisitions were private equity-related and thus inaccessible to arbitrageurs, the underlying trade was worth about $132.5 billion. Assuming leverage of 4:1 (80 percent debt to capital), the total opportunity to employ investors' capital in U.S. merger arbitrage in this particularly inauspicious year amounted to only about $26.5 billion.

Readers need not trouble themselves to dispute any of these assumptions: they are obviously off-the-cuff, and I would not attempt to defend them. In the case of any particular arbitrage situation, *ex ante* estimates can be somewhat more precise. For example, it was known at the time of its announcement that the Sirius|XM Satellite transaction discussed in Chapter 7 would face significant regulatory hurdles. As the news flow concerning regulatory approval of the transaction was bound to create volatility, merger aficionados were aware that there were likely to be numerous opportunities to "trade around" the position, and their estimates of the returns from such trading could clearly be raised. Once Anheuser-Busch had accepted Inbev's sweetened offer (discussed in the same chapter), the probability that the transaction would proceed to completion was high, suggesting much less volatility and thus fewer trading opportunities. However, less volatility, greater certainty of completion, and the market liquidity that the two companies (and the combined entity if the merger succeeded) could be expected to enjoy, supported the risk of leveraging such a trade more highly, and arbitrageurs are likely to have leveraged their exposure to Anheuser-Busch/Inbev by more than 4:1. Again, knowledge of the specific conditions that surround the transaction is needed to lend concreteness to any estimate a risk arbitrageur might wish to make of its potential return.

In other cases, estimates will inevitably be even more approximate. The available capacity in distressed debt markets is probably even more variable than that in merger markets. The opportunity in buy-and-hold fixed-income techniques is inherently bounded by a combination of coupon levels and the extent to which bonds trade at a discount to par, and must be adjusted for the risk of default. Estimates of the global market opportunity for exploiting such a technique are unlikely to be forthcoming, although it is a simple matter to create a fairly precise estimate in the case of any individual trading proposal—and the same is true with respect to any other instrument that has a fixed maturity. However, some such as those employing mortgages, where the convexity introduced by the possibility of pre-payment must be estimated, may involve important additional complexities that make any such estimates dependent on interest rate forecasts and a variety of other factors that are best analyzed using option-analogues, as discussed in the previous chapter.

Trades Bounded by Market Liquidity

The aggregate returns from many directional strategies that an investor might wish to pursue are bounded by the liquidity available in the underlying instrument. For example, directional strategies applied to municipal bonds soon reach significant constraints on their activity that are imposed by that market's comparative paucity of trading opportunities. This lack of liquidity may seem odd, given that the par value of such instruments outstanding exceeded $2.6 trillion at the end of 2008, and that new issuance by states and municipalities was some $391.2 billion over the course of the same year (which experienced a comparatively weak new issuance calendar) (Securities Industry and Financial Markets Association, December 2009, http://www.sifma.org/uploadedFiles/Research/Statistics/SIFMA_USBondMarketOutstanding .pdf and http://www.sifma.org/uploadedFiles/Research/Statistics/

SIFMA_USMunicipalIssuance_GORevenue.pdf). But market size alone is no guarantee of market liquidity. If it were, then commercial real estate would be among the most liquid asset categories of all: one source estimates an "investable" market at the end of 2008 of $21.7 trillion worldwide, of which $6.9 trillion in North America (see Nantamanasikarn (2008)). Investors in municipal securities—both corporate buyers and private individuals—are notoriously even more strongly inclined toward buy-and-hold approaches to investment in those instruments than bond investors generally are inclined to hold their positions to maturity. So, at a guess, there is probably less than $90 billion in municipal obligations actually available for active secondary market trading over the course of a year. This may seem to be a reasonable if not ample level of liquidity, but it is definitely not, as it is spread across some 50,000 issuers and heaven knows how many individual issues.

It is clear, then, that the ability to pursue active trading strategies in municipal bonds is fairly tightly constrained and, consequently, so is the nature of the trades in them that a manager can pursue. Thus, for instance, systematic exploitation of relative value opportunities among individual issuers' bonds is restricted to a very small handful of comparatively liquid instruments—generally those issued by the largest and most profligate states. The ability to extend the trade to those issuers' other instruments is entirely dependent on the accident of those other instruments' availability in dealers' inventories. This explains an otherwise puzzling gap in the market for investment products: on the face of it, hedge funds specializing solely in municipal bonds would seem to be a commercially very attractive proposition to be able to offer to taxable investors. While there are a few such funds, the liquidity of the market in which they operate ensures that they remain limited in number and that they must close to new investment before they can become large. Municipal bonds are exploited by hedge funds, usually on an opportunistic basis, but making a sustainable living from managing a specialized municipal bond hedge fund would be very challenging.

Although futures markets have limitless liquidity in theory, where natural buyers are absent, liquidity is available only from market makers—at a very substantial price. Thus, the opportunities for Commodity Trading Advisors (CTAs) to exploit their trading strategies in comparatively inactive futures such as those available on orange juice or lumber can never be numerous or very sizable. The disappearance of natural buyers has occasionally caused exchanges to cancel trading in some contracts, since futures markets that rely solely on speculators cannot function properly. Similar capacity restrictions affect less liquid options. Although in principle someone will write an option for every would-be purchaser, where hedgers are not present in the market for the instrument sought, market makers' willingness to do so at prices that still leave upside potential for the would-be purchaser's trade is usually quite limited.

Chapters 15 and 17 will discuss situations where liquidity disappears more or less completely from purportedly liquid markets. The experience of 2007 to 2009 serves as a reminder that this can happen in any market, but it is most likely to occur where liquidity even in "normal" market conditions is already in limited supply. When investment policymakers are confronted with an investment proposal that involves participation in such markets, careful study of the market's liquidity and the trading technique's dependence on liquidity for its success (which is most pronounced in the case of directional trades but is an equal if not even more important consideration for arbitrages) is very much in order. An additional consideration is the manager's self-discipline, as the amount of funds it raises will almost certainly affect its ability to generate returns from trades that are pursued in markets that cannot accommodate a major influx of trading interest. Given narrow limits on the assets the manager ought to raise for deployment in such an investment product before closing it to additional new investment, due diligence should also attend to the manager's ability to earn a living off of a limited amount of billable assets under management.

Trades Bounded by Valuation

The aggregate returns that can be generated by directional strategies are subject to constraints that are imposed by valuation. This is the reason that "trees do not grow to the sky." During the speculative frenzy of an asset bubble, it may be difficult to discern what the limits to valuation might be, and all too easy to imagine that there are none. But history has yet to throw up a counter-example to the claim that these limits always find a way to impose themselves, generally with calamitous results for those who have convinced themselves that "this time it is different." In fact, it is a sound rule of thumb that, if that phrase or some variant of it is heard too often, then investors are in the midst of a bubble. The contrast between bounded and putatively unbounded trades is nevertheless significant: valuations are notoriously flexible (giving a diagnostic rule of thumb some value), while bond maturities (for example) or the value of merger opportunities in a given year decidedly are not.

Where market capitalization is very large, where liquidity is much more readily available than in, say, the municipal bond market, and where the range of valuations can be considerably more extreme, making such an estimate is challenging. For example, the average $16.2 trillion in U.S. equities outstanding turned over 8¾ times in 2008, offering some $141 trillion in trading opportunities (World Federation of Exchanges, December 2009, http://www.world-exchanges.org/statistics/ytd-monthly). In this context, it is tempting to imagine that the sky really is the limit and that there are no arbitrary boundaries imposed on an investor's ability to engage in trading activity. However, it is noticeable that the U.S. equity capitalization figure was 66 percent higher only seven months before the December 31, 2008, reading of $11.7 trillion, indicating how widely valuations can change: de-listings for various reasons and share buy-backs contributed to that decline, but only very slightly, and there were virtually no new issues during the period. If there were any investment managers who saw only blue sky ahead when U.S. equity market capitalization was at its peak for the year in May 2008, they were rudely and peremptorily disabused. Valuation capped the opportunities available to long-only directional trading although liquidity remained ample throughout the period. The discussion of short-bias techniques in Chapter 5 indicated that the opportunities available to a directional short book are usually even more limited.

Specifying a valuation boundary is a two-sided problem, as not only do valuation levels change dramatically over time, but the factors on which they are based—whatever it is that in fact is being valued, such as earnings, book value, eyeballs (if anyone still recalls that figment of the Technology Bubble) or what have you—are also quite changeable. In the case of the 2008 decline in U.S. equity prices, it is especially difficult to disentangle the two influences on price levels, since both valuations and what was being valued were changing very rapidly, both in directions that caused prices to decline. It is the general consensus among market participants that security valuations are mean-reverting, given enough time, and as suggested above, there is ample evidence to support this view. But whatever it is that is being valued by valuation multiples is not mean-reverting: that is, corporate earnings and other denominators of value do not fluctuate around some average value. Consequently, even under a strong assumption regarding the mean-reverting character of valuation *levels*, boundaries imposed upon directional trades by valuation are moving targets, and in periods when the *basis* of valuation is highly uncertain, the otherwise comfortable assumption that levels of valuation will revert to a mean is not very helpful.

Further, it is not clear that the prices on investments other than equities do revert so consistently to a mean valuation. While demand destruction, new supply, recycling, and substitution have historically prevented commodity prices from attaining escape velocity and thus defying gravity, it is certainly conceivable that this will not always be the case. Take a rare metal such as ruthenium, for example. Supply at any price has quite restricted elasticity, the fact that it is generally consumed militates against recycling, and while some applications (fountain pen nibs, for instance) are hardly essential and demand from that source could easily be destroyed by persistently high prices, there are other applications for which ruthenium is essentially irreplaceable. It is not at all beyond the bounds of possibility that growing demand for an essential application could drive the price of ruthenium permanently to extraordinary levels, although successive waves of demand destruction for non-essential applications would prevent any such price rise from following an uninterrupted hyperbolic ascent. This situation is not unprecedented: consider Timbuktu, where, until the advent of modern transportation, ordinary salt was worth more *per* unit of weight than gold, a situation which underwrote the commercial viability of trans-Saharan trade for centuries.

However, maturities quite clearly impose a limit on the valuations of instruments that possess them. While non-perpetual fixed-income instruments may trade above their par values over extended periods, redemption at par will ultimately force their reversion to face value. This raises the question whether market interest rates themselves are mean-reverting, which seems likely, at least on an inflation-adjusted basis—but that is a matter for an entirely different discussion.

Boundaries imposed by valuation raise an interesting puzzle: do they affect market-neutral hedge funds? In periods when the entire market is perceived as over-valued, the manager would be expected to hold the least over-valued shares in its long book, and its short book, whether it is short the index or individual equities, would be expected to be more overvalued than its long book. Here the arbitrage-like character of market-neutral techniques is perhaps at its clearest, suggesting that the trade is *not* bounded by valuation.

Boundaries Imposed
by Practical Considerations

As we have seen, constraints on a trade are not imposed solely by the instrument or the markets that exploit it, but also by the management capacity of the funds that are doing the exploiting. While the time and staff required for analysis and ongoing monitoring of trades provide the most important of these constraints, for investment vehicles that do not invest in public markets, attracting opportunities to trade may be an even greater challenge. For this reason, I have stressed repeatedly in Part II that investment policymakers should analyze this or that investment technique at least partially as though it were a private equity investment in an operating business. Issues that ought to be of concern to due diligence may go beyond simply the firm's capacity to manage a diversified portfolio of the investments under consideration, to include questions regarding its ability to discover or attract trades and its ability to capture opportunities where it must compete for them outside of the continuous auction process offered by public markets. Misanthropic loners can still succeed as traders in organized public markets, but beyond the bounds of organized markets, networks of contacts are an inescapable factor in an investment manager's success. Nor is this characteristic limited to investors in private equity or debt: a manager of timber or farm acreage that lacks an extensive network of the relevant contacts will struggle to get its clients' funds invested, and may encounter difficulty in liquidating those investments as well.

For most investment vehicles, there is an inherent tension between the demand for diversification and management capacity. Algorithmic traders and naïve quantitative managers may not feel this tension very strongly—if at all—since automation can be made to handle any volume of data flow. Renaissance Technologies, a well-known quantitatively driven hedge fund manager, is said to measure its daily data feeds in multiple terabytes, and although it only employs a couple of traders, it has been known to account for as much as 14 percent of NASDAQ volume. But for managers whose security selection process cannot be automated, the tension is ever-present and can often be acute. Nor do the challenges to firms that derive from the limits to their management capacity end there. Different trades demand different levels of ongoing monitoring, so that in many cases the burden of monitoring existing investments imposes a constraint on the manager's ability to identify and research new ones that is almost as great as the constraints that trade discovery imposes on itself.

To illustrate this point with an extreme contrast, consider the difference between the obligations that fall upon managers of passive equity products compared with managers of early stage venture capital. For the passive fund manager, trade discovery is handled by the index provider, trade execution can be automated, and ongoing monitoring of position sizes in the context of fund in- and outflows is about all that is required. Even assuming that the manager seeks to replicate the index exactly, running a portfolio of two thousand positions or more is not an insurmountable challenge, provided that the appropriate information technology infrastructure is in place. In fact, managing the portfolio with fewer positions and the aid of an optimization program is in some respects considerably more challenging than simply replicating the benchmark, as it will inevitably introduce situations in which the manager must actually exercise some judgment. Further, where no judgment is involved, compensation arrangements rarely need to be generous. For a venture capitalist, identifying and negotiating purchases is time-consuming, costly, and uncertain, while monitoring the trade after execution is almost equally demanding. Regardless of the venture firm's size, no venture capital manager could dream of carrying even a representative fraction of the positions that its passive counterpart can comfortably manage. Nor would investors benefit if a venture manager were to make the attempt, even if the cost savings were passed on in the form of lower fees: passive venture capital is a fiduciary oxymoron.

Differences in manageable capacity do not relate solely to numbers of positions, but to the dollar amount of assets a manager can accept as well. At the end of 2008 the Standard & Poor's 500 Index had a market capitalization on the order of $8 trillion, so a manager benchmarking to that index faced few meaningful constraints on the size of the fund it could offer. If it replicated the index precisely, position sizes for such a fund ranged from 0.005 percent to 5 percent of its assets under management. One such fund—the iShares S&P 500 Index Exchange Traded Fund—managed investor assets of about $17 billion, so its largest position amounted to some $850 million. In contrast, the National Venture Capital Association reports that at the end of 2008 the average U.S. venture firm had $223.7 million under management and the average individual fund had $104.4 million (see *2009 Venture Capital Yearbook*, March 2009, http://www.nvca.org/index.php?option=com_content& view=article&id=137:online-bookstore&catid=48:membership&Item id=216, 9). Although there are a handful of comparatively large venture funds, that is an average for all venture capital, not just early-stage funds, which tend to be smaller than their later-stage peers. Thus just one of the five hundred positions in what is by no means the largest passive equity vehicle was more than eight times the total assets under management of the average venture capital fund. According to Wade (2009b), the median size of venture rounds is $7 million, and total fund exposure to a single investment is unlikely to be as much as three times that. Again, investors would by no means benefit if it were significantly higher.

There are numerous gradations between these extremes. Where trade discovery can be automated, as in algorithmic trading or "black box" quantitative investment approaches, it imposes few constraints on the numbers or sizes of positions a manager may hold. For high-frequency techniques pursued by numerous human traders operating more or less independently of each other, the significant operating constraint on firm or fund size is the availability of good traders. Managers of conventional fixed-income portfolios who are heavily reliant on credit analysis for their trade discovery are "splitters" who are limited as to the number of positions they can hold by their analytic capacity, but other approaches to fixed-income instruments are not so constrained—on a recent count the PIMCO Total Return Fund sported no less than 20,931 positions. However, the structure of the PIMCO fund illustrates another constraint on trade capacity: the number of positions it holds derives less from a desire for diversity (the bulk of its positions on that occasion were Federal National Mortgage Association [Fannie Mae] mortgage pass-throughs) than from the illiquidity of the fixed-income markets in which it operates relative to the enormous quantity of assets under its management. Reflecting the substantially greater liquidity of equity markets, American Funds' Growth Fund of America, an equity vehicle comparable in size to the PIMCO Total Return Fund, typically carries around three hundred positions.

Apart from simple greed, the egregiousness of the fees that most alternative investment vehicles charge is partly a function of the high cost of their trade discovery processes, and partly to compensate their managers for the limitations on asset-gathering that their trades may impose upon them. Firms that do not suffer from the latter constraint will typically face higher costs from the former: development and continuous improvement of sophisticated proprietary software do not come cheap, and neither do good traders. The infrastructure needed to support products such as the two gargantuan mutual funds mentioned above may be at least as costly, but it can be spread over the fees generated by assets under management that dwarf those of alternative investment managers—the assets controlled by both funds' management companies ($790 billion and $839 billion, respectively at the end of 2008) are an order of magnitude greater than the assets managed by the largest alternative investment management firm or even within entire alternative investment categories such as venture capital or event-driven investing. Blackstone, Carlyle Group, and Man Group, which are probably the largest managers of alternative investments, had a comparatively paltry $91, $86, and $60 billion under management, respectively, at the end of 2008, although some real estate managers are of comparable size, and the alternative investment activities of some investment banks (notably Goldman Sachs) are larger. Nevertheless, the degree of concentration among hedge fund managers is comparable to that of mutual fund managers. For both types of firm, Reilly et al. (2009) estimate that 2 percent of managers account for two-thirds of fund assets under management (8). Roughly the same is likely to be true of other alternative investment categories.

While I am no apologist for the fees charged by alternative investment managers, it is unreasonable to expect them to be comparable to those charged by conventional active managers, let alone index funds. The widely followed rule of thumb that recommends against investment in hedge funds with less than $100 million under management is at least partially justified by the perception that, bearing in mind the volatility of the asset base on which fees are levied, continuing revenues (i.e., neglecting incentive fees) of much less than $2 million militates against a firm's stability. Investors who pursue opportunities with "emerging" managers— which for simplicity can be regarded, at least in the hedge fund environment, as those with less than $100 million under management—do so in the knowledge that they are taking risk with the investment management firm, not just with the investments that the firm manages. They hope to be compensated for this risk with superior performance, but will often hedge their additional risk by demanding fee concessions. Not surprisingly, investors attend to this rule of thumb less rigorously when considering investment firms with less volatile asset bases—whether that reduced volatility is inherent in the trade or simply an artifact of asset values that are estimated rather than marked-to-market—and are correspondingly less likely to be able to extract concessions from them.

This resistance to discounting is most noticeable where the investment firm is active outside of organized public markets. Lack of a mark-to-market regime fosters stability in the asset base, but more importantly, the operating costs of such firms are almost always quite high. While some of the costs of trade discovery and price negotiation are usually passed on to Limited Partners, not all of them can be. Annual revenues of $2 million on a $100 million fund go only so far in covering the costs of legal and forensic accounting advice, finders' fees, travel, background checks, and so forth, in addition to salaries and facilities costs. If an attempted transaction does not reach completion, it may be that only a portion of those sunk costs can be recovered from the fund's investors. Hence the repeated emphasis in Part II on the importance of deal-flow for investors in these investment categories: if an investment management firm is challenged to become invested, it is equally challenged to earn revenue, and its viability as a going concern is questionable. If such a firm expires, its investors are left with illiquid minority positions in whatever assets the fund managed to obtain. These will not be disposed of easily.

A large number of other factors may also impose constraints on a firm's capacity. The extent to which its decision-making is centralized—including decision-making related to management of the firm rather than just management of the investments in its care—the depth and experience of its analytic, trading and/or IT staff, the diversity or otherwise of its product offerings, the intensity of its marketing efforts, and so on can all influence its ability to manage incremental capital. These matters are often treated as a formality on due diligence questionnaires, but they are of existential significance to the firm and therefore should be of great importance to the firm's potential customers.

Further, there seem to be fairly clear developmental stages for investment firms, causing their managerial and operational challenges to metamorphose as they grow into larger-size categories. Firms that are unable to negotiate these step-changes successfully are likely to become unstable, and their investment performance can be expected to suffer as a consequence. The fact that it is a cliché does not make the observation that investors are in partnership with their investment managers any less true. It is essential to the success of the relationship that the manager's operation be a sound business, not just a generator of sound investment results. Investment managers may amass impressive track records as investors, but few of them have lengthy track records as managers of entrepreneurial firms, let alone more established and therefore necessarily more bureaucratic ones. On the other hand, a business can be sound without being a gold mine: investors have every right to expect that the bulk of the fees that they pay be employed in support of the firm's operations rather than to furnish excessively comfortable lifestyles to its principals.

Closing and Re-Opening

Funds close to new investment for a variety of reasons. Private equity and real estate vehicles do so in order to concentrate on investment rather than marketing, and to avoid the conflicts of interest that can arise from simultaneously running more than one fund that is not fully committed. A desire to escape the burdens of marketing is frequently a reason for hedge funds to close as well: many are managed by intensely focused people who do not relish the distractions of client contact. Neither situation requires a great deal of comment. However, funds also close because they believe that they have reached capacity, and this is a more interesting phenomenon.

For obvious reasons, most managers are reluctant to close their funds: a decision to forgo growth is difficult for any business. Their operating budgets are supported by the annual fees they take in, so closing the fund restricts the potential for additional investment in the firm. While capital appreciation should continue to contribute to asset growth, natural attrition—as investors allocate away from the firm or fail to reinvest its distributions back into it—will gradually erode the firm's asset base if flows from new investors are not permitted to take their place. And managers are aware that closing is a nuisance for their customers, insofar as they deign to acknowledge investors' concerns at all. It is an indication of how little those concerns weigh on the behavior of many managers that some hedge funds close, re-open, and then close again frequently and repeatedly. The option of "soft" closing (i.e., accepting new investment only from existing relationships) is a compromise, but if closing is an appropriate response to the capacity-constrained situation in which a fund finds itself, "soft" closing is rarely a satisfactory solution, as it may fail to halt net flows into the fund.

Managers examine the same factors that lead to capacity constraints that were discussed above in reaching the decision to close, but personal preferences, such as an aversion to riding herd over a large staff or a dislike of making investor presentations, may be as important an influence on their decisions as investment or commercial considerations. Particularly those managers who have a sizable portion of their personal wealth invested in their funds may conclude that their personal utility is better pursued through concentrating on performance rather than expending effort on asset gathering. An extreme example is Renaissance Technologies, whose flagship hedge fund has, over time, become an investment vehicle whose investors consist almost exclusively of its own staff.

But it is the decision to re-open a fund that is most interesting. If there were sound reasons to close it in the first place, it is entirely appropriate for due diligence to ask, "What has changed?" It may simply be a matter of a renewal of opportunities as market conditions change. Merger activity, new issuance in certain asset categories, and valuation levels exhibit cyclicality, so a trade that is not productive or can absorb only very limited capital in some market circumstances can become productive or able to absorb considerably more capital in others. The availability of personnel to firms that need to increase their staffing before expansion also varies over time. But there are unsound reasons to re-open a fund, too. A common one is a shrinking asset base as a result of poor performance, perhaps exacerbated by withdrawals. Note that the performance need not be attributable to the manager: an entire investment category may experience poor performance as a result of general market circumstances. But it is not abundantly clear that such a category can therefore automatically accommodate a larger fund: only if market conditions have in fact improved would that be the case. Another reason for re-opening is the perception that the richness of a trade has decreased, so that continued growth in revenues cannot be generated through performance as readily as before. Clearly, investors are well advised to examine a fund's proposal to reopen with a generous measure of skepticism.

CHAPTER 15

Institutional Liquidity

L iquidity, like obscenity, is difficult to define, but recognizable when encountered. In a lecture that was as insightful as it was amusing, Mainelli (2007) introduced his chosen topic of "Liquidity: Finance in Motion or Evaporation?" as follows:

> Liquidity is a fluid concept [*sic*]. While exploring fluidity tonight, I hope to share with you a dark secret at the heart of finance—when we discuss liquidity we're often not sure what we're talking about. Liquidity drips into many financial discussions, but pinning down this watery concept is slippery. Part of the difficulty in pinning down liquidity is due to sloppy phrasing and some is down to different scales of time or size, but at heart, there is still a lot of mystery about some forms of liquidity. (1)

Liquidity is widely regarded as an inherent good, if not of the lofty status of Virtue, Beauty, or Truth, then still a much sought-after characteristic—the "lubricant in the cogs of the economy," "the lifeblood of finance" and all that sort of thing. Mainelli offers a sound working definition of liquidity as "the probability that an asset can be converted into an expected amount of value within an expected amount of time" (2007, 11) and that probability is obviously an attribute of an asset or investment technique with considerable value to its investors.

So it may be surprising to many that liquidity has come under fairly powerful attack in recent years. There is a strong case being made that it is not an especially desirable characteristic, at least for the overwhelming bulk of the assets and investment techniques that might populate an institution's portfolio. Essentially, the charge laid against it is that institutions, in demanding a level of portfolio liquidity in excess of their realistic requirements for it, pay an uncompensated premium to obtain it in quantities that they do not actually need, at a significant and completely unjustified cost to their returns. So, to be completely accurate, the attack has not been directed at the concept of liquidity as such, but at institutions' allegedly exaggerated perception of its importance to their investing activities.

The criticism of institutions' excessive fondness for liquidity has been led by David Swensen (2000, 87*ff* and 2009, 86*ff*), who refers with approval to Keynes's (1964) comment that "… of the maxims of orthodox finance none, surely, is more anti-social than the fetish of liquidity …" (155). He has been forcefully seconded by Fraser-Sampson (2006, Chapter 11). The latter's hyperbolic tone suggests frustration, apparently derived from long experience, over the ability of the more tradition-bound among British institutional investors ever to come to terms with illiquid alternative investments. Neither Swensen, Fraser-Sampson, nor Keynes is so radical as to suggest that liquidity is completely unnecessary to institutional portfolios. Their intent is only to argue that institutions can comfortably and more profitably make do with considerably less of it than they seem to believe they require, at least as evidenced by the asset allocation policies that most of them adopt. Keynes, after all, regarded the preference for liquidity as economically so fundamental that he used it to explain why interest is paid on loans and deposits. None of these three commentators are likely to take issue with institutions' desire for liquidity, but all three are unanimous in condemning them for the "fetish" that they argue that they make of it. However, still another author remarks, in the face of all this talk about an apparently universal "fetish" with something that should not be so great a concern, that in the context of investing, "Liquidity and the lack thereof is probably the one risk that has traditionally received the least focus and yet has inflicted the greatest damage" (Rahl 2000, 15). Which of these views is correct?

Liquidity Issues Relating to Alternative Investments

The liquidity of an alternative investment vehicle is a function of the investments it employs and their wrapper—the legal structure of the vehicle and the restrictions it places in its offering documentation on investors' access to the assets that they commit to it. Certain investments, because of their absolute cost, their uniqueness, or any of a number of other factors, are inherently illiquid. In these cases, transaction costs tend to be high even if the challenges to price discovery are eased by generally accepted, institutionalized transaction arrangements—for example, the fees charged for art auction houses' services. Sufficiently high, in fact, that I am aware of an otherwise impoverished owner of very valuable artworks who refuses to ease his economic situation in order to avoid incurring them.

Other assets have actively traded markets, in some cases twenty-four hours a day. However, even where liquidity is readily accessible, very large transactions or atypical ones (say, the desire to trade 39,439 lb. of frozen pork bellies, given a standard contract size of 40,000) are in most cases difficult to execute. Liquidity is relative to the amount that an investor wishes to trade, the time that the investor is willing to take to effect the transaction, and the investor's tolerance of the costs arising from price discovery, contract negotiation, market impact, and so on. Different assets offer sharply contrasting levels of liquidity, and the liquidity of any particular asset usually varies substantially over time—for trivial[1] as well as deeply interesting economic reasons. **Figure 15.1** illustrates a typical intra-day liquidity pattern, in which activity concentrates in the first and especially the last hours of the exchange session—although it is just as typical for the first hour to dominate activity as heavily as the last hour did in this instance.

Where investors' assets are not commingled—where each investor has full rights of ownership over an individually identifiable and segregated asset—there is no need for restrictions on their access to the funds they have invested, as the assets they hold themselves dictate that accessibility. An investor who purchases a shopping center cannot expect to withdraw capital on one day's notice. An institution that owns 9 percent of the equity of even a very actively traded listed company may be able to sell the position fairly quickly, but only if it is willing to accept a very substantial discount to prevailing market prices. Otherwise, the sale will be protracted, delayed either by the need to "work" the trade in the market over weeks or months or by the time required to locate and negotiate a

---

1. Mainelli claims that an old story ascribing the decrease in the liquidity of Britain's gilts market every day at 11:45 to the no-reservations policy at a popular City of London restaurant is apocryphal, but it seems perfectly plausible to me. My own experience trading Australian dollars in the interval between Christmas and New Year's Day (when senior traders abandon their desks and their juniors are left to hold the fort) suggests that periods of illiquidity engendered by the absence of senior traders can provide excellent opportunities for short-sellers.

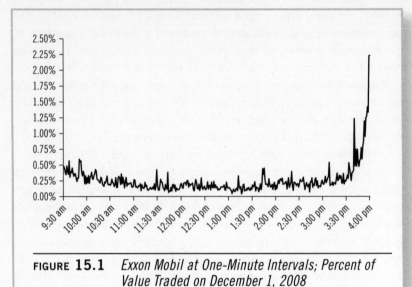

FIGURE 15.1   *Exxon Mobil at One-Minute Intervals; Percent of Value Traded on December 1, 2008*

Source: Bloomberg Finance L.P.

price with a potential buyer for the entire position. Direct control over an asset affords its owner certain real options over its disposition that it may lack if the asset is held in a commingled vehicle, but not more flexibility than the asset itself and the prevailing market conditions for it can offer.

None of this probably comes to readers as any great revelation, but matters are different if investors' interests are commingled, regardless of the legal structure employed. All the investors in such a vehicle share *pro rata* in its expenses, so the transaction and other costs incurred by one investor's withdrawal redound to the disadvantage of all the vehicle's holders. In a large mutual fund, this burden is shared across numerous investors, and the liquid nature of most such funds' holdings keeps transaction costs to a minimum in any case. But the fewer investors a vehicle has, the greater each investor's share of the burden arising from one investor's withdrawal, and if the underlying investments are illiquid, this can be substantial, due to explicit costs including market impact and/or the implicit cost of distortion to the vehicle's investment program that partial liquidation may entail. So, in most such cases, restrictions on withdrawals must be imposed in the interest of equal treatment of all investors—otherwise, investors would resist commingling. These may take the form of outright prohibitions on withdrawal, as are typical of private equity or real estate vehicles, or requirements that investors give advanced notice of the desire to withdraw, ranging anywhere from thirty days to six months. Where withdrawals are permitted, they are typically at fixed dates, either annually, quarterly, or very occasionally, monthly. As a protection to the remaining investors in the fund, disbursals are also typically partial—usually 90 percent of an investor's capital account—pending sign-off on the fund's audit.

In principle, the restrictions that an investment vehicle places on investors' access to their commitments to it should reflect the liquidity of the assets in which the vehicle invests. This works both ways, and is something for due diligence to attend to. Although excessively long lockups or notice periods imposed on investors in vehicles that exclusively invest in liquid instruments may be an unjustified inconvenience, they are not inherently dangerous. But excessively short lockups or notice periods on vehicles that hold less liquid investments can put investors that do not recall their capital at great risk from those that do. Lockups and notice periods are not *just* a nuisance to investors: they also provide protections to them, and due diligence should assure itself that the protection is commensurate to the liquidity risks that a candidate vehicle for investment takes.

This applies to all the vehicle's share classes. Many hedge funds and commodity pools offer different share classes with different liquidity restrictions, or use side-letters to exempt certain holders from all or some aspect of the restrictions that apply to their other Limited Partners. In most cases these are anodyne—merely incentives to investors to accept longer lockups in exchange for lower management or incentive fees, but otherwise the conditions of withdrawal are the same for all investors. But some funds grant privileged status to specific investors, and these should be examined carefully. Typically, those who are granted such privileges are large investors in the fund, so their withdrawal could be calamitous for the investors who remain behind if there is any impairment on the liquidity of the fund's assets. If, for example, it is appropriate on the grounds of the liquidity of the fund's holdings to demand ninety days' notice from ordinary investors in a fund, it is highly questionable that any of the fund's investors should be offered the right to redeem upon shorter notice.

I alluded to the unfortunate phenomenon of misleading claims to low fund volatility in Chapter 4, which can produce attractive and even spectacular Sharpe ratios engendered by the autocorrelation of fund holdings that are not marked to market. Over the last decade there has been a steady tendency for hedge funds to increase the illiquid portion of their holdings, and many allegedly liquid investment vehicles in fact have as much as 30 percent or even more of their assets in venture capital, long-term private loans, European-style options, and so on. Some of them offer quite liberal withdrawal terms, inviting disaster should redemptions begin to outpace liquidity inflows from new investors and realized returns. Under sufficient stress, such funds are forced to side-pocket these illiquid positions, and investors who wish to withdraw funds receive only that portion of their capital accounts that has not been side-pocketed. In many cases, managers continue to earn fees on these side-pockets, raising the question whether their incentives are aligned with the preferences of their investors. In other cases, notably when the fund is in liquidation, the investors' redemption requests are met with distributions of these illiquid assets in kind, and management of the illiquid investment becomes the investors' problem. For all that it alleviates the fee issue, this is not necessarily a more satisfactory solution, as it lands the institution with day-to-day responsibility for an asset that it may not be equipped to manage and of which it cannot easily relieve itself.

But lockups and notice periods certainly *can* be a nuisance, and often an unjustifiable one. Managers of investment products have an obvious incentive to retain assets under management, and making their withdrawal as inconvenient as possible is one way to discourage their flight. More to the point, as many hedge fund investors discovered to their chagrin in 2008, most such vehicles also have the right to impose indefinite restrictions on withdrawals. According to Kishan and Burton (2009), some 18 percent of hedge fund assets under management were subject to some form of restriction on redemptions at the end of that year. Funds will rarely lower such a gate simply in a self-interested attempt to retain assets—having imposed a gate is a stain on a fund's reputation and is often a prelude to its dissolution once investors recover the ability to withdraw from it. Gates are usually imposed in cases where the fund is illiquid and/or where one or more investors request to redeem a very large portion of the fund's total assets under management. But the risk that an institution's assets may be frozen with a manager for long periods is one of which investment policymakers must be cognizant.[2] Unfortunately, the large number of funds that felt themselves forced to impose

---

2. Lhabitant (2004, 307–10), describes a Value at Risk model suggested by Laporte that incorporates a risk factor for the "normal" illiquidity of hedge funds due to their redemption schedules, and so on. Krishnan and Nelken (2003) make the task of adjusting for the periodic availability of liquidity simpler by arguing that reported volatilities for the assets that a fund holds can be adjusted by a formula, so that, for instance, if the reported volatility of a fund offering quarterly liquidity is 6.2 percent, for optimization purposes it should be regarded as having 16.2 percent volatility. However, neither approach can model the ad hoc illiquidity that arises through the imposition of gates, and neither addresses the matter of understated volatility as a result of autocorrelation that was discussed in Chapter 4.

gates in 2008 may reduce the ignominy that previously attached to the practice, as standards that are frequently broken cease to have much normative force. Such a development would be highly unfavorable to users of hedge fund vehicles, and it is to be hoped that this circumstance does not materialize.

How Liquid Are Alternative Investments?

All of the above makes this question difficult to answer. Where the liquidity of the underlying assets is variable, where there is no guarantee that restrictions placed upon withdrawals from the vehicles are congruent with the assets' expected (let alone actual) liquidity, and where withdrawals can be summarily curtailed for indefinite periods, forecasting is confounded. Investment policymakers who submit timely requests for withdrawal can be reasonably confident of obtaining liquidity from commodity pools, but the experience of 2007 to 2009 indicates how ephemeral liquidity can be for virtually every other form of (purportedly) traded asset. In circumstances where liquidity is tightly constrained, commingled vehicles that would typically permit withdrawals are far more likely to impose "gates," as many investors' experience during that period demonstrated. This is a fundamental protection to the remaining investors in the fund, and should not be regarded as dastardly doings. But that is small comfort to those who required liquidity and were unable to obtain it from investments they had been led to believe would provide it in timely fashion and on a regular basis.

Fraser-Sampson is not swayed by these difficulties and argues that the secondary market for many investment products provides ready liquidity. This is deeply implausible. The secondary markets in Limited Partnership interests are informal, and consequently little data of any value is available on the depth of their liquidity. In the specific case of private equity, the estimates I have obtained for U.S. secondary transaction activity in 2007 from participants in that market suggest that it was between $15 and $25 billion on a worldwide basis for the entire period—equivalent to between eight and thirteen average days' turnover in Microsoft's equity that year. It seems to me that Fraser-Sampson is also unrealistically sanguine regarding transaction times and that his views about pricing in the secondary market are certainly not current. He appears to believe that pricing hovers around par relative to fair value. The market for secondary transactions in hedge fund interests is even less liquid, although discounts are narrower: see Cauchi (2009). The market for real estate interests is probably even smaller.

Pricing at par is not the reported experience of funds that purchased private equity secondaries over the last several years, almost always at some discount in excess of 10 percent, and all reports suggest that secondary market pricing for private equity deteriorated sharply over the course of 2008. Both Keehner and Kelly (2008) and Miller and Fabrikant (2008) mention discounts of 50 percent from fair value on top-quality private equity secondaries, the former suggesting that similar pricing for secondary offerings is affecting funds in Fraser-Sampson's British bailiwick as well. So, failing to fulfill any of the three aspects of Mainelli's definition of liquidity, the secondary market for private equity is not what I would regard as a liquid market by any stretch of the imagination. While offers for sale in the wake of the 2007 to 2009 crisis have reportedly increased dramatically, creating the pricing pressures that Miller and Fabricant mention, it does not appear that this has resulted in a correspondingly dramatic increase in transactions that have actually come to completion, so in currency terms, liquidity probably has not increased by much. I am unaware of any comprehensive data on secondary market transactions in hedge funds that are still permitting withdrawals, let alone those that have imposed gates, and the market for interests in private real estate partnerships is so undeveloped that it would be a stretch to claim that it had even reached infancy, although I have the impression that it is growing healthily.

How Much Liquidity Does an Institution Need?

Swensen makes no specific recommendations on this score, no doubt recognizing that this is a decision that will be idiosyncratic to each institution, dependent on its particular spending requirements (note that in some cases, such as foundations, minimum spending levels are dictated by tax considerations) and, perhaps more to the point, by its trustees' comfort with the proposed level of portfolio liquidity.[3] Following his

---

3. However, referring to National Association of College and University Business Officers data, he remarks (2009) that "Target spending rates among endowed institutions range from a surprisingly low 0.1 percent to an unsustainably high 15.5 percent. More than 70 percent of institutions employ target rates between 4.0 percent and 6.0 percent, with about one in six using a 5.0 percent rate" (33). It is interesting to note that the low figure has decreased from 1.25 percent and the high figure increased from 10.0 percent referenced in Swensen (2000, 34).

example in not making generalizations that by their nature are unlikely to have general application, I will draw on a specific example of one institution's liquidity needs. As it happens, there are few better examples than the needs of Swensen's own institution, which are periodically revealed to the public and which are especially interesting in the context of this volume because of that institution's very active program of employing alternative investments. The following is not intended to be tendentious: the Yale Endowment is more transparent about its activities and the needs of the institution that it serves than most, so the fact that it is Swensen's own institution (and my own alma mater) is immaterial to my decision to use it as an example.

Based on the evidence of the assets under his direct control, as shown in **Table 15.1**, Swensen has clearly succeeded in persuading his trustees that high levels of liquidity are unnecessary to the Yale Endowment.

The short position in cash represents an innovation in fiscal 2008: the Endowment has not been leveraged at the total portfolio level in recent memory. It represents nearly a $1.3 billion change in the cash position over the prior fiscal year and 55 percent more than the Investment Office distributed to the University during the 2007 to 2008 period. Borrowing has apparently been used to avoid liquidation of some positions during a period of difficult markets.

Swensen favors U.S. government obligations to the exclusion of all other fixed-income categories. Bearing in mind that Treasuries and

TABLE 15.1 *The Yale University Endowment, Fiscal 2008 June 30, 2008*

	ACTUAL	TARGETED
Hedge Funds	25.1%	21.0%
Conventional Equity	25.3	25.0
Private Equity	20.2	21.0
Real Estate, Timber, Oil, and Gas	29.3	29.0
Fixed Income	4.0	4.0
Cash	−3.9	0

Source: Annual Report.

related instruments settle overnight and that immediate liquidation of the Endowment's relatively modest Treasury portfolio (which amounted to about $915 million on the date shown) would have little or no market impact, completely liquid instruments held in the Endowment portfolio at the end of fiscal 2008 were equivalent to 108 percent of its fiscal 2008 contribution to the University's operating budget, which strikes me (and apparently Swensen and his trustees) as ample liquidity even before considering the cash that the portfolio could be expected to generate over the course of a year.

At the end of fiscal 2008, 49.5 percent of Endowment assets were held in indisputably illiquid private equity and real asset form. It is safe to assume that these are mature programs, exhibiting adequately vintage-diversified portfolios. In "normal" market conditions these two investment categories might be expected in the aggregate to generate cash distributions in the region of 14 percent per annum, although the distributions would not be smooth. The 25.1 percent in hedge funds offers no cash distributions. Swensen is known to favor small capitalization and emerging market equities over large capitalization and developed international equities. For example, Lerner (2007) reports that the Endowment's international equity benchmark is weighted 47 percent to the Morgan Stanley Capital International Europe, Australia, and Far East Index and 53 percent to that provider's Emerging Markets Index (8). Assuming that the equity portfolios are tilted 60 percent toward those equity categories and 40 percent toward large capitalization U.S. and developed countries' shares, the portfolio's dividend yield is probably around 2.3 percent, using early 2009 yield levels. Assuming that Treasury holdings are biased toward long maturities and using early 2009 yields to maturity in the absence of information on actual cash yields, the aggregate yield is probably about 2.6 percent. I have assumed a 3.0 percent financing cost for the borrowing. Thus, assuming normal conditions in the year to June 30, 2009, the Yale Endowment portfolio should have thrown off cash at an annual rate of roughly 7.5 percent of assets—twice fiscal 2008 spending. While cash receivables from investments are unlikely to meet Yale's spending calendar with to-the-day precision, the income to be expected in "normal" market conditions covered 2008 spending by a comfortable margin that allows for portfolio rebalancing without liquidations and makes it unlikely that reserves had to be tapped at all: the recourse to borrowing was almost certainly due to tactical investment considerations.

Note, however, the repeated references to "normal" market conditions. For fiscal 2009, cash returns on private equity are likely to be much lower than in previous years as were the returns on other real assets, with energy contributing weakly and real estate less weakly but still not as strongly as in the past. As a result of this, the aggregate cash distributions received from the illiquid portion of the portfolio during fiscal 2009 will probably be closer to 6 percent than to 14 percent, bringing cash generation for the total portfolio down to 95 percent of the level of spending in fiscal 2008. Given the inaccuracy of these rough estimates, there can be no certainty, but there is a strong probability that the Endowment will either have to tap into assets—although only the highly liquid portion of them—or increase its borrowing just to repeat its fiscal 2008 contribution to the University's operating budget in fiscal 2009.

The period following the Endowment's 2008 Annual Report provided an extraordinarily thorough real world stress test for Yale's and every other institution's portfolio structure. Near the end of calendar 2008, Yale announced that, according to its best estimate, the value of the Endowment had declined by 25 percent from June 30 (Needham 2009). For the sake of argument, it is probably not too unreasonable to assume that, in "normal" conditions, the private equity and real assets could be liquidated at a 15 percent discount over twelve months. In post-crisis conditions, the Endowment would almost certainly have had to accept a much steeper discount to obtain liquidity in the same timeframe. The Endowment's hedge funds offer, in principle, quarterly liquidity. But it is probable that at least a portion of the assets deployed in them has been side-pocketed or gated, and that, at a guess, 10 percent of them are frozen indefinitely. Recalling the small capitalization and emerging market bias to its equity exposure, in normal conditions the total equity portfolio (about $5.8 billion on June 30, 2008) could probably be liquidated without accepting too much market impact in roughly eight weeks. In 2008 to 2009 conditions, a discount of 12 percent is probably a sound rough estimate if a similar liquidation period were required. Short of horrendously short-sighted budgeting, the Yale University Investments Office, for all its famously high alternative exposure, came through the crisis quite capable of meeting liquidity contingencies even in extreme market conditions, thanks to its Treasury market reserve and its significant, if much less than typical, liquid exposure.

Making some rather arbitrary assumptions about the performance of the different components of the Endowment's asset allocation, the portfolio may well have looked something like what is shown in **Table 15.2** as calendar 2008 drew to a close. The figures shown are only rough guesses, however: I am not privy to any non-public information about the portfolio. I have assumed that the strong relative performance of the

TABLE **15.2**   *Yale University Endowment, Subsequent Performance*

	ACTUAL, JUNE 2008	TARGET, JUNE 2008	ROUGH ESTIMATE, DECEMBER 2008	ROUGH ESTIMATE, SIX MONTH RETURNS
Hedge Funds	25.1%	21.0%	26.4%	−20%
Conventional Equity	25.3	25.0	20.6	−38
Private Equity	20.2	21.0	21.8	−18
Real Estate, Timber, Oil, and Gas	29.3	29.0	30.4	−21
Fixed Income	4.0	4.0	4.0	9
Cash	−3.9	0	−3.2	37% reduction in borrowings

Source: Annual Report, author's estimates.

Treasury portfolio (using the Barclays Capital 5–10 year Treasury Index as a proxy) and rebalancing to the target cash position was used to pay down $334 million of the debt. Nevertheless, as a result of the decline in total portfolio value, leverage would have declined only slightly, to 3.2 percent. The numbers assume no withdrawal from other investment categories.

The fact that the Yale Endowment specifies a target allocation indicates that its trustees are quite aware that market conditions can cause the fund's allocation to drift, and the difference between target and actual allocation in the fiscal 2008 Annual Report indicates that Swensen can accept a certain amount of portfolio drift from year to year. But unless Yale has changed tactics significantly, the portfolio at the end of calendar 2008 probably exceeds the limits of his tolerance. Assuming a desire to keep a highly liquid Treasury reserve similar in size relative to annual spending as was carried in June 2008, sales of private equity, real assets, and/or redemption from hedge funds where that is still possible would have been required in order to return to the desired portfolio balance.

In summary, extreme stress on the Endowment's carefully structured but significantly illiquid portfolio has not constrained its ability to fund the University's operations, but it has created some very significant portfolio management problems. Either its management will have to make do with an asset allocation that it deems less than optimal, it will have to abandon some hedge funds in which it might prefer to remain invested, or it will have to accept painful discounting on its illiquid assets to effect the desired changes. Fraser-Sampson's sunny view of illiquid instruments' liquidity and the facility with which they can be tapped for the purposes of a rebalancing neglects the portfolio consequences of such a period of financial market stress—the proverbial case where virtually all "correlations go to one."

Swensen's acute thinking on the attractions of Treasuries compared to other forms of fixed income is amply supported by this result: things would certainly have been very much worse for the Endowment and the University that relies upon it if he had regarded bonds as a return-seeking portion of its asset allocation. A return-seeking approach would inevitably have led him away from the safe haven of Treasuries, and would quite likely have caused the Endowment to incur painful losses on much of its fixed-income allocation. However, despite the extraordinary resilience of its Endowment's investment policy, all is not entirely well with Yale University. Hiring has been tightened considerably, capital projects have been stalled (some of them indefinitely), budgets have been cut for 2009–2010 and 2010–2011, and the University expects to have accumulated more than a $300 million deficit by 2014 (ibid.). Further inroads into the illiquid portion of the portfolio appear to be unavoidable.

All of which suggests that the Yale Endowment's thinking on liquidity is very nearly ideal for the purposes of the institution it supports—a higher level of liquidity as a matter of investment policy would certainly have helped it through this extraordinary period, but at a substantial cost to returns in previous years. There are very, very few institutions that came out of this period of stress that would not have come retrospectively to exactly the same conclusion. Although the Endowment will struggle to support the University and restructure its holdings at the same time, the task is a challenge rather than an impossibility. A windfall from one of its private equity deals would certainly help in both regards.

But it is important to note the specific circumstances of a university endowment, and to consider whether they are equally applicable to every institution. The fiscal year on which Yale operates is revealing: come

June 30, tuition revenues and grant money for the coming academic year are accurately predictable, cost budgets should be fairly firm (at least 85 percent of universities' operating costs are fixed, according to Kochard and Rittereiser 2008, 147), and in "normal" years the Endowment is likely to be at its maximum level of liquidity as a result of the recent receipt of annual distributions from its illiquid holdings. While crucially important to its activities—the Endowment contributed 44 percent of its fiscal 2008 operating budget—at least the University is not 100 percent reliant on the Endowment for funding. Many institutions are not similarly blessed.

Liquidity and Portfolio Structure

Quite apart from the insurance liquidity provides an institution by furnishing it with a reserve against failure to meet its obligations, the preceding discussion indicates that liquidity has an important portfolio role. When markets stage a coordinated conniption, as they did in 2007 to 2009, portfolios are likely to depart significantly from their desired investment allocation structure. Without a liquidity reserve available to employ in rebalancing, managers face a quandary, as the assets or investment techniques that have decreased the most in value are likely to be those that might otherwise have afforded distraught investors the greatest liquidity with which to effect their panicked exit. That is, after a general market crisis, the areas of the portfolio that will probably be in greatest need of additional allocation are those that offer the greatest liquidity while the areas most in need of trimming are those that are least liquid.

Managers must consequently choose between making forced sales of illiquid assets to fund a rebalance—a reliably costly tactic—or trying to make the best of whatever distorted allocation the market rout has left them. That allocation is likely to be short on liquidity, so cash thrown off by investments in excess of required distributions in the quarters following a resumption of "normal" market conditions should probably be husbanded until liquidity is re-established rather than used to re-build the underweighted portions of the portfolio. Prudential hoarding of liquidity argues inconveniently against taking advantage of the many opportunities that the aftermath of a market crisis will probably offer. And conditions following a market crisis are unlikely to favor the large realizations from private equity and other illiquid sources that might otherwise restore the liquidity balance quickly. Consequently, managers who choose to make do rather than to bite the bullet and sell some illiquid holdings are likely to be biting for some time after conditions have calmed down. Neither choice can be expected to engender much enthusiasm among the institution's trustees. This leaves leveraging the portfolio as the institution's only solution, but it is a solution that many trustees would be reluctant to adopt, particularly with memories of a crisis fresh in their minds.

Even assuming that their hedge funds have not imposed gates, it is at this point that the constraints such funds place on withdrawal are a particular irritant. Even where liquidity for 90 percent of the withdrawal is reliably available by quarter's end (recalling the typical holdback provision), a quarter is a long time to watch from the sidelines while opportunities to buy at historically low levels are exploited by others. On the other hand, accepting a large discount on the sale of one asset in order to fund the purchase of another that the manager believes is undervalued requires a confidence in relative valuations that recent events are very likely to have shaken quite thoroughly. Would-be bottom-fishers should be aware that perceptions of value will almost inevitably have become distorted as a result of market turmoil. Take the experience before and after the Crash of 1987 as an example. Going into that debacle, Japanese equities were unquestionably the most overvalued among those traded on major exchanges and German equities arguably the most undervalued. The German market dropped much more sharply during the Crash than any other major market, and Tokyo the least. Japanese equities recovered more rapidly than any other developed country's in the months after the Crash, and continued to rise into 1990, while German shares languished for quite a while after the Crash. Nothing about this tale lends confidence to investors' ability to discern value in and around a period of market crisis.

I am aware of an Employee Retirement Income Security Act pension plan that, as a matter of policy (at least in the late 1980s), was entirely invested in deposits on AAA-rated banks. The plan's trustees had no need for such extreme liquidity, for which the plan clearly incurred substantial opportunity costs, but they justified their policy on the grounds that "we take enough risk in our ordinary business." The fact that they were taking risks with the pension's ability to keep pace with inflation did not seem to penetrate the thinking of the plan sponsors. Institutional investors have no choice but to accept that risk-taking is part and parcel of their mandate, and even apparently "riskless" strategies entail risks. One of the more important considerations that they must address is the liquidity of the plan, not just in order to avoid a failure to meet obligations in the short-term, but to allow for the implications that excessive liquidity may have on their ability to meet them in the long-term.

These implications are many-sided. They do not derive solely from the premium paid for liquidity and thus the impairment of returns to be expected from excessive liquidity. They also relate to the lack of flexibility in investment allocation (and thus the inability to rebalance precisely when this activity is most important to the portfolio's ability to recover from a market crisis) that excessive illiquidity may engender. This may sound paradoxical—a plan that is excessively liquid should in fact have maximum flexibility. But excessive liquidity almost certainly arose in the first place from morbid avoidance of risk, and a sudden appetite for risk in the wake of a market crisis is psychologically implausible for such an investment committee.

Liquidity Premia

The problem of the premium that investors should demand as compensation for taking liquidity risk has been touched upon several times in this book, without receiving much detailed examination. However, it deserves more attention in the context of alternative investments than elsewhere, because it manifests itself in more varied ways. In publicly traded securities, it appears either as a yield premium on income-producing securities that offer a yield, or as a price discount on securities for which yield is not a consideration. The two concepts are not, of course, unrelated—enhanced yield is often the result of a price discount, and a price discount may be largely detectable through the valuation premium exhibited by the discounted security relative to related or at least comparable securities. But these rather trivial observations do nothing to solve the problem of liquidity premia where there are no comparable, freely traded assets to provide a benchmark.

In core real estate and private equity, there are reasonably standard metrics. "Cap rates" on prime real estate are broadly comparable across major markets, and leveraged buyouts can readily be compared on a pre-tax basis with publicly traded equities as well as other private market transactions. However, the more idiosyncratic the transaction, the more difficult comparison becomes: the valuation of real estate that is under development or venture capital opportunities must rely primarily on estimates derived from the details of the proposed investment itself rather than comparison with others. Rational caution dictates that lack of ready comparability will itself raise the bar on required return, but still provides investors with no clear indication of how much caution, and therefore how much of a discount or how great a return premium is appropriate in any particular instance. Where the investment under consideration will never generate cash flow except when it is sold and is thus a purely a directional trade, as in the case of artworks, crafting an estimate that is even within the order of magnitude of what will eventually be achieved upon the sale of the asset may be very difficult, as we have seen.

In Chapter 4, I discussed Andrew Lo's proposals for adjusting the reported return series of hedge funds for their autocorrelation (serial correlation), to achieve a view of what their volatility might have been if their returns had been calculated using fresh, daily pricing. Although he draws some comparisons between his results for hedge funds and those obtained from a similar analysis of mutual funds, he does not extend the analysis to investments generally. Dorsey (2007, 256*ff*), applies similar analysis to the estimation of illiquidity discounts, although he unfortunately does not pursue the topic to completion. Admittedly, doing so would require numerous, challenging analyses of data series that would be difficult to obtain in quantities and quality that would make the effort useful. His preliminary analysis of a sample of real-world cases where illiquidity discounts manifest themselves reaches the probably inevitable but nevertheless disappointing conclusion that liquidity is priced across various investment categories with extreme inefficiency. He finds discounts relative to Treasury strips of comparable duration that range from 0.5 percent to an astonishing 1825 percent. Practitioners will not be surprised to learn that the latter value is his estimate of the discount captured by investment banks in connection with IPOs.

However, the example of artworks reveals that there are significant challenges to any such attempt, as it seems likely that the autocorrelation in the price of every unique artwork is highly comparable to that of every other, but examination of auction histories, which provide the comparatively rare examples of actual price discovery for such assets, reveals that price estimation is far more accurate in some broad categories of artwork than others. That is, if the serial correlation of pricing provided strong indication of relative liquidity, then the errors among price estimates for different categories of artwork should exhibit a comparable dispersion, and this does not seem to be the case. This finding could be interpreted in various ways—perhaps different categories of artwork are more dissimilar than superficial consideration might suggest, or perhaps skill at estimation is more unevenly distributed than one might think, and so forth.

All of which raises the question whether illiquid assets exhibit an illiquidity discount at all. Truth be told, academic research has yet to establish conclusively that such a discount exists in all liquid markets, where its presence should, at least in principle, be far easier to demonstrate. It is unlikely that it can be demonstrated at all for investment products where liquidity is all but absent, in which case, it becomes essentially a theological question that is incapable of decision. Rather than chasing after such rabbits, investors' efforts are probably better spent pondering what the costs or risks of illiquidity are to *them*, given their specific portfolio and institutional circumstances. They are then in a position to judge whether the potential return from the investment, and the probability of achieving it, are justified by the potential costs to the institution of the lack of liquidity that the opportunity entails. That is, rather than seeking to price illiquidity in the market, investment policymakers should contemplate the possibility of pricing it relative to their own liquidity requirements. This is likely to lead to a more illiquidity-friendly investment approach, as the Yale Endowment and others seem to have discovered.

CHAPTER **16**

Tactical Allocation

Transitions between chapters in this volume have probably given the reader a strong impression of non sequitur, so a chapter that addresses tactics and that has the good grace actually to follow rather than precede one on optionality—particularly one that discussed real options—is probably refreshingly logical. Tactical allocation is a real option available to those managers who give themselves permission to exploit the opportunity when they write their private placement memoranda, as many of them do. Managers may actively seek opportunities to exercise these options as a permanent feature of their return-seeking discipline and as an important component of the value-added they seek to offer to their investors. Or they may only avail themselves of those options as opportunistic and occasional responses either to an exceptional market development or to a market-induced lack of opportunities in their primary trading discipline. Investment firms may also permanently alter their investment program, perhaps as the result of a change in personnel, although in such cases it is debatable whether the shift should be regarded as tactical at all—it is arguably a shift in strategy, although investors in most hedge funds would be unlikely to be informed of it, let alone asked for their approval. I mention it because it can happen without notification of investors: for example, many hedge funds with no previous involvement in commodity markets jumped enthusiastically onto the commodity bandwagon in 2007 and 2008.

Which raises the question, to what is the allocation discipline, whether it is perennial or opportunistic, tactically applied? Investment theory provides us with no guidance, as it rejects the proposition that there can be value-added (at least on any sustainable basis) deriving from *any* tactical approach to investing. In conventional investment management, it is not uncommon to refer to even fairly minor departures from the chosen benchmark—whether it is a departure from a blended equity and fixed-income strategy benchmark for a balanced fund or even from the industry sector composition of the Standard & Poor's 500 Index when it is used as the performance benchmark for a large capitalization manager—as an example of tactical allocation, even though, in the latter case, no difference in asset category or security selection technique applied to that category is actually involved. "Tactical allocation" is yet another term that has come to bear far too much freight. This is largely because Modern Portfolio Theory can offer us no indication of how it should be defined: finance theory would regard any departure whatsoever from the chosen benchmark as tactical and therefore suboptimal, more or less by definition.

For my purposes here, it is useful to regard the object upon which tactical allocation is exercised as the investment technique that a manager employs rather than to relate the notion to assets or benchmarks. This definition has the advantage of being in less in danger of becoming so all-embracing as to include under the banner of "tactical allocation" virtually everything that an active manager might choose to do. Thus, for example, my definition would not regard a shift in the bias of an opportunistically long/short vehicle as an instance of tactical allocation, for all that it is clearly a tactical maneuver. The manager's decision to implement such a change is consistent with the return drivers that the manager pursues in the ordinary course of its trade discovery process—the possibility of executing such a maneuver is built into its fund design, and its investment methodology incorporates decision tools that are explicitly intended to identify such opportunities and implement the appropriate changes. In fact, it may not be the product of a decision at all, but the fund's bias might instead "bubble up" from its security selection discipline. However, if a long/short manager decides to embark on a true arbitrage trade—for example shorting an issuer's equity against long exposure to its debt (which is a typical distressed investment technique)—I choose to regard this as an instance of tactical allocation. As with so many things this volume touches upon, my treatment of tactical allocation is somewhat idiosyncratic. I ask the reader to bear with me.

Implications of This Treatment

The most obvious consequence of my treatment of this topic is that it entails that any decision to allocate tactically is a decision to enter a trade with different dynamics. This will typically involve different risks and require different expertise and decision support compared to the trades in which the manager was previously accustomed to engage. The nature of the asset on which these techniques are exercised is not material, so that in the example above it is not the decision to use debt, but the decision to engage in arbitrage that, in my view, constitutes tactical allocation. Although the contrast involved in the example of the long/short fund may not seem to be very extreme, entry into distressed investing techniques requires knowledge of bankruptcy and other matters that are not universally familiar to long/short equity managers. "Trading around" positions—a tactic so common that it can easily escape notice—is another example of tactical allocation. The manager chooses to overlay high-frequency trading on an existing trade, thereby introducing a new and different set of risk factors into its return-seeking, which requires trading skills that may not previously have been so necessary to it. In particular, the manager may expose itself to operational risks that were present but essentially inconsiderable before it embarked on a course of trading more actively.

An advantage of this treatment of tactical allocation is that it does not exclude the possibility that investment vehicles that operate on very long time horizons in private markets, such as private equity or real estate, might engage in it. One might be inclined to think that, once their Limited Partners' capital commitments to these vehicles are deployed, long horizon funds are incapable of executing tactical maneuvers. Although some of them may change tactics during their commitment periods—the shift toward distressed investing on the part of recent-vintage leveraged buyout vehicles has already been mentioned—it would seem that their capital, once invested, is largely frozen in the tactic that dictated that investment. But this neglects the real options that active management of their investments affords these managers. While these options are not unlimited in scope—a venture investor in a biotechnology firm cannot realistically choose to transform that firm into a media company or a miner, and only the very fortunate owner of farmland can convert it to oil production—the managers' active role in the investments' governance allows these investors to make significant changes in the investments' strategies, business plans, and, as a result of control over their financing, their return characteristics.

But in some cases it is not even necessary for the manager to institute change in the underlying investment. For example a "value-added" real estate investor (a gold-plated term for a buyer of fixer-uppers) may initially plan a directional strategy of selling a property at a profit once it has been renovated but may subsequently shift to a cash flow strategy of holding it as a premium real estate investment in response to a change in market conditions or to any number of other factors. Granted, many funds deliberately set limits on their investment programs, restricting their tactical freedom in order to increase their appeal to institutions that wish to be certain what it is to which they are committing their capital. But the managers of many other alternative investment products grant themselves wide latitude in the sorts of instruments that they may employ and the investment techniques that they may choose to apply to them. This sort of change of horses midstream is by no means unusual.

Attentive readers have probably already noticed that this definition of tactical allocation makes no reference to the underlying assets at all, implying, for instance, that the decision to shift allocation from fixed-income to real estate held for income generation is in some sense a "lower-order" tactical decision than shifting from directional- to cash flow-oriented real estate exposure. I am certain that many will balk at this and regard it as grounds for dismissing this treatment of tactical allocation out of hand. However, it seems appropriate to me that there should be "higher" and "lower" orders of tactics, and relating them to the strategy objective rather than to the asset or vehicle chosen to realize it strikes me as natural. From this perspective, maneuvering between strategies as I have defined them—directional, cash flow, and arbitrage—is in some sense a "higher order" tactical decision than, to refer again to the example above, shifting exposure between equity and debt in the context of a long/short strategy, or for that matter reallocating assets from directional, long-only equities to directional, long-only commodities. The comparative ease with which many institutions (let along opportunistic hedge funds) have persuaded themselves to implement the latter allocation decision supports the view that this is a "lower-order" decision.

Another feature of this treatment of tactical allocation is that it need not involve an actual movement between assets—the example of the "value-added" real estate investment, after all, involved no sale of one property to fund purchase of another. Different strategies can be applied to the same asset, and a more traditional definition of tactical allocation that is focused upon the assets involved cannot take account of such a change. But if the original asset is deployed differently, a fundamentally different investment stance has been adopted, and a different pattern of returns is to be expected, for all that the asset itself is the same as before. This raises the specter that, if a manager becomes too emotionally attached to a position, claiming different strategic roles for it may be a way to justify retaining a position that should, on emotionless investment grounds, be abandoned.

I do not regard the fact that it allows for equivocation as an objection to my account of tactical allocation but rather as confirmation that I might be on the right track, because this is an empirically accurate description of something that regularly takes place in the investment world. The manager of the "value-added" property may well have sound investment reasons for retaining the building once it has been refurbished, but on the other hand may simply be attempting to rationalize the failure of a directional trade. Similar equivocation between the return-seeking and the hedging functions of positions has already been mentioned, and this example of behavioral psychology is so common in financial markets that to pretend that it does not occur would be perverse. Because real options offer the possibility of return, it follows that they also have their risks, and the risks arising from such self-deluding reinterpretation of the facts are by no means the least of them. An understanding of tactical allocation that did not allow for such equivocation would fail to account for the inherent difficulty that all investors experience in distinguishing between strategy and tactics. Such a loss of psychological realism would, in my view, almost certainly indicate that there was some flaw in that understanding.

Chapter 2 made the claim that a hedge is a matter of intention, not a property inherent in the specific investment itself. Something similar appears to be happening with this account of tactical allocation. A multi-strategy fund may allocate to a new trade—say, convertible arbitrage—involving assets and a trading strategy to which it had no pre-vious exposure—as a deliberate decision to take a risk that it perceives as attractive. This is a straightforward directional investment decision based upon that perception. But a superficially identical pair trade may be put on as part of a long/short strategy. The difference is likely to lie in the extent to which the option embedded in the convertible is in or out of the money, and the form of the trade (i.e., which position is long and which is short). The allocation to convertible arbitrage is made in order to obtain returns from a reduction in a pricing discrepancy, and presum-ably a multi-strategy manager chooses to allocate to that trade because it perceives the discrepancies to be rich, because exposure to arbitrage would have desirable portfolio diversification effects and/or because it has encountered a dearth of other, superior opportunities. The long/short manager is certain to be less concerned with that opportunity to capture returns than with the risk that further price divergence will spoil its hedge—achieving gains on the arbitrage embedded in its trade is largely beside the point, and the trade is unlikely to be sufficiently lever-aged for any gains that may be realized to be of much interest to it.

So, essentially the same trade (or at least two very similar ones) may be a matter of tactical allocation or not, depending on the manager's intent.

The point here is that my treatment emphasizes the source of returns, not from the perspective of the underlying asset but from the perspective of what kinds of risks the manager regards itself as taking in order to achieve those returns. Different sources of risk, such as reliance on forecasts, use of leverage, or dependence on the persistence of observed correlations, can be analyzed independently of the underlying assets, and in many cases they are more material to returns than the risks that are specific to this or that individual asset or even asset category. For example, an equity-oriented manager may take long positions in oil futures because they offer more purity of exposure to oil prices than the equity of most oil producers, because the manager is aware that an oil producer may hedge its position, may have entered into long-term fixed-price sales contracts, or may engage in activities such as refining, marketing, or petrochemical manufacture that have different return profiles from oil production. Isolation of these risks permits investment managers, and ultimately investment policymakers, too, to manage them through diversification and overlay hedges. Use of an allegedly "exotic" instrument such as an oil future or a swap in no way changes the fundamentally conventional nature of the manager's activities.

It is customary, for example, to analyze the risks attached to conventional, long-only fixed-income investment in terms of duration, issuer category, and issue-specific risks. Duration is a risk that attaches to any fixed cash flow investment, and the discussion of liquidity in the previous chapter should indicate why this source of risk is important to institutions. The discussion was intended to imply that it is appropriate for them to apply the concept to assets beyond just those that comprise the fixed-income portion of their portfolios—perhaps to their portfolios as a whole. Issuer category as conceived in fixed-income analysis is largely exclusive to that asset category, but issue-specific risks may well be duplicated by an institution's equity holdings.

Thus holding Lehman Brothers' subordinated debt in the autumn of 2008 did nothing to diversify a position in its equity—it only aggravated issuer-specific risk exposure. Recall that a corporate bond can be analyzed in terms of a short position in a put option on the issuer's equity: when the equity comes under severe pressure, the bondholder finds itself the unhappy owner of equity-like exposure of the most unattractive variety. To focus solely on the type of asset held, and to neglect the investment characteristics that it may share with other assets, is to compartmentalize the aggregate risk exposure of a portfolio in ways that interfere with the need to manage that risk where possible. Because these exposures will only be apparent to factor analysis if the issuer has been close to failure long enough for the bond's high correlation to the issuer's equity to be apparent to regression analysis, such exposures are not transparent to standard forms of analysis such as those offered by multi-factor or Value at Risk models. This is not to say that different asset categories do not have risks that are sui generis—they clearly do—but often those risks are less important than those that they share with assets in other categories but that may be exploited by similar techniques. This, of course, is an argument for the analysis of portfolios according to their factor loadings, but with an overlay of common sense and stress-testing that gives due attention to tail risks, which will feature prominently in the remainder of this book.

Tactical Allocation within an Alternative Investment Portfolio

The relative performance of different alternative investment techniques is certainly volatile, and tactical allocation depends on such volatility to generate its returns: without volatility in relative performance, there would, after all, be little value added to be achieved from allocating tactically among them at all. **Table 16.1** shows the performance of thirteen Hedge Fund Research sub-indices of different investment techniques to indicate that they certainly do provide the volatility relative to each other that would be requisite to allow tactical allocation among them to be potentially fruitful. Inclusion of private market assets is largely irrelevant—on the one hand, the illiquidity of the vehicles makes them poor instruments among which to allocate tactically in this way, and on the other, the fact that they do not mark to market and thus exhibit a high degree of autocorrelation would distort the comparison.

Interestingly, returns for the Multi-Strategy and Funds of Funds indices fairly consistently clustered around the median ranking and offered roughly the median cumulative return. This suggests that either these managers

❑ concentrate their efforts on strategic rather than tactical allocation;
❑ their tactical maneuvering failed on average to add much value; or
❑ the benefit from sound tactical decisions was largely offset by mediocre implementation.

TABLE 16.1   HFRI Indices: Annual Returns

	1999	2000	2001	2002	2003	2004	2005	2006	2007	2008	MEDIAN
Convertible Arbitrage	14.41%	14.50%	13.37%	9.05%	9.93%	1.18%	−1.86%	12.17%	5.33%	−33.71%	**9.49%**
Distressed/ Restructuring	16.94%	2.78%	13.28%	5.28%	29.56%	18.89%	8.27%	15.94%	5.08%	−25.20%	**10.78%**
Emerging Markets (Total)	55.86%	−10.74%	10.36%	3.70%	39.36%	18.42%	21.04%	24.26%	24.94%	−37.35%	**19.73%**
Equity Hedge	44.22%	9.09%	0.40%	−4.71%	20.54%	7.68%	10.60%	11.71%	10.48%	−26.63%	**9.79%**
Event-Driven	24.33%	6.74%	12.18%	−4.30%	25.33%	15.01%	7.29%	15.33%	6.61%	−22.12%	**9.74%**
Fixed Income (Corporate)	7.35%	−3.03%	5.37%	5.80%	21.30%	10.49%	5.27%	10.78%	−0.74%	−23.44%	**5.59%**
Funds of Funds (Diversified)	28.46%	2.47%	2.79%	1.17%	11.42%	7.19%	7.46%	10.18%	9.72%	−20.82%	**7.33%**
Macro (Systematic Diversified)	26.17%	11.79%	4.09%	−3.25%	15.36%	6.42%	14.40%	16.84%	10.34%	18.08%	**13.10%**

Macro (Total)	17.62%	1.97%	6.87%	7.44%	21.42%	4.63%	6.79%	8.15%	11.11%	4.79%	**7.16%**
Market-Neutral	7.09%	14.56%	6.71%	0.98%	2.44%	4.15%	6.22%	7.32%	5.29%	−5.96%	**5.76%**
Merger Arbitrage	14.34%	18.02%	2.76%	−0.87%	7.47%	4.08%	6.25%	14.24%	7.05%	−5.00%	**6.65%**
Multi-Strategy	10.98%	3.42%	10.36%	6.48%	11.53%	8.20%	5.66%	8.99%	1.81%	−20.38%	**7.34%**
Short-Bias	−24.40%	34.63%	8.99%	29.17%	−21.78%	−3.83%	7.28%	−2.65%	4.72%	28.41%	**6.00%**
MEDIAN	**16.94%**	**6.74%**	**6.87%**	**3.70%**	**15.36%**	**7.19%**	**7.28%**	**11.71%**	**6.61%**	**−20.82%**	

It is probable that each of these explanations applies to some portion of the managers whose returns were aggregated to construct these indices, although in any given year there were obviously some whose performance was substantially better than the median for the techniques among which they allocated and others whose returns badly lagged behind the median performance. There may well have been managers who demonstrated consistent levels of value added or value subtraction over the entire period shown. It is also interesting to note that their median returns were nearly identical, which suggests (as their providers like to claim) that the higher fees associated with funds of funds are offset by superior implementation through the selection of better-performing managers to exploit the investment techniques their funds employ. However, the HFRI Multi-Strategy Index is in fact a sub-index within its Macro category: it is probably not representative of all multi-strategy vehicles.

Not the least of the challenges that confront funds of funds that wish to enhance returns through tactical allocation derives from hedge funds' restrictive liquidity policies and lack of transparency. Lengthy notification periods, holdback provisions pending annual audits, and fixed redemption schedules that may not allow for smooth and timely transfers between funds cause the project of steering among fund positions to be a sort of elephantine waltz. And this is without considering the possibility that a fund might impose a gate to prevent redemptions or hold back a portion of invested assets indefinitely in illiquid side-pockets. The underlying funds' lack of clear investment mandates makes it difficult for funds of funds managers to be certain that allocation to a new vehicle will in fact accomplish what that manager had in mind. These issues, and fees, are the arguments in favor of multi-strategy as an alternative to fund of funds investment.

Leaving aside the extreme impediments to tactical allocation raised by long-horizon, illiquid investments such as private equity or real estate, and ignoring the possibilities offered by separate account management[1] or multi-strategy vehicles, tactical allocation among alternative investments cannot in most cases be a matter of short-term opportunism. Of course, opportunism based on a perception of value is possible for the institution that is already liquid at the time the value is recognized. While a tendency toward return-chasing is rarely helpful to investment performance, in

---

1. This is a common arrangement with CTAs, in real estate and (largely in the form of co-investments alongside a fund holding) in private equity, but a fairly rare one in the hedge fund world, largely because such accounts have difficulty obtaining prime brokerage services. However, separate accounts seem to be gaining ground in the hedge fund arena, too: see Timberlake (2009).

the world of alternative investments it is likely to be a fairly sure route to disaster. Would-be investment allocators must resign themselves to a deliberate approach reliant on comparatively long-term forecasting. This suggests that trades dependent on relatively long-term economic fundamentals, rather than those that attempt to take opportunistic advantage of transient valuation discrepancies, are most adaptable to allocation among alternative investments. In **Table 16.1**, it is notable that the three investment techniques that demonstrate any appreciable serial persistence in their relative performance are emerging markets, systematic diversified macro, and distressed investing, all three of which exploit macroeconomic trends rather than transitory trading conditions as the most fundamental drivers of their returns. In another period, merger arbitrage might also have exhibited similarly persistent rankings—as in fact it did through much of the 1990s—but the dominance of leveraged buyouts during the mid-2000s acquisition boom did not favor that investment technique.

Given the time horizons involved, tactical allocation among alternative investments melds imperceptibly into strategic allocation, nowhere more clearly than where long-tail investments such as private equity or real estate are concerned. The decision to enter into such investments is a long-term commitment, and while the perception of the commitment may change, as suggested by the "value-added" real estate example, the underlying asset itself does not. However, perceptions matter. In that example, a directional trade became a cash flow trade. While this may be a matter of rationalization, it may also be a decision based on an analysis of market conditions and a realistic assessment of the available investment opportunities. If, for example, the building was acquired in 2005, refurbished and fully leased for ten years to top-quality non-financial tenants by the second quarter of 2007, maintaining the exposure, perhaps in place of a portion of the institution's corporate bond holdings, will probably turn out to have been very a sound investment decision. Fluctuations in the building's value would have been painful, but not as painful as the subsequent experience with most corporate bond positions, and the yield would have been higher than that achievable from a comparable credit at the time the reallocation to fixed income might otherwise have been made. Meanwhile, the inflation protection offered by a real asset might turn out to be quite valuable in the wake of the extraordinary monetary stimulus of 2008 to 2009.

Once again: the underlying asset has not changed, but its portfolio function has changed from one of pursuing directional price appreciation from an equity interest in a property to reaping cash flows from corporate lease obligations. Even if an institution's trustees stubbornly persist in the rather unfortunate habit of thinking in terms of asset allocation "buckets," the investment should nevertheless be moved from one conceptual category to another, because its return characteristics are dramatically different from the ones that were initially contemplated for it. This may seem an odd procedure considering that the asset remains the same building and the plot of land upon which it sits, but otherwise an investment that might be an excellent cash flow generator would instead be regarded as a failed directional trade. If such a change makes the new "bucket" to which the institution assigns the asset (corporate credit exposure) seem over-full, then the decision to hold or dispose of the investment should most appropriately be measured against the contents of its new "bucket" rather than those of the "bucket" it previously occupied.

Apart from what might be termed "perceptual re-allocation" of this sort, tactical maneuver in long horizon investments proceeds at a leisurely pace that allows macroeconomic forecasts to dictate behavior. It is probably appropriate for institutions to review their allocation policy with each vintage year, to allow them to tilt their mix from, say, office to industrial properties or leveraged buyouts to venture. Although macroeconomic visibility is unlikely to be clear far enough into the relevant future to provide enormous conviction to these allocation choices, in conjunction with more useful current valuation data it provides reasonable grounds for decision-making. Current valuation conditions should probably weigh particularly heavily in such calculations, as sound purchasing discipline will trump guesses about market conditions in the distant future ninety-nine times out of a hundred. In our real estate example, the risk of inflation, the comparative certainty of receiving the negotiated lease payments, and the likelihood, on a ten-year view, that commercial real estate liquidation values will be less depressed than at the time of a general market crisis during which the decision had to be made, constitute a reasonably persuasive case for retaining the building for its cash flow generation rather than selling it and holding corporate bonds in its place. However, if the secondary market liquidity for these sorts of investment interests that Fraser-Sampson imagines does actually develop, matters may become somewhat different, and changes of allocations involving real estate investments and similar long-term commitments may no longer need to be, perforce, so leisurely.

Tactical Allocation through Overlay Hedges

A perfect hedge in effect turns a position into cash less the cost of putting the hedge in place—clearly a protective rather than a return-seeking allocation decision. Some alternative investment exposure is more readily hedged than others. Most directional strategies can be more or less accurately hedged with publicly traded derivatives, and in many cases over-the-counter derivatives can be crafted to hedge other directional exposures. For example, the CIO of the University of Virginia Endowment was able early in 2000 to negotiate a remarkably well-timed over-the-counter hedge for venture capital exposure, which had achieved its IPO exit but for which Limited Partners' interests were still restricted from sale and no publicly traded options were yet available (Kochard and Rittereiser 2008, 99).

Other ways to hedge illiquid exposures involve use of short positions in leveraged loans and commercial mortgage securities issued by borrowers with a profile that is similar to that of the position being hedged. Hedging may be more difficult to accomplish for trades with uneven or irregular cash flows and especially arbitrage exposures, but the creativity of investment banks' structured products desks approaches limitlessness, or at least the marketers for those origination desks believe that it does. So with a will, a way can usually be found—most likely through a structure involving total return swaps—if the institution is willing to accept what may be a not inconsiderable cost and the (very considerable) risk that its analysis of the effective exposures it obtains through the proposed hedge is incomplete. As always, the institution must make substantial efforts to assure itself that the return outcomes of the hedge it purchases are structured in the way that it thinks they are. Complex over-the-counter hedges are the source of most of the more unfortunate cases of disastrous derivative exposure and are primarily responsible for the fear of derivatives that so widely pervades the markets.

Development of hedge fund replication technologies contributes to investment banks' ability to offer at least partial hedges for most alternative investment exposures. Replication products have been marketed heavily, and the increased liquidity they make available to the banks' trading desks also benefits potential users of such structured products. I am convinced, in spite of concerted efforts to persuade me otherwise, that these replication offerings are deeply flawed—well, most of them. Some that rely on algorithmic trading may in fact be of some value to investors. Those that rely on factor replication are, in my opinion, nothing other than complex recipes for underperformance and potentially disaster—and those are the ones upon which such a hedge would be constructed. In general, my objection to these products is the use of the term "replication"—in my view they replicate nothing, but create a new, sui generis hedge fund, and in every instance that I have seen, not an attractive one (see Chapter 24).

However, the inherent inaccuracy of factor-based hedges, which will inevitably manifest itself most starkly precisely during those periods of market stress when the hedge is most needed, and the very real risk that the portfolio could obtain unintended exposures or notional leverage through them, should give institutions considerable pause for thought. The CIO of the University of Virginia Endowment, mentioned above, was able to hedge with confidence and with the full support of her trustees—but hers was a comparatively simple hedge to construct and analyze, and her confidence (and her trustees' confidence in her) was no doubt reinforced by her own background as a trader. Many institutions' investment staff may not have these luxuries. They and their trustees should think twice, and after a pause a third time, before entering into complex swap agreements.

Although hedging can be cumbersome and expensive, and in some cases must rely on very approximate estimates of the appropriate hedge ratio and even the appropriate hedging instrument to use, it can have a value beyond portfolio protection. Many of the most desirable alternative investment vehicles are accessible essentially by invitation only: it is very difficult to become a member of these exclusive clubs, and once an investor has withdrawn from them, in most cases it is highly unlikely that it will be welcomed back to the fold in the future. If an institution expects that it will want to have exposure to some provider's new vehicle at a later date (or subscribe to a successor fund managed by the General Partner of a closed vehicle to which the investor currently wants to reduce its exposure), then withdrawal of exposure may not be advisable, and a hedge may offer an alternative to liquidation. But it is not a riskless alternative.

In venture capital circles in particular, memories are long and networks are tight: a reputation as anything other than a "good" Limited Partner, which may take years and no small amount of dues-paying for an institution to build, may interfere with its investment program over the long-term. A "good" Partner is, of course, one that subscribes, keeps its mouth shut, and then subscribes for each succeeding fund. In these cases, even an inadequate and expensive hedge may be preferable to exit. At the time of writing, General Partners are likely to be more forgiving of "transgressors" than they have been in the past, and perhaps the risk of closing oneself out of funds by redeeming from them (or not subscribing to the one that is currently open to new investment) is not so high as it has been, but it will probably manifest itself again when these products return to investors' favor and institutions generally are under less stress than at present.

Swensen (2000, 286*ff*) recounts a parallel cycle of arrogance, temporary remorse, and a return to arrogance in private real estate fund management. Institutions will not go far wrong if they consider a well-regarded manager's systematic abuse of its investors on terms and conditions as a signal that the manager or even its entire asset category is or will shortly become unattractive, as it is a clear sign that a trade has become overcrowded. This may, in fact, be one of the more reliable tactical allocation signals available to institutions, and it is certainly one that they should be on the watch for. Too many investors' decisions are swayed by the perception, fostered by the General Partner, that in being offered access to an investment they are receiving a privilege for which they should be uncritically grateful.

Tactical Allocation between Alternative and Conventional Investments

I have already implied that I have more that a minor aversion to "bucket-think" in investment allocation. I believe that portfolio constituents should be analyzed functionally, in terms of their contributions to the performance, risk, and diversification of the aggregate portfolio, rather than in terms of assigned categories based on some or other definition of their asset class. I elaborate considerably on this point in Chapter 19. As the choice of examples in Part II was intended to illustrate, portfolio function is largely independent of the underlying asset upon which one or a combination of the three investment strategies is employed. The treatment of tactical asset allocation in this chapter follows on from that, and adds the wrinkle that even identically the same asset's functionality can change over time, depending on market conditions and the asset's return characteristics when deployed in different strategies and relative to the other holdings in the portfolio. In this connection, Alice Handy, the CIO of the University of Virginia Endowment who made the timely hedge of her institution's restricted stock positions in 2000 notes,

> Yale puts a manager in one block, [the University of Virginia] puts it in another, and it's the same manager. One classifies it as a hedge fund and another as a traditional long-only manager. Virginia Retirement System puts all hedge fund strategies into its global equity allocation as opposed to a hedge fund box. Asset classes make no sense anymore as they don't really describe enough about the portfolio. The old categories don't address liquidity or leverage. The problem is that the nomenclature academically hasn't

caught up with what is happening with investment people. (Kochard and Rittereiser 2008, 101)

She might add that the community of investment consultants has made little or no effort to move beyond asset class "buckets" and essentially superficial style differentiation within them, because this construct is ideally suited to

❏ their limited due diligence capabilities, especially with regard to operational issues;
❏ their lack of understanding of portfolio change both in general and in the case of any specific portfolio example; and
❏ their commercial imperative to recommend ever more manager searches on which they can bill.

"Bucket-think" is a simple, linear classification scheme applied to the multi-dimensional and occasionally discontinuous reality of portfolio management. It attempts to force a static model onto what is in fact a process. Portfolio management is dynamic both at the most general level of analysis and in each of its subsidiary parts. Any advocacy of asset allocation "buckets" is so clearly in its proponents' self-interest that it should be deeply suspect, rather than Gospel, to investment policymakers. While there are many consultants that add value to institutional thinking, there are many that subtract it, and agency issues abound in this sphere.

All of which raises the question whether there is anything distinctive about allocation—either strategic or tactical—between alternative and conventional investments. At the level of trustees, all but the most fortunate investment staffs have found that there certainly is: trustees' levels of familiarity and the comfort it entrains are noticeably different between conventional and alternative investments. Whether justifiably or not, most investment committee members feel that they have a sound working knowledge of stocks, bonds, cash, and possibly real estate, but if the issues confronting the portfolio under their stewardship require them to stray too far from their accustomed path, in many cases their comfort levels decline precipitously. For psychological reasons that are familiar to everyone, unaccustomed risks are more daunting than customary ones, and trades that derive their returns from multiple moving parts are inherently more difficult to grasp than those that derive their returns from one, obvious source such as directionality or cash flow—all of which accounts for a large part of institutions' reliance on precedent, consultants, and peer comparisons. This, however, is an externality, and is not the issue at hand. The question is whether there is anything inherent to alternative or conventional investments that requires special accommodation when allocating between them. None of the examples explored in Part II suggests any such thing.

Having witnessed an at least partial (and I hope definitive) demolition of any firm distinction between alternative and conventional investments in the Introduction of this book, the reader has probably already inferred that, other than the practical difficulties involved, *there is in fact no distinctive issue regarding allocation between alternative and conventional investments.* This is true regardless of whether the allocation in question is tactical or strategic. But the practical difficulties of tactical allocation involving alternative investments are by no means inconsiderable, and for most investment policymakers most of the time, it probably makes more sense to seek returns from tactical allocation either within the confines of funds that specialize in it or in their selection of conventional investments. This is less true where separate accounts for liquid alternative investment activities can be employed, as is typical with CTAs, but as a broad generalization over the universe of alternative investments, I believe that the observation holds true.

Investment allocation is a unified, holistic set of interrelated problems, and it is inappropriate to separate it artificially into steps or stages. However, the human imagination is limited in its ability to visualize beyond our accustomed three dimensions and the linear processes for which evolution and education have adapted us. In this chapter I have already slipped in some mention of "higher-" and "lower-order" allocation decisions, without commenting on what distinguishes them. The task of Part IV resembles the problem of Mercator in accommodating a higher dimensional world within the confines of a flat and, I fear, rather pedestrian description. This is the "complex simultaneity of the asset management process" to which the Introduction alluded. For a foretaste of the challenges that lie ahead, readers might wish to consult A. Square's (Edwin Abbott's) fantasy about life on just two axes, *Flatland: A Romance of Many Dimensions.*

CHAPTER 17

Portfolio Liquidity

In the wake of an extremely damaging global economic and securities market crisis of the sort that began in 2007, diversification is likely to be a very sore topic. Even granting that many alternative investment vehicles performed well relative to equities and corporate credits, all those shiny claims for diversification look rather shopworn after "correlations go to one." Investors who tolerated weak relative performance from some of their investments while markets were rising discovered that some of them offered little or none of the advertised protection when markets fell dramatically and in unison. Hedges ceased to hedge, collateral became evanescent, and the only apparent safe haven offered, on a few occasions, the "security" of guaranteed negative returns. In 1987, all this was unfamiliar territory, and in the aftermath of the Crash that year, market practitioners wandered about among the wreckage in complete bewilderment. But twenty-odd years later, the phenomenon of correlations rising in unison as markets descend into panic has become an all-too-familiar one, even though investors are not much (if any) better equipped to protect themselves against it than they were the first time they encountered it in the 1980s.

Alternative investments began to attract substantial amounts of investor attention only after they proved their ability to skirt the worst consequences of market drama during the collapse of the Technology Bubble at the beginning of this decade. Although many institutions already had exposure to alternative investments prior to that episode, it was those vehicles' strong relative performance during and after the collapse that released a flood of institutional funds into alternative investments. But even during the bursting of the Technology Bubble, not all alternative investment techniques proved equally defensive, and venture capital investments in particular suffered from that calamity—from which, in many respects, they have yet to recover fully. Nevertheless, the failure of most alternative investment vehicles to offer substantial portfolio protection from the multiple crises of 2007 to 2009 came as a shock to investors. Although many funds performed strongly relative to conventional benchmarks, a loss of, say, 18 percent during a period when the Standard & Poor's 500 Total Return Index was down about 37 percent, as it was in 2008, offered limited comfort at best. "Absolute return" did not, after all, turn out to be as "absolute" as many had thought.

Chapter 3 discussed how spasms of financial panic disturb the markets' statistical signposts, but these episodes are likely to interfere with other indicators upon which investors rely, too. Relative valuations will almost certainly have been altered significantly, and macroeconomic conditions may have changed out of all recognition—having either been the cause of the drama in the first place or having been radically altered in the course of central banks' and finance ministries' attempted responses to it. In some cases, these events have clear implications for at least certain parts of the investment landscape—the bursting of the Technology Bubble provided a fairly obvious clue to the future development of returns from venture capital, and the Credit Crunch has made it quite clear what will become of the returns of recent and at the very least a few subsequent years' vintages of leveraged buyouts (see Meerkatt and Liechtenstein, 2008) and commercial real estate. This renders Swensen's comment (2009) that "market returns contribute very little to ultimate results" from private equity completely unaccountable (54). We can only conclude, with Horace, that sometimes even Homer nods. But other cases, most notably including the Crash of 1987, have been inscrutable, largely because their macroeconomic implications—which, as we have seen, are an important driver of tactical decision-making—were unclear. Thus, quite apart from their effects on the fundamental assumptions that underlie long-term, strategic investment allocation, these high standard deviation events interfere with the trading indications upon which tactical allocation relies as well.

Yet invest we must, and given the arithmetic of percentages, having an appropriate asset allocation when markets have hit bottom and begin to recover is the best means of recouping the wealth that has been so wantonly destroyed. Rebuilding a sense of how different assets and investment techniques will behave relative to each other, and of the returns that they will offer in the first year or so subsequent to the crisis, becomes more crucial than ever. On the one hand, the window of opportunity is likely to be narrow—depending on a variety of circumstances, three to nine months is generally a good guess—and on the other, the opportunity cost of failing to implement an allocation that can exploit those transient circumstances (assuming the institution has the liquid resources to do so) is very great. If the episode has discernable macroeconomic implications, they will usually provide some valuable guidance with respect to some portion of the assets, strategies, and/or investment techniques to which an institution already has exposure, but not to all. They may also suggest additions to the institution's investable universe. Otherwise, analysis must focus on determining in what respects the future will resemble the "normal" *status quo ante* and in what respects the post-crisis markets have entered a new phase.

Correlations during Market Crises

Bookstaber (1999) has produced a vivid description of markets in turmoil that provides the groundwork for an insightful analysis of such phenomena. It furnishes the superstructure upon which the discussion that follows has been erected, and it is a valuable contribution to investment thinking in its own right. Consequently, it deserves citation at length:

> In a normal market, investors have time to worry about the little things: the earnings of this company *versus* that company, P/Es, dividends, future prospects, and who is managing what. As the energy level goes up in the market, investors . . . need to concentrate on sectors. If the technology sector is underperforming, all technology stocks look the same. If oil prices go up, an oil company's management and earnings prospects no longer matter; all that matters is that the company is in the energy sector. Turn up the heat further to a crash environment and all that participants care about is that it is a stock and that they can sell it. All stocks look the same. . . . The market is different; the habitat has changed.
>
> An analogy from high-energy physics helps to illustrate the situation. As energy increases, the constituents of matter blur. At low energy levels . . . molecules and atoms are distinct and differentiated. As energy goes up, the molecules break apart and what is left are the basic building blocks of matter, the elements. As energy goes up even more, the atoms break apart and plasma is left. Everything is a diffused blob of matter.
>
> As the energy of the market increases, the same transformation happens to the constituents of the market. In a market crisis, all the distinct

elements of the market—the stocks (e.g., IBM and Intel), the assets (e.g., corporate bonds and swap spreads)—turn into an undifferentiated plasma. Just as in high-energy physics, where all matter becomes an undifferentiated "soup," in the high-energy state of a market crisis, all assets blur into undifferentiated risk.

One of the most troubling aspects of a market crisis is that diversification strategies fail. . . . The reason for the lack of diversification is that in a high-energy market all assets in fact *are* the same. . . . What matters is no longer the economic or financial relationship between assets but the degree to which they share habitat. What matters is who holds the assets. If mortgage derivatives are held by the same traders as Japanese swaps, these two types of unrelated assets will become highly correlated because a loss in the one asset will force the traders to liquidate the other. What is most disturbing about this situation is . . . that there is no way to determine which assets will be correlated with which other assets during a market crisis. That is, not only will diversification fail to work at the very time it is most critical, but determining the way in which it will fail will be impossible. (10–11)

At the heart of Bookstaber's account of market crises is a rejection of the idea that there is continuity between the behavior and trading structure of "normal" markets and of those of the same markets when they are in crisis mode. He bases his distinction on the behavior of liquidity demanders and liquidity suppliers in different market circumstances, and thus his analysis skirts around the entire infrastructure of the Efficient Market Hypothesis and the standard academic account of how markets function. In the process, he is able to make sense of a peculiarity of markets, which is that, in certain circumstances, a sort of negative demand elasticity plays a prominent role in market participants' thinking—declining prices make assets *less* rather than *more* attractive. Interestingly (and a confirmation that Bookstaber is almost certainly onto something here), this is consistent with the opposite situation that may be witnessed in the later stages of a speculative bubble, a form of negative demand elasticity in which price increases foster increased demand for assets.

Both phenomena—if they can in fact be regarded as distinct—relate to what Bookstaber describes as the markets' energy state. They are likely distinct, and bullish negative elasticity is a state of intermediate energy (where security-specific features are ignored but where asset categories remain significant for investors' behavior) that is preliminary to markets entering the high-energy state that constitutes actual panic.

At least, that seems to have been the progression during the Technology Bubble, which collapsed after Bookstaber had written this analysis. A similar progression from boom to indiscriminate revulsion affected commodities and commodity-related equities in 2007 to 2008. Notably, the phenomenon of negative demand elasticity is more familiar to commodity traders—at any rate, I first heard the notion explicitly articulated in conversation with one—than it is to commentators on equity or fixed-income markets, although Wilmott (1998, 370) gives it implicit formal expression in connection with his discussion of the feedback effects of hedging as they relate to the Crash of 1987.

Such market conditions are all but incomprehensible to conventional financial economics, and during the question-and-answer session after he presented his paper, Bookstaber explicitly stated that "Low-energy diversification is the Markowitz diversification," which his analysis consigns to irrelevance during periods of market crisis (18). His thinking about crises rejects the information-based approach to understanding market function that lies at the root of the Efficient Market Hypothesis, replacing it with a liquidity-based understanding of markets. That is, rather than regarding all asset price movements as responses to new information that has suddenly reached the market, he segregates price behavior into different categories. In one of these—the crisis state—he regards changes in asset prices as responses to changes in investors' liquidity preferences and the availability of liquidity from market makers and other liquidity providers such as hedge funds and speculators. Thus, he offers an answer to a puzzle that finance theory finds intractable: what information could suddenly have entered the market on October 19, 1987, to which a greater than 20 standard deviation event was a commensurate response? His answer is, quite simply, "none." On Bookstaber's analysis, that event was caused by trading behavior itself, rather than the advent of news that influenced trading behavior.

As might be expected from an analysis based on a model of market participants' trading behavior and the microeconomics of the trading business that underlie it, the sort of diversification Bookstaber proposes as protection from what he calls high-energy states is diversification by counterparties and what he refers to as trading "habitats" rather than diversification by asset or factor exposures. That is, the diversification that he thinks will offer (comparative) safety in high-energy markets is not in terms of portfolio holdings but in terms of trading relationships and the exposure to risk in the trading "habitats" that an investment manager chooses to occupy. However, as he also notes, that choice cannot always be well-informed.

Unfortunately, Bookstaber's description of the sort of diversification that might protect portfolios during high-energy market episodes has been overtaken by events—as he seems to have feared it might be at the time he was writing, and as he acknowledges has in fact occurred in a more recent publication (Bookstaber 2007). Ten years after he presented his paper, the globalization and consolidation of markets and market participants has rendered his recommendation to diversify among counterparties and "habitats" largely moot. The "malling of Wall Street" that he predicted has occurred, so that every trading "habitat" seems to feature the same collection of "big box" liquidity providers and the same crowd of customers clamoring for liquidity. The result is, or approaches being, a single global trading "habitat" that seems to offer few if any opportunities for diversification. **Figure 17.1** illustrates one day's activity in a specific liquidity "habitat." Although it does not depict a market transaction environment, its implications are fairly clear for any liquidity environment in which interconnectedness is similarly tight and concentration on a few principle nodes is similarly great.

There has been ample recent evidence of this phenomenon. When the soundness of the Belgian banking system is tested by mortgage defaults in Nevada or one-month LIBOR resets receive comment in the Akron *Sentinel*, the world's trading "habitats" have clearly coalesced to a very substantial degree. The market turmoil of 2007 to 2009 differed from

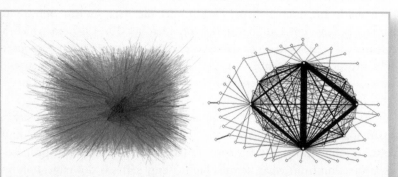

The figure on the left represents one day's Fedwire® interbank payments network activity among more than 6,600 banks executing more than 70,000 transfers between them. The figure on the right represents the activity at the core of the network (dimly perceptible as the dark center of the figure on the left), consisting of 66 banks and accounting for 75 percent of payments by value.

FIGURE 17.1 *Tight Coupling in Financial Networks*

Source: Soramäki et al. (2006, 2); used with permission of the Federal Reserve Bank of New York.

the crisis case studies that Bookstaber uses to support his 1999 analysis because of its intimate linkage with a deep recession in the global real economy. This suggests that there *may* be reason to hope that diversification among "habitats" can offer *some* protection to portfolios against *some* future crises, provided that the future crises lack this sort of linkage to global macroeconomic developments. But the cat is clearly out of the bag, and investors are probably wise to assume that diversification among "habitats" will offer at best limited portfolio protection during future crises, particularly since, as a consequence of the 2007 to 2009 episode, securities industry consolidation has progressed even further, at the same time that the liquidity available from market makers and speculators has decreased. Poorly conceived regulatory responses to that episode are likely to ensure that a shortage of liquidity to facilitate transactions remains in place for some time to come.

The Aftermath of the Recent Market Crisis

Many authors have commented on the misfortune that diversification is least useful when it is most needed, but few that I am aware of have devoted much attention to what is to be done with portfolios after this problem has manifested itself during a market collapse. Chapter 15 discussed the likely need for portfolio rebalancing as a risk-control measure in the wake of a market crisis, and this chapter emphasizes the importance of such rebalancing in order to optimize recovery from the portfolio consequences of such an episode. Just as the protection offered by diversification fails when it is most desperately needed, so the challenges to investment allocation are greatest when clear signposts for investors would have the greatest value to them. To our sorrow, high standard deviation events alter those signposts. I am reminded of the time my wife and I were lost in the Tetons, dusk was falling, it began to rain, and we saw sign of bears. An unaltered signpost would have been most welcome, but having become lost in the first place because someone had tampered with the trail signs, we could not trust the directional markers we saw and were left without guidance until it became dark enough to see headlights on a road. Investors would be unwise to assume that an analogous indication of the path out of their predicament will be available after a crisis, although an occasional guiding light may glimmer through.

In several places I have mentioned the need to stress-test conclusions that are based on correlation analyses, but of course, real-world stress provides a far better test than simulation or study, and few portfolios escaped its effects in 2007 to 2009. Chapter 4 suggested some ways to perform such a test in terms of the fundamentals that drive the volatility, correlations, and relative value of different assets and investment techniques. Bookstaber's analysis of market crises offers some additional suggestions. While I believe he deliberately leaves his concept of market "habitat" somewhat vague,[1] the "habitats" they occupied certainly played a significant role in different portfolios' performance during the recent trial by fire, and examining recent history in light of his idea may help give some concreteness to his notion.

So, for example, leveraged buyout and commercial real estate funds clearly found themselves together in a single corporate credit "habitat." Investors Diversified Realty (2008) estimates that commercial real estate leverage averaged as much as 1:20 (indebtedness of 95 percent) prior to the beginning of the Credit Crunch (15), and while leveraged buyouts were not as highly leveraged as that, debt issuance of $669 billion in 2007 alone (Meerkatt and Liechtenstein 2008, 2) suggests that they had borrowed plenty. With energy- and commodity-related shares providing essentially the sole support for equity prices in the first half of 2008, equities and commodities shared "habitat," with alarming consequences for equity benchmarks when commodity prices collapsed that summer. Venture capital funds, unable to find exits for their mature holdings given the condition of the equity markets and the reluctance on the part of trade buyers in an environment of uncertain credit availability (see Wade 2009b), also faced challenges to obtain mezzanine funding. They are always, to a greater extent than their proponents would typically allow, a part of the equity "habitat," but environmental influences from the equity world made themselves even more strongly felt on venture capital than usual, and they found themselves with comparatively unaccustomed exposure to credit market developments as well. Major currencies, having more than a minor functional role in every market "habitat," behaved with atypical volatility amidst all the other dislocations, which in turn fed back into the markets for all other assets, especially through the medium of the short-term Treasury market. Meanwhile, the consolidation

---

1. However, it is quite clear that he does not intend what Lo calls an "ecology" (2004, 23), which is an information-based construct governed by behavioral considerations, rather than a liquidity "habitat": see the next chapter. Use of metaphors from biology is on the rise in financial discussions: May et al. (2008), all the authors of which are biologists, draw analogies from environmental science and, not surprisingly in light of recent events, Haldane (2009) finds useful comparisons to epidemiology.

among investment banks, in an environment of increasingly tight credit, had significantly reduced the liquidity available to participants in all of these markets.

Within the universe of liquid alternative investment techniques, trades that by their nature were always vulnerable to the evaporation of liquidity were early victims—notably naïve quantitative long/short equity managers (as a result of overcrowding in their trades) and those techniques that employ corporate bonds, especially convertibles. As the markets' "energy levels" continued to rise—particularly after the mid-September 2008 bankruptcy of Lehman Brothers—margin calls began to put pressure on all leveraged trades, and traders that did not experience margin calls nevertheless experienced a contraction in available credit. As we saw in Figure 11.4, event-driven trades held up better through the summer than long/short techniques, but event-driven funds eventually came under significant pressure, too, although not to as great an extent as long/short vehicles. As a general rule, neither technique is especially highly leveraged, but as the equity "habitat" deteriorated, all investors who populated it were affected, although event-driven investors in particular were less affected than many others.

There is no benchmark for high-frequency traders, but anecdotally, my impression is that most of them weathered the debacle fairly well, which is consistent with their market neutrality, but is also a function of their role as liquidity providers. In line with Bookstaber's analysis of the economic function of liquidity provision (1999, 9), as liquidity became scarce, these traders' margins for providing it actually improved. According to the HFRX Volatility Index (see Figure 8.2), volatility traders also performed well, probably for the same reasons. Nevertheless, high-frequency traders experienced some difficulties, in a few cases withdrawing from trading activity entirely as market volatility went beyond the ability of their trade identification and risk management systems to cope with it—high-frequency strategies that stick to pure arbitrage strategies seem, as would be expected, to have been most affected. In the extremely choppy markets at the beginning of 2009, trend-following traders also suffered, as might be expected in such conditions: see Cui (2009). Among illiquid trades, vulnerability to the market crisis was largely a function of the source of revenue. While private equity and real estate valuations suffered to some extent, cash flow generation from these sources was not necessarily impaired, and provided that new financing or exits were unnecessary, the investments performed relatively well. However, funds that were in need of financing or an exit suffered, in some cases very dramatically. Some short-term direct lenders experienced a rise in defaults, but others—and also mezzanine debt providers—reported improved lending opportunities, if not necessarily better terms, as competition from banks and other providers of financing decreased.

The challenge for investment policymakers, in light of such a litany, is to sort through the wreckage for opportunity. Investment techniques that exhibited strong relative performance during the crisis may in some cases merely have postponed longer-term underperformance, particularly if their outperformance was largely due to the fact that they mark infrequently to estimated markets. This seems quite likely to be the fate of private equity and at least some (although more likely all) categories of directionally oriented commercial real estate, because leverage levels will not recover quickly, exits will remain difficult, further delay of exits will erode internal rates of return and corporate profits, and property leasing and occupancy rates will continue to be under considerable pressure for some time after markets in liquid instruments begin to recover. But for precisely the same reasons, opportunities for mezzanine and some other direct lenders are likely to continue to be good, which should fairly quickly feed through into an improvement of the terms on which they lend. The handful of naïve quantitative long/short funds that survived the debacle may find that their opportunities improve as their trades become less crowded, and in general, the depletion of hedge fund assets as a result of negative performance and withdrawals can be expected to bolster the subsequent performance of the survivors that are able to continue the pursuit of whatever trades they engage in.

But some trades will be under a cloud for a considerable time. Convertible arbitrage recovered smartly in the first half of 2009, but it is questionable whether it will be able to continue to thrive. Fixed-income strategies in corporate debt generally will probably fail to attract the investor interest that they had recently enjoyed. These trades were strongly touted as "absolute return" techniques, but as with many such techniques, they displayed unacceptably "fat tails." However, assuming a return to more "normal" credit conditions, neglect of such vehicles will likely turn out to be a mistake. Distressed debt has yet to show much for all the hundreds of billions raised for that trade during 2008, and it seems likely to me that this trade is overcrowded before it has even had an opportunity to perform. However, the capacity available for exploiting opportunities in distressed mortgage instruments is limited by the paucity of loan processing capability, and more opportunity may lie there and in other instruments structured from retail loans than in corporate distress. As a consequence, some entirely new trades have opened up: for instance, purchase and work-out of distressed automobile loans.

Note that this very rough sketch of the aftermath to the recent drama in world markets does not rely very strongly on fundamental analysis or any assumptions about correlation among assets that were dramatically revalued by events. In the wake of a market crisis, liquidity considerations remain significant, as traditional sources of liquidity may have been exhausted or at least severely impaired. In particular, the winnowing of the ranks of investment banks' trading desks, greater credit discipline at deposit-taking institutions, and the dramatic shrinkage experienced by hedge funds have changed the picture for the availability of liquidity very significantly. In some markets, economic fundamentals may take years to reassert themselves, and while this spells opportunity for investment policymakers who are confident in their ability to be successful contrarians, they also will almost certainly have to be patient. There is a stock market adage that "a bargain that remains a bargain is no bargain," and in the aftermath of a market crisis there are a lot of those to be found.

But investors must exercise considerable caution in looking to the pre-crisis environment for clues to the "proper" valuation of certain assets in its aftermath. For example, eight years after the collapse of the Technology Bubble, the best closing level for the NASDAQ Composite Index was 57 percent of its March 10, 2000, peak value, in contrast to the broader market's full recovery to pre-Bubble levels within five years. Yet the correlation history exhibited in Figure 17.2 indicates that, once technology issues' relationship of value relative to the broad market had been adjusted by the brutal sell-off in those shares subsequent to their March 2000 peak, technology stocks established a very strong and highly stable correlation with the broader market. This suggests a one-off adjustment to their relative valuation with little or no prospect that earlier, extraordinary levels of relative valuation will be recovered—a conclusion to which common sense might have led in any case. Because venture capital occupies the same "habitat," it too has failed to recover its earlier rates of return. The assumption that valuations are mean reverting may be true, but investors are wise to consider carefully what the appropriate period is from which to draw the mean to which values can be expected to revert.

The "Normal" Market "Habitat"

I have stressed throughout this book that correlations change over time unless there is a systematic reason for them not to. This is not categorical, however, and Chapter 10 touched on an alternative situation, where anomalous relationships between some instruments, in particular fixed-income securities, are likely to persist over time but do not seem to be fully systematic, as there is no mechanism other than the attentions of arbitrageurs that forces them to converge, although they always seem to do so eventually. Market drama will usually offer up discrepancies in quite a few of the latter sorts of price relationships, and reversion to "normal" in these cases is one signal that markets are departing from crisis mode—although, given the reliance of correlation calculations on time series data, it is necessarily a lagging indicator. Thus, many market participants looked to a narrowing of high-grade corporate credit spreads as an indicator of a return to equity and other market normality late in 2008. All of which raises the question: are non-systematic correlations mean-reverting?

On the face of it, there is no reason in principal that they should be. Figure 1.1 illustrated a situation—the relationship between oil prices and the value of the dollar against an index of the currencies of the United States' most important trading partners—in which correlations may be in the process of being permanently reset. However, it is important to remember that correlation is a matter of relative price movements, which accumulate to become relative values. If there were no mean reversion, then we would be faced with the possibility that some trees might actually succeed in "growing to the sky." Although relationships between asset prices may reset, once that process has occurred (and it may be a sudden occurrence or a gradual development over time) they will tend to revert to their new mean value. A fairly sudden readjustment—completed over the course of only six months—was illustrated in **Figure 17.2**.

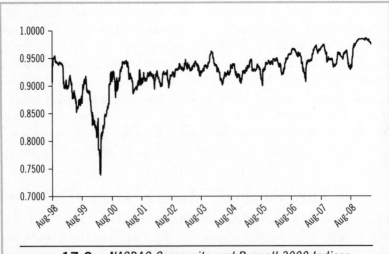

FIGURE 17.2 *NASDAQ Composite and Russell 3000 Indices: 90-Day Trailing Coefficient of Correlation*

Figure **17.3** and **17.4** show the correlation histories of the actual and residual returns of two rather dissimilar large capitalization equities— that is, Figure 17.3 shows the correlation of their daily price changes, and Figure 17.4 exhibits only that portion of their daily returns that is not ascribable to their market βs relative to the Standard & Poor's 500 Index. The data exhibit a statistically significant trend, indicated by the trendlines, which have virtually identical slopes. That is, the change in the correlation between the two stocks can be explained more or less entirely by the change in the market's perception of their specific risks.

This indicates that relative valuations *do* revert to the mean, but that the return derived from specific risk does not. In other words, assets do not depart indefinitely from market-derived relative valuations, which cause them to maintain a relationship of correlation with market metrics and thus with each other, but their idiosyncratic return characteristics (or the market's perception of them) may change over time, and the contribution of those characteristics to their returns does not revert to a mean but may permanently change, either suddenly or over an extended period. In other words, market participants definitely distinguish between the α and β components of a security's price behavior. It is interesting to note from Figure 17.4 that the market seems to be deciding that the specific risks of General Electric and Procter & Gamble Co. are (or have become) significantly less similar than it had previously thought.

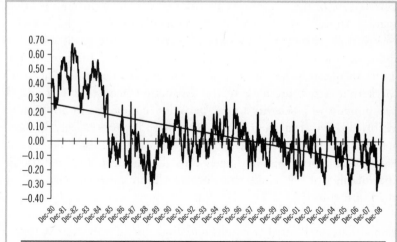

Source: Bloomberg Finance L.P.

FIGURE 17.3 *Procter & Gamble and General Electric: 90-Day Trailing Coefficient of Correlation*

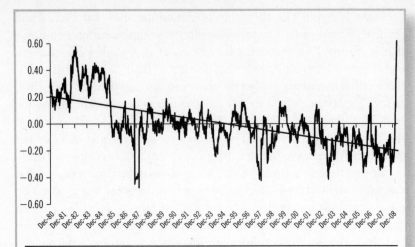

FIGURE 17.4   *Procter & Gamble and General Electric: 90-Day Trailing and β-Adjusted* Coefficient of Correlation*

*Adjusted to remove correlation to the Standard & Poor's 500 Index.

The charts also offer further detail on the behavior of markets during a "high energy" or "phase-locking" episode. In Figure 17.4, note that the correlations of the stocks' specific risk was very high during the 2008 market panic. This suggests that Bookstaber's analysis of the behavior of investors in such an environment—their tendency to ignore even quite significant information that might otherwise differentiate the assets in question—is quite a powerful one. Although in "normal" markets investors are alive to the distinction between the α and β components of a security's price behavior, conditions in 2008 quite visibly drove it from their minds. The sharp increase in negative correlation in 1987 would seem to provide a counter-example, but as **Figure 17.5** shows, this was largely caused by a substantial increase in the volatility of P&G, and thus shows up more clearly in Figure 17.4 than in Figure 17.3.

All of which provides a partial clue to determining what correlation in "normal" market conditions might be. To the extent that a strategy or instrument correlates with the broad market, its correlation should revert to a mean value over significant periods of time— Figure 16.2 and other examples scattered throughout this volume

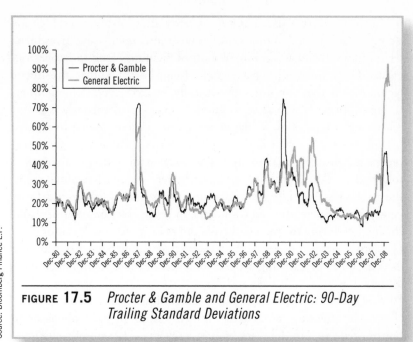

FIGURE 17.5 *Procter & Gamble and General Electric: 90-Day Trailing Standard Deviations*

suggest that in most cases such reversion has a roughly three-year periodicity. But the residual portion of the instrument's returns that derives from its idiosyncratic characteristics does not revert, although it will change as those characteristics change relative to the characteristics of the investment technique or asset to which it is being compared. A single-factor analysis such as this one is rather a blunt instrument, and multi-factor analysis, for all its embedded statistical assumptions, is likely to be more revealing of where correlations will settle out. In the case of General Electric and P&G, for instance, one undoubted reason for the divergence of their specific risk characteristics is General Electric's factor loading toward financial activities. However, my result for a single-factor model is consistent with the Capital Asset Pricing Model, which requires a linear relationship between asset returns and their β, not between their returns and their total risk. Lhabitant (2004) comments that ". . . one could say that the CAPM philosophy is the exact opposite of traditional stock picking, as it attempts to understand the market as a whole rather than look at what makes each investment opportunity unique" (71). This is a rather more elegant formulation of the contrast I have drawn between "lumpers" and "splitters."

In the recovery phase after a crisis, correlations may remain high for a considerable period of time—just as most instruments and investment techniques suffered as a group, so most of them may tend to recover as a group. This raises special challenges for long/short and other investment techniques if they are not systematically hedged. Determining when the returning tide will cease to raise all boats simultaneously is by no means a simple matter. While in some cases differentiation in relative performance may occur fairly rapidly, in others it may be a fitful and protracted process, particularly if the initial stabilization of markets is followed by the re-entry of specialist buyers seeking bargains among the wreckage. Acquisitive corporations, investors in distressed debt or equity, and dealers who had withheld non-perishable commodities from the market during the period of crisis can prevent expected relationships of relative value from re-asserting themselves immediately, making life difficult for return-seeking hedgers for a year or more after markets have clamed down.

Practitioners of naïve quantitative techniques are especially vulnerable to the attentions of predatory traders and to the entry of corporate bottom-feeders into the markets after a severe correction of valuations. Restricted liquidity will tend to make their hedging trades vulnerable to traders who can anticipate their activities. At the same time, their simple screens are likely to put such quantitative managers into hedges that become acquisition targets while their long positions in "quality" issues, which fail to attract similar buying interest, underperform the stocks in which they are short. On the other hand, these conditions are clearly ideal for practitioners of risk arbitrage, distressed investing, those private equity funds that have managed to retain "dry powder," and so on. Lucretius noted that "one man's meat is another's poison" more than two millennia ago and in an entirely different context, but his observation remains pertinent to market participants today.

Correlations do not present the only statistical challenge to investors in the aftermath of a market crisis. As Chapter 3 discussed, hedge ratios are strongly affected by the difference between individual instruments' or strategies' standard deviations, not just their correlations relative to each other. The statistical history for these will, more or less by definition, have been altered by a market conniption, but it is not clear that there is reason to expect the instruments' volatility to revert to a mean or that the relationship between the standard deviations of different instruments or investment techniques will revert in that way.

Figure 17.5 indicates that, as would be expected, standard deviations drop back quickly after a high standard deviation event such as the two market crises that occurred during the period shown there, and they can be expected to decrease after the crisis that was still in process at the time the chart was created. However, the behavior of the two series for several years after the collapse of the Technology Bubble in March 2000 indicates that, at the very least, there are few grounds for believing that mean reversion will in every case be rapid. Consequently, even though (as Figure 17.3 indicates) the correlation between these two instruments did not depart noticeably from its "normal" levels and trend in the aftermath of the Technology Bubble, their hedge relationship to each other (and consequently their ability to diversify each other) remained for a protracted period quite different from what it had been before the Bubble burst in 2000. For a long-term (1871–2000) history of the standard deviation of a broad market measure, see Jones and Wilson (2004, 103). Their findings tend to confirm the idea that standard deviation is relatively stable over time, but nevertheless exhibits some quite noticeable departures from trend for protracted periods.

In the wake of market calamities, investment policymakers must re-examine the assumptions behind their pre-existing investment allocation as well as those supporting any opportunistic changes they may be interested in making. In the absence of the familiar sources of guidance based on valuations and correlations that can be relied upon in "normal" markets, fundamental economic considerations and an analysis of the liquidity "habitat" provide the best support for sound decision-making. Neither the assumption that markets will return to their *status quo ante* nor a tendency to regard the post-Crash market landscape as having been radically and inalterably changed are likely to be very helpful points of departure. Time is pressing, and the data that might be used to support decision-making accumulates slowly, so investors are not at leisure to rely on the gradual accumulation of data histories to provide the basis for forecasts of market relationships and relative returns. But the opportunity to recover the wealth destroyed by a high standard deviation event is too precious to waste. Although investment committees cannot prepare action plans in advance for such eventualities, they can at least prepare themselves with a shortlist of the questions for which they will want, as soon as possible, to find answers.

Liquidity-Takers and Liquidity-Providers

Recalling Mainelli's (2007, 1) definition of liquidity as "'the probability that an asset can be converted into an expected amount of value within an expected amount of time," the denizens of liquidity "habitats" can be divided into two broad species—liquidity-takers and liquidity-providers. The former are primarily concerned with the time required to execute their business and the latter with the price at which they execute it. Obviously, neither type of investor is completely indifferent to the other concern, which is why Mainelli combines these considerations in his definition, but the distinction between these species is a matter of the trader's priorities. These priorities may change with the trader's circumstances— for most firms, there will be occasions when getting the transaction done is paramount, and other occasions when the trader has the leisure to "work" the trade in pursuit of the best available price.

Arbitrageurs represent a hybrid species. On the one hand, their trade is, by definition, motivated by the desire to exploit transitory pricing relationships, and its success is thus crucially dependent upon their traders' ability to execute both legs of it at the price differential that will deliver their required returns. On the other hand, the risk of acquiring unhedged directional exposure requires that they be equally sensitive to the immediacy of their executions—otherwise, in the attempt to "work" one leg of the trade they would be directionally exposed until their orders are filled. This accounts for arbitrageurs' preference for highly liquid markets, where the risk that one leg of the trade fails to execute at the desired price is kept to a minimum. It also accounts for the careful attention they devote to their trading infrastructure. Where arbitrageurs tread in less liquid "habitats," as is frequently the case, for instance, in capital structure arbitrage, the price differentials that they seek to exploit must be correspondingly richer, to compensate them for this operational risk.

As long as they are not under obligations to make markets, liquidity-providers are generally better defended against market crises than liquidity-takers, and may even benefit from crises, as volatility generally contributes to the opportunity sets that their opportunism seeks to exploit. This is perhaps most apparent in the case of investment techniques that exploit distressed situations. In "normal" conditions, these traders can afford to wait for prices to reach their targets before transacting, as the liquidity-taking seller is likely to be highly motivated and competition for damaged goods is generally low. There is a spider-and-fly aspect to many liquidity-providing techniques that however unfairly, does nothing to enhance their practitioners' reputations. But many of these trading techniques are highly vulnerable to overcrowding: if too many traders seek to exploit distress, pricing discipline breaks down, and the transactions occur at prices higher than their target purchase valuations. In these circumstances, practitioners of distressed investing face an unattractive choice between transacting at levels that offer less than their required levels of return or failing to transact at all.

It is the liquidity-absorbing characteristic of private market investments that causes their sensitivity to crises in liquid markets. If the investment technique does not require recourse to the markets for an exit, and interim funding (for example, a mortgage refinancing) is not required while the crisis is under way, then despite illiquid investment techniques' liquidity-taking characteristics at the time of initial investment, they are partially insulated from any drama in the markets. Although their mark-to-market value is likely to be affected by developments in liquid markets, holders of such investments should be comparatively indifferent to such price behavior, particularly if their participation in those investments is driven by demand for cash flows from them. In principle, investors in private market directional trades, provided that the intended exit is sufficiently remote, might be indifferent to marks-to-market, too. But the evidence since the bursting of the Technology Bubble is that serious impairment of exit channels can last for years after the crisis in liquid markets has abated, so any indifference to their marks-to-market on the part of these investors is probably misplaced.

Outside of crisis periods, practitioners of directional and cash flow strategies seek to be liquidity-providers—that is, to avoid situations where the need for immediacy of execution takes precedence over achieving an attractive price—but circumstances can militate against this. Unanticipated flows of funds into or out of their investment vehicles, margin calls, and similar events may force them to transact when market conditions would otherwise argue against trading. There are a variety of stratagems that can cushion the risk from forced transactions. A highly diversified vehicle can choose between transacting in a few of its most liquid positions, without much fear that doing so will unbalance its portfolio, or it may transact in all of them, in the expectation that the market impact of each individual trade will be relatively small. Through trades that lean against the prevailing market wind and that consequently alter their long/short bias, long/short vehicles can, at least in principle, remain liquidity-providers in most market conditions. High-frequency directional traders lean against these winds as a full-time occupation, accounting for their performance advantage relative to trend-followers in the choppy markets of the first half of 2009. In general, hedge funds are able to manage this problem by permitting only occasional redemptions or contributions and imposing notification periods for withdrawals, but as was seen in 2008, these offer them only limited protection from the effects of a severe and protracted crisis.

Certain alternative investments can provide at least partial protection from liquidity crises through diversification of "habitat," although leverage and short exposure may also make them more vulnerable to them. One lesson that investors should certainly have drawn from the 2007 to 2009 episode is that vehicles that sport an "absolute return" moniker but that are highly leveraged may be especially vulnerable during periods of market turmoil. However, as Bookstaber warned, the "malling" of financial markets is now almost complete, and even the merely partial protections that certain liquid alternative investment techniques may offer were unavailable to investors in conventional vehicles during the recent crisis.

CHAPTER 18

Alternative Investments and Information Theory

In keeping with the environmental metaphor that occupied much of the previous chapter, here I turn to Andrew Lo's (2004) concept of information "ecologies" (23). In contrast to Bookstaber's idea of liquidity "habitats," Lo's notion is defined in terms of competition among different "species" of investors to uncover and react promptly to new information. The use of "promptly" here suggests that there are some respects in which the two strands of analysis intertwine, as does Bookstaber's account of how relevant certain forms of information are in different liquidity conditions. I will scratch the surface of this commonality between their two notions to some extent below, although it is really a topic for a different book entirely. But Lo's analysis is primarily information theoretic rather than an account of the way that liquidity conditions affect market participants' trading behavior.

The liquidity environment in which the considerations of information theory are most relevant is Bookstaber's "low energy" state, the "normal" market condition where the full range of fundamental considerations concerning individual investments affects their pricing and where what he calls "Markowitz diversification" retains its full relevance. In Bookstaber's account, as the "energy level" of the markets rises, highly specific information becomes progressively less influential on an instrument's price behavior. First market participants lose sight of information regarding the idiosyncratic characteristics of individual investments, and in the ultimate "plasma state" of crisis they ignore all information about the investment except their ability to transact in it. From this it is clear that this chapter will devote itself to a discussion of investment in "normal," "low temperature" circumstances rather than the "high energy" state of extreme crisis conditions.

Lo's information "ecologies" are the competitive environments in which investors' trade discovery activities vie with each other to identify and exploit new opportunities. While an enormous amount of information is common to all participants in any given market, the outperformance that can be achieved by some firms relative to those practiced by similarly disciplined managers depends upon information that other participants in that market have yet to uncover or to process, and reacting to it before those others can. These "ecologies" may overlap to a greater or lesser degree. For example, a merger arbitrageur operates to some extent in the same information "ecology" as a conventional, long-only equity manager. However, in other respects, merger arbitrageurs occupy an information "ecology" of their own, distinct from that of the broader equity market "ecology" in which it is "embedded." "Ecologies" may be less or more remote from each other, and the distance between them can vary over time. Thus developments in the fixed-income or commodity markets may be largely irrelevant to equity investors for long periods of time, but become information that is crucially important to their decision-making at other points in the market cycle. It is notable, for instance, that there are times when equity investors hang on every word from the Federal Open Markets Committee, and others when they may well be unaware that its minutes have even been released.

Investment Strategies in Information "Ecologies"

All three investment strategies may be part of wider or narrower information "ecologies." This may sound peculiar for arbitrages, which are in most cases trades in comparatively liquid public market securities, implying that the information underlying these trades is widely disseminated to a varied and rich "ecology." However, the information requirement for arbitrageurs is different from that of non-arbitrage traders in the same instruments, and in many cases not so easily accessible to them. Note, for example, my emphasis in Chapter 7 on merger arbitrageurs' intellectual capital requirements and the necessity for them to internalize a fair portion of that intellectual capital. Although other arbitrage trades may not be quite so demanding of research support, they nevertheless require analytical resources that may not be available (at least in timely fashion) to other traders in their markets. Thus, for instance, while pricing discrepancies in, say, the Treasury market may be plain for all to see, the hedge analytics necessary to exploit them with reasonably consistent success are not present on every trading desk. Further, a long-only constraint and lack of access to leverage prevents many investors from pursuing these opportunities even if they are quite aware of them and are otherwise capable of exploiting them. Without the leverage required to make the returns on these trades attractive and without the protection offered by arbitrageurs' ability to hedge with accuracy, conventional investors are unlikely to exploit the opportunities that constitute fixed-income arbitrageurs' bread and butter. But they are hardly oblivious to them. To push the biological metaphor further, arbitrageurs have adapted to thrive on a diet that is inadequate to the return requirements of other traders in the same instruments.

If we take seriously Bookstaber's analysis of liquidity "habitats," then diversification among these "habitats," however imperfect, is a valuable thing. Lo does not explore the notion of diversification among "ecologies," but it is difficult to imagine that the same would not be true. The differential performance between equities and credit spreads as economies tumbled toward recession during much of 2008 supports this view. Yet the globalization and homogenization of investment impinges upon the isolation of "ecologies" just as it does for liquidity "habitats," and in many cases it is likely that liquidity travels faster than knowledge. In the 2007–2009 crisis, such obscure but seemingly well-insulated enclaves as the stock exchange of Botswana were affected by the global contagion. Long before investors in major markets even become aware that there is such an exchange, let alone acquire the information and familiarity necessary to invest on it, the global liquidity network apparently extends to that distant node as well. Even these comparatively obscure corners seem to have been included within the scope of the "malling" of financial markets that Bookstaber describes. But the degree to which liquidity serves as a transmission mechanism for knowledge is likely to vary in unpredictable ways.

Private market investments are obviously in an at least somewhat different liquidity "habitat," in Bookstaber's sense, from similar publicly traded investments. An investment's failure to mark-to-market should not be confused with differences in timing or time horizon relative to publicly traded investments, but it does constitute an at least marginal difference in "habitat." But to a much greater extent, private market investors inhabit "ecologies" of their own, isolated from outsiders, because the information available to them is not available to others. Assuming that they are not dishonest, for private market directional strategies that require an exit through public markets, this may not be much of advantage, since most of their valuable information must be publicly disclosed prior to an initial public offering. But where the exit is through a trade sale, the ability to protect information behind non-disclosure agreements can preserve its value to both pre-existing investors and the eventual purchaser. Here, as in the case of arbitrage, an analogy might be drawn with the parallelisms sometimes observed between different environmental niches: for example, swallows and some species of bats occupy much the same niche, but at the same time it is as different (literally) as night and day.

While the "ecological" isolation of private market investments is not generally complete at the time exposure to them is acquired—it is only seldom that their investors are not in competition with other potential investors to make a purchase—once exposure has been obtained, its information value is largely exclusive their purchaser. The ability as a matter of course to avoid such competition to purchase is a rare and highly privileged position, generally available only to a few firms such as the "Golden Circle" of venture capitalists (Hsu [2004] attempts to quantify these firms' pricing advantage). Even then, their pricing is certain to have at least some reference to the marketplace, for all that their privileges are likely to extend to more attractive pricing. Networking is an important aspect of private market investing not least because it occasionally offers such opportunities to investment managers who do not belong to such charmed circles. But once the purchase of such an investment is completed, even less privileged private market investors can keep a great deal of potentially valuable information to themselves. For example, it may be difficult to hide the identity of the beneficial owner of farmland or the price it paid for it from other interested parties. But once it is purchased, the financing structure of the transaction, negotiated lease rates, any planned improvements, the investor's time horizon, and anticipated exit strategy need not be disclosed to anyone.

High-frequency trading is of necessity an alternative, long/short technique. For all that they are abundantly visible to them, high-frequency trading and information environs are inaccessible to conventional investment techniques, because long-only high-frequency trading is virtually an oxymoron. Note the howls of protest from market makers when regulatory authorities imposed bans on short-selling during 2008, and the special exemptions that regulators soon felt obliged to grant to them. Although high-frequency techniques are pursued in the familiar world of liquid instruments and their derivatives, they have the effect, like Alice's rabbit hole, of transporting those who employ these techniques into a different investment realm from those who operate on longer time horizons. Clearly this is a separate liquidity "habitat," and Chapter 8 argued at length that high-frequency trading operates in its own "ecology."

Some might object that characterizing the high-frequency environment as an "ecology" in Lo's sense is a conceptual error, in that the very short-term actually contains no information at all. The theoretically orthodox, who view short-term price volatility as "noise" and nothing else, would deny that it contains any information, and they would argue that the fact that many people believe that it does says more about human psychology than about the markets. I am not clear on whether Lo would regard an informationless environment as an "ecology" or not, although I can see no reason in principle why he would not. In any case, his interest in technical analysis (see Lo [2000] as well as Lo and Hasanhodzie [2009]) indicates that he is willing to commit the grave finance theoretical heresy of entertaining the notion that there is information in price movements themselves. Actual practitioners of high-frequency techniques have never had any doubts. It is interesting to note, however, that this information is about liquidity. The transaction environment is, not surprisingly, the point at which "habitats" and "ecologies" coalesce. This is not the place to attempt a synthesis of Lo and Bookstaber, which I am not in any case qualified to do, but I think that this observation is very suggestive.

While alternative investment techniques might seem to have an edge over conventional ones in breaking new "ecological" ground, this is not to imply that there are no conventional investment techniques that occupy at least partially isolated information "ecologies." They tend to be comparatively obscure and illiquid, but the same might be said about many alternative investment techniques as well. Micro-cap U.S. equities and "pioneer" emerging markets are examples of environments where market-specific information generally overshadows the more widely available inputs from the global equity "ecology." Many might in fact regard these conventional, long-only investment areas as "alternative," and it is noticeable that most providers of hedge fund indices offer an "emerging markets" category, for all that in both equity and fixed-income this is an almost exclusively conventional, long-only investment technique. However, as my earlier reference to Botswana suggests, the isolation of even these markets is by no means splendidly complete.

Information Vacua

The marketing materials for many long/short investment products, particularly those that are quantitatively driven, often argue by implication that their short book operates in a distinct information "ecology" from that of conventional, long-only investors, and indeed, from that of their own long book. The point rests on the contention that security analysts generally work with an eye toward their firms' "Buy Lists," and that once a candidate is rejected for inclusion on that list, little further work is performed to determine whether it is in fact a "Sell" and thus a candidate for short-selling. This point is generally made by way of introduction to the sorts of claims for the information efficiency of naïve quantitative techniques that were mentioned in Chapter 5. There I dismissed these managers' pretensions with comments on their neglect of other risks attendant on carrying short exposure, but here I will go farther.

While I believe that there probably are some differences between the "ecologies" of candidates for short selling and potential long positions, I do not believe that naïve quantitative techniques are positioned either to identify or exploit these points of differentiation. By applying unaltered, off-the-shelf models to unfiltered, publicly available data, I believe that naïve quantitative techniques offer essentially no value added and approach a state of near perfect informationlessness. Screening sell-side analysts' estimates, after all, will not correct for their alleged tendency to concentrate their efforts on candidates for their "Buy Lists." It requires adoption of only the weakest form of the Efficient Markets Hypothesis to make such a claim: as Grinold and Kahn (*ibid.*) remark, "consensus in implies consensus out" (94), and this is hardly the road to adding value. Many funds of this sort were structured as 1940 Act mutual funds and sold to the general public as "130/30" vehicles. Daniel (2009, 20, Figure 9) illustrates quite plausibly the performance differential to be achieved through the application of "proprietary," "mostly proprietary," and "more well-known" quantitative strategies.

Fundamentally driven, return-seeking short sellers certainly seem to operate in a different information "ecology" from long-only investors—or at least, they seek to, and I believe that the most skillful of them succeed in doing so. The tales surrounding the intensity of the Feshbach Brothers' research in the 1980s and the unusual indicators they employed in connection with their spectacularly successful short positions in ZZZZ Best, Canon Group, Texas Air Corporation, and a long list of others[1] would certainly suggest that short sellers who devote sufficient resources and creativity to their trade discovery processes can insinuate

---

1. Matt, Kurt, and Joe Feshbach ran a short-sale fund from 1982 with considerable success until it fell on hard times in 1990. It was liquidated in 1992.

themselves into new, rich and largely unpopulated "ecologies." Short sellers who do not, cannot.

Is there an informationless "ecology"? The experience of naïve quantitative techniques in 2007 and again in 2008 (having learned no lessons) would seem to suggest that there is. It resembles a puddle on a hot day: it will not support life for long, but the niche fills rapidly until it begins to dry up. The reason for such a puddle's fecundity is that information-lessness is cheap and readily accessible. The first firm to enter the puddle thrives for a while, and its visible success spawns numerous new entrants. The competition among these firms for the same trades reduces the aggregate return achievable, and when the sun of the market begins to evaporate the puddle, what was perceived as opportunity becomes a trap. Naïve quantitative techniques provide excellent examples of the greater fool theory in action.

Additional Perspectives on Diversification

Referring specifically to hedge funds, Lo (2008) notes that "the long-only constraint imposes a limit on the amount of factor timing that can be accomplished [by conventional investment vehicles], and this limit can be a severe handicap in environments where factor risk premia change signs . . ." (169). This is a distinct claim from suggesting that alternative investments increase diversification through providing investment access to factor loadings that are unavailable to long-only techniques. It explicitly refers to returns to timing that are inaccessible to conventional investment managers. Alternative investments can provide exposure to time and timing in ways that are not possible for conventional investment techniques.

Lo is referring specifically to the timing benefits that can be extracted from hedge funds' ability to take short exposures, but there are a variety of other ways that alternative investment techniques can provide diversity of timing opportunity and time horizon. Many of these relate to the real options embedded in various private market investment techniques, and where an investment involves control (whether directly or through an agent such as a General Partner) they are substantially different from the options available to the managers of conventional investment techniques, which are binary options that only permit a choice between buying or selling. Activism may seek to arrogate some of these managerial real options, yet the information that is available to public market activists is substantially different from and inferior to what is available to corporate insiders. This is in fact one of the drawbacks to activism in public markets: even if it succeeds in obtaining the options it seeks, it may lack the information that lends them much of their value. Private market investments inhabit a different "ecology" in Lo's sense than even very similar public market investments, as the information available to managers and the variety of ways they are able to act upon it are quite different from what they are in public markets.

Investment Strategies in an Environmental Context

With the partial exception of the somewhat isolated information "ecology" inhabited by arbitrages, representatives of all three investment strategies populate all of Lo's and Bookstaber's biomes. It is the assets they are applied to, but more particularly the techniques that are applied to those assets, which provide environmental differentiation among them. However, it is possible to make some broad generalizations about the environments in which different investment techniques are pursued.

Investments in private market instruments—whether directional or cash flow trades, and whether long-term or short-term exposures—are not entirely insulated from either the liquidity "habitats" or the information "ecologies" of liquid public markets. Their relationship to those markets is closest at the points of entry and exit, but marks-to-market artificially keep them in touch with liquid markets, based on information analogies between liquid and illiquid instruments. As we have seen, where there is little or no information analogy, as in the case of unique works of art, marks-to-market become problematic to say the least. Or is this a matter of illiquidity, which causes the artwork to occupy its own "habitat"? Here, as in the very short-term environment of high-frequency traders, "ecology" and "habitat" seem to coalesce, and for similar reasons. This is an elegant and unexpected symmetry that suggests there might well be considerable value in attempting a synthesis of Lo's and Bookstaber's ideas.[2] However, in the case of unique artworks, the scarcity of information encounters an equal paucity of liquidity—the price

2. If there are investment circumstances in which there is liquidity and no other information, and circumstances in which there are neither liquidity nor information, are their circumstances in which there is information but no liquidity, which would complete the symmetry? There is such a circumstance—the Market Portfolio itself, which represents the limit-case for a wide range of investment ideas. Its "ecology" is the sum of all possible investment information, but it is not even observable, let alone transactable.

movements that may be said to constitute the information "ecology" of high-frequency traders are unavailable to potential investors in these illiquid assets.

Another aspect of potential synergy between Lo's and Bookstaber's ideas comes from a consideration of how the results of multi-factor analyses are affected by "high-energy" markets. When equities, credit spreads, commodities, and foreign exchange all respond similarly in a crisis, a multi-factor model is unable to distinguish which factor is actually affecting a given investment. It would appear that "ecologies," like "habitats," expand to embrace virtually the entire investable universe when the markets are in a "high-energy" state. As Bookstaber (1999, 10–11) suggests, the only relevant information is the ability (or inability) to transact: this is Hegel's "night in which all cows look black." Information "ecologies" coalesce because there is only one item of information that matters.

I have repeatedly drawn a contrast between the comparative indifference of cash flow investors to price movements in the underlying asset and their crucial importance to directional investors in the same sorts of asset. This is because, although they inhabit the same information "ecology"—as suggested by similar marks-to-market—they clearly inhabit different liquidity "habitats." The example in an earlier chapter of the real estate investor who reclassifies a directional trade as a cash flow exposure indicates that, by changing investment technique, the manager can migrate to a new "habitat." A change of "habitat" that does not require "virtual reallocation" occurs when a longer-dated bond crosses the one-year maturity threshold and becomes a money market instrument: entry into a new liquidity environment can occasionally be to the advantage of conventional fixed-income investors. Yet the relevant "ecology" does not change in either instance.

I argued, in the case of that real estate investor, that "virtual reallocation" can result from a legitimate reconsideration of the optimal means of exploiting an investment that was originally made with another strategy and outcome in mind. But in the case of equivocation between hedge positions and return-seeking investments, discussed in Chapter 3, the situation is quite different. Here there is a change of neither "ecology" nor "habitat," merely an *ex post* reinterpretation of the facts surrounding the initial decision to take on the exposure. While this might be considered a minor, even amusing peccadillo, along the lines of what happens in the retelling to the size of a fisherman's catch, it is a symptom of a lack of intellectual discipline that could have unfortunate consequences. After the fact, no damage can be done, but what does a tendency to rewrite history say about the manager's understanding of and control over its current exposures? The real estate investor may or may not be guilty of equivocation, but the hedger who slides too easily between a risk-reducing and a return-seeking understanding of its positions certainly is.

A long-only directional trade may become an event-driven one, at which point it might enter a different "ecology," for all that its liquidity "habitat" may remain the same. Hedge funds can in fact add considerable value through their ability to shift with comparative ease between information "ecologies." Although this ability is not completely inaccessible to conventional directional managers, it is less common among them, in part because the hedging and leveraging capabilities that may be required to maximize returns from such situations are generally not available to them.

Information Efficiency

The information ratio cannot easily be pressed into the service of analyzing alternative investments. Although superficially this ratio resembles the better-known Sharpe ratio, it divides active return rather than excess return by the standard deviation of the investment technique being analyzed. Active return is most conveniently defined in terms of benchmark tracking error, and because alternative investments generally are not benchmarked, the ratio as it is usually calculated is inapplicable to them. Although "absolute return" vehicles might arguably benchmark to the risk-free rate, in which case their Sharpe and information ratios would be identical, as will be argued below, this is not a very satisfactory benchmark for these investment techniques. In any case, the burden of much of this volume has been to call into question the value of reported standard deviations for many alternative investment vehicles, rendering an analytic comparison among vehicles that employs a metric for which standard deviation is the denominator rather questionable.

However, this inconvenient result does not render the information ratio irrelevant to the analysis of alternative investments. Although it cannot easily be applied to them in practice, it can be demonstrated that it applies to them in an idealized sense, and thus its properties apply to alternative investments in principle. Grinold and Kahn (2000) demonstrate that the information ratio can be decomposed into what they call the "information coefficient," which represents the actual performance outcome of each investment decision relative to its forecast outcome—that is, the actual return less the return required of each individual investment decision that the vehicle's manager acts upon (148). Multiplied by the square root of the number of decisions reached, this "information coefficient" is equivalent to the information ratio. Although as a practical matter the "information coefficient" is unanalyzable, the fact that it can be shown to be equivalent to the benchmark-based calculation of the information ratio in this way indicates that general observations about the efficiency of investment information apply to alternative investment managers just as they do to conventional investors. Thus alternative investment vehicles are subject to Grinold's and Kahn's Fundamental Law of Active Management, and as a consequence, their concept of investment vehicles' value added applies equally to alternative investments as well. Though immeasurable in practice, the principles underlying these analytic concepts are still valid for alternative investments.

Thus, in conformity with the Fundamental Law, excess returns are a function of the quality of the information upon which a manager acts and the frequency with which it does so. The relevance of this to our recurring discussion of the information content (or otherwise) of high-frequency trading techniques is obvious: frequency makes up for whatever weakness there is in the quality of their information. However, a feature of the theory that receives far less attention than it deserves is also relevant to this discussion. The Fundamental Law is couched in terms of *independent* decisions, and in fact these are taken far less often by most active managers than might be supposed. To be truly independent, two decisions cannot be based upon the same analysis of economic and market conditions—a very difficult requirement for fundamentally or quantitatively driven investment techniques to meet. It requires that the information that causes a manager to take on long exposure to, say, energy producers must be unrelated to the information that causes it simultaneously to build short exposure to airlines—in effect, a requirement of psychopathology. Despite appearances, most managers actually reach comparatively few independent decisions over the course of a year. By contrast, each decision at which a high-frequency trader arrives is independent of every other. As mentioned, a common trading desk discipline is in fact to discourage traders from forecasting at all, not least in order to preserve the independence of their decisions from each other. Consequently, what limited information high-frequency traders do possess is exploited with much greater efficiency than the mountains of information that determine many other managers' decisions.

At the other extreme of time horizon, the managers of long-term, private market investments make comparatively few investment decisions, and therefore must have access to information of a depth and quality that is unavailable to their public market brethren if their returns are to justify their risks. And this is, of course, what they aspire to. However, their situation underlines a point that is obvious but all-too-frequently overlooked: quality of information is one thing, but ultimately it is quality of analysis that determines investment performance. The difference between a top-tier venture capitalist and all the rest is not the quality of the information available to it but its ability to translate that information into superior corporate (and thus fund) performance. It follows that, for all that purchase and sale discipline are crucially important to the returns on long-term, private market investments, in most cases it is the decisions regarding the exercise of real options in the intervening period that separate the top quartile from all the rest. However, this will differ by trade: the options available to a mezzanine lender or a timberland investor are fewer and of less scope than those available to venture capitalists. Consequently, purchase and sale discipline bulks all the larger for those investment techniques.

Grinold and Kahn bring these concepts together in a measure of investment value added, which they define in terms of the information ratio divided by a measure of investor utility. That is, the success of the manager's risk-adjusted decisions, adjusted by the number of decisions taken, is further adjusted by the individual investor's risk preferences. As a consequence of this definition, a high information ratio on its own is not enough to make an investment vehicle add value to a portfolio, and a corollary that is of relevance to investment policymakers is that, insofar as they seek value added from their portfolio managers, they should seek it especially from those engaged in risk-seeking trades. This provides interesting support for Swensen's arguments against the use of credit and currency exposures in an institution's fixed-income portfolio, but its implications are broader than that.

"Absolute return" may offer diversification benefits, but it subtracts from value added if it does not achieve fairly high, equity-like returns. Market-neutral techniques frequently fall short of institutional requirements by these standards. The aggressiveness of many other alternative investment techniques contributes to their value added under Grinold's and Kahn's definition precisely because it allows them to take full advantage of information that may be known to all market participants but from which the alternative investment managers' leverage and/or short exposures allow them to extract a more attractive return. However, the fruits of the fortunate employment of leverage should not be mistaken for the possession of superior information. Given most funds' poor disclosure levels, disentangling the two is often not easy to accomplish, but it is an unavoidable requirement of due diligence: committing to trades that the broad market passes over because most participants are unwilling to leverage them to the extent required to meet an acceptable level of return is unlikely, if unaccompanied by superior information, to be a recipe for investment success. It is notable that most trades—apart from arbitrages—in which access to superior information is fundamental to success, tend to be relatively lightly leveraged. Grinold and Kahn regard as important enough to put in boldface type the comment that "[t]he information ratio is independent of a manager's level of aggressiveness" (116).

When applied to long-term, private market investments, this concept of investment value added has been used to argue that inherently less risky techniques applied to such exposure, including mezzanine investment, are in principle less attractive than riskier categories such as private equity, and consequently should be avoided. However, it is important to recall that, insofar as it is specifiable at all, the information ratio and therefore this concept of value added that relies upon it, are *ex post* analyses of returns, and have limited forecasting value. There have been and will continue to be vintages in which mezzanine debt funds will post superior returns to more aggressive private equity vehicles, and in general mezzanine debt offers returns that justify its use relative to, say, equities. In making these very difficult timing decisions, investment policymaking exhibits its own value added.

Information Efficient "Ecologies"

The idea that we might be able to identify "ecologies" that offer inherently greater information efficiency is an attractive one, but it is not entirely clear what this happy circumstance would entail. I can think of a few possibilities: these would include "ecologies" where

- ❑ forecasting tends to be consistently more accurate than elsewhere;
- ❑ the competition among investors for actionable information is comparatively low; and
- ❑ unexpected outcomes tend on balance to be favorable rather than unfavorable.

The first of these is likely just to lead to more efficient pricing. Investors would be certain to notice such circumstances, so gaining an information advantage would just be correspondingly more difficult than elsewhere. Prices would probably be less volatile than in other instruments, and because prices would adjust to certainty, the additional effort required in order to gain an information advantage would not in most cases be well compensated. Short-term Treasury instruments and their related derivatives would seem to offer such a marketplace, which would fail the value added test mentioned above for all but investors with virtually unlimited access to essentially zero cost leverage—that is, broker-dealers that specialize in dealing in those instruments. Note that this is a high-frequency trade, to which the visibility of trading interest at the point of price formation is crucial. That is, money is only to be made in an ultra-efficient information environment by ignoring that information, and attending instead to the information embedded in prices themselves.

The second of these alternatives could come about either because there are few investors seeking the information or because the information is deliberately rationed. The former situation might arise in "pioneer" emerging markets and the latter in private market investments. In the first case the information advantage is likely to be transitory, and the more productive of return the relevant information is, the more transitory the advantage is likely to prove. On the other hand, the latter situation may be fairly permanent, but it would take a firm a long time and a solid performance history to develop it. That is, an investment firm does not become a "preferred investor" that attracts exclusive or semi-exclusive proposals over night, but once it attains that status it may be able to retain it in the face of other pretenders to this advantage for long periods.

The third possibility is paradoxical. Over time, market participants will surely notice a bias in outcomes and price it into the instruments that exhibit it—such a feature of forecast outcomes is highly unlikely to go unnoticed forever. It is tempting to think that pricing would take full account of this, as in the first "ecology," but the element of uncertainty involved embeds an option-like element into this environment. These are essentially the conditions under which hedged trades operate, and the pricing will vary based on market participants' perception of the value of the hedge.

The Efficient Market Hypothesis was formulated with a steady-state universe in mind, and it was not designed to handle situations where the efficiency of a market might change. For well-established markets, steady-state efficiency might provide an adequate or at least plausible description much of the time (that is, outside of Bookstaber's elevated energy situations), but certainly not elsewhere in the developing world (see for example Allen et al. 2008, 21$f\!f$). If the cost of obtaining information is high and its accessibility limited, as with most private market investments, information efficiency will be low, for all that the quality of the information may not be. Where an information "ecology" occupies a point of intersection between liquidity "habitats," as is the case, for instance, with option markets, strong claims for information efficiency are also likely to be implausible. The managers of alternative investment vehicles are frequently to be found in these environs. However, any claims they may make to enjoying an information advantage need careful examination: as Rutherford D. Rogers noted, "We're drowning in information and starving for knowledge." As chief librarian at different times for Stanford and Yale Universities, Rogers' opinion on this matter is worth taking to heart.

PART IV

PORTFOLIO CONSTRUCTION

CHAPTER 19

Classification
of Investments

A scrupulously attentive reader may have noticed that the term "asset class" has been used sparingly throughout this volume. In a work about the allocation of investments, this probably seems idiosyncratic at the very least, if not an astonishing oversight. But its omission is entirely intentional, and in fact it has required a certain amount of less-than-elegant circumlocution to avoid use of a term that is so ubiquitous in discussions of this type. And it has demanded even greater contortions to avoid use of the term "asset allocation." The reason for these acrobatics is that I believe that the notions of asset classes and asset allocation "buckets" have become impediments to investment thinking, "idols of the marketplace," to borrow again from Francis Bacon, and that it is high time that they are replaced with something that is useful rather than a hindrance to investment policymaking.

A replacement is necessary because we cannot simply abandon the idea of classification and proceed to allocate among the wide and bewilderingly disparate range of investment possibilities without some guidance from organizing principles. As William James noted, in the absence of concepts that help us to sort and categorize it, our experience is nothing but "blooming, buzzing confusion." Life is difficult enough for investors without that. Even an inadequate system of categories such as that offered by the notion of asset classes is preferable to no system of classification at all.

There is no single, "correct" system of classification for anything: we mentally organize things to suit our particular purposes, and our purposes change with our circumstances. For all that it is an arbitrary system of categorization, if we are creating a directory of asset managers, then alphabetization is likely to provide the simplest way of ordering them—provided that we know the name of the firm for which we are looking. To help us if we do not, cross-referencing by investment instruments employed, investment discipline, or the amount of assets under management may provide useful supplements to our primary categorization by alphabetical ordering. For reasons that escape me, *Nelson's Guide to Investment Management* categorizes firms by state: it would be interesting to know what information requirement its editors think this serves. Other arbitrary systems are likely to be equally unhelpful: grouping managers by the color of their CIOs' eyes or their headquarters' distance from Ulan Bator are as valid classification criteria as any, but probably do not serve many of our purposes. This chapter will explore various proposals for replacing the categorization of investments by asset classes. But first it will be useful to the project of replacing the construct to investigate how we arrived at the place we find ourselves, and what the problems with the traditional notion of asset classes are.

A History of Asset Classes

Categorizing investment vehicles by what they invest in is a fairly natural criterion to choose and remains useful for some purposes. Not so very long ago, institutional investments consisted all but exclusively of stocks, bonds, cash, and possibly real estate. Hybrids such as convertible bonds or warrants were rarely encountered, high-yield debt was not issued but only resulted from credit deterioration, and institutions essentially ignored them. Real estate provided something of a gray area in this scheme, but that was of concern only to a minority of institutions. Whether cash should be classified as fixed-income was the only other point that might have been contentious, but that, too, was generally ignored. Assets were held long-only and commodities were not considered investments. Organized financial derivative exchanges did not exist, and leverage was only used by the most desperate of retail brokerage customers. It was thought that there is a clear dividing line between investment and speculation—one was respectable and the other decidedly less so. Anything that did not fit easily into the four asset classes and the accepted norms of institutional behavior fell into the latter category and was unacceptable to polite society.

Categorization of investments by asset class seemed to make intuitive sense in terms of the risks to be expected from different portions of the portfolio and so furthered the interests of investment policymakers, thanks to this happy congruence between asset classes and portfolio function. Allowing for some overlap between fixed-income and real estate, the four asset classes were recognizably different and performed distinct functions in portfolios. With the same allowance for real estate, each asset class had its own role to play, which could not be performed by the other available choices, and lacking derivatives, leverage, and so on, investment policy made do with those functions performed by those assets or simply did without.

The situation began to change under the influence of investment consultants, who introduced institutions to a stratified sampling approach that eventually led to an array of subcategories that provided the basis for the Morningstar Style Box.[1] Confusingly, these subcategories also became known as asset classes, for all that "mid-cap value" is simply equity, no more and no less so than "small-cap core." When foreign equities began to enter into U.S. institutional portfolios in the early 1980s, they too were regarded as an asset class, which (apparently through mitosis) became two as emerging market equity gradually gained the status of an asset class in its own right and then three as "small-cap international" began to gain favor with institutions. Can "mid-cap international" be far behind? The fixed-income sector experienced a similar proliferation of assets classes, and eventually real estate did as well. Only cash remained cash, pure and simple, although the rise of a commercial paper market began to lend pointedness to the question of the relationship between cash and fixed-income.

Apart from consultants' commercial self-interest—the constant proliferation of asset classes leads inexorably to more, very lucrative search assignments—the seemingly relentless pursuit of ever more finely drawn distinctions among asset classes traces to Modern Portfolio Theory's concept of the Market Portfolio, the sum of all investment opportunities. Theory claims that only the maximally diverse Market Portfolio is truly efficient, and portfolios are less efficient to the extent that they are less diverse than it. To ensure, within the constraints of practicality, the maximum efficiency of their clients' portfolios (while at the same standing Modern Portfolio Theory on its head by applying

---

1. Grinold and Kahn (2000) note, "When a portfolio manager says he uses stratified sampling, he wants the listener to (1) be impressed and (2) ask no further questions" (394). Interestingly, Morningstar® seems to be moving away from strict adherence to the Fama-French three factor model, and reportedly plans to introduce more factors into its analysis of mutual funds: see Mamudi (2009).

its thinking to the recommendation of active managers), investment consultants sorted the investment universe along two or more axes to facilitate monitoring of the range of exposures across them. The equity universe was classified by capitalization and security selection technique, the fixed-income universe by credit exposure, by duration, and latterly by security selection technique as well, while the real estate universe came to be subdivided by property type and investment technique—that is, core, "core plus," "value-added," or opportunistic.[2]

All three asset classes were further categorized by the geographical location of the investment. Constructing portfolios that exhibit a balance between these various categories excludes fewer securities, so balance tilts a portfolio away from the Market Portfolio less than a bias toward one or the other category would. In their own commercial self-interest, investment managers colluded in consultants' efforts by taking vows of rigorous "style purity," which allow consultants to craft such a balance without risk that active managers might spoil it through the creation of redundant exposures. In the process, the previously unsuspected sin of "style drift" was born.

The system of asset classification along these lines received academic support, initially from research to test the Market Efficiency Hypothesis, which uncovered the small capitalization equity effect and eventually led to the identification of size and value sensitivities as factor loadings distinct from β. The former apparently began with Banz (1981), and the latter is the contribution of a well-known paper, Fama and French (1993). This approach to classification had some unquestionable peculiarities. For example, "growth" or a BBB-rating are not inherent in the instruments to which they are ascribed, so that exogenous influences alone could transform an instrument into an allegedly different category of asset. The failure to distinguish between super- and subcategories resulted in ever finer parsing of putative asset classes in a horizontal system of classification, confronting investment policymakers with what

---

2. Real estate categorization is comparatively recent, and does not seem yet to have settled into a rigid system. REITs may be regarded as real estate or as an asset class of their own, and farmland, some forms of infrastructure, and timberland may or may not be regarded as real estate. I would classify timberland and possibly the relevant forms of infrastructure rather differently, as forms of private equity, because in both cases returns are generated from operating the asset rather than leasing it to a third party. Dorsey (2007) contends, "From an investment perspective, real estate is more often defined by its strategy approach than its property type" (113), but this is not confirmed in my experience, and is at any rate inconsistent with the inclusion of the latter categories as asset classes within the real estate super-class.

were properly tactical decisions about exposure to micro-cap Chilean growth equity or east Javanese value-added three-star hotel properties. Difficulty in determining the size of asset classes made benchmarking somewhat arbitrary: without knowing the size of the relevant Javanese or Chilean markets, it was essentially impossible to determine what neutral exposure to them might be. This point is not as trivial as it might seem—the paucity of data on the size of commodity markets has been no small inconvenience to index-producers and consultants alike. The system invited what I have called "bucket-think," where investment committees are encouraged to take on exposure simply for the sake of having it—a "tick-the-box" approach from which nothing good is likely to come. Nevertheless, the scheme may have been of some value to investment policymakers.

Institutions' increasing employment of alternative investments created the categorical contortions and endless exceptions that have brought many practitioners to the point of despair regarding categorization by asset classes. Crossovers and hybrids demanded ever more "buckets," at the same time that hedging, leverage, and previously unfamiliar security selection techniques transformed the return patterns of the putative asset classes to which they were applied out of all recognition. While some alternative investments were truly and fundamentally different from the traditional asset classes, others such as long-biased long/short equity were only different in degree, and in many cases not that great a degree. Trade structuring, such as that employed by arbitrageurs, produced distinctly different patterns of returns from those of the underlying assets, but meanwhile many long-only, conventional investment techniques exploited some of the same investment situations without use of hedging. Portfolio function became increasingly divorced from the asset class employed, so that diversification by asset class no longer ensured diversity of economic and market exposures. And so on: what worked fairly smoothly when there were four quite distinct asset classes broke down under the weight of alternative investors' wealth of innovation—and this without even bringing exotica such as life insurance settlements into consideration. "Confusion now hath made his masterpiece!" exclaims Shakespeare's Macduff: the rationale for classifying investments by asset classes was undermined.

Some Proposals

Practitioners' dissatisfaction with the prevailing scheme of classification has mounted steadily, yet the project of erecting a replacement structure has not attracted as much attention as one might expect. This is because there is no consensus on what such a classification is meant to accomplish. I am sure, however, that there have been many other proposals than just those I list below. Further, it is likely that some of these schemata were offered more in the spirit of exploration than as carefully considered proposals, and they should almost certainly be regarded as suggestive for discussion rather than as attempts at definitiveness. It is doubtless unfair of me to dissect them, but the exercise will illustrate some points about classification, and if it appears to be an exercise in knocking down straw men, I apologize to the reader and to their authors. Proposals that I have encountered include

1. return generators, inflation hedges, and deflation hedges;
2. market exposure, risk reducers, return enhancers, and inflation hedges;
3. value creation, subordinated cash flows, relative value, and priority cash flows;
4. capital assets, consumable/transformable assets, and assets that are stores of value; and
5. α-drivers and β-drivers.[3]

Each of these collections of categories represents only one dimension of a scheme that would probably, if further elaborated, involve several dimensions: I will discuss such matrices below. With the exception of number four, which is clearly focused on the assets themselves, and perhaps number three, which is somewhat inconsistent in its application of a single criterion of categorization, all these authors focus on investment function as the foundation of their classifications. However, the first views function economically while the second and fourth link function explicitly to the assets' or investment techniques' role in portfolios.

Although in other respects it is certainly an improvement over the traditional asset-based approach to classification, the categories shown in number four share some of its problems. Certain assets, such as gold, seem to straddle asset classes, and it is not clear where real estate would fit into this schema. It offers no obvious place to hedged trades, particularly arbitrages, which carry no (intentional) exposure to any of the

---

3. These derive from William Spitz, Jonathan Hook, Daniel Kingston (cited in Kochard and Rittereiser 2008, 132, 214, and 234), Greer (1997), and Anson (2004), respectively. The addition of real estate to Greer's categorization offers the different categorization that Anson suggests in 2002, 2*ff.*

asset classes. Number three would have a hard time accommodating commodities or non-arbitrage high-frequency trading, and some real assets would probably fall between the value creation and subordinated cash flow categories. Further, it is not clear what, other than (presumably) degree of risk, distinguishes subordinated from priority cash flows. But a more fundamental objection to both approaches to classification is that they have no strong implications for portfolio management: it is not clear, for example, that their categories necessarily diversify each other, and they offer little intuitive sense of the extent or nature of their risks.

The categorization by economic criteria shown as number one, while more obviously suggestive for portfolio construction, also suffers from overlaps and difficulty accommodating hedged trades. These problems in fact seem to be inherent in classifications that are asset-based—number four skirts around the latter objection by introducing a category, relative value, which clearly is not asset-based and seems inconsistent with the others in that schema. To my mind, numbers two and five are more suggestive for the way forward toward an investment classification, as their criterion of classification is portfolio function, differentiating among investments based on how investment techniques contribute to performance, rather than criteria that are descriptive of the assets or investment techniques themselves. They do not actually apply to assets but to investment techniques, which allows them to accommodate hedged trades. And while it is arguable that some assets could straddle categories, that criticism is irrelevant to schemata that categorize investment techniques, not assets. Further, such schemes can accommodate investment techniques that fall between categories, provided that an estimate can be formed of the extent to which the contribution of different techniques affects the vehicle's return characteristics. This possibility is not available to asset-based classifications.

However, proposals two and five have their weaknesses, too. While it may be immaterial that assets might fall into more than one category, if investment techniques can, then the classifications are somewhat less than ideal, unless an estimate of the relative contributions to returns of the different category components can be formed. In the case of the second proposal, it would be difficult to imagine an investment approach that offered enhanced return without a substantial measure of exposure to *some* market, or for that matter, an approach that offered an inflation hedge without similar exposure. Here the contributions of the different categories to the vehicle's return characteristics cannot be isolated. In the case of number five, unless the distinction is between purely passive vehicles and all others, then there very few investment techniques that do not fall into both categories. If Anson intends "β" to refer to a variety of factor exposures, as is likely, there are no investment techniques (including both passive and active ones and fully-hedged arbitrages) that manage to escape having such exposures except systematic arbitrages, to which few institutions are likely to be exposed. And if the concept of "β" is stretched sufficiently to include factor loading to volatility, not even systematic arbitages would qualify. Further, the exposures may be very numerous and may even, in some cases, be unknown. Thus the two categories are not two at all, but an indeterminate number of so-called βs, with considerable overlap between them, plus a residual for α that is largely determined by the thoroughness of investment policymakers' search for the numerous βs. This provides little basis for classification at all.

Categorization by Investment Strategy

My proposal is to use the investment strategies described in Chapter 1 as the basis for classifying investments. These are not asset-based, but they are not really based on portfolio functions, either: they are vehicle-based. Compared to an asset-based categorization, my approach has the advantage that it allows for hybridization and the contrasting uses that different managers may make of the same asset. It also explicitly allows for investment techniques such as arbitrage that carry no net asset exposure at all (although they do carry factor exposures, however difficult they may be to isolate). It differs from functionally based criteria of classification, but subtly and in ways that improve on those criteria. In particular, it does not carry any implicit reference to investment policymakers' intentions, which on a functional scheme can allow the same investment technique to fall into different categories, depending on the purpose intended for it. However, the types of trades in which an investment product engages clearly have implications for that product's portfolio function. My hope is to show that vehicle-based classification combines the comparative objectivity of an asset-based approach with the nuance and implicit connection to the decisions that confront investment policymakers that functionally based approaches attempt to offer.

As I have stressed, investment vehicles may employ one, two, or all three of these strategies, but this does not create a problem of overlap between categories, because the contributions of the strategies to the return characteristics of individual vehicles can be isolated for analytic purposes, and more readily than in the case of a functionally based categorization. Conventional long-only equity or fixed-income provide fairly trivial examples: the extent to which the returns achieved by such vehicles derive from the cash flows received versus the directional price change of the instruments employed is easily measured. In other cases the difficulties are greater, and quantitative precision may not be so easily obtained, but they are not insurmountable. For example, untangling the contribution of arbitrage returns to hedged trading techniques may not be possible without the ability to perform the sort of trade-by-trade analysis that is generally not permitted to investors in hedge funds— but at least in principle it might be done, if only by the manager of the fund itself. In contrast, if functional categories are defined as in example one above, it is difficult to imagine what the inflation hedge provided by an investment might be other than its return generation in excess of the inflation rate—on close inspection the categories collapse into each other, and no separate contribution to returns can be identified.

Another virtue of this approach is that the categories are conceptually distinct: there are no arbitrages between them. In a conventional, asset-based categorization, commodities such as oil may be used to hedge equities such as airlines, and the same may (but need not necessarily) be true of functional classifications. This is inelegant, in that it means that hedged trades automatically spawn hybrid categories within these classification systems. While my different categories diversify each other to some extent, and as discussed previously, there is an element of hedging and thus of arbitrage involved in the use of more than one category for diversification purposes, I believe that my discussion of the relationship between diversification and hedging in Chapter 2 addressed this. There I distinguished between them on the basis of intentions—a hedging trade may be successful whether it produces a positive or a negative return, while an investment made for purposes of diversification is return-seeking. In most situations, an investor who pairs airline holdings with a position in oil derivatives is hedging, while an allocation across two or three of my vehicle categories would typically seek returns in addition to diversification. My treatment can accommodate this distinction.

The obvious relevance of functional classifications to the task that confronts investment policymakers is a very attractive feature of any classification scheme that is based upon them, and the relevance of classification by my criteria to investment policy decisions is not so immediately apparent. However, I do not think their relevance is unreachably remote from policymakers' concerns—at the very least, the functional contribution of cash flow strategies should be quite clear. And while it is a generalization that is vulnerable to numerous counter-examples, directional strategies can be regarded as portfolios' return-drivers while arbitrage strategies can be characterized as diversifying sources of absolute returns. As might be expected, a focus on investment strategy meshes conveniently with a focus on risk, and with the same caution about exceptions, directional strategies can be regarded as continuously volatile, cash flow strategies can be seen as having less extreme volatility (partially mitigated by their distributions), and arbitrages can be classed as low volatility strategies, although susceptible to negative high standard deviation events.

Classification Matrices

Lhabitant (2004) proposes a classification of investments along three axes—the instruments employed (bonds, equity, options, and hedge funds), the types of risks to which they are exposed (liquidity risk, credit risk, etc.), and "other" (which is something of a catch-all, including geographical location of the asset, time to maturity, and so on) (291f). This is a matrix, similar to those that underlie factor models, rather than a hierarchical system of classification, because investments can obviously belong to more than one category of risk and/or "other." Because Lhabitant actually offers a pictorial illustration of his schema, he is restricted to three axes, but I think this is an accommodation to graphical necessity rather than his considered opinion on how many dimensions his schema should have and how they should be populated.

The contents of Lhabitant's "other" axis are obvious candidates to be distributed among additional dimensions. For example, a division of geographic exposure to whatever fineness investment policy believes to be relevant (by country, continent, etc.) would constitute one dimension, provided that it included an "irrelevant" category for assets such as commodities for which location is not in most cases an investment issue. Maturity buckets—again drawn to whatever degree of fineness, but necessarily including a "perpetual" category—could provide another dimension. The axis for types of risk is more problematic, but I would be inclined to distinguish between operational risks, risks inherent in the asset category, risks that attach to economic geography or regulatory jurisdiction, and risks that relate to the specific investment technique employed. Note, for example, that there is some form of liquidity or credit risk that attaches to each of these broad risk buckets, but that the risks are in fact quite distinct from each other, despite their shared names. Clearly, we are quickly confronted with an n-dimensional array that is beyond the bounds of graphical illustration.

However, a peculiar construct results from this excursion into higher dimensions. While some of the cells of the array could, at least in principle, be populated by numerical values similar if not identical to factor loadings, others are simply boxes that may or may not be checked. For example, the "locationlessness" of some commodities cannot be quantified. In other cases, particularly those involving non-market risks, it may be necessary to assign subjectively derived comparative ranking scores to a cell based on an intuitive but fundamentally immeasurable sense of their scale. Thus there is no time series against which counterparty credit risks might be assessed, for all that we have every reason to believe that there are degrees of such risks, so that they are much reduced in markets that enjoy a central counterparty compared to those that do not. Given our inability to model non-Gaussian distributions with assurance of the accuracy of our model's "fit," where the relevant risk is a high standard-deviation event, it is essentially unquantifiable even in circumstances in which, as with systemic liquidity risks during 2007 to 2009, we have unfortunately ample experience of it.

Further, such a matrix-like array obscures any "natural" hierarchy of categories. There is nothing about it that enlightens investment policy-makers as to where to begin their task. This is not a minor concern, as is revealed by examining the end result of allocation, when *ex post* analysis seeks to determine the contributors to portfolio performance. The conclusions of performance analysis will differ depending on what the initial allocation decision is thought to be. Much criticism of the widely discussed paper by Brinson et al. (1986) depends on the observation that the results of performance attribution are significantly determined by the sequence in which the contribution analysis is conducted. That is, answers to performance attribution questions are influenced by the order in which the questions are asked. Thus, for example, the conclusions will differ if the first and most fundamental allocation decision is regarded as, say, between geographical exposures rather than between asset categories. It follows that performance results are influenced by the order in which allocation decisions are made, suggesting that the hierarchy that may (or may not) be embodied within a classification of investments is no trivial matter.

Lacking broadly diversified benchmarks for directional, cash flow, and arbitrage strategies, it is difficult to make a compelling claim that my criterion for the classification of investments provides such a basis for ranking investment decisions. Nor are such benchmarks likely to be forthcoming. However, I believe that I can make a reasonably convincing case for the fundamental nature of my classificatory scheme by taking a step back from Lhabitant's approach and rethinking it.

Regardless of what we might believe is the most fundamental characteristic of investments, there are some dimensions within Lhabitant's matrix that are clearly less fundamental than others. For example, investment policy is unlikely to embark on an allocation project from the perspective of accepting or avoiding instruments' credit risk as its primary consideration, to which all other allocation decisions are subsidiary. Proceeding in that fashion would give no guidance for allocating among investments that do not involve such risk. If instead it were counterparty credit risk that was regarded as fundamental, then decisions between instruments that are exchange-traded versus those that are not would become a primary consideration for investment policy. Given differences in market structure, in this instance risk aversion would recommend naked positions in soybean meal futures over holding short-term U.S. Treasuries, which is clearly a strong counter-example for choosing counterparty credit risk as the most basic determinant of allocation. To be functionally useful from the perspective of investment policymaking, the fundamental categories must

❑ be all-inclusive, so that no possible investment fails to fall within the scope of at least one of them;

❑ lead to intuitively sensible conclusions about diversification, so that they provide useful indications for portfolio construction; and

❑ have implications for risk budgeting that are consistent with common sense.

Nothing prevents us from applying different subsidiary criteria of classification across different fundamental categories—this after all is the procedure of biological taxonomy, which does not have to worry itself over empty categories such as dicotyledonous crustaceans or feathered protozoa. This leaves geographical-, asset-, or strategy-based criteria of classification as the most likely to be fundamental.

However, we have already observed that a geography-based system of classification requires a category for "locationless" investments—that is, a place for those things to which, from an investment perspective, geographical considerations do not apply. If geography were fundamental to investment classification in the sense I have described, then the "locationless" cell of the categorization should be empty. But gold is gold, regardless of whether it originated in South Africa, Nevada, or Queensland—and arbitrage aside, with essentially no difference in its investment characteristics if it is held in Madras, San Jose, or Zurich.

For that matter, it makes only a minor difference if it is held in the form of jewelry, electrical contacts, or bullion. Because a geographic categorization cannot meet the first criterion above, it cannot meet the second, either—an investment that falls outside of the fundamental diversification framework will tend to attract all of an institution's allocation to it. Thus it fails on the second criterion and therefore on the third as well. Having already argued for the advantages of a strategy-based system of classification over an asset-based one, it is appropriate to turn to a consideration of how sub-categorization in such a scheme should be organized.

Secondary Categories within a Strategy-Based Classification

It lends elegance to the system, but more importantly provides some assurance of its inclusiveness, if the sub-categories parallel each other at different levels of the classification hierarchy. That is, while it is not necessary that the sub-categories used to distinguish among directional, cash flow, and arbitrage strategies be the same, it is useful if they follow parallel rules of construction. Thus, while biological taxonomy does not concern itself with empty categories of the sort mentioned above, it draws parallels between the plant and animal kingdoms in proceeding with its division of life. Plants and animals are categorized in phyla according to gross anatomical features—for instance, possession of exoskeletons in the case of one animal phylum, or vascular systems plus another differentiator in the case of several plant phyla. While the criteria of biological classification by no means proceed in exact parallel, the basic principles of classification—at this level, structural differences that are impossible to ignore—are the same.

Applied to investments, geographical classifications, for example, might appropriately be applied differently to different strategies. If we test this, in my opinion we come up with optimal schemata that are something like this:

❑ *Directional Strategies:* by country plus "locationless," except for real estate, which would be by city or region (see below regarding collectibles);
❑ *Cash Flow Strategies:* by home currency, developed currencies, and emerging-market currencies; and
❑ *Arbitrage:* "locationless" except merger arbitrage, which is classified principally by the legal and regulatory domicile of the target and secondarily by the domicile(s) of the acquirer(s).

Although there is obvious parallelism here, it is not so pronounced that it seems to me that geographic categories should provide the next level of classification after investments are differentiated by strategy. That is, as a criterion of classification, geography requires too many exceptions and special considerations, so it probably should not play "phylum" to strategies' "kingdom" and should instead make its appearance lower down the classification hierarchy. What, then, is the most appropriate secondary category?

The geographic exceptions, which are largely dictated by what instrument the investment strategy is employed upon, provide a clue—what better than asset class? Strategies must be applied to something, and why not use the instruments they are applied to as the primary differentiator among them? Geography affects what strategies are applied to rather than the strategies themselves, so it seems reasonable that it should be a subsidiary consideration. How subsidiary? I think at least one level of classification should intervene. For want of a better term, I have called this "investment technique." This encompasses the various types of trades discussed in Part II, as well as many that were neglected there, and takes a more prominent place in the classification hierarchy than geography because pursuit of a technique is more likely to dictate entry into a geography than the other way around. This is illustrated, for example, by the scramble in which some merger arbitrageurs must have engaged in order to acquire expertise on Belgian corporate governance in connection with the Anheuser Busch/Inbev deal. Their realization that knowledge of Belgium was necessary to the pursuit of their accustomed technique, rather than a sudden desire to know more about the home of Van Eyck and Rubens, instigated this scramble. Belgian equity investors who were not participants in the arbitrage experienced considerably less pressure to learn the details of U.S. corporate governance practices. If, one day, there is a takeover transaction in Mongolia, distance from Ulan Bator (mentioned above as a conceivable, if not especially useful, criterion of classification) may suddenly become a relevant cross-reference within a putative directory of arbitrageurs, but would remain a classification criterion that is irrelevant to most other types of investment managers.

Table 19.1 summarizes the system of categorization I am constructing. Bookstaber (2007, 245f) offers a fairly similar classification system by asset class, directionality or the lack of it, investment technique, geographic region, and liquidity. However, it is not clear that these are hierarchically ranked—he refers to it as both a "categorization scheme" and a "matrix." I have placed "implementation" beneath geography in the

TABLE 19.1 *Outline of a Taxonomy of Investments*

TAXONOMIC ANALOGUE	CRITERIA OF CLASSIFICATION		
Kingdom	Directional Strategies	Cash Flow Strategies	Arbitrage Strategies
Phylum	Asset Class	Asset Class	Asset Class
Class	Investment "Technique"	Investment "Technique"	Investment "Technique"
Order	Geography	Geography	Geography
Family	Implementation	Implementation	Implementation

classification hierarchy; by this I mean specific characteristics of how the investment technique is employed, such as a growth or value orientation to long-only equity security selection, a credit- or yield curve-driven approach to bond selection, and so on. It would also capture differences in the hedging techniques employed by long/short investors, the specific types of loans that direct lenders pursue, the core, "core plus," and other categorizations of real estate, and so forth. At this point, I believe classification has gone as far as it can usefully go, because below the level of implementation, differentiating features are very much specific to the individual vehicle or manager. That is, I am inclined to think that there is no need to proceed on to genera and species (see **Figure 19.1**).

But readers may wonder what has become of the risk axis of Lhabitant's matrix scheme. It is a hidden dimension, and leaps vertically out of the page at each level of classification, as will be discussed in more detail in Chapter 21. The risk that is relevant to directional strategies, at the highest level of generality, is forecasting error. Subsidiary to that are risks that appear at one or more levels of the hierarchy—operational risks, risks inherent in the asset category, risks that attach to economic geography or regulatory jurisdiction, and risks that relate to the specific investment technique or implementation that is employed. Ever-more-specific forms of operational risk are found at each level of classification. For example, all trades involve counterparty risk to a greater or lesser degree, long/short involves timing risks when hedges are implemented,

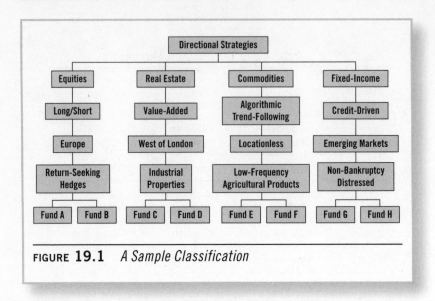

FIGURE 19.1 *A Sample Classification*

market practice governing short positions vary by regulatory jurisdiction, and return-seeking hedges may have specific implementation issues related to Δ-hedging. Risks at higher classification levels manifest themselves as specific instances at lower levels: for example, the old up-tick rule for U.S. equities was a geographical feature that affected some but not all forms of return-seeking hedging activity in that country alone.

The perennial investment outliers—collectibles—provide a useful stress test for any system of investment classification. Clearly, investment in these instruments is a directional strategy, and I doubt that there would be much dispute that they merit an asset class of their own. I am not a habitué of galleries or auctions, but I can imagine that there are various investment techniques that apply to artworks: no doubt there are value/contrarians and others who seek to build value by assembling comprehensive or representative collections within an asset sub-category, and from what I read about contemporary British art there are plenty of trend-followers, and so on. Collectibles' geographical category is "locationless," because where they are held is largely irrelevant to their value, although there is probably a form of return-enhancement to be achieved by lending items to sufficiently prestigious museums. This may seem odd, as the whole edifice of art history is built around classification by temporal and geographic categories—note the title of Erwin Panofsky's classic *Early Netherlandish Painting*, for example—but these are distinctions at the asset class level, and are not determined by where the object ultimately finds itself. Implementation may be harder to fathom, but distinctions might be drawn by purchase method (auctions, galleries, flea markets).

All of which seems to work surprisingly well for collectibles in the abstract, but it runs into problems of implementation when applied to unique items. Uniqueness causes most of the problems relating to the classification of collectibles as investments, because at some level of subdivision within the asset class, each such item inhabits a category all to itself. Even items that are not unique can be highly specified at that level, such as the print hanging on my library wall, described in **Table 19.2**.

Here period takes precedence over nationality, but that would not always be the case—Hans Memling was a contemporary of Botticelli, but at a time when there was a world of difference between Flanders and Italy. In the case of this print it is not clear that nationality is relevant at all: Romanticism was a Europe-wide movement. But at least the print is

TABLE 19.2 *Classification of a Collectible*

Investment Strategy	Directional
Asset Class	Collectibles
First sub-class: type	Engraving
Second sub-class: period	Early Romanticism
Third sub-class: nationality	Italian
Fourth sub-class: artist	Giovanni Piranesi
Fifth sub-class: series	Carceri d'Invenzione
Sixth sub-class: specific print	Plate XV
Seventh sub-class: print run	Fifth estate
Eight sub-class: condition	Good
Investment Technique	Just liked it
Geographic Category	"Locationless"
Implementation	Purchased from a Brooklyn print shop

fungible with others similarly specified, so that I can obtain a reasonably accurate estimate of its value (based on a 2008 sale at Christie's, in London, not very much) without putting my own copy up for sale in order to assess the bids it attracts.

Kritzman and Page (2003), referring to allocation among long-only, multination fixed-income and equities, argue for a fixed decision-making hierarchy based on their analysis of which decisions (asset, country, sector, security) add the greatest value, arguing somewhat cynically for ranking the decision with the least value-added first, on the theory that it "has the least potential for damage" (23) to portfolios. Assoé et al. (2004), adjusting the decisions Kritzman and Page discuss for active risk, come to the conclusion that the decisions are equally important and imply no hierarchy. I am unimpressed with both conclusions, because the methodology employed is blind to the factors that drive the decision in the first place. By constructing random portfolios and then ranking their *ex post* performance by their return dispersion, both papers largely assume what they claim to demonstrate. While these papers may have something to offer from the perspective of *ex post* performance measurement, I do not believe that they are helpful to those tasked with making decisions in ignorance of their outcomes. The decomposition of performance after the fact involves a different set of problems from those involved in creating that performance in the first place.

The decision model described in Singer et al. (2004), employing Monte Carlo simulation, at least does not have this look-back feature. Having predefined the investable universe, they employ a brute force approach (multiple runs of 1000 ten-year periods) to achieving a portfolio with a specified level of volatility. They do not claim optimality for their result, only "appropriateness," subject to an *ad hoc* liquidity constraint. One particularly valuable result of their method is that it gives explicit forecasts of the extent to which the portfolio is likely to drift from its policy targets: for example, the 5 percent recommended allocation to private equity grows to 14 percent or more in 5 percent of the simulation periods (108). While their approach holds some promise, it is clearly very cumbersome to implement and lacking in intuitive power. It does little to help investment policymakers determine what the investable universe *should* be, and any active factor tilts that they might wish to incorporate would have to be imposed through additional constraints. The latter is a less than satisfactory procedure, since it prejudges "appropriateness"—that is, the value-added of the allocation does not come out of the model itself but is imposed on the model *ex ante* and thus is not transparent to the model's analysis.

As with any system of classification, the most interesting things about mine are the gray areas and apparent exceptions. Just as biological taxonomy is by no means fixed in a definitive form—Linnaeus identified only two kingdoms, plants and animals, but current debate centers on whether there are five or six, and that is by no means the only bone of contemporary taxonomic contention—I suspect that my division is eminently revisable. For example, should futures or options be regarded as asset classes in their own right? Are there cases—most likely real estate, which is notoriously a matter of location times three (or is it to the third power?)—in which geography should take precedence over investment technique? Is there a role for further levels of classification before we reach individual investment products? I suspect that further investigation will find that my scheme is simplistic—that there is much less parallelism between the way categories that are subsidiary to the investment strategies are drawn than I have suggested, that the ordering of classification criteria must be far more fluid than I have implied, and so on. I do not mean to be facetious in leaving these as problems for the reader: I am convinced that devoting attention to these matters is likely to be productive for investment policymaking.

Classification by Factors

Inklebarger (2009) reports that the $30.2 billion Alaska Permanent Fund Corporation has adopted a classification system that is partially based on factor loadings, and notes that both CalPERS and CalSTRS are considering such an approach to classifying their investments as well. I say "partially," because Alaska's schema is in fact a mixed one, consisting of

- ❑ "company exposure," comprising equities, corporate credit, and private equity;
- ❑ "opportunity pool," including "absolute return," "real return," and distressed debt;
- ❑ "real assets," consisting of real estate, infrastructure, and TIPS;
- ❑ "interest rates," comprising government securities other than TIPS; and
- ❑ cash.

Compared to its previous practice, this new system of classification significantly reduces the number of categories that the Fund employs, as shown in **Figure 19.2**.

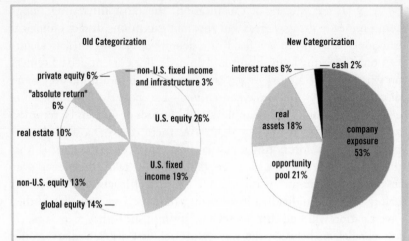

FIGURE 19.2 *Alaska Permanent Fund: Old and New Classification Systems*

Source: Inklebarger 2009.

The reduction in equity categories alone provides a significant improvement in comprehensibility: the Fund's previous division of equity exposure into three overlapping categories plus private equity was clearly the product of consultant-driven "bucket-think." But the scheme is not comprehensive—"opportunity pool" is a grab-bag category that might equally be labeled "other," and the inclusion of distressed debt there rather than in "company exposure" seems odd. The distinction between "real return" and "real assets" is unclear, and I doubt that it can be factor-based. The scheme is not internally consistent.

However, it suggests a useful alternative to the approach I have outlined and deserves serious consideration. It is certainly an interesting development, and with high-powered sponsors such as those that Inklebarger mentions, it will doubtless receive extensive elaboration. My major concern with a factor-based approach is that factor loadings change over time, and can appear in unexpected places, such as the oil loading exhibited by Houston office buildings, to which I have already referred. While classification along these lines is undoubtedly an improvement on asset classes, I believe that it will encounter numerous problems and gray areas.

CHAPTER 20

Diversification among Strategies

Investment policymakers are not accustomed to thinking in terms of the investment strategies I have identified as the most fundamentally distinguishing features of investments. And the ways in which they diversify each other may be less intuitively obvious to them than they have been (incorrectly) persuaded to believe that they are for the traditional asset class "buckets" to which they are more accustomed. So this chapter will explore the portfolio function of investment strategies in some detail. First, however, it will be useful to look more closely into just what it is that a "portfolio function" might be, because like so many terms of the investment arts, it has come to mean a great many things.

The most basic portfolio functions are the preservation of capital, the generation of returns, and the maintenance of spending power. With a few nevertheless notable exceptions, any institution that fails to achieve these imperatives will have failed in its task at a cost either to its beneficiaries or to the source of its funding. Although there are a handful of institutions for which preservation of capital and purchasing power may not be a priority—foundations with finite lives or defined benefit plans that are well along the path to being wound down—these can be neglected for the purposes of the discussion in this chapter. However, the tasks and priorities vary a great deal among institutions, depending on their structure and circumstances.

Although preservation of capital is an inescapable priority for virtually all institutions, for foundations, which generally cannot expect much if any supplemental contribution to their initial capital, it is existential, while for other institutions (and for their investment staffs' continued employment) it may "merely" be crucially important. A charitable endowment in support of an essential service, particularly in a highly inflationary sector such as education or healthcare,[1] is likely to have greater concerns about maintaining purchasing power than an investment account related to fire or casualty insurance policies, where underwriting terms can, at least in principle, be adjusted to inflation conditions, generally on an annual basis. Achieving high returns is likely to be a greater priority for an under-funded pension plan than for a fully funded or over-funded one, or for a commercial insurer compared to a mutually owned one. All of which indicates one of the key features of portfolio function: it is only in the context of an institution's needs and resources that it can properly be understood.

From this it is clear that portfolio function is not primarily an attribute of investments themselves, but of the way that an institution makes use of investments in pursuit of its non-investment goals: for most institutions, investment is a means rather than an end in itself. The exceptions are fiduciary institutions, such as mutual funds or endowment pools, whose ends are beyond their trustees' control and possibly even their knowledge—the ends for which the investment is undertaken are determined by their underlying investors and are usually not transparent to the managers of these vehicles. Institutions in the latter category will pursue an investment program that they believe is likely to serve the ends of some large number of potential customers for its services, while the investors will seek out the fiduciary institutions that offer investment programs that they believe are most likely to further their non-investment goals.

An example will illustrate the point. A perpetual foundation with ambitions to expand its grant-giving programs is likely to be attracted to high-return investment vehicles. However, increasing its capital is certain to be a lower priority for it than maintaining its tax-free status, which according to the U.S. Tax Code entails distribution of at least 5 percent of its capital each year, because losing its tax status would seriously endanger its indefinite survival. If the investments under consideration involve long lockups with little prospect that they will make

---

1. Swensen (2009, 34) notes that the Higher Education Price Index had, for the forty-six years through 2006, exceeded the GDP deflator by about 1.4 percent per annum. Inflation in the health-care sector is probably even higher: see PricewaterhouseCoopers (2008).

distributions to the foundation for four years or so, the foundation must balance its return-seeking preferences against its tax-aversion, and will allocate less to those investments than it might otherwise prefer to do. That is, institutional goals that are unrelated to investments will override an investment priority if the investment means available conflict with those goals—in this case, operation in perpetuity. In general, distributions from the portfolio that must conform to a fixed and predetermined schedule are the most frequently encountered constraints on institutions' pursuit of return maximization.

In environments where yields on riskless instruments such as U.S. Treasuries are high, the challenge of meeting distribution requirements is much reduced by making a large allocation to them. Institutions that took advantage of them in the early 1980s still have a few more years to enjoy the benefits of having invested at Treasury yields well above 10 percent. However, these are likely to be the same environments in which inflation is high and economies are depressed, making the demands on institutions to increase their distributions greater. The twin realities of the economic environment and of markets' response to it entail that the basic portfolio functions of preserving capital, generating returns, and maintaining purchasing power are in constant tension. A crucial task of investment policymaking is to employ diversification among investment strategies in order to reduce that tension to the extent possible.

Investment Strategies and Portfolio Function

It is tempting, but erroneous, to link the investment strategies that I have identified directly with the basic portfolio functions discussed above. The fit is not precise. Each of the strategies can be employed to fulfill each of the functions: none of the functions demands the strategy-specific characteristics that only one of the strategies offers. For the most part, the same can be said of the next level of classification, by asset class—even commodity investment can be transformed into a cash flow strategy through exploitation of roll yield when available. Strategies' and asset classes' effectiveness in fulfilling the various functions begins to be differentiated at the level of what I called "investment techniques" in the previous chapter. Thus, for example, neither long-only directional nor cash flow strategies, when applied to fixed-income instruments, contribute to the goal of maintaining purchasing power—but arbitrage and long/short strategies employing bonds or interest rate futures can.

These are the sorts of considerations that underlie the rankings in my classification hierarchy.

This suggests that diversification among investment strategies may be unnecessary. It would require some contortions, but fulfilling the functions of preserving capital, generating returns, and maintaining purchasing power might be achieved by careful selection among different implementations of only one investment strategy. The resulting portfolio would probably be required to employ short positions and leverage in unusual ways, and practical constraints would probably make it difficult to construct, but in principle it could probably be done. However, it would in effect be a very complex arbitrage, almost certainly exhibiting severe optionality, obscure factor exposures, high kurtosis, and strongly negative skewness. Just because something can be done does not recommend doing it, as I argued in Chapter 12 in commenting on the suggestion that institutions substitute hedge funds for all of their fixed-income exposure. Such a portfolio would be more of a stunt than a sound investment policy.

This possibility, however inadvisable it may be to realize in practice, underlines the point that investment strategies are tools for fulfilling portfolio functions rather than functions themselves. Further, it suggests that each is better for performing some functions than others. There is a stronger argument for diversification among investment strategies based on suitability for use than there is based on risk reduction. In fact, the two strands of argument are complementary. Ultimately, portfolio risk is reduced when the three imperatives of preserving capital, generating returns, and maintaining purchasing power are addressed through the use of the optimal combination of tools for the task in hand. Just as the tensions among portfolio functions create the major challenge to investment allocation, exploiting the complex interplay among the strategies is the best way to overcome it. In the final analysis, it is the same set of forces that create those tensions that the investment strategies, in their different ways, seek to exploit.

Cash Flow Strategies

The functional virtue that is peculiar to cash flow investing—its distributions of liquidity that can be used either for institutional or portfolio management purposes—is also its disadvantage, as it creates reinvestment risk if the asset is not perpetual or if cash flows remain in the portfolio rather than being fairly promptly distributed. If term bonds are the asset class employed in this strategy, laddering and similar techniques can smooth the income received over time, but they cannot eliminate reinvestment risk, and a long secular downtrend in interest rates will eventually feed through to the income line.

Earlier chapters have made the attractions of predictable cash inflows obvious—if they were not already abundantly clear—from the perspectives of both portfolio management and institutional demands on the portfolio, and there is no need to belabor them. It should come as no surprise that institutions have long experience with the asset classes that offer them—fixed-income and high-quality real estate. However, institutions' interest in real estate waxes and wanes dramatically compared to their perennial interest in bonds. Because the volatility of real estate is roughly comparable to that of fixed-income, this is probably because of its illiquidity, which most institutions will tolerate only when real estate offers the prospect of significant directional gains, apart from its cash flow contributions. The intermittent interest that real estate receives from institutions is unfortunate: real estate is eminently suited to financial engineering, permitting investors considerably more flexibility with this asset category than is available from their more conventional fixed-income sources of cash flow. This is almost certainly a case where what Keynes (1964, 155) calls the "fetish for liquidity" has resulted in missed opportunities for institutions.

Assets and investment techniques that distribute cash flow unevenly or intermittently are less useful than those with fixed distribution patterns for the purposes of funding either budgeted distributions from the portfolio or periodic portfolio rebalancing. Making a case for the portfolio employment of these investments must, in most instances, rely on their expected total return—regarded strictly as sources of cash flow most of them are somewhat unsatisfactory. However, there are exceptions to this generalization. For example, the appreciation of timber acreage is a fairly insignificant contributor to its returns, most of which are distributed to its investors, although unevenly. Thus Caulfield (1998, 72) finds that returns from timberland derive 6.2 percent from property price appreciation, 33.3 percent from changes in product prices, and 60.5 percent from biological growth. Wasting assets such as oil or gas properties usually have little terminal value, and again the returns they deliver must be from their exploitation rather than their appreciation.

Further, many such investments' distributions can be inconveniently large when they do come in, creating substantial reinvestment risk. The risk-adjusted returns required of them must consequently be higher than those available from assets and techniques that offer predictable distributions. It is difficult to quantify these disadvantages in terms of cost or risk, but they can be quite significant, and the management of them can be costly in terms of both time and expenditure. This may seem ungrateful—oversized distributions are hardly an unwanted investment result—but the reinvestment problems they engender are not inconsiderable.

However, variability of cash flows is generally tied to these investments' ability to protect purchasing power—even those categories of bonds that offer inflation protection often depart from the norm in having somewhat variable distributions. Quality real estate is an exception, as its value will tend to respond to inflation, but its cash flows much less so if at all, and if lease income does adjust to inflation, it generally does so with a significant time lag. This is one of the opportunities that institutions may be missing in this asset class. Otherwise, distributions of cash flow that vary with inflation, such as those from timberland or oil and gas production, tend to a greater or lesser degree to be uneven and irregular. Diversification among such investments can smooth this considerably, resulting in relatively stable aggregate distribution income for the institution. A portfolio of, for example, mezzanine debt, timberland, public infrastructure, and natural gas–producing properties, once it has reached maturity, is likely to produce fairly stable, inflation-responsive distribution streams. Maturity is crucial, however: the first two investment categories, with their J-curve effects and the finite life of the relevant vehicles, require vintage diversification, while natural gas, as a wasting asset, will also require eventual reinvestment. Both initiating and maintaining broad diversification among such investments is very demanding of investment policymakers' time and resources.

Cash flow return on investment is generally lower than the returns that investors require of directional investments, although some of the more volatile sources of cash flow can produce very high returns. Figure 9.2, shows, among other things, a 426.8 percent increase in charter rates (i.e., gross income rather than the value of the vessels that generated it) in the period February 2006 to November 2007, from levels that were already historically high. An investor would have enjoyed that increase in return without recourse to the directional proceeds from selling its vessels, although the increase in their earnings potential would have been reflected in the vessels' market price, suggesting that the total return on well-timed entry into and exit from this investment would have been truly extraordinary. It is this relationship between the amount of income it generates and the asset's price that usually prevents cash flow investing, unless it benefits from such perfect timing, from achieving returns comparable to those on directional trades: prices adjust upwards

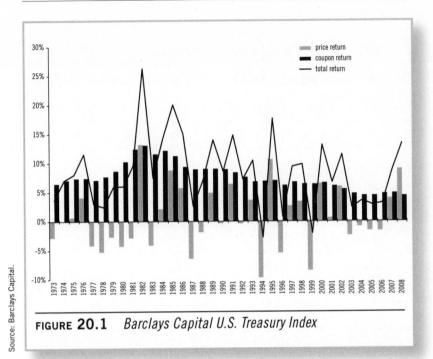

Source: Barclays Capital.

FIGURE 20.1 *Barclays Capital U.S. Treasury Index*

to prevent yields on assets from becoming stratospheric. **Figure 20.1** illustrates how "riskless" bond prices have reacted over the last several decades to keep coupon yields relatively stable: over the thirty-six-year period shown, the annualized standard deviation of monthly bond price returns was 7.05 percent, while the figure for their yields was only 0.63 percent. The statistic for their total returns was 5.46 percent.

For many portfolio purposes, investors should be indifferent to whether their returns are in the form of distributions or capital gains, and taxable investors will generally prefer the latter. In fact, it is often a considerable convenience that returns come in the form of asset appreciation rather than exclusively in the form of distributions, as it obviates the need for reinvestment, although at the cost of increasing the portfolio's directional risk. However, capital gains are not currency, and budgeting that relies on realizing capital gains to fund portfolio rebalancing or an institution's spending obligations crystallizes directional risk repeatedly, with every turn of the budget cycle. The result is a drag on performance— such an approach to funding is, in effect, the reverse of dollar-cost averaging, and will tend to whittle away at returns over time. Underlying this calculation is well-known and essentially trivial arithmetic: as **Table 20.1** indicates, recovering from a decline in portfolio value is

TABLE 20.1 *The Arithmetic of Percentages*

LOSS	RETURN TO RECOVER	LOSS	RETURN TO RECOVER
5%	5.3%	55%	122.2%
10%	11.1%	60%	150.0%
15%	17.7%	65%	185.7%
20%	25.0%	70%	233.3%
25%	33.3%	75%	300.0%
30%	42.7%	80%	400.0%
35%	53.9%	85%	566.7%
40%	66.7%	90%	900.0%
45%	81.8%	95%	1900.0%
50%	100.0%	100%	infinite

challenging enough without further reducing the investable resources upon which any recovery from a loss must rely.

One of the primary advantages of investments that distribute cash flows evenly and regularly is that they remove such timing issues for that portion of the institution's cash requirements that they can fund. Accepting lower returns from the cash flow allocation in order to avoid placing such a drag on the performance of the total portfolio is often, but not in all cases, an appropriate tradeoff.[2]

In this respect, cash flow strategies contribute to the amelioration of portfolio risk. If an institution has no spending obligations, and if portfolio rebalancing is kept to a minimum or executed only opportunistically

---

2. Issues associated with spending of principal are especially acute for endowments, many of which bumped up against restrictions (derived from §2 of the Uniform Management of Investment Funds Act, which has been adopted by forty-seven states since it was introduced in 1972) on doing so in the wake of the recent market turmoil. This has resulted in frantic lobbying to amend the legislation. These are not simply investment issues, but relate to the purpose of endowments in the first place, and the extent to which they should respect the wishes of their donors. See Hechinger and Levitz (2009).

when market conditions are supportive of it, then it would have little use for regular cash flows. The exceptions would be those cash flow investments that offer the safe haven of local currency government debt or those that are judged to be superior sources of total return relative to other available investments. Some sovereign wealth funds have entertained this notion, although none of which I am aware has entirely abandoned allocation to fixed income or real estate (Norway's Government Pension Fund, which despite its name invests the nation's oil income for future generations, perhaps comes closest). The Yale Endowment, as discussed in Chapter 15, carries a small allocation to Treasuries for their safe-haven characteristics, but its real estate portfolio is very substantial, it receives cash flows that are incidental to its directional strategies (i.e., equity dividends), and it allocates heavily to high-return trades that generate uneven cash flows, across which it is broadly diversified.

Arbitrage

In principle, provided that the arbitrage strategy is riskless, regression analysis should be unable to detect any correlation between it and much of anything else, except perhaps the volatility of the underlying instruments, suggesting that arbitrage makes an ideal diversifier. To the extent that an arbitrage is less than "pure," correlation inevitably creeps into its return pattern, but in no case should its correlation to another financial time series be very high if the correlation that the arbitrage exploits is not a spurious one. Given solid if not generally spectacular returns, the attractions of such "absolute return" strategies for the purposes of portfolio construction are compelling, and it is no surprise that they have come to take a prominent place in portfolios—although many investment techniques that sport the "absolute return" label do not in fact offer the desired characteristics. However, regression analysis is virtually blind to optionality, and the options embedded in arbitrage strategies exercise into a variety of market-correlating factors, generally with disastrous consequences. Further, the financing structures that arbitrage vehicles employ will in many cases cause them to have some appreciable factor loading to interest rates.

These features pose significant challenges to investment policymakers. The more familiar quantitative approaches to analyzing investment allocation are unhelpful, while identifying, isolating, and putting a value on the embedded optionality of arbitrages is excruciatingly difficult, if possible at all. Without the ability to model a wide range of trading opportunities over a significant period of time, as Duarte et al. (2007) do for a selection of fixed-income arbitrages, optionality may not be isolable even in principle. And the issue of identifying all the possible sources of optionality is fraught: there is no way that an analyst can prove comprehensiveness, so the risk of being blindsided by unforeseen exposures can never be completely eliminated. However, because these options are generally similar to short put positions, identifying as many of them as possible is a very high priority, because they "explain" the reasons that the arbitrage might collapse and determine the magnitude of the resulting damage to the portfolio if it does. As a result, investment policy finds itself in a quandary.

Consequently, for all that such trades are clearly attractive constituents of a portfolio, investment policy should enter somewhat gingerly into arbitrage. While "normal" market conditions support its claims to be a valuable diversifier, its tail risk is substantial, and in many cases that risk is likely to be fairly highly correlated with the tail risk of other investment strategies employed in the portfolio. However, it need not be, and investment policy can mitigate this risk through careful diversification among arbitrage techniques. Commodity markets provide numerous arbitrage opportunities, with minimal correlation to each other or to other sources of return. Merger and Treasury arbitrages are unlikely to be significantly correlated, but merger arbitrage and any such trade in credit markets are likely to have significant commonality in both their factor loadings and their sensitivity to market volatility. High-frequency arbitrages should not, in most cases, correlate highly with longer duration trades, and so on. I noted in Chapter 7 that there may not be much benefit to investment policy in diversifying broadly *within* an arbitrage category (more on this below), but policy can best exploit the portfolio attractions of arbitrages through well-diversified exposure *across* arbitrage categories.

While arbitrage does not provide a hedge against inflation as such, the expected returns on any arbitrage vehicle to which investment policy should give serious consideration should be high enough to preserve purchasing power in "normal" inflationary conditions. However, if inflation rises to the extent that it stimulates a significant tightening of monetary policy, the cost of the leverage that is essential to arbitrage strategies' ability to generate satisfactory returns may reduce the trading opportunities available to them. As the costs incurred in financing the trade rise in response to increasing inflation, the richness of exploitable pricing discrepancies must increase correspondingly, or the economics of the trade begin to become unattractive. I have remarked on the cyclicality of available opportunities in merger arbitrage, and while in most cases it is unlikely that other arbitrage trades exhibit a similar cycle, an environment of sharply rising interest rates might be just such a case. If so, diversification across arbitrage categories can do little to reduce the risk, as the performance hurdle for all arbitrages will rise at the same time. Unless there is a mechanism to offset this through an increase in the arbitrages' richness when interest rates rise—and it is not clear to me what that would be—arbitrage is not only unlikely to preserve purchasing power during periods of high inflation, but its returns are likely to be lower than their long-term averages during them.

Over long periods, arbitrage strategies will not generally produce returns that contribute strongly to the growth of capital. Barring use of leverage to rival that of Long-Term Capital Management, they cannot match the long-term returns that are generated by more volatile trades, and any that claim that they do are probably repeating that firm's mistakes. Offering returns that, in most cases, fall somewhere in between those of fixed income and equities, arbitrages are effective in preserving purchasing power outside of hyperinflationary conditions, but only modestly supportive of an institution's ambitions to increase its spending or reduce its reliance on contributions. Their low volatility and high contribution to diversification in most market conditions is the compensating factor. However, in keeping with the comparative stability of their returns, arbitrages lack correlation to directional strategies rather than counter-correlating to them. That is, they provide portfolio diversification, but they do not provide a hedge. The ability of arbitrage to generate returns in virtually all but the most extreme market circumstances smoothes the portfolio's aggregate returns and thus improves its compounding, but an exposure to arbitrage that was sufficient to preserve a substantial portion of the institution's capital during market crises (assuming the arbitrage positions do not themselves succumb to those market conditions) would significantly constrain the growth of its capital. And given the difficulty of identifying all the risks in arbitrage, even a broadly diversified exposure to it, if large enough, could in a worst case scenario expose the portfolio to catastrophic loss.

Directional Strategies

Directional strategies are preeminently investment policy's means of generating returns and maintaining purchasing power, but notoriously at odds with the third investment imperative of preserving capital. This is not to say that either of the other two investment strategies is incapable of inflicting punishing losses on an institution's resources, but noticeably, they do so by becoming directional. The failure of an individual cash flow or arbitrage strategy consists precisely of that undesirable transformation, and in market crises of the sort that seem to weigh on all strategies equally, the correlations that have "gone to one" are with directional strategies that have come under severe pressure, and are likely in most cases to be the causes of the crisis in the first place. Note that the two most recent crises began with directional trades—in technology stocks and in housing—where valuations became overextended and reverted abruptly and painfully to the mean. These in turn fed through to destabilize trades in convertible arbitrage after the Technology Bubble and to both arbitrage and cash flow trades in mortgage and credit instruments during 2007 to 2009. However, the emerging-markets crises of the late 1990s were sparked by the collapse of cash flow and arbitrage trades, indicating that there are destabilizing risks in every part of the markets and therefore every part of an investment portfolio. Despite these notable exceptions, the "usual suspects" in most crises are directional strategies and the assets that they employ.

Directional strategies derive their returns from price volatility—where there is no price movement, then by definition there are no returns from them. As we have seen, Modern Portfolio Theory interprets price change as the consequence of information becoming available to market participants, while Bookstaber offers a liquidity-based explanation. These explanations are not mutually exclusive but are most relevant to different time horizons. The information-based explanation is unable to account for the empirical fact of second-to-second price fluctuations, while Bookstaber's explanation would be hard-pressed to explain the long-term, economically driven trends exhibited by assets and investment techniques in "normal" market environments. A reductionist interpretation would favor Bookstaber's account, because in the final analysis all price movement is the result of the accidents of the timing and size of orders that reach the markets' points of price formation, but such reductionism neglects the second-order economic explanations that result in fluctuations resolving themselves into trends. While analogies to games of chance are frequent in discussions of the markets, if that were ultimately all that they amounted to, they would not demonstrate observable trends, and the interest in them would be considerably less than it is.

Arbitrages also rely on volatility to create the pricing discrepancies that they exploit. The short put optionality of these trades indicates that once the trade has been entered into, excessive volatility is anathema to them, but their trading opportunities would not arise in the first place were it not for the volatility of the underlying instruments that gives rise to the price discrepancies upon which arbitrages rely. Practitioners of "pure" buy-and-hold cash flow strategies perceive volatility solely as risk at the point of entry: once they have achieved the desired exposure at a price that suits them, the subsequent price behavior of the underlying asset is largely immaterial to them. However, few institutions have the luxury of ignoring the total return contribution of such investments to the values of their aggregate portfolios, which Figure 20.1 indicates is not inconsiderable even for riskless assets of on-average intermediate duration. The discounting mechanism that makes timing at entry of crucial importance to all cash flow investors persists over the life of the investment, and only a very small minority of fortunate investors is completely untroubled by its effects.

Thus, volatility is not uniquely the concern of directional investors, but it is their predominant concern to an extent that is less true for practitioners of the other strategies. Consequently, the use of hedges against volatility is far more pervasive in their trades than in arbitrage or cash flow disciplines. Although arbitrages are hedged trade structures, it is a rare arbitrageur (do any in fact exist?) that attempts to hedge the short put optionality embedded in its trade structures. To do so would probably hedge away all the potential returns from the trade. Hedging of cash flow trades will generally be at significant cost to the net cash flows received, which in many cases would defeat the purpose of entering into the trade if it is the pursuit of those cash flows—rather than total return—that motivates entry into it in the first place.

It is the higher return expectations in the context of consistent volatility that attach to directional exposures that make hedging of them economical and tolerable. If there is an arbitrageur that hedges its embedded optionality, it must spend large amounts of time justifying its tolerance for continuous hedging losses to itself and its investors, as profits on those hedges will be rare, resulting only when the catastrophic tail risk against which they are designed to protect manifests itself. Expected returns and their "normal" volatility also both underwrite and provide the explanation for a degree of diversification among directional techniques that is not so commonly applied to the other investment strategies. For example, the typical institution will pursue at least two or three security selection techniques among conventional long-only equities, across three or four capitalization size categories and in international and perhaps emerging as well as domestic equity markets. Even a very roughly similar degree of diversification among the conventional fixed-income techniques that institutions employ is rare.

Funds of hedge funds will tend to be comparably diversified—or even more so—but again, their high and volatile targeted returns justify the attendant expenditure of time and effort.

The Traditional Tools
of Portfolio Construction

In abstraction from practical considerations of cost, finance theory will always reply to the question, "How diversified should a portfolio be?" with the answer, "As much as possible." However, a fairly straight-forward application of theory is able to determine at what point the benefits of diversification might begin to be negligible relative to costs, which **Figure 20.2** suggests is somewhere around two hundred positions. Given the degree of diversification institutions typically maintain, this may seem extremely low, and it is—two hundred is by no means a definitive answer.

The analysis shown there depends upon dated assumptions about transaction costs, which tend to reduce the figure, while the methodology employed by Statman (1987), selecting randomly among the components of the Standard & Poor's 500 Index as a proxy for the Market Portfolio,

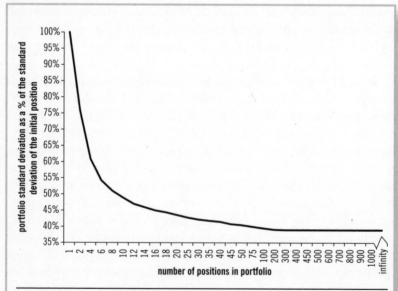

FIGURE 20.2 *Diversification Benefit of Adding Positions to a Portfolio*

Source: Adapted from Elton and Gruber (1977) and Statman (1987).

tends to have the same effect. Use of a broader proxy for the Market Portfolio and lower transaction cost assumptions would push the point of *de minimis* improvement further to the right in the illustration. And deliberate rather than random security selection would, at least in theory, increase the diversification benefit beyond the 61 percent reduction shown. Even apart from a correlation-based selection procedure, the recent examination of that index shown in Table 4.1 finds that its twenty-five largest constituents account for 40 percent of its weighting, so selection based simply on size would provide closer tracking to the proxy than a random selection. But here as in so many cases, the familiar Pareto principle provides a handy rule of thumb, and index coverage in the region of 80 percent (which, as it turns out in the case of the Standard & Poor's 500, works out to about two hundred positions) will in most cases be as close to optimal as makes no difference.

Diversification can reduce risk only so far.[3] Market β—however that is specified for the assets and investment techniques under consideration—and the individual instruments' volatility together define the lower limit. In Figure 20.2 "The Market" is the equity index. Were the coefficient of correlation between each incremental position in Figure 20.2 zero, and assuming equal weighting of positions (as is assumed by Statman and reflected in that chart) the resulting diversification benefit would be a linear function of the square root of the number of positions. Consequently the reduction in standard deviation would be much more rapid, and its asymptote would be zero rather than some larger fraction of the average standard deviation of the instruments employed, as was shown in Figure 20.2 (see Clarke 2006, 181). However, if it were possible to identify eight investments, each with zero correlation to each of the others, it is likely that such a portfolio's expected return would approximate

---

3. And perversely, in some cases diversification among alternative investments may actually *create* risk, notably if a portfolio diversifies within a specific arbitrage strategy: see Lhabitant and Learned (2002, 30*f*), who find that, although a limited number of hedge funds (five to ten) achieves virtually all the reduction in volatility that can be achieved through diversification, diversification among certain categories of funds, notably those engaged in arbitrage, increases kurtosis and especially skewness. Co-kurtosis and co-skewness are beginning to attract academic attention: see Harvey et al. (2004), although as indicated above, I am unconvinced by their application of them. Singer et al. (2003, 103) maintain that the more diversified the institution's exposure to virtually any alternative investment category, the greater the correlation of that portion of its portfolio to public markets is likely to be, but this is probably a consequence of *excessive* diversification than just diversification per se.

to no more than the risk-free rate, with at best equivalent volatility. But unearthing eight such mutually uncorrelated investments is extraordinarily unlikely, if not outright impossible, particularly if we attend to any optionality that might be inherent in them. Recall Lhabitant's comment, cited in Chapter 12, that low β is most likely to be a matter of failure to identify the appropriate factor loadings for the instrument under consideration.[4]

This brings into high relief the fundamental problem of investment allocation over a universe that includes alternative investments, as that is the universe of all possible investments, for which there is no proxy or benchmark. Within long-only equities, it is not unnatural to benchmark against a capitalization-weighted index that embraces all or at least most of the relevant investment universe. But what guidance does this provide us toward identifying the appropriate allocation we should make to strategies that employ futures, given that the net value of all futures outstanding is, by definition, zero? However, we do not need to penetrate into the realm of derivatives to be confronted by this issue: no investor of which I am aware looks upon the aggregate value of fixed-income instruments outstanding as a reference point in determining the size of its allocation to bonds. Thus even the most elementary allocation decision for conventional portfolios lacks a benchmark. We should not be surprised that the situation when alternative investments are included in the investment universe is no better.

Nevertheless, in the days when available investments were limited to equities, bonds, cash, and real estate, the allocation decision was relatively straightforward. Cash and real estate were regarded as substitutes for fixed income, so the fundamental decision reduced to choosing a spot on a two-investment efficient frontier. Overlaid on this choice, as lower-level decisions, were issues such as liquidity requirements, the perceived need for a cash reserve, and any enhancement the institution might wish to make to the fixed-income portfolio through the use of real estate or cash. If, in time-honored academic fashion, we simply ignore all the difficulties with optimizers' statistical foundations, with estimating the statistics that feed them and with the special problems that surround arbitrage and other fully hedged trades, then, in principle, there is no challenge in calculating an efficient frontier for any number of investment categories

---

4. On techniques for identifying factors, none of which can guarantee completeness, see Elton and Gruber (1994, 35*ff*), Campbell et al. (1997, 233*ff*), and Grinold and Kahn (2000, 57*ff*); for a list of factors that might typically be employed in tactical allocation among categories of long-only equities, see de Silva (2006, 4).

or techniques. Those difficulties are hardly insignificant, and are probably insurmountable—hence Michaud (1989) calls optimizers "estimation error maximizers" (33). But even assuming that they can be overcome, the allocation that an optimizer suggests will not, in many cases, address all the requirements of investment policy.

Optimizers are notably single-minded: the efficient frontier for which they solve takes no account of institutional requirements, such as a need for liquidity, that are independent of the imperatives to maximize (total) return and preservation of capital. If the model is unconstrained, then it will throw off proposals that do not allow for lower-level decisions concerning issues such as liquidity needs, preservation of purchasing power, and so forth. Thus it may recommend allocations, such as the 100 percent hedge fund portfolio discussed in Chapter 12, that fail to address important institutional concerns. Attempting to skirt this problem by imposing constraints on the model's parameters—for instance, by specifying a minimum allocation to investments that correlate negatively with inflation—is not neutral for the rest of the portfolio. The optimizer will mindlessly attempt to offset this exposure elsewhere in the allocations that it identifies as optimal. As optimization is driven solely by returns and volatility, it cannot tilt its allocation proposals to reflect desired factor loadings. While optimizers have been constructed that incorporate considerations such as liquidity into their allocation recommendations (see Lo 2008, 97–120), these strike me as rather blunt instruments, and the sense of "liquidity" involved is not the one that is of most importance to institutions that must meet periodic distribution deadlines.

None of this comes as news to investors, and multi-factor analysis, which is common in long-only equity management, has gradually gained traction in other fields of investment. However, multi-factor analysis is benchmark dependent. Without reference to a benchmark of some sort, the completeness of its analysis cannot be verified (see Elton and Gruber 1994, 33f). Application of this form of analysis to equities is uncontroversial because there are numerous benchmarks, many of which are highly specific to subsets of the equity universe, against which the model can be calibrated. There is no benchmark for the Market Portfolio, and thus no means of testing a multi-factor model when it is applied to the universe of all possible investments. As already discussed, building a multi-factor model for the analysis of portfolios that include allocations to alternative investments is an empirical task of identifying factors one-by-one, in which there can be no guarantee that an important factor has not been missed. Once again: it is impossible to prove a negative existential proposition of the form "No other factors are relevant to the price behavior of this investment." In equities, it is possible through analysis of the benchmark to assure ourselves of the adequacy, if not the complete comprehensiveness, of a multi-factor analysis. That is, we can estimate the unexplained portion of returns. This is not possible if there is no benchmark.

Recognizing only the two imperatives of maximizing return and minimizing volatility, optimization cannot distinguish between degrees of priority in investment allocation decisions. Relying on a comprehensive metric for the investment universe against which it can measure the explanatory power of their conclusions, multi-factor models cannot fully address the allocation problem associated with a universe that is unconstrained in its use of assets and investment techniques. The point of a hierarchical classification of investments is to facilitate investment policymaking by creating a basis for distinguishing between higher- and lower-order decisions, in order to provide some guidance forward from where theory seems to have left us stranded.

Higher- and Lower-Order Allocation Decisions

Institutions must, of course, decide for themselves what their investment priorities are. Some of these, such as foundations' requirement to distribute 5 percent of capital annually, are imposed on them from without, while others, such as a desire to increase distributions at a rate in excess of inflation, are self-imposed. But a disciplined approach to investing also requires due attention to the priorities that investment itself imposes.

Which take priority depends on circumstances. The 5 percent distribution requirement, as already discussed, is existential for a foundation, and must take a prominent place in its thinking, particularly if its portfolio of illiquid investments is not mature, for example if it is a new entity. Institutions have life cycles just as private investors do, and these can have important implications for their behavior. But in the majority of cases, as Markowitz recognized, the parameters of mean and variance that underlie optimization are where investment policymaking must begin. The higher moments of statistical distributions and considerations such as liquidity requirements or preservation of purchasing power are secondary to these, and to some extent their ranking may be dictated by them. For example, liquidity needs may be met more or less automatically if the institution's risk tolerance is very low, but concerns over preservation of purchasing power will then probably be quite significant. An institution that has the luxury of long-term planning—such as the Carnegie Corporation, which funds major new projects once a decade—may feel less constrained by the demands of liquidity than others. Institutions with more of a return orientation may be unconcerned with preservation of purchasing power provided that they perceive inflation to be "normal," believing that portfolio returns will compensate for whatever the inflation outcome turns out to be.

Beginning a paragraph with "Having established a return requirement and the tolerable level of volatility ..." is reminiscent of the economist joke with the punch-line "Assume a paddle ..." Although it is understandable that commentators would prefer to avoid matters as fraught and obscure as reaching such a determination, investment policy-makers hardly deserve to have their most difficult challenge trivialized. Bismarck's caution against inquiring too closely into the making of legislation or sausages is unhelpful to those who must make either. As with sausages, there is a visceral element to investment policymaking in the raw that the overscrupulous would prefer not to confront. Though rational considerations relating to the institution's requirements and to the analysis of its investment universe can certainly be brought to bear on the question, it is fundamentally an emotional one—ambition, fear, a sense of mission, and a sense of the crushing weight of responsibility are all at play. As Lo (2008) notes, "Ironically, despite all of the many tools offered to individual investors—risk tolerance surveys, "what-if" scenario simulators, and lifetime financial-planning software—there is virtually nothing comparable for helping institutional investors determine their collective risk preferences" (239). The most likely reason for this apparent market failure is the "collective" nature of the relevant decision-making body. It is difficult enough to elicit an articulation of risk preferences from a single investor—an effort in which the insights provided by behavioral finance have perhaps made their greatest contribution to investment thinking—let alone a committee of trustees.

Nor is the task ever completed: for all that policy committees attempt to decide matters once and for all, in tacit if not explicit recognition that second-guesses motivated by market activity are likely to be less than optimal, it is virtually impossible to avoid the temptation. It is far easier to recommend disciplined rebalancing and contrarianism than it is to carry them out in practice. All of which may be more suggestive of Hunter Thompson than Bismarck, but Iron Chancellors of the investment world are few and far between. Leave it to a practitioner to provide what comfort investment policymakers can obtain on this score, which amounts to little more than the observation that we are all in the same boat:

> For many investors, defining the efficient frontier represents the ultimate goal of quantitative portfolio analysis. Choosing from the set of portfolios on the frontier ensures that, given the underlying assumptions, no superior portfolio exists. Unfortunately, mean-variance optimization provides little useful guidance in choosing a particular point on the efficient frontier. Academics suggest specifying a utility function and choosing the portfolio at the point of tangency with the efficient frontier. Such advice proves useful only in the unlikely event that investors find it possible to articulate a utility function in which utility relates solely to the mean and variance of expected returns. (Swensen 2009, 121–22)

So—having established a return requirement and the tolerable level of volatility, choice among investment strategies is a matter of addressing lower-order questions of liquidity needs and so on. Many of these are best addressed at the level of asset classes and investment techniques. For example, given a high disbursal requirement, investment policy can choose to focus its directional exposure on long-only, dividend-paying equities at the expense of hedged strategies, increase its fixed-income credit risk and/or build a diversified portfolio of investments that produce irregular cash flows. Note that the decisions are comparative, and inevitably involve tradeoffs between volatility, liquidity, and sensitivity to inflation. While this is confusing, it also leaves ample room for creativity—investment allocation is a cat that can be skinned numerous ways, so investment policymakers need not obsess over finding a sole, optimal solution. Mean variance optimization has, in this respect, done them the disservice of implying that there in fact is such a thing. Systematic arbitrage is something of an exception to the idea that all choices involve tradeoffs: it is only occasionally liquid, but otherwise it is a low volatility, moderate return trade that makes no factor contribution to the portfolio other than its (often unanalyzable) tail risk. These are the characteristics that cause the term "absolute return" to be bandied about so loosely, but the crowdedness of many of these trades and their tail risks should temper an institution's enthusiasm for excessive allocations to these techniques.

The task of investment policymaking is iterative: lower-order decisions may reflect back on higher-order ones, so that the steps taken in investment thinking need to be continually retraced. Thus, for example, the decision to use lower-quality credits to enhance income must be referred back to decisions taken on the desirable level of directional exposure in general and equity exposure in particular. Here Swensen's notion of "complex simultaneity" confronts us starkly. To avoid falling into a hopeless muddle, it is helpful to maintain a sense of which consideration ranks higher in the allocation decision hierarchy. In this instance, investment policy should consider the importance of the income enhancement to the institution—is the incremental income necessary to its distribution or rebalancing program, or is it a return stream that would be equally valuable to the institution in the form of an embedded capital gain on a directional position? Would increased exposure to fixed income affect the portfolio's sensitivity to inflation in ways that conflict with the policy view? Reaching down rather than up the hierarchy of decisions to something approaching the tactical level, what are the anticipated distributions from irregular cash flow investments, which might make the additional injection of cash liquidity into the portfolio unwelcome? Would extension of fixed-income duration without changing credit quality (and thus increasing equity-related exposure) achieve the same goal? Amid all these decision loops, we must not lose sight of the decisions on risk and return requirements that are most fundamental and that should inform all of the others.

An example of a consideration that may be of importance to institutions at any level of allocation beneath investment strategies is so-called social responsibility, which has become an unavoidable concern for many institutions. Superficially, this seems to be a matter of security selection rather than investment allocation, and in most cases that is the decision level at which the relevant choices are made and implemented. But Sharia-compliant investors shun the entire conventional fixed-income asset class, Taft-Hartley plans may steer clear of leveraged buyouts or investment outside of the United States, university endowments will avoid investment in whatever individual countries are currently out of liberal favor, corporate pension plans sponsors may not look kindly on investment techniques that involve short selling or activism, and so on. Regulation or tax considerations may impose similar constraints at any level of decision-making beneath allocation among investment strategies—for example, many institutions are constrained by their tax treatment from employing investment techniques that involve leverage or by state law from those that employ leverage or short exposure. Where such considerations affect investment portfolios, they may entail iterative reexamination of investment allocation. For example, an ecology-minded constraint at the level of security selection on investment in the oil industry may have significant implications for a desire to preserve purchasing power.

A constraint on investment in the oil industry illustrates my point about the hierarchy of decisions. Although at the level of optimization it may appear to be an afterthought, it can substantially affect portfolio balance. Yet it cannot usefully be considered before other, higher-order investment decisions have been made: thus it may bulk very large for an institution that allocates heavily to fixed income, as it removes a standard way of addressing concerns about purchasing power with which such an institution is unavoidably faced. And it may have significant implications for other parts of the investment allocation, such as a recommendation to concentrate real estate holdings in Houston-area office properties. Though a linear hierarchy is an aid to investment thinking, and probably a necessary one, I take "complex simultaneity" to mean that allocation is ultimately a holistic endeavor.

CHAPTER 21

Multi-Dimensional Risk

Many people are unaware that Jules Verne was not exclusively a science fiction writer, but *Michael Strogoff*, a conventional adventure tale, was a childhood favorite of mine. Among its other virtues, at one point it lists all the titles of the Czar, which as I recall occupy most of a page—Prince of Nijni-Novgorod, Governor of the Hyperborean Regions, and so on. Attempts to catalog investment risks soon become even lengthier and more obscure, because every aspect of an investment, from the initial impulse to make one to the reinvestment risk that usually attaches to receipt of the final proceeds from it, involves one or in most cases several risks. Distinction piles on distinction, and the number of separately identifiable risks adumbrates to the limits of time and patience. I will refrain from offering such a list, because I doubt that it would have much value. There is in fact an infinity of investment risks, or near enough as makes no difference, so a complete enumeration is impossible, and a lengthy one offers only a misleading illusion of comprehensiveness.

Academic discussion of risk tends to focus on the risks associated with the performance of investments themselves, rather than operational risks or credit exposure to counterparties, let alone the risk of fraud. This neglect is not perhaps so surprising, because organized markets in conventional investment instruments cut the latter risks to an irreducible minimum, or very close to one. For example, a market-making and arbitrage unit of one of my former employers executed hundreds of trades in several different markets daily over three years without experiencing a single trade failure. But many alternative investment vehicles are far more heavily exposed to operational and counterparty risks than conventional, long-only managers, which places a significant additional burden on those who perform due diligence on them. Further, as I have stressed, investors in illiquid instruments may find that trade discovery—or rather, the possibility that the fund may fail to discover trades—entails risks that are not nearly so familiar to investors who are accustomed to liquid instruments traded in continuous auction markets.

However, academic neglect of transaction-related risks derives most fundamentally from the distinction that Modern Portfolio Theory draws between risks that can be reduced through diversification and those that cannot be. Finance theory instructs us to eliminate the former to the extent possible and gives us essentially no guidance on how to reduce or otherwise manage the latter, among which transaction risks are included. Interestingly, however, as the example of my former employer suggests, careful management of risks that are not diversifiable can to a large extent eliminate them, while diversifiable risks can only be reduced so far, after which they are not further reducible through diversification. Even if our portfolios were able to achieve the maximum diversification of the Market Portfolio, they would continue to exhibit some level of volatility (and based on the experience of 2007 to 2009, when investments ranging from artworks to zinc to houses in the Hamptons were affected, probably not a trivial level), but the experience of my old firm and many others suggests that, while transaction risks always remain as possibilities lurking in the background, with diligent and continuous effort to control them, traders need not suffer their consequences.

Another category of risk that has attracted considerable study is agency risk, which has been recognized as a legal issue since law began with Hammurabi, and has received considerable attention from economists from Adam Smith on. There are features of some alternative investments that magnify this risk considerably, or that manifest it in unexpected ways, but by and large the agency risks that attach to alternative investments are very similar to those that attach to conventional ones. The most notable of these, at the level of third-party investment managers, are herding behavior in the interest of retaining assets under management and excessive focus on asset-gathering. However, their unregulated status and the lack of transparency that characterizes many alternative investment vehicles provide enormous scope for agency risk and conflicts of interest, and the Madoff affair indicates that they can also facilitate outright theft. Vehicles that employ assets that do not permit of custody make instances of fraud even more difficult to detect and consequently more likely, while investments that require day-to-day operating management are immensely hospitable environments for agency risk. I recently read with cynical enjoyment the disclosure in a private placement memorandum for a real estate vehicle that the due diligence on the manager had been conducted by one of its own affiliates: why even go through the pretense?

One form of risk that is universal in the field of investments but that comes in for surprisingly little attention, is opportunity cost. This tends to be mentioned somewhat dismissively in connection with "regret" as an aspect of behavioral finance, and otherwise ignored. But it is peculiar that a risk that attends all but the one, best-performing investment over any given time period is treated so cavalierly, particularly because attempts to avoid it have considerable real world effects. For example, much of the widely disseminated advice against market-timing depends at least partially on the observation that returns on cash are low (for example, see Swensen 2009, 66), which is nothing other than a warning about the potential opportunity cost of moving portfolio exposure into then out of risky assets. I will return to this subject below.

Risk within the Hierarchy of Investments

There are risks that are common to each level of the investment allocation hierarchy, and others that are quite specific to certain levels or even to specific assets or investment techniques. Thus, counterparty risk manifests itself in every investment of every type, but in a wide variety of ways and with different implications for management of this risk in each specific instance. The sole exception is where it has been socialized away, for example with respect to cash deposits of less than the maximum insured by the Federal Deposit Insurance Corporation. On the other hand, from what I can gather, the risk of catastrophic loss from trematode infestation is exclusive to catfish aquaculture in the lower Mississippi basin.

This is the intention behind the analogy I have drawn between risk and the geometry of higher dimensions: some risks pervade the entire hierarchy of investments, while others touch on it here and there or only at a single point. It is as though the two dimensional flatland of a linear hierarchy that I have drawn is embedded in a three-dimensional world, with risk providing the third dimension (**Figure 21.1**). As Edwin Abbot recognized well over a century ago, the denizens of a planar world would perceive the intrusion of three dimensional beings among them as familiar lines or points—they could not, in fact, perceive anything else from a single vantage point, although given the ability to move around the plane, they could determine the the cross-sectional contour of a three-dimensional object insofar as it intrudes on the plane they inhabit. They would be unable to conceive of the portions of those beings that did not impinge on the plane in which they live or that simultaneous appearances in different parts of the plane could possibly be appearances of the same being. Movement of three-dimensional beings with respect to the plane would be perceived as inexplicable expansions and shrinkages or sudden appearances and disappearances.

We are frequently in a similar situation with regard to risk. Superficially dissimilar risks pop up without being recognized as being fundamentally the same, while risks that are in fact different in kind may appear quite similar from our limited perspective. Thus, for example, the liquidity and counterparty risks that—as is now all too clear—became increasingly pervasive throughout the financial system in this decade, were perceived as peculiar to only a few, comparatively obscure investment sectors before the experience of 2008. Most commentators hailed a new paradigm (it is always a new paradigm) of risk transfer and diversification, while failing to notice that the risks that

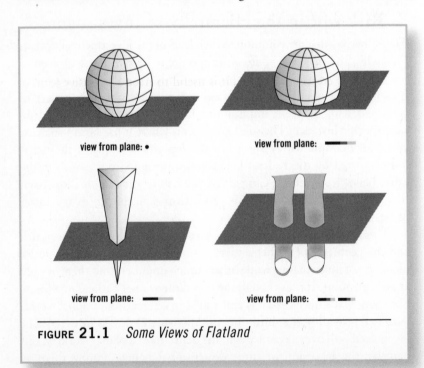

FIGURE 21.1 *Some Views of Flatland*

were being spread throughout the system were not diversifiable: they did not offset each other, so multiplying them simply multiplied risk, and transferring them simply spread risk more widely, to recipients who in many cases were unprepared for it. This is the difference between the naïve, "eggs in one basket" understanding of diversification and Markowitz's insight into the behavior of assets whose price fluctuations are at least partially correlated with each other. It is astonishing that this fundamental distinction was ignored: the few who did notice and comment on the rapidly mounting systemic risk, among them Bookstaber, were dismissed as Cassandras.

Risks that appear similar but are in fact quite different are equally dangerous. Often this is a function of hidden optionality. For example, corporate bonds embed a short position in a put option on their issuer's equity, which Treasuries, of course, lack entirely. Most of the time, even for mediocre credits, such options are so far out of the money that they are irrelevant to the pricing of the bonds, which are priced off Treasuries in a clear implication of "like-for-like with minor adjustments." But if the issuer's credit comes into question, the options' presence is suddenly and unpleasantly felt. In 2008, AA credits of some of the best-known U.S. financial services issuers saw these options come into the money—disastrously for those, who through ownership of the bonds, had effectively sold put options on the underlying equity—while the industrial and other AA issuers with which such bonds are typically more or less fungible were significantly less affected.

In lieu of creating a catalog, it is useful to trace a pervasive form of risk through the various ways that it manifests itself up and down the investment hierarchy. One risk that is nearly universal in some form or another, and thus provides a good illustration, is credit risk. It is, of course, the fundamental risk to cash flow strategies, but manifests itself in the other strategies in the form of counterparty risk, call risk for short positions, and so on. At some point or another, every investment involves exposure to the risk of non-payment, or exposes its investor to margin calls, or exposes other credit providers whom the investor itself puts at such risk. When it is remarked that finance is a fabric that is held together by trust, this is what is meant. The asset that is most immune to this risk is physical gold, but even there, some risk attaches to the transaction and to the subsequent storage of the bullion. Drawing on my analogy, credit risk is one of the higher dimensions in which the entire lower dimension of investment activity is embedded. The fact that the investor becomes a credit risk for the other entities that become exposed to it is satisfyingly symmetrical. This is not always so apparent. For example, it would seem that the issuer of a bond carries no exposure to the holders of that instrument, but this is only true once the instrument is in issue: during underwriting, the issuer runs the not unnoticeable risk that those who subscribe to the issue may fail to honor their commitments.

How many such all-pervading risks are there? This can quickly degenerate into semantic considerations—counterparty risk is in some cases quite clearly a form of credit risk, but in others it may be operational. Operational risk in one form or another is, in any case, certainly another pervasive form of risk. It might be thought that bringing investment management in-house would relieve an institution of agency risk, but an institution's own staff members are agents, too, and arguably even more vulnerable to group-think and herding behaviors than third-party agents. Lacking a commercial imperative, in-house staff feel no countervailing pressure to distinguish themselves, and consequently may be even more vulnerable to these tendencies than third-party providers. The entirety of Wu (2005), but especially Chapter 4, might be regarded as an essay in how agency risks manifest themselves inevitably and unexpectedly in virtually every aspect of economic activity.

Risks that derive from illiquidity are also likely to be all-pervading across all levels of my investment classification. In an age where many assets have been dematerialized and off-site record keeping is widespread, Acts of God may seem a less universal risk than they once were. But the failure of Bank of New York's systems in 1985[1] and the furor over the potential systemic consequences of "Y2K" indicate that we are not as protected as we might hope from a sufficiently aggrieved Supreme Being. While it is probably unlikely that investment activity requires the burgeoning profusion of dimensions employed by String Theory to account for all its inherent risk categories, the requisite figure is probably somewhat greater than just these five.

Then there are the highly specific risks that attach only to particular investment techniques. To my knowledge, trematodes are a threat only to investors in a particular form of aquaculture in a particular region.

---

1. On November 20, 1985, a programming error interfered with the processing of more than 32,000 transactions (about 19 percent more than the average volume for the entire market at the time) in government securities at one of the largest clearing banks for these instruments. The bank was forced to turn to the Federal Reserve for a then-unimaginable $32 billion overdraft facility. It is a measure of our misfortunes that $32 billion is certainly not unimaginable anymore. See Berry (1985).

As a broader category of risk, parasite infestation is only an issue for biology-dependent investments, and would not seem to pose risks to investments in mines or commercial paper. However, the controversy over the health of the CEO of Apple during 2008 suggests that biology might be a more pervasive influence on investments than it would at first appear. Economics is, after all, a social science, and society and all its works are built upon biological foundations. With sufficient perseverance, I suspect that many so-called specific risks can be found to belong to some or other category of risks that affects most if not all investments.

Could it be that all risks are manifestations of one or other of the all-pervading risks? I do not know, but it would be convenient if they were. This would permit a hierarchical classification or risks in parallel with the classification of investments already offered, and would facilitate the identification of all the risks that any specific investment entails. If one can be developed, it will be of great value to investors, but the project requires considerable caution: a flawed classification could be a dangerous source of false confidence that all the risks relevant to a particular investment had been identified.

Identification of Risk

The management of risk has become a major industry, not just within academia and among software vendors but in institutions and at the managers they employ. Models such as Value at Risk have been elaborated in considerable detail, and numerous firms apply substantial resources to their development and extension as well as their day-to-day care and maintenance. Whereas much of this effort is of great value, a fair amount of it is misplaced, or seeks to accomplish for the entire portfolio what can only be accomplished for certain portions of it. As Bookstaber notes,

> ... those strategies with the most complex and quantitative risks also have the best tools in place to deal with them. Those strategies with more subjective risks do not generally have these tools, but then, those tools would not do them much good. That is, along this spectrum the capability to do risk management is in phase with the meaningfulness of the results. The level of detail to which risk management can reasonably be performed is in line with the degree to which that detail would have any value. There are those who can and already do and those who don't and probably can't. (Bookstaber 2007, 249)

By subjective risks, I believe that Bookstaber intends those that are not susceptible to statistical analysis, either because they have not occurred so that their frequency and extent cannot be measured or because they occur so seldom that the likelihood of their occurrence and their potential magnitude cannot be reliably estimated. Unfortunately, this category includes some very considerable risks. Thus, the risk that an institution will be unable to exit from its direct venture capital investments, causing realization to be delayed with potentially severe consequences for returns, is largely immeasurable. Such risks need not arise from unprecedented events such as earthquakes in Indiana, although these certainly fall into the immeasurable category. The risk that the equity market will be unable to accommodate IPO exits when that would be desirable is hardly a bolt from the blue—the cyclicality of the new issue market has long been well recognized, if never completely understood. The fact that a risk is not measurable does not mean that it is *de minimis*, and it need not even mean that it is wildly improbable.

Thus some of these immeasurable risks are truly tail events, but others are seemingly quite "normal" occurrences. The latter probably belong more properly under Bookstaber's rubric of subjective risks. These risks are occurrences that can be expected, based on experience, but for which the timing is uncertain, and any judgment of their probability is, in fact, fairly purely "subjective." An institution that invests in venture capital creates a hostage to fortune that is known at the time of its subscription, since there is no reason to expect that then-prevailing new issuance conditions will persist until access to the IPO market is required. Vintage diversification is the recommended way of managing this risk, but it is only a partial solution, in that it smoothes rather than eliminates the risk. If a vintage becomes mature during a period when IPOs are difficult to achieve, the time denominator of the internal rate of return calculation can rapidly erode the investment's returns. If, as experience in this decade suggests, weak conditions in at least some parts of the IPO market can persist over long periods, vintage diversification will provide only very limited risk reduction to investors whose exits rely on that portion of the new issuance market.

As discussed in the previous chapter, multi-factor models are only useful in identifying exposures to risks for which factor exposures and a metric for them have been identified. Although these models may occasionally uncover unanticipated exposures in this or that investment, in most cases their contribution is just to quantify a risk that those who were taking it already knew was present. And they may not succeed at that: occasionally factor loadings will reveal exposures that are entirely unaccountable, and may be spurious. But as with the "false negative" that results from the failure to identify explanatory factors, we can never be certain that these "false positives" are in fact false. In my experience, the systematic explanation for most of them can be uncovered after a little cogitation, but occasionally a factor exposure will be offered up by the model that cannot easily be elucidated or explained away. I regard these as challenges to further research—in fact, yet another call for stress-testing in the peculiar sense I have been using—but in the meantime my prejudice under the press of events is to regard them as spurious until research suggests otherwise.

Despite Bookstaber's assurances, I am inclined toward caution concerning any form of quantitative risk modeling except where its input is at least weekly data and the time horizon of the investor is not too dissimilar to that—not much more than, say, quarterly or perhaps biannually. Virtually all institutions adopt a longer-term horizon, which suggests that they may find such analyses of limited value. This modeling frequency requires enormous data-handling capacity if the analysis is performed position-by-position, as in a Value at Risk model, but multi-factor models can make good use of what a risk manager of my acquaintance characterizes as a "prudent level of transparency" by focusing on returns, provided that the nature of the underlying positions is well known. Where such transparency is not available, selection of factors for the risk manager to investigate is impeded, and the unexplained portion of returns may well be so high as to render the modeling essentially valueless. There is a tendency among many less-than-sophisticated users, strongly and irrationally encouraged by regulators, to think that modeling is risk control: in many cases, modeling simply dissembles risk, especially when the risks have not been identified before the model is run.

At the end of the day, regardless of its elaboration and sophistication, quantitative risk modeling cannot tell us what is most crucially important for investors to know: when, where, and how our portfolios will be affected when confronted by market crises. Although occasionally an institution is completely blind-sided by an undetected risk, in most cases the damage done to its portfolio can be ascribed to the exposures that were taken with return maximizing intent. Thus, for example, the reasons behind the dismal history of U.S. municipalities and their attempts to maximize their returns from supposedly riskless, cash-like investments are plain to all serious investors. The municipalities' professions that they were misled have plausibility only on the assumption of utter, near criminal incompetence—come to think of it, perhaps not such an implausible excuse. Although serious investors may occasionally be surprised when the markets uncover unexpected exposures in their portfolios, they are not astounded to discover that excess returns entail exposure to risk.

Where risk is completely unanticipated, it will generally be found to be the result of failure to recognize the extent to which unusual market conditions or the way a strategy is implemented can stress a risk that was in fact fully recognized. For all the enormous turmoil that financial markets experienced in 2007 to 2009, few senior obligations of AA-rated issuers actually defaulted. For buy-and-hold investors, these instruments' price gyrations were no doubt alarming but largely insignificant, and for opportunists they provided a bonanza. But for institutions that were employing these bonds as collateral or that were heavily exposed to them in situations where marking them to market would have significant effects on their operations, the consequences were in some instances catastrophic. But in *no* case were they unthinkable. One must assume that all investors in such instruments are aware of their credit exposure and of what that implies when credit exposure becomes anathema to the markets. F. H. Bradley commented that "It is not that he never thinks; he is always thinking—about something else." These institutions were thinking about returns, not the function of collateral or the consequences of employing credit exposure in a context of mark-to-market risk.

We cannot know in advance from where, among all the risk dimensions in which our investment activities are embedded, the next extraordinary risk is going to appear. Quantitative tools, when employed in the context of stress testing, are dedicated to fighting the battles of the past: they cannot identify risks that are not anticipated by those who construct the models. Even if their inputs include forecasts, the forecasts themselves must be built on an understanding of market history. Our ability to imagine all the potential forms of investment horror is limited—which, inconvenient as it is, is also consoling for those of us who require at least occasional sleep. Diversification can reduce some risks, and others can in fact be controlled through obsessive managerial attention to the details, such as their operational capabilities, over which management actually exercises significant control. But risk is a fundamental fact of investment life: if we take the relationship between risk and return seriously, then we have no choice but to recognize and even embrace this. Investors' task is to take the risks that they wish to take, rather than to avoid risk entirely or to find to our sorrow that we have taken risks that we wish we had not taken. We can never assure ourselves that we have taken no unknown risks—we can only continually reexamine our position.

Opportunity Cost

This segues nicely into a discussion of an aspect of investments that is too frequently dismissed with snide remarks about "would'a, could'a and should'a." Regardless of the apparent fact, which has been explored extensively by behavioral economists' development of prospect theory (see Barberis and Thaler 2003, 1067*ff*), that we are not accurate forecasters of expected utility, if we nevertheless accept that the attempt to maximize returns is at least one of the important functions of investment management, then we as investors operate in an environment that always reminds us that we could have done a better job. We are, indeed, playing a "loser's game," but in ways that Charles Ellis's famous article of that title (1975) did not discuss. Even if we do somehow stumble on the best-performing investment over some period, unless that period coincides precisely with our investment career, our career will unavoidably have been one of lost opportunity.[2] And even then, that investment's volatility will doubtless have created opportunities, some of which we will inevitably miss, to enhance its returns by trading around the position. Further, in the context of the Market Portfolio, we can never in fact know that we have succeeded in identifying the best-performing investment, as one of the myriad investments that comprise the Market Portfolio that are not marked to market might well have outperformed those that posted returns with which we are familiar. Investors are unavoidably haunted by opportunity cost, or at least the nagging sense that they might have suffered it unknowingly.

All of which may be of passing interest to a psychologist or two, but is investors' fragile emotional state really subject matter for a book on investing? I think not. However, opportunity cost is not merely an occasion for tearing of hair and gnashing of teeth, but a fundamental concept that pervades all investment activity. From the establishment of investment policy to the process of selecting which individual position exposures to liquidate, all investment decisions involve a weighing of comparative attractions, often complicated by

---

2. A portfolio manager of my acquaintance told me that, upon learning that his was the best-performing U.S. mutual fund one year, he told his boss not to expect a recurrence and that he wanted a raise. It is unclear to me how the one follows from the other, but it was doubtless worth a try.

non-investment considerations. The decision to deploy capital in one way is, *ipso facto*, a decision not to deploy it in another. I have already drawn upon the example of a foundation that chooses not to make what it believes would be return-maximizing investments in the interest of preserving its tax-protected status—an obvious loss of opportunity. Imagine the contrast in its behavior if the foundation's return forecasts were completely reliable: given a sufficiently lucrative opportunity, it would be likely to forgo its tax advantages, since the anticipated returns would more than compensate for the cost of incurring taxation.

So opportunity cost is closely related to uncertainty. Much has been written about the distinction between uncertainty and risk, but it is really not so very profound. Whether justifiably or not, I feel no uncertainty that the sun will rise tomorrow, and thus perceive no risk that, if I survive the night, I will freeze in darkness in the morning, even though I am uncertain about the time that sunrise will occur. However, the latter uncertainty does not translate into risk unless I take some action that depends on the timing of sunrise—for instance, placing a wager on when it will be. Uncertainty is simply ignorance, while risk results from acting in ignorance. Opportunity cost results from the necessary specificity of our actions—my bet on the time of sunrise must be for 6:57, 7:12, or some such, as I am very unlikely to find a bookie who would accept "in the morning" as a wager. We cannot choose to invest in general but must always select this or that particular investment. Some might convince themselves that they can avoid choice through investment in broadly diversified passive vehicles, but that is simply to choose, quite specifically, the weighted average return of their constituents.

Diversification reduces opportunity cost by spreading exposure over a wide array of investments. We do not enjoy full exposure to the best-performing of them, but with any luck we do not miss out on those winners entirely. However, it is interesting that the practice of diversifying portfolios generally proceeds in the opposite direction. That is, we typically identify what we believe will be the best-performing investments and then reduce our anticipated returns by mixing in second and third choices. Thus uncertainty drives us into seemingly paradoxical behavior. The paradox is resolved when it is recalled that diversification need not be so naïve as the "eggs in one basket" caricature would suggest.

As already discussed, in most cases diversification is not among independent return streams: the volatility of any portfolio is not just the weighted average of its constituents' individual volatilities. It would only be so if all the instruments involved had correlations with each other of one—hardly the portfolio that even the most naïve investment policymakers would be likely to choose. Although the return of the best-performing asset will unquestionably be diluted through diversification, there is a compensating reduction in the aggregate volatility of the portfolio if the less promising assets are carefully chosen. The opportunity cost is made acceptable through a reduction in the expected volatility of the portfolio, which, as discussed in Chapter 3, is no small thing. Even so, this is tolerable only as recompense for having to operate under uncertainty. If we could reliably pick the best performer (in absolute terms: volatility adjustment would cease to be relevant) it would be irrational to diversify.

Thus, the concept of opportunity cost is built inextricably into the most fundamental of portfolio disciplines. It is clearly another dimension in which all investment activity is embedded, but should it really be classified as a risk? I cannot easily think of anything else it might be called, other than perhaps an existential fact of investment life. But if we take the intimacy of the relationship between risk and return seriously, that is what all the pervasive risks I have catalogued are. However, opportunity cost is different from all the other pervasive risks in one important respect. While operational or credit risks relate to things that *may* go wrong, but against which we can take preventative measures, opportunity risk is an ironclad promise that something *will* turn out other than as desired. Opportunity cost embodies the relationship between risk and return in its purest form: as the *Devil's Dictionary* defines it, an opportunity is unavoidably "a favorable occasion for grasping a disappointment."

Tail Risk

In the Introduction to Lo (2008), the author imagines a hedge fund, Capital Decimation Partners L.P., that pursues a strategy of monthly sales of out-of-the-money index put options. After discussing the danger that a strategy that entails such substantial tail risk may be pursued without becoming apparent to external analysis, he concludes with the comment,

> This is not to say that the risks of shorting out-of-the-money puts are inappropriate for all investors—indeed, the thriving catastrophe reinsurance industry makes a market in precisely this type of risk, often called *tail risk*. However, such insurers do so with full knowledge of the loss profile and probabilities for each type of catastrophe, and they set their capital reserves and risk budgets accordingly. (Lo 2008, 13)

While Lo is probably too sanguine about these insurers' ability to judge the probability of these risks and so to price them with precision (or even rationality), his point is clear. There can be no objection to taking extraordinary risk for the investor that is fully equipped to take the consequences if things turn out other than as anticipated. But unfortunately, the analogy between security investment and catastrophe insurance is imperfect in several respects.

For one thing, catastrophes have essentially no correlation with each other. Although the adage that "bad things come in threes" seems to apply here as elsewhere, there is certainly nothing systematic that connects a tornado in one region with an earthquake in another. Each catastrophe constitutes an isolated exposure that does not have implications for others in the way that a crisis in one part of the investment world (whether it is an asset class, a geography, or an investment technique) can bleed over so easily into others, as Bookstaber describes in his discussion of markets' energy states, which we encountered in Chapter 17. After suffering catastrophic loss, insurance premia more or less automatically rise, underwriting the recovery of the sector in ways that most other investors can only envy. And for all the inaccuracy that the procedure inevitably involves, at least the risks that these insurers take can be priced explicitly—they receive a known premium for taking on carefully specified exposure. This contrasts with the situation in which most investors more typically find themselves, where both returns and risks are uncertain. Lo's comment about reserves is very much to the point, however, and contrasts noticeably with the behavior of most institutions, which tend (with some notable partial exceptions such as the Yale Endowment) to regard all the components of their portfolios as return-seeking.

As mentioned in Chapter 15, the Yale Endowment's practice of maintaining a reserve in Treasury and other federal government-backed instruments has been amply justified by the events of 2007 to 2009. For all the criticism that Swensen's arguments in support of the practice have received,[3] his reasoning has proved correct on every point. But there are circumstances in which even supposedly riskless assets offer little

---

3. In particular, his willingness to forego the higher yields obtainable from "safe" credit exposures and his dislike of foreign currency-denominated instruments. The criticisms have been sufficiently vocal that he apparently felt it necessary to defend himself at length in the second edition of his classic (Swensen 2009, 349*ff*). Events overtook publication, and the arguments he presented there were made very forcefully for him by the markets themselves during the fourth quarter of 2008.

protection. We do not have to engage in apocalyptic speculation about U.S. government default to regard the return of high inflation as a real possibility, which one way or the other (through the erosion of returns or through an aggressive monetary policy response) would impair the value of such a reserve. This threat can be addressed by other parts of the portfolio, but that is not the point, which is that there can be no ultimately safe "safe-haven" reserve. In fairness to Swensen, he does not claim that government-backed instruments provide a reserve, but refers to them as the Endowment's deflation hedge.

This comment is reminiscent of the point made in Chapter 2 that each position in a diversified portfolio is closely analogous to a hedge against some factor exposure in at least some of the other positions it holds. To maintain some semblance of a distinction between hedging and diversification, I suggested there that a hedge is a trade for which a successful outcome could equally be a gain or a loss, while a trade that is regarded as a failure because it generated a loss is unquestionably return-seeking and thus a diversifying investment rather than a hedging one. In the context of a diversified portfolio, the intention of investment policymakers is to incur opportunity cost in the form of underperformance for a portion of the portfolio in exchange for reduced volatility for the total portfolio. If in fact their intention were to hedge their positions fully, success would entail that they would achieve zero volatility and no return at all other than the losses resulting from transaction costs.

Yet the penalty to performance that results from attempting to diversify in ways that offset tail risk, while certainly real, need not be a hair shirt: the Yale Endowment, for example, assiduously pursues whatever return maximization it can achieve from its government securities positions. The inability of gold to generate anything other than directional returns explains its failure to achieve a place as a reserve against inflation and/or financial market dislocation in most institutional portfolios. It does not detract from the occasionally very considerable speculative attractions of bullion that, as a reserve against inflation, various inflation-linked cash flow trades are likely to be more satisfactory to institutions, whereas Yale's use of government paper as a reserve against financial crises, when combined with a number of other, inflation-sensitive investments, is also more appropriate. This is because returns on gold are entirely due to favorable timing: the opportunity costs of holding it in a reserve capacity are simply too high, a conclusion that has come to be shared by many central banks over the last several decades.

This applies even more strongly to dedicated short sellers. Because most financial time series are kurtotic, maintaining a short position against them would seem an ideal way to hedge against their tail risk. However, the negative skewness of most such series implies that the bulk of their return periods exhibit performance above the median level of the distribution. Assuming the median return is positive—a safe assumption, as otherwise few would be attracted to taking a long position in it in the first place—then the short position is a loss-maker (even before consideration of financing costs) over most of the life of an institution's exposure to it. If the position were sufficiently large to provide meaningful protection against tail events, the results for the portfolio's returns over significant time horizons would be disastrous. Self-financing structures using combinations of short call options to fund purchase of protective put options can be more attractive for this purpose, particularly when market volatility is high, but entail substantial opportunity costs resulting from the sale of upside potential embodied in the short call portion of the trade.

Since 1987, it has become abundantly clear that tail risk is not just a statistical residuum, something the equations throw out that will never actually occur. While investors are not much better equipped to manage those risks today than they were thirty years ago, the concept of holding a reserve is a step in that direction. Unless it is large enough to constrain returns unacceptably, a reserve clearly will not protect a portfolio from severe loss, as the Yale Endowment's 25 percent decline in the second half of 2008 indicates. However, catastrophe insurers' reserves are not intended to defend them against losses either. For such an insurer these reserves serve the twin purposes of maintaining liquidity for operating purposes and a core of solvency that will allow them to return to the fray and underwrite again. For other institutions, such reserves can provide some room for maneuver to readjust the portfolio in the wake of a crisis. This is not an unimportant contribution: the ability to invest decisively when the portfolio is in shreds is what distinguishes institutions that recover from crises with relative aplomb from those that may not recover at all.

CHAPTER 22

Filling Out the Allocation

The expression "There's many a slip twixt cup and lip" dates to a time when the cups in use made "slips" both frequent and voluminous. In classical Greece, wine was drunk from *kylikes*, shallow footed goblets that could be as broad as dinner plates. Drinking from these cannot have been easy at the best of times, and although the ancients diluted their wine, sometime after the third or fourth round, unintentional wine baths must have been fairly common, particularly because they drank lying half-prone on couches. Implementation of allocation decisions is never easy, but the inclusion of alternative investments in an institution's investable universe both magnifies and multiplies the problems that can arise. Implementing the allocation can be at least as challenging as devising it in the first place.

Later, in Chapter 24, I will discuss some of the issues surrounding the scope of investment policymakers' responsibilities; this and the following chapter will lay the groundwork for it by arguing that in almost all cases they go beyond just the decision to include this or that investment category within the institution's investable universe. This decision only leads to a new set of questions, but the answers to some of them must inform the initial decision regarding inclusion—"complex simultaneity" yet again. So it is appropriate that they fall within the functional competence of policymakers, or at least that policymakers insist that their investment staff or advisors consider them carefully and advise them appropriately, to facilitate them in reaching their higher-level decision. Many of these subsidiary choices involve judgments of risk, both regarding the new investment category and for the institution's portfolio as a whole, so they are certainly relevant to policy, and arguably they are in fact policy decisions. However, occasionally they may involve technical considerations for which an institution's fiduciaries are unprepared, and it is here that delicate issues surrounding the interaction between policymakers and their staff or advisors may arise.

There is a wide variety of such issues, but among the most important and least escapable of these subsidiary (but certainly not secondary) questions are

- ❏ what should be the neutral allocation;
- ❏ how should it be funded from the existing allocation; and
- ❏ what parameters should be placed around tactical decisions to depart from neutral exposure?

In most cases, policymakers will probably want the last-mentioned decision to be made consistently with similar parameters that have already been set for other investment categories. But private assets are likely to require special accommodation in this regard, and in some cases regulatory considerations may supervene, for instance where an institution's taxable status is affected by ownership of more than a specified portion of its portfolio in a particular type of investment. Further, the expected volatility of the new addition may make it appropriate to require tighter or looser constraints than those placed on other portions of the portfolio. This sort of decision may be motivated by either risk or operational considerations. This is a decision that must be made holistically: note from Table 15.2 that the comparative lack of volatility in investment techniques that seldom mark-to-market has very considerable implications for the investment allocation when other, more liquid investments have displayed high volatility.

The first two decisions, however, should unquestionably be made with reference to the specific characteristics of the investment category being added to the institution's investable universe. The return characteristics of the new addition will have implications for the total portfolio (otherwise, why make the allocation at all?) that demand investment policymakers' attention. In the case of most private assets, given the long lead time between commitment and final drawdown, the interim disposition of the funds that will be deployed to them should also be considered—if only to underline to the committee that such interim measures will be necessary. Here a very specific aspect of the implementation of policy must at least be brought to investment policymakers' attention.

The Neutral Weighting

The considerations that investment policymakers must bring to bear on their decisions regarding the level of neutral exposure primarily concern the way that the new addition relates to the current composition of the portfolio and what the new addition is intended to accomplish for the portfolio. Naturally, these must be judged in the context of the institution's overall goals and existing exposures. Some of these concerns are quite clear—if the institution is in need of current income and the planned addition to its investment universe does not offer it, then the allocation obviously should not be so large as to impair the income-producing portion of its investment allocation. If the institution is risk-averse and the new addition is a risky investment category, then its primary function can only be to enhance diversification, and the allocation to it should be comparatively small unless its diversification benefits are unusually great.

But some of the necessary considerations are not nearly so transparent. If the institution with current income requirements is considering a cash flow investment that distributes unevenly, it must consider whether substantial fluctuations to the income it receives interfere with its goals and allocate more or less to the investment accordingly. If the risk-averse institution is contemplating a conservative investment that involves a long lockup period, it should consider whether its attitude toward risk is likely to change over the holding period. This situation may seem somewhat unlikely, but there are numerous actuarially driven institutions that were fully funded a few years ago, and that consequently adopted quite conservative investment policies, that found themselves in considerably different circumstances after the carnage of 2007 to 2009. If they were excessively exposed to conservative investments from which they could not reallocate, their ability to recover from the crisis was tightly constrained. Investment policymakers should be alive to the unfortunate fact that risk aversion has its own, not inconsiderable risks.

However, some rules of thumb apply to the problem of setting the neutral level of allocation. Perhaps the most important is simply that investment policymakers should have the courage of their convictions. If they are not certain enough of the investment category to make a meaningful allocation to it, then they should not include it in their institution's investable universe at all. "Meaningful" is largely in the eye of the beholder, and will be partially dependent on how deeply into the decision hierarchy the committee's deliberations reach. That is, minimum allocation sizes should vary depending on whether the decision is simply to include some hedge funds in the mix or reaches a level of specificity that involves choosing between long-biased or opportunistically long/short funds, and so on. The more specific the decision, the smaller the minimum investment size can appropriately be. By and large, however, I would suggest that decisions that affect less than 5 percent of the total portfolio are not properly the concern of policymakers.

This rough guideline is supported by operational considerations. Given the costs and effort involved in coming to the determination to add an investment category to the investable universe, there is little point in doing so if the decision will not appreciably affect returns at the aggregate portfolio level, which should be the primary focus of investment policymakers' concern. Referring to another rule of thumb—the three-year limit to economic visibility—a position sized at 5 percent of the portfolio would have to achieve a fairly remarkable 26 percent per annum return during that period just to contribute 5 percent to the total portfolio's return. Put in terms of risk, if the existing portfolio has an annual standard deviation of 6.5 percent, then reducing total portfolio standard deviation by 0.25 percent would require that a proposed 5 percent position in an investment that has zero correlation to all the other components of the portfolio must exhibit an annual standard deviation of 1.5 percent. This is probably only achievable, if at all, with cash. Investment policymakers may want to delve into portfolio minutiae where the proposed investment is extremely risky or where it is a question of creating an essential reserve, but in general, 5 percent of assets under management seems a reasonable threshold for their decision-making responsibility.

Turned on its head, this conclusion implies that the maximum number of decisions that an investment policy committee should make regarding the institution's investment universe is twenty. Unless the decisions about investment categories are extraordinarily specific, even this is a degree of hyper-diversity that few institutions would probably entertain. Put in terms of a strictly conventional portfolio, twenty decisions implies the ability to allocate among each of the nine equity Morningstar Style Box categories and three international equity categories, still leaving an ample eight categories for cash, real estate, and fixed-income decisions. Investment policymakers leave the realm of policy and have become closely involved in implementation and tactics if they go much further down the decision hierarchy than this, and arguably they would already have done so at this level of specificity. For the institution that allocates among alternative investments as well, defining part of their universe in terms of broader categories such as stocks, bonds, cash, and real estate implies sixteen categories of alternative investments that might be considered, which also suggests an excessive degree of discrimination among them.

It is difficult to generalize at the other extreme. As I have mentioned, I am aware of one ERISA pension plan that allocated 100 percent of its assets to cash (exclusively on deposit at AAA-rated banks: the fact that it still had a reasonable number of choices suggests how long ago that was), and there have been many institutions that have shifted to a 100 percent allocation to fixed income at one time or another. There are some, although not many, institutions that carry 100 percent of their portfolios in hedge funds, and probably more than a few with similar exposures to real estate. However, the overwhelming majority of institutions practice a much more balanced approach to allocating their investments. In a universe defined (for the purposes of illustration) as stocks, bonds, cash, real estate, hedge funds, and real assets, a maximum permissible exposure of 50 percent to any one category is probably ample.

However, these considerations should not be taken to suggest that investment policy should confine itself to only the most abstract decisions and airy generalities. Concerns specific to the institution may dictate allocation decisions and even economic biases to investment policy that are of crucial importance to its investment decision-making. Two that I have already mentioned are unusual liquidity requirements and the special attention that endowments in support of activities in highly inflationary sectors such as education or health care must pay to the preservation of purchasing power. Apart from non-investment considerations such as support for regional development or principles-based avoidance of certain types of exposures, institutions may encounter other influences on their investment behavior. If they are sufficiently important to the institution that failure to address them would imply a failure of fiduciary responsibility, by definition they become matters for the investment policy committee. The next chapter discusses some of these that relate to plan termination, which can be especially difficult to negotiate for institutions that allocate to alternative investments. Large and unexpected demands on the portfolio or, for that matter, comparably large inflows, may require similar high-level decisions.

Funding a New Allocation

Having decided to add an investment category to their investable universe, investment policymakers must determine which existing exposure(s) to reduce in order to fund its acquisition. Even if the institution expects to be able to use cash inflows to fund the entire allocation, this is effectively a decision to reduce every other exposure *pro rata* in order to fund the new one. More commonly, institutions must sell part or all of one or more positions to fund an allocation to a new investment category. Consequently, the addition of a new category to the investment universe usually has broader portfolio implications than just the incremental contribution of the new exposure to the portfolio's volatility and return characteristics.

In establishing the new allocation, investment policymakers must consequently decide what it is that they hope to accomplish with it. Depending on how it is funded, the new position may add to portfolio risk, reduce it, or have very limited effect (although it will always have some), and similarly regarding the expected returns, income generation and other characteristics of the portfolio. Though to state it may belabor the obvious, reduction of a low-risk exposure to fund a high-risk one will usually have a much greater effect on aggregate portfolio risk than funding the new exposure from an equally risky one (although this needs to be confirmed through correlation analysis in any particular instance). Addition of new investment categories may also affect portfolio skewness and kurtosis—if the new allocation is to an alternative investment category, it typically will, even if it is entirely funded from existing alternative exposures. Investment policy must concern itself with how as well as what additions are made to the portfolio, because the "how" may in some cases influence its fundamental concerns with risk and return even more than the "what" does.

As a result, additions to the investment universe are easiest when investment policymakers wish to change the total portfolio's characteristics. If they do not, the tradeoffs among return characteristics quickly become quite complicated. And given the uncertainty regarding their future correlations to each other, the effort is fated to achieve only approximate success at best. For example, the institution that would like both to add exposure to real estate and maintain its current portfolio's return characteristics faces some difficult decisions concerning the source(s) of funding, and these may depend on characteristics that are quite specific to the properties in question. Real estate exhibits both equity- and bond-like characteristics, and the degree to which it resembles one or the other depends on property type, its occupancy rate, tenant quality, the financing structure employed, and local market conditions, among numerous other factors. Retaining the portfolio's return characteristics may involve the investment policy committee in detailed, technical decisions with which it is far from comfortable. On the other hand, leaving implementation decisions entirely in the hands of staff or agents can easily result in unwanted changes to the portfolio's risk characteristics that may not even be apparent to the policymakers.

There are some issues connected with portfolio implementation in which policymakers may wish to involve themselves that do not give rise to these sorts of quandaries, however, such as restrictions that trustees may place on the types or size of providers employed, limitations on permissible leverage, and so on. All too often, however, such risk policy decisions are imposed reflexively by trustees who have not thought through their implications. If such restrictions are not fully informed by knowledge of their effects on portfolio implementation, they may have the effect of increasing risk or constraining implementation in undesirable ways. For example, as seen in Chapter 14, the average size of venture capital funds is quite small: if an institution places an unrealistic minimum requirement on its service providers' assets under management, it may unintentionally restrict itself to venture firms that in many cases will not in fact be accessible to it. Once imposed, the restrictions tend to cut short the consideration of investment possibilities that might highlight the restrictions' shortcomings, so their effect may never become apparent to policymakers.

As discussed in Chapters 15, employment of alternative investments has considerable effects on portfolio liquidity. While I argued there, in broad agreement with critics of the "liquidity fetish," that the importance of portfolio liquidity is often overestimated by investors, the experience of many institutions with large allocations to alternative investments in 2008 was certainly a reminder that portfolio liquidity is nevertheless of considerable value. With a few exceptions, such as separate accounts with CTAs, allocations to alternative investments reduce portfolio liquidity and, commensurately, the flexibility available to the institution should it wish or need to make changes to its investment allocation. As I have stressed, options have a value, and this ability to change is a real option that can be extremely valuable in certain circumstances, which need not be restricted to the aftermath of a market crisis. Among the most psychologically distressing forms of opportunity cost are those that result from "landed poverty"—the inability to exploit an attractive opportunity because liquidity is not available.

Funding of investments with long lead-times between commitment and final capital call poses special problems for investment policymakers. There may be a gap of as much as six years between subscription and the end of the commitment period for some of these vehicles.

Meanwhile, what is an institution to do with the capital committed but not yet called? Although REITs may provide a plausible substitute for private market real estate exposure, there is no obvious public market analogue for many other such long-tail investments. And as plausible as REITs may be as a surrogate for the intended eventual exposure to real estate, their volatility raises timing issues, because there can be no assurance that capital calls will coincide with opportune moments to liquidate REIT positions in order to fund them. The same is true of any other return-seeking investment technique that is liquid and therefore likely to be volatile that might be used as a parking place for such funding. On the other hand, holding the funds in reserve in low-risk, low-volatility investments runs counter to the risk-seeking intent behind most private market allocation decisions. If the intention of adding an investment category to the investable universe is to increase risk in order to increase returns, then it is a highly perverse result if its consequence is to reduce risk and returns over a significant number of years.

In the case of private market directional trades, once sufficient vintage diversification has been obtained to make the allocation self-funding, this issue is largely moot, but in most cases that will take seven years or more from the initial commitment to such investments. The issue is recurrent and inescapable for private market cash flow trades unless they are perpetual in nature. Reinvestment of the cash flows received is unlikely to allow an institution to maintain a stable level of exposure: as each partnership liquidates the institution has to rebuild its exposure. The larger distributions that directional vehicles make as successful positions are liquidated over the life of the fund eventually allow an institution to achieve a more stable exposure to their trades.

Exposure Parameters and Rebalancing

All the issues surrounding rebalancing are vexed, and based on the evidence, they are unlikely to achieve comfortable resolution. Recommended frequencies range from continuously to never. Many commentators suggest that rebalancing be carried out at regular intervals from monthly to once every three years, and others recommend rebalancing only when the portfolio departs from its target allocation by specified threshold amounts, although there is similar lack of agreement about what the size of those thresholds should be. Some of this variety is because many of the participants in the discussion are talking at cross-purposes. Rebalancing is quite a different thing for investors who perform their own security selection compared to those that invest solely through third-party managers. And given lockups, specified redemption periods, and so on, it can to some extent be a largely academic discussion for investors that employ alternative investments.

Except where there is a commercial incentive to persist in it (and a wide variety of firms, from institutional consultants to retail investment advisors, share this incentive), the obsession with investment allocation as allegedly the only significant contributor to excess return has, for the most part, dissipated after considerable and occasionally heated debate (for a summary see Goldman Sachs [2004, 1*f*], and for a full, if rather intemperate discussion, consult Nuttall [2000]). Enthusiasm for the idea was sparked by widespread misunderstanding of the conclusions reached by Brinson et al. (1986), whose paper did not in fact address excess returns at all. The currently more fashionable fixation with the pursuit of α, widely and mistakenly identified with investment skill, has largely replaced it. Yet the fundamental logic behind the idea of rebalancing is clear enough. Assuming that a significant amount of effort has been expended on creating the portfolio's allocation target, at the very least it would be pleasing to think that occasionally the portfolio will actually resemble it. In principle, the allocation target, too, is a potential source of α, so investment policymakers' interest in seeing that it is adhered to is not solely a matter of justifying their contribution to the institution's management.

Rebalancing is arguably a form of risk control, but it has contrarian elements to it that resemble a return-seeking discipline, and these elements, particularly in combination, have natural attractions to many investment policymakers. It can also have an objective and mechanistic aspect that some find compelling—in fact, it has a widely accessible appeal similar to that of dollar-cost averaging, for many of the same reasons, not the least of which is that it is simple to understand and explain. None of which is meant to belittle the idea of rebalancing, which I, like most others, accept as an essential element of the investment toolkit. However, like any tool, rebalancing can be wielded more or less skillfully, and in the context of portfolios that employ alternative investments, a fair degree of skill is crucial to its successful employment.

The costs and difficulty of rebalancing differ markedly, depending on the composition of the portfolio. In addition to the challenges that liquidity constraints may place on the project of rebalancing, the uncertainty as to exposure levels if the portfolio includes investments that infrequently mark to market, and numerous other factors mean that rebalancing may pose quite different challenges to each institution. At one extreme, changing exposure to large capitalization developed market equities or to commodity futures, either upward or downward, has fairly trivial costs and can in most cases be accomplished in a week or less, while reducing direct real estate exposure is costly and can be expected to consume at least six months. Increasing direct exposure to real estate is even more of a problem, as it will typically involve the acquisition of new properties rather than just an increased commitment to existing positions. In the case of illiquid investments, rebalancing is performed, as it were, in the dark. Because price discovery takes place through transactions, exactly what will occur in the process of rebalancing only becomes apparent in the course of performing it. When rebalancing of illiquid positions is forced, it is unlikely that the institution will be able to obtain "fair value" (or in many cases, anything even approaching it) for the investments it liquidates.

For these reasons, investment policy is well advised to design its rebalancing program around portfolio exposure thresholds rather than to schedule it rigidly according to a calendar, and to adjust the size of the permissible departure from the target allocation to the difficulty and cost of rebalancing for the different categories of exposure. However, this creates new problems in turn, as liquid instruments will rebalance much more frequently than less liquid ones, creating potentially quite thorny timing issues. For example, as the prices of equities and credit instruments plummeted in the fourth quarter of 2008, estimated values for commercial real estate were comparatively stable. However, market participants recognized that this was an artifact of the estimation process for real estate rather than a matter of its relative economic performance, and while the performance of commercial real estate was an imponderable (in the course of exploring secondary sale of a real estate partnership, I encountered a new term: "squishy" valuation), it certainly was not positive. What was the appropriate rebalancing response? Price movements in equities and corporate credits certainly recommended additional purchases, and lack of movement in real estate prices suggested that those positions might be an appropriate source of funds. But given transaction times in real estate, by the time a sale could be accomplished, pricing might well have caught up with that of more liquid instruments, and the institution could easily find itself selling into a market that was falling sharply, in order to purchase instruments that, at that point, could well have recovered some ground. Even if secondary markets for these investments were as liquid as Fraser-Sampson imagines them to be (2007, 6f), in these conditions investors could only escape their illiquid positions at very painful discounts, and transaction times would still be considerable.

The simplicity and mechanistic appeal of rebalancing rapidly disappears when the instruments involved are illiquid—especially if they are not marked to market. But periodic liquidity for instruments that do mark to market can also raise problems. Many hedge funds only permit annual withdrawals, and frequently these are for December 31 value dates. This arbitrary structure is only occasionally a problem for investors, but if the markets collapse in the fourth quarter, it creates considerable consternation among would-be rebalancers. If they do not redeem when markets are depressed, they will not have an opportunity to do so for another year. Further, 10 percent of the value redeemed will typically be held back until the fund's audit is complete, and this may not be until June (the slowness of hedge fund audits is one of the great mysteries—and irritations). So even if a fund allows more frequent redemptions—say, quarterly—if the institution intends to reallocate quickly to some perceived short-term opportunity, either 111 percent of the desired amount must be redeemed from the fund or only 90 percent of the opportunity can be exploited.

Then there are the issues that surround an institution's relationships with General Partners. Many of these have convinced themselves that it is a privilege for investors to do business with them, a privilege that can only be maintained through undying loyalty. Withdrawal of funds or failure to subscribe to their latest offering may result in permanent black-balling, so that if the institution wishes to reinvest or to subscribe to a later fund, it may receive a chilly reception or not be received at all. Investment in Limited Partnerships is always subject to the General Partner's approval, which can be withheld for any reason and need not even be explained. Although the experience of many alternative investment vehicles in 2008 will probably reduce funds' anxiety to demonstrate their exclusiveness for some period, a few good years and their self-regard will doubtless recover.

Additional Policy Considerations

Where an institution applies quantitative risk analytics to its exposures, inclusion of a new category of alternative investment in its portfolio creates a not inconsiderable research and development burden for it. First, assuming that the necessary data is actually available (which it is not for illiquid investments) and that the manager is willing to provide it (which many are not), the type and frequency of data must be determined. Daily position data are in many cases likely to place an overwhelming burden on computing resources, offering the possibility of precision in principle at a substantial cost to comprehensibility in practice. Yet even this degree of data overload is unlikely to give an accurate indication of the activities and the attendant risks of high-frequency techniques. Daily return data are more readily analyzable but much less revealing, unless the underlying manager's activities are tightly circumscribed to a few known trades. A risk manager of my acquaintance demands what he describes as "rational transparency," which in his view consists of weekly return data backed up by full position transparency as the occasion demands. For most purposes, this is probably more than adequate, provided that the trades are known and tightly circumscribed. In most situations, it is more than can be expected.

Research and development become issues because most alternative investment vehicles include option-like exposures that are not transparent to the regression analysis that underlies standard risk models, and must be separately accommodated for analytic purposes. Further, many vehicles carry factor exposures for which commercially available analytic models do not solve. Without doing the research required to identify these factors and to devise a metric for them, and employing a model that allows its users to introduce customized metrics into it, off-the-shelf risk products simply consign these exposures to their model's unanalyzed error term. Although some institutions draw comfort from their outlays on risk analytics, if the risk monitoring process is not a dynamic development effort staffed by knowledgeable (and expensive) professionals capable of original research, it represents little more than wasted expenditure to acquire misleading comfort. To my mind, less quant and more thought are likely to be far more valuable to an institution that is unwilling to invest heavily in this effort than off-the-shelf software (which is nevertheless by no means cheap) run by a handful of uncritical MBAs of recent vintage. Quantitative techniques are only a tool for and supplement to informed analysis, and useful analysis requires expertise.

One way that an institution can ensure that it has transparency to any degree of detail that its risk department might require is to invest through separate accounts rather than commingled vehicles, which affords it transaction-by-transaction data if it so requires. Separate accounts offer the additional advantage compared to commingled vehicles that the institution's investment is unaffected by the new commitments or redemptions of other investors, which impose costs that are borne by all investors in such vehicles, not just the Limited Partner that initiates the change. Further, there are likely to be few constraints on withdrawing from the account at will, and control of the audit is in the institution's hands. As mentioned previously, separate account arrangements are fairly common with CTAs, and the idea seems to be gaining traction with institutions for their hedge fund investments, too.

Putting the idea into practice requires finding a manager who is willing to take on separate accounts, and many hedge fund managers are not at all enamored of the idea. Futures accounts have leverage and the ability to sell short built into the instruments they employ, but the institution must acquire a prime brokerage account in its own name if it wishes to establish separate hedge fund accounts that trade in equities or fixed income. This is becoming more difficult than it might have been just a few years ago (see Pulliam and Strasburg 2009). However, probably the greatest objection to separate accounts is that they do not protect the institution from liability if, for instance, the manager engages in improper trading practices on the institution's behalf. Nor do they protect the institution's assets from margin calls if the manager's activities on its behalf turn out disastrously. An institution can, in principle, insulate itself from these liabilities by placing its ownership of the account in a limited liability structure, but then it is questionable whether it would be able to obtain prime brokerage services. It remains to be seen how enthusiastic institutions will actually become for separate hedge fund accounts in the light of these disadvantages, the resistance of hedge fund managers, and the reduced availability of prime brokerage services generally.

Institutions are often invited to co-invest directly in the underlying investments of the private market investment vehicles to which they have subscribed, and there can be significant attractions to doing so. Apart from properly investment attractions, not the least of these is the chance to enhance their status as "good" Limited Partners in the eyes of General Partners to which they would like to increase their exposure. In the process, however, they acquire liabilities parallel to those that attend upon separate hedge fund accounts, including liability for environmental, labor, and similar violations. However, in many cases it is comparatively easy for them to shield themselves from these through use of limited liability structures, although this will not protect them from reputational risks. The major impediment to institutions taking on co-investments is staff time. If they are to obtain full benefit from their direct ownership position, they will want to participate in the oversight of their investment, and this can be very demanding. Investment policymakers must be sensitive to the operational and administrative implications of their decisions: staff resources are a finite and valuable commodity. The decision to embark upon direct investments has significant implications for an institution's investment decision-making capacity.

CHAPTER **23**

Time and Tide

In attempting to find the source of the expression "time and tide wait for no man," to which I alluded in an earlier chapter, I was intrigued to discover that it is truly ancient—the first known reference to it, in an English still in transition from its Germanic roots, dates to 1225, but there is reason to believe that it is considerably older. And "tide" referred, not to the movement of the waves, but to time (the modern Dutch for "time" is *tijd*, which is pronounced like "tide"). However, its use here is not simply poetic alliteration, because "time" and "tide" carried slightly different connotations. The phrase originally meant something like "neither the passage of time nor the opportune moment wait for anyone." I referred to the distinction between "time" and "timing" in my first chapter in ignorance of its pedigree.

In some Hindu traditions, the primary aspects of godhood are Brahma the Creator, Vishnu the Preserver, and Shiva the Destroyer. In this schema, the relationship between the idea of divinity and the temporal development of creation is fairly obvious, but there is another feature of these gods' roles that is suggestive for our discussion. Shiva is often depicted performing the Dance of Destruction on the back of Maya, the demon of illusion and uncertainty. The implication is that time and uncertainty are intimately linked, and that it is only when time has come to an end that uncertainty is vanquished. As investors, we are always under the veil of Maya, and even though we may engage in perpetual investments, we can only obtain true understanding of our performance when the investment has been liquidated. My discussion of opportunity cost in Chapter 21 would appear to have metaphysical sanction. While it is true that in many Hindu mystical traditions, gods, time, and all creation are themselves considered nothing more than the illusions of Maya, these traditions do not much concern themselves with investment matters.

Time and timing have lurked in the background of much of this volume, as they do in virtually all discussions about investments, where they are usually hidden under the guise of "t" or "r_t," respectively, in the more obscure parts of some equation or other. "Lurking," in fact, is what time generally does, because it is so extraordinarily difficult to talk about explicitly. Dictionaries, for example, attempt to define it in terms of "period," "duration," "occasion," and so forth—that is, in terms of itself. And while philosophers since Thales have struggled mightily to come to grips with time, for the most part it has eluded their grasp, and their efforts have been to very limited effect. But time and timing are central considerations in every investment endeavor—all those equations would be rendered meaningless if their references to time periods or specific moments were removed—so time and timing demand our attention, as much as it would be convenient to avoid them. Fortunately, we need not delve further into the nature of godhood in order to give time and timing their due, as investments are concerned with their effects rather than their essences.

Institutional Time Horizon

Most commentary about institutional investment assumes a long time horizon—if not the perpetual horizon of most endowments or foundations, at any rate one spanning generations. There are several reasons for this, not the least of which was the rise of a group of articulate and highly sophisticated endowment managers in the 1980s and 1990s. Before their arrival on the scene, it is unlikely that anyone would have turned to that source for investment insight. But the traditional defined benefit pension plan, which had been the main focus of most earlier discussions of institutional investment, also has a long tail, and if it is assumed that the plan sponsor will prosper and grow, it extends indefinitely into the future as the number of contributors to the plan increases at least as rapidly as the number of plan beneficiaries. Life insurance has a comparatively short time horizon, but nevertheless one that may span decades.

It continues to be the case that most institutional investors have such long-term horizons, but it is by no means as near to being universally true as it once was. The termination of defined contribution pension plans by most corporations has created numerous plans with finite lives that, while of indeterminate duration, become shorter with each passing day. The number of project-oriented foundations not intended to be perpetual has increased, in part because of donors' desire to prevent the mission-creep and agency issues that affect many perpetual endowments (I am told, for instance, that the Ford family has long wished not to be associated with the activities of the eponymous foundation). And numerous fiduciary institutions, such as funds of private equity funds and private real estate partnerships, are themselves designed to liquidate upon completion of their investment programs, typically after ten years or so. If it is borne in mind that the relevant "information" includes information regarding the institution's liabilities, and with an eye toward the roughly three-year limit to economic visibility, the following comment from Grinold and Kahn (2000) might be taken as a general rule: "The choice of time period may affect information analysis. As a general comment, the investment time period should match the information time period" (319n.). However, Campbell and Viceira (2005) offer some possible reassurances regarding longer-term forecasts at least from the standpoint of strategic policymaking.

Institutions' investment responses to limited time horizons vary. Fiduciary institutions—which are, in most cases, simply conduits for the investment activities of longer-horizon investors—tend to pursue long-term return maximization goals congruent with the needs of their Limited Partners. In principle, there is no reason for them to have finite lives, and in the case of those that invest in liquid instruments, most of them do not. In principle, funds that invest in illiquid instruments could be similarly structured, although the task of marketing a perpetual vehicle of this sort would doubtless be a considerable challenge. In general, managers of illiquid investments offer limited duration funds in series, allowing longer-lived institutions to reinvest and fashion vintage-diversified portfolios. Not infrequently, investments will be handed forward from earlier-vintage vehicles to later-vintage ones, so that Limited Partners' exposure to the underlying investment may persist if they subscribe to later funds, although the vehicle through which that exposure is effected does not. Often, institutions will co-invest in the same assets alongside the partnerships in which they have interests, allowing them to retain exposure to some of its investments after the partnership has been dissolved.

Foundations that are intended to liquidate themselves usually pursue an investment program designed to preserve purchasing power over their intended life spans. Cash flow considerations are in many cases lesser priorities, as they tend to have few operating costs and little concern about reducing the endowment to meet their grant-giving goals. The original donor funds the foundation appropriately to accomplish its charge, factoring some investment returns into its calculations, but the greatest risk to the donor's intent is that inflation could leave the endowment with insufficient funds to fulfill it. The imminence of the foundation's demise will determine most other investment choices made for it, but the necessity of a five- to seven-year investment program to achieve vintage diversification will in most cases militate against use of private equity. To the extent that the concept of vintage diversification is applied to commingled commercial real estate vehicles—and I suspect its application will increase in the wake of recent market developments—the same is true of those products. If the life of the foundation permits, other private assets such as mezzanine debt, timber or farmland, oil and gas production, and so on, may be appropriate investments. Use of hedge funds would seem uncontroversial, but given the proclivity of many of them to make illiquid investments, their use would require some caution: about the last thing the donor would want would be for assets to be frozen in a side pocket at the end of the foundation's mission.

Closed pension plans must incorporate actuarial considerations into their investment planning, which are largely determined by the demographics of the plan beneficiaries at the time that the plan is closed and the contractual obligations that the plan sponsor has incurred under the plan, for instance regarding cost-of-living adjustments. The inevitable conflicts of interest between the plan and the plan sponsor, for instance regarding return assumptions or the choice of a discount rate, are rarely alleviated by plan termination. Given that the reason for closing a plan is most often the sponsor's desire for cost-savings, if anything these conflicts are likely to be even more fraught. On the other hand, closing a plan crystallizes its demographics and relieves actuaries of the need to incorporate estimates about new entrants into their calculations. Having acquired a termination point—even though its date is uncertain—investment considerations for closed plans begin to resemble the "life cycle" advice given to private investors. Plans will tend to become more risk-averse and income-seeking over time, but provided a sufficiently young demographic, use of most forms of alternative assets may still be appropriate until the portfolio approaches termination.

For the perpetual (or at any rate long-lived) institution, the weight of years presses heavily. The institution's future needs, and the investment environment and inflationary conditions under which they will have to be met, can only be guessed at. The institution's ability to forecast its own needs may penetrate more or less deeply into the future, but economic visibility is notoriously constrained. Those institutions that have hope of funding from external sources discover that the market conditions that cause them to fail to achieve their required returns may also affect those sources' ability or willingness to provide such funding. Where investment policy rather than (or at least, in addition to) the market environment is the source of poor performance, potential contributors to charitable endowments may become particularly unenthusiastic about making up the difference. This was the experience of the Yale Endowment in the 1970s, when donors virtually went on strike, and the Endowment experienced a "perfect storm" of poor returns, low contributions, and sharply rising demand on its resources from the University as a result of high inflation. Institutions that have little prospect of bolstering their capital base from external sources, such as most foundations, find periods of poor performance, from whatever cause, especially challenging—these are the circumstances under which their prospects for existence in perpetuity can all too easily come into question.

Investment Time Horizon

Long-tail, even perpetual investments seem ideally suited to similarly long-lived institutions, but there is no reason in principle that they should be more attractive to them than to other investors with reasonably long time horizons. Nor is there any fundamental reason that long-tail investments should be more attractive to these institutions than short-tail investments. The long run is nothing other than the accumulation of shorter periods, and if short-term investment targets can be met with reasonable consistency, the long run will take care of itself. Along with encouraging interest in alternative investments, the recognition that the capital market assumptions that underlie strategic allocation are not written in stone, so that investment policymakers can add value through periodic adjustment, is one of the key contributions of the so-called Endowment Model to contemporary investment thinking (see Viceira (2006) and Chapter 24). Perpetual institutions should be largely indifferent to time horizon.

A horizon of fifteen years or so accommodates virtually every known form of alternative investment other than direct investments for cash flow. Fifteen is a somewhat arbitrary number, but it allows for investments with a planned ten-year life, permits the General Partners to impose or request two-year extensions (rights that many funds reserve for themselves), and allows a year for liquidation. Among illiquid term investments, this is the longest required commitment that, to my knowledge, an investor is likely to encounter. As discussed in Chapter 9, there are numerous investors whose holding periods make fifteen years look almost like day-trading, but in most cases these are investors that take an active role in the management of the long-term investments they hold. Planning to invest in perpetuity without access to real options other than the choice to liquidate (assuming the investment even offers that choice) is probably not ideal investment policy for even the most long-term of investors, which accounts for the marketing challenges that would face any manager that wished to offer such a fund. Very long-tail investments, such as public infrastructure, that might suit such a vehicle, are generally packaged either in exchange-listed form or passed on to the managers' future fund offerings to allow for the possibility of liquidation.

Consequently, where the amounts of the assets under their management permit and perpetual investors are otherwise equipped to do so, they tend to invest directly rather than through commingled vehicles, precisely in order to be able to exploit such options. But whereas a perpetual institutional time horizon certainly makes the idea of entering into perpetual or very long-tail investments easier for an institution to contemplate, there is no reason in principle for it to do so. Such institutions have the luxury to engage in very long-term investment activities, but having the capability is not an argument in favor of exercising it. Equivocation between the length of the institution's mission and its investment horizon is very common and can result in considerable confusion. This is never helpful to investment policy, and may be quite deleterious to it.

Consider the caricature of two investments with equivalent twenty-period returns illustrated in **Figure 23.1**, and note that the numerical values on both axes have deliberately been left vague. If the periods are seconds, most institutions, whether perpetual or even quite short-lived, would be essentially indifferent between the two investments. Although in terms of its Sharpe ratio and similar measures Investment A is clearly preferable to Investment B, it is unlikely that risk-adjustment over less than half a minute has much meaning. The institutions' reactions are likely to be similar if the periods are minutes and quite possibly hours. But indifference is likely to fade if the periods are weeks, will unquestionably decrease significantly if they are months, and will almost certainly become active repugnance if they are years, let alone decades.

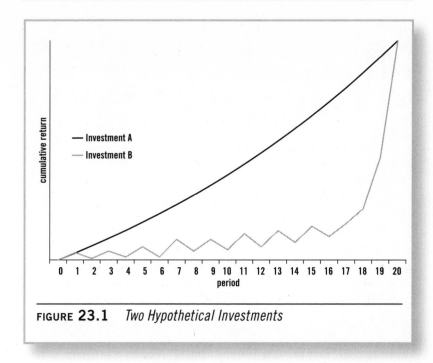

FIGURE 23.1 *Two Hypothetical Investments*

A thought experiment of this sort may in some cases help investment policymakers to determine what their time horizon should be. One contributing factor is likely to be the institution's reporting frequency. Any non-investment obligations related to the institution's budget or its distribution requirements under tax legislation will, in most cases, relate to an annual reporting schedule. That institutions' indifference is likely to decrease markedly somewhere between five months (twenty weeks) and a 1⅔ years (twenty months), as my comments above suggested, is not coincidentally related to such an annual cycle.

However, if the periods shown in Figure 23.1 are half-years, the return profile of Investment B is not too dissimilar to what might be expected from a successful private equity investment (note that this is a cumulative return profile, not a cash flow profile, so that J-curve effects are not apparent). Assuming a sound average exit value of 3× purchase price from the underlying holdings of Investment B, the zero-volatility Investment A would have to return an unlikely 14.87 percent per annum over ten years to keep pace with it. But trustees' repugnance for Investment B's return profile is likely to remain, and this is a strong reason, quite apart from risk mitigation, to seek vintage diversification for these investments. Trustees are almost certain to be far more accepting

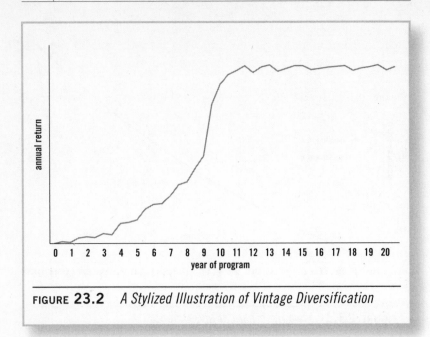

FIGURE 23.2 *A Stylized Illustration of Vintage Diversification*

of Investment B if they see it transformed, through a program of new investment every six months in a fund with an identical return profile, into the investment program illustrated in **Figure 23.2.**

The evidence of institutional exposure levels to private equity suggests that charts exhibiting a similar degree of stylization have proven to be quite persuasive to many investment committees. Of course, its assumption of investment in a fund with an identical return profile every six months is completely unrealistic, and in the interest of lending some verisimilitude to the illustration, I have added more volatility to the return stream shown there than idealized calculation of such a program would in fact generate. But it hardly needs to be emphasized that stylization conflicts with realism, and given the real-world constraints on the availability of funds with identical return profiles, few investors are likely to obtain returns even as smooth as these in the mature phase of their private equity programs.

Timing and Time Horizon

In general, opportunism and long-tail investments are a poor mix, for the reasons illustrated in the two charts above. Quite apart from the operational difficulties of employing such investments in this way, ten years is so far beyond the range of economic visibility that Investment B amounts to little more than a leap of faith. It is justifiable only in the context of a dedicated program of vintage diversification, which is, as any institution that has embarked upon one can amply testify, the antithesis of opportunism. Even so, and despite all the efforts of investment policymakers to accustom their trustees to its probable return characteristics in advance of the decision to invest, few institutions that have established such a program have managed to avoid considerable impatience from that source. Once the program has matured, the virtues of a vintage-based approach to these investments should be clear, but the period leading up to maturity offers trustees numerous occasions for demonstrating their failure to understand the need for patient structuring of the portfolio.

In the context of institutions that expect to operate in perpetuity or at least over several generations, this may seem remarkably short-sighted, but quite apart from the psychological challenge of maintaining equanimity in the face of extended fallow periods for returns, there are institutional considerations that must unavoidably be faced when embarking upon such an investment program. That portion of its portfolio that produces low returns drags on total portfolio performance until its returns kick in, reducing the institution's flexibility to increase its distributions to the causes it supports in the meantime. If it is an actuarial entity, poor performance may require it to tap its source of funding for greater contributions or to refrain from underwriting new risks if the growth of its regulatory capital is too greatly constrained as a consequence of that performance. When returns do materialize, they are often extraordinary and unbalancing for the portfolio as a whole. Given that, at the time of initial commitment, economic visibility is no better for the prospects of reinvestment than it is for the returns on the investment in the first place, opportunistic policymakers in effect take two leaps of faith rather than just one with these sorts of investments. Without much in the way of intervening cash flow distributions, long-tail directional investments are difficult to value and consequently difficult to justify opportunistically.

This issue of valuation pervades the whole question of investment timing. At the other, short-term extreme of time horizons, investment policy should probably think twice before engaging in opportunism as well. Again leaving operational considerations aside, novel investment decisions that depend primarily on short-term price developments, like very long-term decisions, require information that is unlikely to be within investment policymakers' range of visibility. Even where all of an institution's assets are managed internally, its trade discovery processes and the data upon which they rely will be focused on the trades it pursues in the normal course of its investment activities. It is difficult to guess what near-term trading signal its fixed-income, real estate, or equity managers might receive that would suggest acquiring short exposure to, say, six-month orange juice futures—and provide them and their investment policymakers with the confidence to act on that signal. While short-term trading conditions are not unknowable in the way that market conditions ten years into the future are, as a practical matter, managers can attend to only so much information at a given time, and a given datum's relevance to their primary task is a screen that they must apply fairly rigorously. If an institution is already active in agricultural futures, it may be in a position to react quickly and with confidence to trading signals from the orange juice pit, but otherwise it is probably best served to ignore any signals upon which it happens to stumble.

The task of investment policy is to decide which price signals the institution wants to put itself in a position to respond to, either directly or through agents. In the example above, the institution has installed capacity for discovering trades in fixed-income, real estate, and equities. Given that there are costs and time involved in acquiring such capacity—policymakers' decision-making, acquiring resources if it is to be managed internally, a manager search and allocation of capital to the manager if it will be managed externally—practicalities militate against rapid reaction to perceived opportunities. Institutions should view their minimum timing horizon in terms of the speed with which these practical considerations can be addressed. But all of these represent sunk costs that should be measured against the perceived opportunity. A single short position in an orange juice futures contract would have to be either extraordinarily lucrative and/or extraordinarily large to justify such effort, while a program of such investment activity can recompense the institution over time without having to rely on extraordinary returns or risks to justify its sunk costs.

Although I am unaware of any scientific support for the view, it is more or less an institutional rule of thumb that the timing horizon should be about three years. Intuitively, that seems about right. Three years is roughly the limit of meaningful economic visibility, and three years of returns that are modestly better than the portfolio's required return seem appropriate recompense for the cost and effort involved in making such a decision—if returns are better than "modest" improvements or remain above the required return for more than three years, that represents the upside potential to the investment of time and effort.

I mentioned in Chapter 3 that three years of monthly returns were not statistically so terribly significant, but that period has become important to investment thinking as a result of these non-scientific considerations. However, positions that massively outperform expectations dictate reexamination of the initial investment thesis. Occasionally, institutions pleasantly surprise themselves, and achieve such extraordinary returns in the short-term that economic visibility suggests that retaining the asset longer would be an unwarranted investment risk. For example, I am aware of an institution that had the unheard-of good fortune to achieve more than a 100 percent return on a large investment in timberland in the space of only about a year. In these cases, opportunism should unquestionably trump whatever intuitive attractions a three-year timing horizon may offer.

Positions that underperform expectations are, inevitably, more problematic for investors. If Investment A in Figure 23.1 represents the required return, and the periods shown represent calendar quarters, then it would take strong conviction to retain the allocation to Investment B even into the third year, let alone until it finally produced the required return after five years. In many cases, an institution that did not lose heart early on would congratulate itself on achieving anything like a return in the fourth year, and sell just as the investment was beginning to produce what it had so long desired. "Conviction" is a term that is used far too freely in investment circles (does the existence of "Conviction Buy Lists" imply that firms also maintain "Lack-of-Conviction Buy Lists?"), but it is nevertheless a very important attribute. Assuming Investment B is a liquid instrument, only conviction would typically allow a holder of it to obtain its required return from it. The ability to maintain that conviction is likely to depend heavily on the nature of the investment and the investor's detailed knowledge of it—if it were private equity, an investor would be unreasonable to expect much if any return in the first three years, but for most other investments, the performance shown in Figure 23.1 would indicate either that the manager had failed to become invested or had obtained unexpectedly poor results in doing so.

As conviction falters, it is important for investment policymakers to consider where the conviction was misplaced—was the opportunity misperceived, or did the attempt to exploit it fail in implementation? This is yet another place where investors may be tempted to equivocate—it is generally easiest for trustees and institutional staff to blame the (third-party) manager, but there are in fact numerous points along the decision path where things may have gone wrong, and most of them are unquestionably the responsibility of the institution and within its power to avoid. While self-knowledge has a value in its own right, a more valuable result from raking over the coals of failed decisions is that they can serve as stress tests for the institution and its processes.

Timing and Tactics

A timing horizon of three years suggests somewhat glacial tactical flexibility, but that is not really the case. Once a commitment has been made to exposure at the upper levels of the investment categorization, lower-order decisions that gradually enter into the realm of tactics should follow fairly easily, and it should be possible to implement them quickly without bureaucratic encumbrance. An institution's ability to capture the returns offered by opportunism depends on its preparedness to grasp the opportunities that present themselves. Thus, for instance, if it has been decided to invest in quality office buildings, the subsidiary decision between purchasing in Minneapolis or Houston can be made opportunistically on short notice, once the infrastructure for making a decision regarding office investments in any location has been put in place.

It might be objected that some of the best managers are narrow specialists who add considerable value but only within their niches. Where an institution perceives this to be true, then the degree of expertise it must internalize (or access through consultants) must be correspondingly higher. Otherwise it is likely to violate its own hierarchy of decision-making, which will result in inappropriate predetermination of the investments that the institution eventually makes. To take a trivial example, if the response to a decision to invest in real estate is to select a Minneapolis specialist prior to deciding that Minneapolis is an appropriate location in which to invest, then there is clearly something flawed in the institution's understanding of its decision hierarchy and of how its decisions must be implemented. Specialization undoubtedly has an important place in investments, but that place is put in context by investment considerations that extend beyond this or that narrow specialization.

As discussed in Chapter 18, these hierarchies are not rigid and may even be changeable as the investment environment or the portfolio changes. But in the course of preparing itself for entry into a new investment category, an institution should acquire a thorough understanding of these dynamics. To continue with the real estate example, in the course of designing its investment program, the institution may conclude that it wants the essentially bond-like returns offered by core exposure to office buildings that are fully occupied by high quality tenants on long leases. Or it may be attracted to the equity-like returns of "value-added" investment in buildings that are in need of work and/or repositioning. In the first case it may be largely indifferent to the choice between investing in Houston or Minneapolis, and its decision is more likely to be determined by relative valuations than location. Although it will not entirely ignore the differences between the two local economies, particularly regarding their exposure to the oil industry, the equity component of core real estate is so far out-of-the-money that it will have limited effect on returns, so those are likely to be comparatively minor considerations. In the latter case the institution certainly cannot afford to be indifferent. If an institution is considering "value-added" exposure in Houston, with its attendant equity-like exposure to an oil-dominated local economy, it would be well advised to examine the rest of its portfolio for factor exposure to oil. And it should determine whether exposure through a real estate vehicle is optimal relative to other ways that it might achieve (or has already achieved) its energy exposure, as that is part of what it is likely to be getting.

If the institution's real estate interest steers it instead toward investing in medical facilities, the analytic considerations involved in reaching that decision may be quite different. Although the oil factor will play a significant role in determining long-term demographic trends in the Houston area, the microeconomics of local medical provision are likely to be the most important intermediate-term influence on returns. But this begs the question of how the institution chose between medical facilities and office buildings in the first place. This decision could, perhaps, have been affected by desire for factor exposure to oil, in which case Minneapolis probably did not figure in its thinking, but Edmonton might have. That is, the institution's decision hierarchy may have driven it to seek real estate opportunities in Houston, and failing to uncover any in the office building market segment, it may have looked elsewhere. It may have been attracted by a return profile in which the oil factor is a long-term influence but valuation considerations might affect returns sooner, in which case investment in Minneapolis might well have been a realistic alternative to Houston. Or, having made a decision to allocate to medical facilities based on nationwide demographic trends, subsequent investigation may have revealed that values were most compelling in Houston, irrespective of its factor loading to oil.

This is Swensen's "complex simultaneity" in action, and clearly it is only made possible by thorough institutional preparation. The glacial aspect of an institution's ability to respond to opportunity is due to the time required to decide to build the necessary infrastructure for making such decisions and then implementing them. Once that commitment has been made, there remain only internal impediments to institutions' ability to react quickly to opportunities. If the institution typically relies on external experts—in this case, a real estate consultant—the decision to seek investments in real estate must first be made, and some parameters must be set around the sorts of investments that the institution will seek. Identifying a consultant in whom the institution can comfortably put its trust will unavoidably require that the institution gain significant understanding of the investment category under consideration in order to be able to do so. Unfortunately, there is no Royal Path to enlightened opportunism.

Investment Policymakers' Involvement with Timing Questions

Every decision that is made can be dated, and every decision that is postponed is avoided at a specifiable time. Strategic decisions to extend an institution's investable universe—or not to do so—do not occur in mystical timelessness, and thus they unavoidably have a tactical element to them. They are influenced by the context in which they are taken, and the history of institutional investment practice over the last half century is one of rapidly changing context. It is a rare institution that has not in recent years taken a decision, yea or nay, about adding some or other alternative investment category to its investable universe.

Consequently, for all that received wisdom recommends strongly against the involvement of investment policymakers in tactical decision-making, they cannot entirely avoid it. A proposed new investment category will prove timely or otherwise, and whereas short-term investment considerations should not influence the decision, psychological realism suggests that they cannot help but doing so. A properly functioning committee may well contemplate adding investment categories that it might eventually use, even if they are obviously ill-timed when they come up for consideration, but unless it is remarkably prescient, such a committee is unlikely to have approved every possible investment category that might in fact be currently opportune. A policy of blanket pre-approval (apart from the fact that it would constitute no policy at all) would accomplish very little, unless it includes specification of the conditions under which the investment category might actually be employed. These are considerations that verge on the tactical (and also require a degree of prescience that would be even more remarkable). Investment risks from approval, and opportunity costs from failure to approve, are unavoidable.

The distinction that Anson (2004) draws between strategic and tactical allocation, based on their relationship to fulfilling policy goals *versus* "beating the market," respectively (10*f*), is not terribly helpful in disentangling investment policymakers from their problems of timing. It is advice for a steady-state world in which the range of allowable investments does not change. A new candidate will be proposed for inclusion in the investment universe on the assumption that, at some point or another, it can contribute to policy goals—otherwise, why waste the committee's time? Once approved, the inevitable "Now what?" demands a timing decision. That decision may be outsourced, but it cannot be avoided. Anson's generalization that investment policy should concern itself with β and leave decisions that affect the portfolio's α generation to the tactical implementation level of decision-making strangely neglects the situation where an institution adds an investment category to its investable universe.

The question for investment policymakers is not whether to involve themselves in matters of timing, but the extent to which they allow themselves to do so. To return again to my real estate example, policymakers may decide to include a real estate allocation in their investable universe, and perhaps set a long-term target of 10 to 25 percent on exposure to it. They may then turn all other questions of implementation over to consultants. But in doing so, they have effectively decided to take on at least 5 percent exposure in the intermediate-term. They may instruct their consultants to proceed deliberately, but having made the addition to their universe they can reliably expect their consultants to reach half the minimum exposure level on their behalf within the horizon of economic visibility. The result for the portfolio is unlikely to be different if they choose instead to internalize all real estate decision-making down to a level that is as obviously tactical as the decision between prime office building investments in Minneapolis and Houston. Someone—whether a consultant or on staff—has been hired to do the job, and can reasonably be expected to do it.

This conclusion does not result from just a cynical pretence to psychological realism. Allocation targets, if they have any meaning, are meant to be achieved. The imperative of diversification argues strongly in favor of employing any investment category that is approved. Within three years of the decision to add a category to the investable universe, if half the target exposure is achieved, the portfolio is still 50 percent underweight its minimum allocation to that category. As evidence of the force of the imperative to gain exposure following the approval of an investment category, one need only point to the perennial friction between trustees and those who implement investment policy after a decision has been reached to add private equity to the investable universe. Given the difficulty of building exposure to this investment category, investment staff are virtually guaranteed that they will receive pointed questioning from trustees within the three-year horizon of economic visibility subsequent to the approval of the investment, regardless of how much effort they have put into preparing the trustees for the realities of building private equity exposure.

So the pretence that strategic decisions can be taken in splendid isolation from tactical ones is just that—a pretence. This should not really come as a surprise. Strategy that has no tactical implications (for instance, blanket inclusion of all possible investment categories in the investable universe) is no strategy at all. And severing the feedback loop between tactical conditions "on the ground" and strategy formation is obviously a recipe for disaster. We need not accept Goethe's rather idiosyncratic judgment that "we do not understand the strategy until after the campaign is over" to recognize that strategy and tactics are and should be intimately intertwined. Strategy informs tactics, and tactics give concreteness and meaning to strategy.

This is not to say that the decision between Minneapolis and Houston necessarily has implications for strategy. It depends how the decision is reached, and what is intended by it—which in turn depends on the decision hierarchy employed. The greater its portfolio repercussions, the more strategic consequences a decision entails. Thus the decision between cities in which to make core investments in office buildings is, comparatively, a stand-alone decision of an almost purely tactical nature, while "value-added" investment in Houston may have portfolio consequences well beyond the tactical implementation of a real estate investment program. On the other hand, "value-added" investment in Minneapolis may not have such broad consequences for the portfolio, or at any rate, given my ignorance of the local economy there, does not suggest ones that are as obvious to me as Houston does.

Portfolio Termination

As already suggested, few alternative investments fit well with plans that are approaching termination—hedge funds or CTAs that engage exclusively in short-term strategies and some short-term direct lenders are possible exceptions. But the risks of missing a distribution obligation or retaining illiquid exposures after the portfolio should have been liquidated are too unattractive to support brinksmanship. Institutions with finite lives that make use of alternative investments should plan well ahead for their final days. An undistributed surplus at termination may be a boon or a major nuisance, and the planning obviously must take this into account. In this discussion, I assume that the plan sponsor would prefer to avoid such an eventuality, and that the institution wants to depart the stage as gracefully as possible, with a zero balance on its investment account.

If portfolio assets are committed to investments with the potential to be locked up for fifteen years, prudence suggests that the institution should cease making such commitments sixteen years in advance of termination. However, these lockups are a function of commingled fund structure rather than of the underlying assets, and an institution need not refrain from direct commitments to the same sorts of investments so early. To avoid having to make a disposal under pressure, institutions should probably allow themselves two years to liquidate direct investments in built real estate and similar long-tail assets, and perhaps three for private equity positions. This places a termination program within the bounds of economic visibility, allowing the institution some room for tactical maneuver. Real estate under development is a trickier matter, and planning should focus on time to completion plus three years' leeway to allow for construction delays, and so on.

Hedge funds, where opportunism frequently knows no bounds, are another matter. Too often, their Limited Partners only discover that a portion of their positions is illiquid the hard way—in a fund's response to their submission of a redemption request. If a gate is imposed or they are side-pocketed, then they are simply frozen in some portion of their exposure, and if a "stub" is distributed to them in kind, it is unlikely that they will be able to find a buyer for it readily. Institutions on the road to dissolution should probably instigate a concerted program of direct contact with their hedge fund managers five years before planned termination, to emphasize to those managers their concerns and to obtain what assurances they can that their fears will not be realized. Where such assurances are not forthcoming, institutions should probably redeem at that time.

CHAPTER 24

Managing the Allocation Decision

I t may seem peculiar that a book addressed to investment policy-makers has made no effort to identify who they are. It is, of course, to be hoped that they already know. But as a general rule, issues of institutional portfolio governance are rarely explored, and the nature of the oversight function, including the depth of its involvement in what I have described as "lower order" decision-making, varies widely. "Institution" is yet another portmanteau term, embracing everything from large insurers for which investment is a core commercial competence to small eleemosynary establishments overseen by unpaid but nevertheless deeply committed volunteers. Included within the term's scope are giant state pension organizations governed by political appointees, corporate plans with personnel department administration under bank trusteeship, and university endowments supervised by professors drawn from the economics or finance faculties and alumni with extensive investment experience. Institutions are supported by large cadres of investment staff or have no staff at all, and their terms in office range from the annual to the perpetual. So generalizations about institutional governance are made at our peril.

Institutional governance is a subject for another book entirely, and one that I lack the expertise to write. However, institutional interest in alternative investments has increased the frequency with which most institutions have had to make decisions regarding their investable universe, and in the process has highlighted aspects of those decisions that can benefit from some discussion here. I would not presume to make a recommendation about how institutions should structure their policymaking processes, and in any case, those processes are likely to be idiosyncratic to the institution and even to the individuals who play a role in them. Not the least of the factors that determine how these decisions are reached are matters of personality, trust, interpersonal dynamics, and self-knowledge, about which it is difficult to generalize. Yet these have influenced institutions' allocations to alternative investments in numerous and not necessarily subtle ways. Without entering the realms of social psychology, there are still aspects of the decision process that bear investigation.

The management of institutional investments, like virtually every other human endeavor, is subject to fashions. By the early 1980s, the last of the self-managed corporate pensions were fading from the scene, and it was the received wisdom that the function of investment policy-making was to set strategic goals, which should be executed by third-party managers chosen with the aid of consultants. Insurance companies continued to manage the bulk of their assets internally, but virtually all other institutions were committed to this model of outsourcing large portions of their decision-making. Fiduciary trusteeship came to be regarded as a non-executive oversight role, for which investment expertise was unnecessary and possibly even undesirable. But change was in the air, and it came from the unlikely direction of university endowments.

Perhaps this was not so unlikely after all. By the mid-1980s, academic financial theory had become market orthodoxy, and the research taking place in university economics departments no longer seemed so removed from practice as it once had. Further, certain developments in the markets, such as the launch of index options in 1983, caused Wall Street to turn increasingly to academia for the technical expertise that it lacked. Inevitably, talent and ideas began to flow in both directions. But the damage done to university endowments by the economic and market conditions of the late 1970s probably provided the most important catalyst for universities to permit their investment committees to migrate closer to the Wall Street community. Conditions were ripe for endowments to take a more active role in the formation and implementation of investment policy at a time when the need for change was strongly felt. This was the period when the previously unknown role of the endowment CIO was created.

Governance and Investment Decision-Making

From an investment perspective, probably the most important of the very wide range of differences among institutions' governance structures is the amount of technical investment support that the fiduciaries with ultimate responsibility for the portfolio receive. Given the extent to which strategic decision-making bleeds imperceptibly but inevitably into tactical consequences, this is no small matter, and it is a two-sided proposition. On the one hand, trustees with limited investment experience must rely heavily on this support, whether they receive it from the institution's staff or from external advisors. On the other, trustees with substantial investment experience rely on an investment staff or third-party advisors in which they have strong confidence to help them resist the temptation to engage in micromanagement of the portfolio, recognizing that, for all that it is a significant responsibility, trusteeship is not a full-time job, while the day-to-day tactical management of portfolios unquestionably is.

Contrast, for example, the composition of the portfolio oversight committees shown in **Tables 24.1** and **24.2**. It is no reflection on the quality of the CalPERS Committee to note that investment expertise is rather thin on the ground there. Oversight of the state pension plan is firmly in the hands of representatives of its sponsors and beneficiaries, which is entirely appropriate, assuming that the political appointees are responsive to *their* sponsors—California's taxpayers. The committee is structured for oversight and nothing more, analogous to the purely non-executive corporate boards found in Germany. And it is inclusive: all the members of the ultimate CalPERS governing body, its Board of Administration, have a seat on its Investment Committee. The Board of Directors of the Harvard Management Co. includes representatives of its owner (the university) and its operating staff through the presence of its CEO, as well as a large contingent of investment professionals and academics in relevant disciplines, who presumably represent alumni and faculty as well as providing the Board with their expertise. Only the representatives of the university administration have a role on the main governing body of the institution. The Board of Directors of the Harvard Management Company is obviously intended to fulfill a consultative as well as an oversight role, similar to the role that corporate boards play in the United States, but only with respect to its activities, which are restricted to the management of the endowment, and not those of the institution it supports. It is interesting to note that the expertise of one faculty board member is in corporate management rather than finance: presumably consultation extends beyond strictly investment matters.

The CalPERS Investment Committee is suited to the institutional investment model that prevailed in the early 1980s, and the fact that the CIO is not a member suggests that the relationship between the

TABLE 24.1 *CalPERS Investment Committee*

George Diehr, Chair	professor of management, CSU San Marcos; research in education management
Priya Sara Mathur, Vice Chair	financial analyst, Bay Area Rapid Transit District
Rob Feckner	glazier, Napa Valley Unified School District
John Chiang	*ex officio*; California State Controller
Patricia Clarey	senior vice president (regulatory affairs), Health Net, Inc.
Dan Dunmoyer	head of State Legislative and Regulatory Affairs, Farmers Insurance Group
David Gilb	*ex officio*; Director of the California Department of Personnel Administration
Henry Jones	CFO (retired), Los Angeles Unified School District
Bill Lockyer	*ex officio*; California State Treasurer
Louis F. Moret	former Board member, Los Angeles Fire and Police Pension Board
Tony Oliveira	member, Kings County Board of Supervisors
Kurato Shimada	supervisor of operations (retired), Oak Grove (San Jose) School District
Charles P. Valdes	deputy attorney, California Department of Transportation

Source: CalPERS.

Committee and those who implement its decisions is kept at arm's length. It seems likely, in fact, that internal investment staff could be replaced with third parties without much affecting the Committee's structure or its deliberations, and this is probably not accidental. Although certain decisions are no doubt cumbersome, there is value to the institution in reaching any strategic decisions deliberately, given that Committee members must be able to represent them to their varied constituencies.

TABLE **24.2** *Harvard Management Co. Board of Directors*

James F. Rothenberg, Chair	*ex officio,* Treasurer, Harvard University
John Y. Campbell	professor of economics; research in financial econometrics
Drew G. Faust	*ex officio,* President, Harvard University
Edward Forst	co-head, Goldman Sachs Asset Management
Jacob Goldfield	hedge fund manager; former CIO, Quantum Fund
William W. Helman	partner, Greylock Partners
Glenn H. Hutchins	partner, Silver Lake; chairman, SunGard; Board member, NASDAQ OMX Group
Robert Kaplan	professor of business; research in corporate strategy and optimization
Martin L. Liebowitz	managing director, Morgan Stanley Investment Strategy research group
Jay O. Light	professor of business; research in investments; former CIO, Ford Foundation
Jane Mendillo	*ex officio,* CEO, Harvard Management Co.; former CIO, Wellesley College
Peter A. Nadosy	president (retired), Morgan Stanley Asset Management
Hilda Ochoa-Brillembourg	CEO of two investment management firms; former CIO, World Bank

Source: Harvard Management Co.

The dynamics of Harvard's board are doubtless quite different. As a private entity, the university can internalize its representative function in the board itself. While no doubt board members feel an obligation to various constituencies, ultimately the Harvard Management Co. answers to the university and no one else. Whereas the board might also choose to deal with those who implement strategy at arm's length, there would hardly be a need for such investment expertise at board level if that were its procedure, nor would there be a need for representation from the management company. In fact, there would be no a need for a board at all, and if the university chose to rely entirely on external investment service providers, no need for the management company, either. The members of this board are obviously expected to involve themselves intimately with matters related to the implementation of strategy to a much greater degree than the members of the CalPERS Committee.

Since the 1980s, bodies such as these have been asked to make increasing numbers of decisions regarding the inclusion within their investment universes of investment categories with which at least some of their members were probably unfamiliar. Many were novel, with little in the way of a track record. They were at least superficially much riskier than the investment categories to which they were accustomed, and some no doubt had unfamiliar time horizons or return characteristics. Neither the CalPERS nor the Harvard governance structures need have interfered with this. However, the CalPERS Committee is very unlikely to have initiated any such proposals, whereas it is hard to imagine that the Harvard board refrained from doing so. Given the previous chapter's discussion of the intimate connection between strategic and tactical decisions, the CalPERS structure results in a decision mechanism whereby the strategic changes that might have tactical implications are proposed by those who must implement them, while at Harvard, such decisions might equally come from the ultimate fiduciaries.

The Harvard structure creates the risk that part-time trustees encroach on matters that require full-time attention: hence the importance of the Harvard Management Co.'s representation on the board. Those who implement policy are best-positioned not only to supply the board with the information regarding a proposed new investment category that they might require to make a decision, but also with an analysis of the consequences of allocating to the category for both the portfolio as a whole and for the institution's investment management processes and structures. For example, if the proposal is to allocate 5 percent of the Endowment to rare postage stamps, through the CEO the management company can communicate its analyses of

❑ the characteristics of the market (its transaction processes, asset categories, and the investment techniques that might be pursued);
❑ the effect that investing $1.4 billion (assuming the October, 2008 endowment value) in this narrow market might have and the time required to invest that amount without creating market disruption;

❏ the quality and availability of external advisors *versus* the cost of internalizing the required expertise; and

❏ the portfolio role that this investment category would play in relation to existing and anticipated holdings.

While the CalPERS Committee could certainly request similar analyses if it wanted to see them, the extent to which it and its investment support staff could work together to reach a conclusion is unclear, while a process involving considerable give-and-take between trustees and staff would seem natural in the Harvard context.

The "Endowment Model"

Not the least of the reasons why fashion shifted toward institutional use of external managers were the liabilities placed on corporate pension plan sponsors—the institutional thought-leaders of the time—by the Employee Retirement and Income Security Act of 1974. Use of external consultants and managers shielded sponsors from much of the liability that, under that legislation, their investment activities might engender. Not the least of the influences that caused endowments to reject the received wisdom of external management was the recognition that they did not suffer from similar constraints—it is notable that private institutions pioneered this innovation and remain its thought-leaders. And they tended to be larger ones, because they were able to garner economies of scale. Investment expertise is expensive, but spread over enough capital, savings relative to the cost of third-party investment services were achievable by larger endowments, and provided a further encouragement to institutions that contemplated a move in that direction primarily for other reasons. El-Erian (2008) indicates that, for Harvard, internal management saves about half the cost of outsourcing, although it raises delicate issues over staff remuneration and retention (266*ff*).

The desire to achieve cost savings was dwarfed by the desire for returns, and as academic research in finance progressed beyond the consideration of conventional, long-only equities and fixed income, so did universities' investment interests. There were few external sources to which they could turn for advice on alternative investments, which had not then attracted the interest of other institutions, so it became necessary to build the expertise themselves. They were extremely well positioned to do so, given that the universities were the ultimate sources of many of these developments in investment thinking. Because most of the successful Wall Street practitioners had passed through their schools, opportunities for cross-fertilization were high. Finally, access to computers, to those with the then comparatively rare ability to program them and to econometricians with the skills to design those programs, was not a challenge for the universities. Because of their intellectual authority and investment success, thought-leadership gradually shifted to the university endowments.

Then as now, the endowments pursued an interesting mixture of investment techniques, resembling the "barbell" structure sometimes adopted by fixed-income managers, in which investment is concentrated in the most and least risky parts of the yield curve with little or nothing in the intermediate-duration, intermediate-risk part of the curve. In the interest of cost savings, many endowments manage routine portfolios of indexed equities and fixed income internally, while in the interest of return maximization they pursue direct exposure in private market investments such as co-investments in private equity and direct holdings of real estate, energy properties, and so on. The middle ground of risk—active investment techniques in marketable instruments—is generally outsourced to commercial investment management firms. This is consistent with certain precepts of information theory discussed in Chapter 18.

Despite the experience of 2007 to 2009, the "Endowment Model" appears to be on the verge of becoming the new institutional orthodoxy. Although endowments remain small relative to the sum of institutional assets, the previous investment model that particularly addressed the needs of corporate pensions is no longer so influential now that defined benefit pension plans themselves are disappearing. While the new model certainly has not displaced investment consultants from their central role in the industry, it has forced them to adjust to an environment where, at least with respect to the largest institutions, they are more truly consultants, usually hired on a project basis, rather than the effective managers of strategy implementation and perhaps even the sources of strategy itself. However, the cost of internalizing investment expertise should not be accepted uncritically. In what may soon come to be regarded as near-heresy, Allan Bufferd, Massachusetts Institute of Technology's former Treasurer, notes that

> Gifts to the endowment are really important factors in building the endowment over time. Part of my judgment about the endowment in mid-size institutions is to wonder whether the marginal dollar of the budget should be spent on development rather than on the investment budget. People and organizations have to tune themselves to where they are. (Kochard and Rittereiser 2008, 87)

His point is especially pertinent to institutions that are considering adding alternative investments to their investable universe. Sound expertise in this area is neither readily available nor cheap, the risks from insufficient diversification in portfolios that are not large enough to allow for it are great, implementation is unlikely to be optimal, and management of the positions taken by the institution will in many cases be burdensome. Before committing itself to an investment program that will unquestionably entail significant costs, an institution should consider carefully whether this is the best use of its resources. As Bufferd suggests, the incremental dollar in the endowment that was obtained through fund-raising is no less valuable to the institution than the incremental dollar from superior investment performance, and endowed institutions should ask themselves which they think they have the greater probability of achieving. Ultimately it is the value of the endowment, not how that value was obtained, that is of importance to the organization that the endowment supports.

Outsourcing

The theory of interpretation is also known as hermeneutics, and a key concept of the discipline, introduced by the theologian and textual critic F. D. E. Schleiermacher in the nineteenth century, is the "hermeneutic circle." This is the paradox that, in order to gain understanding of something, we must already understand it to some extent. If confronted by something that is completely unfamiliar to us—for instance, *Geisteswissenschaftsbegriffsbildung*—we are at a loss. If we discover that this monstrosity means "concept formation in the humanities and social sciences," then we at least have a place to start. This is the circular aspect of understanding: we survey the territory, return to where we started a little wiser, retrace our steps repeatedly, and gradually learn the lay of the land. The hermeneutic circle is at the root of the problem of outsourcing investment functions. In order to perform our fiduciary duty and obtain quality third-party service, we must be able to recognize quality. This requires that we attain sufficient expertise to do so, but the desire to avoid that requirement is probably why most institutions' policymakers turn to outsourcing in the first place.

This is fundamentally a problem of agency risk, and essentially the same problem many of us face in selecting a lawyer or car mechanic: we do not trust them, but we do not know enough about their specializations to recognize a good one. So we ask around, and that is, in effect, what most institutions do. In light of the "six degrees of separation," it should be no surprise that this procedure has resulted in a concentration of general investment consultancy business in a few firms—although there are many such consultants, the overwhelming bulk of the business, and especially that portion of it that consults to large institutional investors, is in the hands of a fairly small number of firms. But of course, this begs the question whether the advice of the people we have turned to is sound. This is one of those inconvenient subjects that people tend to want to slide past with eyes averted, but it is becoming an issue—potentially even a regulatory issue—for many investors, and is at last beginning to receive the attention it has long deserved: see Wright (2009).

This is not to imply that consultants are as disreputable as car mechanics are thought to be (let alone lawyers), but only to underline the fact that an institution's experience with a consultant is specific to its own needs, which may not mirror the needs of another institution that turns to it for a recommendation. A good experience during a search for a multi-strategy manager or a general review of portfolio strategy does not guarantee good experiences on other consultancy assignments. Every consultancy firm has its strengths and weaknesses, and the weaknesses may not be apparent to an institution that happens to have turned to a consultant for advice in an area that is among its strong suits. Institutions seeking recommendations should be certain that the advice they heed is based on experience with the specific service they require. Most consultants' experience with alternative investments is considerably shorter and less comprehensive than their experience with conventional investments. Further, the universe of alternative investments is so disparate and rapidly changing by comparison to the universe of conventional investment vehicles that experience with alternative investments must be very deep indeed to be comparable to a consultant's expertise in conventional instruments. These circumstances further emphasize the need for caution about referrals.

For the most part, consultants are only the first in a two-stage process of outsourcing, because they are retained to identify third-party managers on behalf of the institution that engages them. The risks inherent in hiring an intermediary to hire an agent need no comment. If the consulting assignment is to identify a fund of funds, then it becomes a three-stage process of hiring an intermediary to hire an intermediary to hire an agent, implying further adumbration of those risks. In the alternative investment environment, where transparency and investment discipline leave much to be desired, these risks can quickly become quite substantial. The further removed the institution is from the agent that executes transactions on its behalf, the more it should question the extent to which it has fulfilled its fiduciary responsibility of due diligence in selecting that agent.

This is not intended as a counsel of despair to institutions that do not have large resources of qualified investment staff to give them a point of departure on the hermeneutic circle, but only as an encouragement to caution and realistic self-appraisal. With every fashion, there are always some people whom the current one does not suit, and that is as true of the current enthusiasm for the "Endowment Model" as it is of any other fashion trend. Even more than institutions, consulting firms tend to be dedicated followers of fashion, and this should be borne in mind when seeking and implementing their advice. Unfortunately, self-knowledge cannot be outsourced: when trying on a new outfit, if we ask the store clerk whether it looks good on us, in most cases we are unlikely to be told that it does not.

Apart from funds of funds, there are also a variety of firms that supply outsourced alternative investment management services on a separate account basis. This gives the institution direct access to the funds on the provider's platform, without the mediation of a fund of funds. But in general the institution should not expect to receive a truly customized solution: apart from any investment providers or techniques the institution specifically excludes from its mandate, it can expect its fund holdings to be essentially identical to those of the platform provider's other institutional clients. Because the provider will inevitably have limited access to different providers of underlying investments, in effect it offers a range of choices that the institution can take or leave, with little—or more typically, no—ability to customize beyond the specification that this or that product on the platform must be excluded from consideration. The desirability of this solution depends entirely on the funds to which the provider has access—which the institution must determine for itself, because the platform provider obviously cannot offer unbiased advice. If, as is often the case, the funds on the platform refuse to offer transparency to the platform's users, the institution is given little upon which to base its decisions. Although these services are structured differently than funds of funds, their risks are similar: their clients rely on the platform manager's selection of investment choices, although they have the freedom to reject some of them and perhaps to allocate their percentage exposures to the vehicles that they retain for consideration.

For an institution with limited resources of highly qualified investment staff, the alternative investment landscape is, frankly, a potential minefield. Quite apart from the risks that these vehicles present to its portfolio, the legal risks to the institution of making an unfortunate decision may be substantial. Some reliance on third-party advisors is, in all but a very few cases, essential. Although careful selection of consultants, fund of funds managers, or platform providers reduces agency risk, the risk from reliance on these resources must itself be carefully judged. Bufferd's advice about the use of the institution's resources is well taken: even if investment calamity is avoided, alternative investment risk that produces performance below its investment category's median is generally not worth the not inconsiderable trouble of taking and almost certainly represents uncompensated risk.

When it comes to relying on third parties for allocation advice, I would hope by now that this volume has indicated the pitfalls of making such allocations among alternative investments. As a general principle, to which I doubt there are exceptions, if an institution's trustees, with the aid of whatever investment staff they have, cannot determine for themselves at least the broad categories of alternative investments that are suitable to its investment purposes, then the institution should not seek such exposure at all. Swensen (2009, 297) implies that the basic organizational choice facing institutions regarding their investment activities is between building staff to support *any* allocation to actively managed investments and restricting themselves to purely passive exposures. This strikes me as rather extreme, but in the realm of alternative investments it has sufficient merit that investment committees should give it serious consideration. Which leads to the question, are there attractive passive approaches to alternative investments?

Hedge Fund Replication

It is not possible to replicate private equity, real estate, or many other alternative investment categories. Investable long-only passive commodity vehicles are widely available, including some that use rules-based approaches designed to capture roll yields and other features of futures' returns apart from their direct relationship to the price of the underlying. Long-only instruments are also available for a few individual commodities, notably precious metals and energy sources. These have become sufficiently commonplace that they require no further discussion, although it might be questionable whether, as long-only vehicles now frequently packaged as Exchange-Traded Funds, they qualify as "alternative" at all. But the proposal that hedge funds (or at least, their alleged β) can be replicated through the use of carefully chosen positions in indices and derivatives has attracted considerable attention. Broadly, two replication procedures have been proposed. One involves the use of mechanical trading algorithms to mimic various trend-following or mean reversion-based trading techniques, such as those that are often pursued by CTAs, foreign exchange traders, and other, often high-frequency approaches to investment. The other employs factor replication of hedge fund indices or even the reported returns of individual hedge funds, or an option-based approach that mimics their payoff characteristics.[1]

The first alternative does not replicate anything, but simply creates a unique new fund that implements whatever trading rules its sponsors install in its software on whatever instruments they choose to trade. It is not in principle different from any other fund that employs algorithmic trading, except that in aspiring to passive credentials, its sponsors are likely to be far more willing to disclose the algorithms that drive its trade discovery processes, more or less guaranteeing that their algorithms will be rather less than state-of-the-art. The attraction of these products, if they have any, lies in a calculation that their reduced fees offset the opportunity costs of trading without value-added programming. These vehicles are, in effect, the algorithmic counterparts of what I have labeled naïve quantitative techniques. Because they are highly vulnerable to predatory traders, interested investors should be very cautious about how liquid the instruments to which they devote their attentions are (as being lost in the crowd offers such traders a measure of protection) and how much they leverage their exposure to them. In my view, this approach to "synthetic" trading vehicles is only appropriate to the currency and futures markets and to the most liquid equity index options.

The second set of alternatives more properly deserve to be described as "replication" vehicles, because their returns are in fact derivative of the performance of other instruments. The proposal that a handful of judiciously chosen positions in derivatives and indices could replicate hedge funds has, not surprisingly, horrified the α-obsessives of the hedge fund community, who are quick to point out what no proponent of replication would dispute, that this sort of replication can only generate the returns attributable to so-called hedge fund β, and there are grounds for questioning the legitimacy of that concept. Lo (2008, 121–167) offers detailed procedures for creating what he calls "linear

1. For a review of the literature related to the latter techniques see Amenc et al. (2007).

clones" of individual hedge funds. Interestingly, he finds it difficult to create satisfactory "clones" for fixed-income arbitrage, event-driven and emerging market style indices (ibid. 145)—which he ascribes to the illiquidity of their trades. But the factor exposures of arbitrages are inherently difficult to isolate, and I suspect this is a bigger impediment to replicating them than illiquidity. Also, the latter two categories are trading techniques where individual skill might be expected to make a particularly strong contribution to returns.

Proponents of factor-replication approaches argue, like those who recommend algorithmic approaches, that the sacrifice of α is compensated by lower fees. While in both cases this is asserted rather than proven (and Amenc et al. give significant grounds for doubting it), in light of the level and structure of hedge fund fees, it is at least superficially plausible. Dissatisfaction with fee levels probably biases many to accept the claim. However, I am inclined to think that this is yet another instance where the fact that something is possible does not constitute a recommendation for doing it. Because replications are constructed through the application of analysis to the returns of the vehicle being replicated, they are perforce backward-looking: the input that would motivate a change in the replication portfolio is a change made in the underlying portfolio during a previous reporting period. Changes to the underlying portfolio that have not yet had a measurable effect on its performance are opaque to these analyses and thus will not be incorporated into the replication—all of which assumes active rebalancing of the replication portfolio, but many replication programs are in fact seeking static replication portfolios that do not rebalance. Although this sort of replication sacrifices any returns to the underlying portfolio from α, it is likely that it accepts all of that portfolio's systematic risk, which is consequently uncompensated. As putative passive alternatives to active hedge fund management, it seems to me that replication vehicles require most of the same expertise to evaluate them that active ones require, and thus they do not meet Swensen's stricture.

I stressed in Chapter 13 that models, however useful they may be as explanatory analogies, should not be mistaken for what is modeled. I suspect that there is a very real risk of such equivocation in hedge fund replication. Although replication portfolios might be expected to perform as desired in "normal" market conditions, they are in fact complex structured derivative products, and history has shown that, under stress, these may offer highly unattractive return characteristics, including unanticipated exposures and, through margin calls and escape clauses for those that offer them, may require of their investors perverse responses to certain market situations. One problem with a passive approach to alternative investment is that it does not allow for a human in the loop, capable of exercising real options in response to unanticipated developments.

Notably, some of the most enthusiastic proponents of hedge fund replication are investment banks. There are two reasons for this. On the one hand, replication portfolios are attractively profitable to offer: the cost of a few quants and some Linux software is not much overhead, and although fees are lower than for hedge funds, they are still fairly generous by mutual fund standards. On the other hand, the products offer the investment banks significant trading opportunities because they are volatility generators. Many replication algorithms are in fact sold in structured product form—as swaps or notes—which allows the investment banks to trade with them as principals.

Up and Down the Decision Hierarchy

To return to the postage stamp example, let us assume that the investment staff has concluded that an investment program of this sort is feasible and recommends that it be pursued. The judgment of the proposal's feasibility requires a combination of objective and subjective judgments. The liquidity of the market and the ability of the endowment to transact anonymously in it can be readily and objectively determined, as can the transaction costs, the costs of safe-keeping, and so on. Identifying quality agents or potential staff members to carry out the program is far more a matter of spending time with the investment category and getting familiar with the lay of the land, the players, and so on. Judging the attractiveness of the proposition is still another matter, which must be explored from several directions.

First, the investment characteristics of the underlying asset must obviously be identified. In the case of ownership of postage stamps, it is clearly a purely directional trade, and no doubt it offers some—possibly quite substantial—inflation protections. Price behavior probably bears some correlation to that of collectibles in general, although this may not be so easy to pin down. I suspect, for example, that price developments in rare stamp philately relate fairly closely to those in the numismatics of rare modern-period coins, but not to those of ancient coins, which are probably more vulnerable to supply shocks from the occasional archaeological find. The finer sub-categorization of the asset category, presumably by country of origin, needs to be understood, and whether this implies any currency exposure—it seems reasonable that the primary source of demand for a given country's stamps would be from collectors in that country, and thus pricing would tend to be dominated by transactions denominated in that country's currency. But this would require confirmation.

I imagine that there are various investment techniques that can be applied to the pursuit of stamp collections—I would guess that there are trophy investments and out-of-favor contrarian categories, that there are techniques that rely on the appreciation of largely uncorrelated individual assets and others that build value through creation of comprehensive or representative collections. The extent to which individual stamps or investment techniques diversify each other must be explored, and this is likely to vary depending on the asset sub-categories or investment techniques employed. An exit strategy must also be considered, and this will probably vary with the technique employed. For example, if the technique is to assemble a collection that has value as a collection that exceeds the value of its individual components, then once it is assembled there are may be few reasons to continue to hold the position. As a directional trade, philately relies on an exit to produce a return—I suspect the assets' value as collateral is low, so that they cannot provide funds for institutional or investment purposes short of liquidation—and an understanding of its market cycles is essential.

Postage stamps' place in the portfolio, both as it is currently allocated and as it is expected to be within the limits of economic visibility, must be investigated in detail. For example, the gradual accumulation of exposure to an asset that offers purchasing power protection might be very welcome to a portfolio with oil or gas properties that are approaching depletion, but much less so if their production is expected shortly to ramp up. Philately has negative cash flow from the costs of safekeeping, of insurance, and of expertise to manage the exposure, whether that is internalized or retained. Because its positions probably cannot reliably be liquidated on short notice, its effect on the liquidity of the total portfolio must be considered.

Doubtless there are numerous other matters requiring consideration that the investment staff will uncover in the course of its research. It will return to the board with a detailed proposal, the contents of which may be hard to predict in advance. Perhaps the staff will reach the conclusion that philatelic markets cannot readily absorb a $1.4 billion investment, and that the capacity of the trade over the horizon of economic visibility is only, say, $850 million. The trustees will then consider whether the projected returns justify the cost and operational inconveniences of a 3 percent position. Or the discovery of an entirely unexpected and desirable factor loading, such as high positive correlation to the level of interest rates (this is a random example, not intended to imply that postage stamps actually display such behavior—I have not the slightest idea), may recommend greater use of the investment category than was originally proposed. The degree to which trustees are asked to consider lower-level decisions, such as the investment technique to be employed, will probably depend on their investment consequences: for example, it seems reasonable to expect that a value strategy of building a collection has a noticeably different return profile from buying and holding trophy specimens.

Having received the go-ahead, the investment staff will implement the program in whatever way the trustees have approved, largely without additional consultation. However, this is where the separation of institutional responsibilities can easily break down, and if it has been the lifelong ambition of one or two trustees to actually hold the "Treskilling Yellow" (which last traded at SF 2.5 million) in their tweezers, second-guessing and interference in the program's implementation are likely. This is where the sharp separation between oversight and implementation designed into the CalPERS Investment Committee structure proves its value. In an environment, such as that of a state pension, where decisions are sensitive and highly visible, even the appearance of inappropriate influence on execution, let alone the reality of it, is likely to be unacceptable. In the more private deliberations of an organization structured the way that the Harvard Management Co. is, issues of this sort can arise more easily, but they have fewer deleterious consequences beyond their possible portfolio effects. Although this caricature of a strategic investment decision regarding postage stamps makes this potential problem look rather silly, it is noticeable, for instance, that two of Harvard's board members are quite successful private equity professionals. It is hard to imagine that they do not have strong views on very detailed matters of the tactics to be adopted and the best means of implementing them in their areas of professional expertise. No doubt their presence on the board is largely due to the management company's desire to avail itself of that expertise, but it is likely that the line between consultation and interference is sometimes difficult to discern. Selecting trustees with the necessary discernment is presumably a delicate matter.

In compensation for this, an engaged and well-informed board affords Harvard Management Co. a strategic flexibility and a source of advice of which other institutions can only dream. For example, it is inconceivable that an institution would permit its staff to leverage the portfolio at the endowment level without the prior approval of the ultimate fiduciaries—I suspect that for most institutions, approval at the highest policymaking level would be a legal or regulatory requirement. Yet precisely this tactic is apparently a matter of policy at Harvard Management Co., which has been consistently short cash (i.e., in debt) for some years. Consistency might suggest strategy rather than tactics, but the borrowing is actively managed, varying with each reporting period, and is presumably employed for tactical purposes. The Yale Endowment leveraged its portfolio in 2008 with what seems to be quite clearly tactical intent. Prompt responsiveness to the sort of opportunity that would have motivated such borrowing is only possible where trustees and investment staff can work together closely.

CHAPTER 25

Concluding Remarks

G iven that I have not reached one, I can hardly entitle this chapter the "Conclusion." I have not succeeded in erecting a grand theory, and if I have managed to offer any insights, most of them create more problems for investment policymakers than they solve, muddying rather than clarifying the waters. I am apologetic but unsurprised about this: for all that I would like to have "solved" at least one of the important problems facing institutions when they confront the issues surrounding alternative investment, I am skeptical that definitive solutions to most of those problems are possible. On the whole I believe that sowing confusion in these matters is preferable to offering pat answers or false hope. Although the final section of this book has offered some rough empirical generalizations, they constitute at best an indication of the way forward, and offer only limited guidance on how to proceed.

Given what is by now quite clearly the considerable nuisance that attaches to allocating to alternative investments and to monitoring that exposure once such vehicles have been selected, the enhanced returns and increased diversification that comprise the reasons generally offered to justify their employment must be very compelling. All too often, they are not. Largely out of impatience with the topic, I have avoided all the discussion of survivorship bias, back-fill bias, and so on, that has taken a prominent place in the commentary on the returns offered by alternative investment indices (see Lhabitant [2004, 90*ff*] for an outline of these). Most of this discussion focuses on demonstrations that hedge fund index returns are not as attractive as advertised. Although metrics for private asset returns do not easily lend themselves to similar analysis, it is safe to say that much the same can be said for the returns offered by benchmarks for those types of investments as well. Instead, I have stressed that the standard deviations reported for both indices and individual alternative investment vehicles are systematically understated in a variety of ways. Not surprisingly, in a field where both the aggregate returns and the vehicle-specific volatility levels are suspect, it is a widely accepted rule of thumb that achieving median returns is not worth the candle.

Various commentators have claimed that alternative investments lost the confidence of investors during 2007 to 2009, having come through the crisis with nothing resembling the aplomb they displayed in 2000. The volume of redemptions they suffered and the sharp increase in offers of funds for sale in the secondary markets are said to provide evidence for this view. However, although there were certainly some funds that put in execrable relative performance, there always are. By and large, indices for alternative investments outperformed those of conventional vehicles other than U.S. Treasuries for the period. Whereas "absolute return" may not have turned out to be so "absolute" after all, with correlations between alternative and conventional investments proving in many cases much higher than investors had been led to expect, I think that it is fairer to say that alternative investments disappointed than that they were discredited. Disappointment, as we have seen, is an existential fact of investment life.

In the Introduction, I belabored the point that the differences between alternative and conventional investments are a matter of degree, not for the most part differences in kind. Although in certain periods of stress—including the collapse of the Technology Bubble in 2000—substantial performance differentials between them might suggest otherwise, these are likely to prove the exceptions rather than the rule. Not the least of the reasons for this is that substantial institutional inflows into these investments have moved many alternative investments closer to the same liquidity "habitat" and information "ecology" as conventional investments. And even the 2000 episode threw off categories of alternative investments—those employing convertible bonds and venture capital, for example—that were badly damaged, although the damage was not immediately apparent in 2000. In the prologue to the bursting of the Bubble, long/short funds struggled to match the performance of markets that offered few rewards to their short books. Those who turn toward alternative investments seeking completely uncorrelated generators of returns that are reliably in excess of those they achieve on their conventional investments can expect the markets to disabuse them. The creativity of their managers has yet to overcome the basic principles of economics, and is unlikely to do so.

Additional Benefits from Alternative Investment?

Although I do not believe that recent experience destroys the case for alternative investments, it certainly weakens it. Some may object to my view that the nuisance factor is a further strike against them, but if use of alternative investments imposes a burden on institutions, that is a cost that must be compensated in terms of returns, risk reduction, or in some other way. Apart from purely investment considerations, search, administration, and institutions' other incremental operating costs from engaging in a program of alternative investment are real and must be compensated. Are there other ways that alternative investments can accomplish this that we have yet to explore?

Conforming to fashion has significant psychic rewards. People are gregarious by nature, so that few want to be so dowdy as to stand out ridiculously in the crowd. The terms "conventional" and "long-only" have pejorative connotations of fustiness and narrowness of vision with which institutions that think of themselves as forward-looking are unlikely to identify. The impulse to blend in is reinforced by the fact that many institutions benchmark themselves against others of their kind: despite what our parents told us, "because everyone else is doing it" *is*, in fact, a reason for institutions that are subject to the Prudent Man Rule to do it. The institution's dependents or beneficiaries as well as its trustees are likely to take comfort from its attention to fashion, for all that the current vogue may not really suit it. Although few institutions would probably be willing to admit it, such considerations are in many cases enough to compensate for the nuisance of engaging in a program of alternative investment. Insofar as the nuisance is simply that—a nuisance rather than a substantial cost burden—this is not even a criticism. If the psychological benefits boost institutional morale, they are not to be sniffed at. Particularly given the challenges of attracting quality staff, a creative and fashionable investment policy may have benefits for the institution that are difficult to quantify. But feeling good about themselves or their work is not within investment policymakers' fiduciary remit. Insofar as a program of alternative investment imposes significant incremental management costs, these can only be justified on investment grounds.

And that is what we will inevitably circle back to. The benefits that are relevant to the investment decision are investment benefits, and these come in the form of enhanced returns or reduced risk. The value of collateral benefits to the organization, such as enhanced investment skills, improved employee retention, or what-have-you, must ultimately be measured in those terms, too. Given the relationship between risk and return, reduced risk will in all but a very few, idiosyncratic cases come in the form of increased diversification. The question, then, is whether alternative investments offer forms of diversification that are conceptually distinct from what might be achieved by simply adding previously unconsidered equities or bonds to conventional portfolios. Here we are on somewhat firmer ground, because the answer we seek is in terms of investment benefits. We may not in all cases be able to measure them reliably—much of this volume has argued that we cannot—but if we can conceptualize them we can make a case for them. And thus we return to the question, is there anything—that is, anything that is not a matter of fashion, nuisance or cost—that differentiates alternative from conventional investments? Much of this book has pursued a "lumper's" agenda that argued that there is not. It is appropriate in conclusion to do some "splitting." As a Scholastic might say, *distinguemus*—"let us distinguish."

Alternative versus Conventional Investments

The area where it will probably be most fruitful to hunt is in the distributions of investment returns that alternative investments seek to exploit. In a Gaussian distribution, just over two-thirds of observations lie in the interval between one and minus one standard deviation. This is where conventional investment managers primarily make their livings, and where Modern Portfolio Theory most plausibly holds sway. Alternative investors concentrate much of their attention to the left and right of this central zone, and the fact that, for most financial series, this is a more populous domain than the illustrious Johann Carl Friedrich Gauss would have suspected provides them with more opportunity than theory would suggest. However, it is important to note that the managers of alternative investments do not necessarily seek to exploit this region—although many do. Simply paying greater attention to avoiding the negative tails of return distributions, rather than suffering them in silence, can distinguish them from the managers of conventional vehicles.

A dedication to exploiting unusual, if not necessarily high, standard deviation events is most explicit among "macro" hedge funds, but in various ways it pervades the realm of alternative investments. Arbitrages would have nothing to arbitrage if the price discrepancies they seek to exploit were not atypical. Long/short investors rely on the fact that βs are less stable over time than theory suggests. Private market investors of all types seek their returns from opportunities that are removed from public market scrutiny entirely, whereas high-frequency traders exploit the price discontinuities generated by liquid markets' microstructure that are beneath the notice of theory. Investors in distressed situations, CTAs and direct lenders flirt with the peripheral opportunities thrown off by the more conventional marketplace—it is a notable rule of thumb, for instance, that commodity markets that are dominated by speculators rather than "natural" buyers and hedgers cannot function properly. In the Introduction I characterized this as alternative investors' obsession with being different from the crowd, but it goes further than just teenager-like contrariness. The managers of alternative investments seek, by various means, to enter different information "ecologies" from those inhabited by conventional investors. Often they succeed, at least until those "ecologies" become overpopulated.

But the unusual information environments found at the farther reaches of return distributions can be difficult to negotiate. During crises, most if not all investors unwillingly find themselves in this territory, but permanent residence is another matter. By their nature, these regions are not normally thickly populated, but if they become so, they soon loose their ability to support acceptable levels of return. The disappointment generated by alternative investments in 2007 to 2009 was largely due to population pressures that denuded what are sparse environs at the best of times. Alternative investments' reward for being able to survive in these regions is reduced competition for the information and liquidity that nourishes their excess returns. Increased competition within that environment cuts sharply into the returns they can achieve.

Managers of conventional investment vehicles operate in less exacting environments. While they face greater competition for the information that leads to outperformance, an abundance of information presents fairly consistent opportunities to achieve returns. Their trades are unlikely to become crowded out. Conventional investment management techniques have a perennial character that is lacking in most alternative techniques—and this brings us back to fashion.

Contrarian Investment Policy

The bargain bins at secondhand shops are at least the temporary fate of all but the most perennial fashions. Excessive enthusiasm for alternative investments has resulted in pressure on their returns, cheap knock-offs, and not a few costume failures that, in less pressurized circumstances, might not have occurred. It is likely that the enormous institutional appetite for these investments has, for the time being, been sated. This is no bad thing. Although it will be uncomfortable for a few firms whose names and fortunes were most closely associated with the vogue for alternative investments, and it will doubtless make life even more difficult for emerging managers, a return to more normal demand conditions will improve the offering and allow returns to recover.

Reflexive contrarianism might seize upon this as an opportunity to make commitments, but reflexive *anything* with regard to investments, and especially alternative investments, is almost certainly a mistake. The burden of this book's argument has been to emphasize the need for a carefully considered approach to alternative investments, and a few bad quarters is by no means enough to clear out of the system the excesses that accumulated in this decade. My suspicion is that commercial conditions for hedge funds will not stabilize before 2010, and the consequences of recent pressures on the returns of leveraged buyout, venture capital, and commercial real estate will have considerably longer tails—not coincidentally like the investments themselves. While some trades will almost certainly recover more quickly than others, and some will even prove to have benefited from the dislocation, the clouds over alternative investing as a broad category are unlikely to lift in a hurry.

Yet enthusiasm for alternative investment was not baseless, and as fashions often do, it will come round again. This is unavoidable: at some point, neglect will result in the creation of such compelling value in trades that are so visibly under-exploited that even investors who were burnt before will reconsider them. It is not necessary to successful employment of alternative investments to identify that turning point precisely. Investment fashions are sinoidal, as caricatured in **Figure 25.1**: in the transition from a situation where risks are inadequately compensated to one where rewards outweigh risks, fashion traverses a zone in which risk and reward are in approximate balance, which is a perfectly good time to invest. It is difficult to tell when even that region, let alone

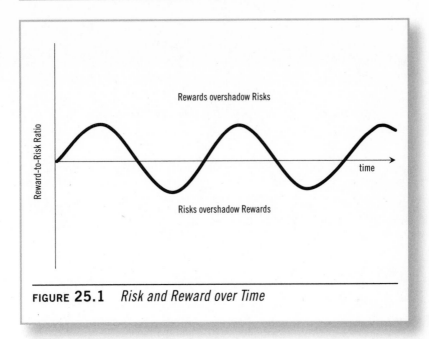

FIGURE 25.1 *Risk and Reward over Time*

the point of maximum returns relative to risk, has been reached. But it is coming as surely as wide ties or long skirts will eventually return to favor, and in some cases, such as convertible arbitrage, it may already have arrived. Given the speed with which institutions have unloaded their alternative investments for liquid trades, it may be coming sooner than most observers think.

Table 3.3 shows that tail risks manifest themselves more often than theory would suggest. Although the recent episode demonstrated that alternative investments cannot entirely avoid these risks, many were able partially to ameliorate them. Less overcrowding will enhance their ability to do so. I see nothing to suggest that tail risk will manifest itself less often in future than it has in the past—if anything, quite the reverse. From the perspective of risk as well as return, I believe that the case for institutional exposure to alternative investments remains sound and timely. I hope this book will help institutions take advantage of this opportunity.

Bibliography

Agarwal, Vigas and Naik, Narayan Y. 2000. "Performance Evaluation of Hedge Funds with Option-based and Buy-and-Hold Strategies." Centre for Hedge Fund Research and Education working paper, available at http://www2.gsu.edu/~fncvaa/benchmark.pdf.

—— and ——. 2004. "Risks and Portfolio Decisions Involving Hedge Funds." *Review of Financial Studies*, vol. 17, no. 1, pp. 63–98.

Allen, Franklin, Qian, Jun, Qian, Meijun, and Zhao, Mengxin. 2008. "A Review of China's Financial System and Initiatives for the Future." Working paper 08-28, Wharton Financial Institutions Center, University of Pennsylvania.

Amenc, Noël, Géhin, Walter, Martellini, Lionel, and Meyfredi, Jean-Christophe. 2007. "The Myths and Limits of Passive Hedge Fund Replication." EDHEC Research Center publication, available at http://facluty-research.edhec.com.

Anson, Mark J. P. 2002. *Handbook of Alternative Assets*. Hoboken, NJ: John Wiley & Sons.

——. 2004. "Strategic versus Tactical Allocation." *Journal of Portfolio Management*. Winter, pp. 8–22.

Assoé, Kodjovi, L'Her, Jean-François, and Plante, Jean-François. 2004. "Is There Really a Hierarchy of Investment Choice?" Les Cahiers du CREF of HEC Montréal: Working Paper no. 04-15, November.

Bacmann, Jean-François and Pache, Sébastien. 2004. "Optimal Hedge Fund Style Allocation under Higher Moments." In Barry Schachter (ed.), *Intelligent Hedge Fund Investing*, pp. 393–422. London: Risk Books.

Banz, Rolf W. 1981. "The Relationship between Return and Market Value of Common Stocks." *Journal of Financial Economics*, vol. 9, no. 1, pp. 3–18.

Barberis, Nicholas and Thaler, Richard. 2003. "A Survey of Behavioral Finance." In George M. Constantinides, Milton Harris, and René M. Stulz, (eds), *Handbook of Economics and Finance*, pp. 1053–121. Amsterdam, NL: Elsevier B.V.

Barv, Alon, Jiang, Wei, Partnoy, Frank, and Thomas, Randall S. 2008. "The Returns to Hedge Fund Activism." *Financial Analysts Journal*, vol. 64, no. 6, pp. 45–61.

Berk, Jonathan B., Green, Richard C., and Naik, Vasant. 2004. "Valuation and Return Dynamics of New Ventures." *Review of Financial Studies*, vol. 17, no. 1, pp. 1–35.

Berry, John M. 1985. "Computer Snarled N.Y. Bank: $32 Billion Overdraft Resulted from Snafu." *Washington Post*, December 13.

Black, Fischer. 1976. "The Pricing of Commodity Contracts." *Journal of Financial Economics*, vol. 3, nos. 1/2, pp. 167–179.

Bodie, Zvi and Rosansky, Victor. 1980. "Risk and Return in Commodity Futures." *Financial Analysts Journal*, vol. 36, no. 3, pp. 27–39.

Bookstaber, Richard M. 1999. "A Framework for Understanding Market Crisis." In *Risk Management: Principles and Practices* (AIMR Conference Proceedings), pp. 7–19. Charlottesville, VA: Association for Investment Management and Research.

——. 2007. *A Demon of Our Design: Markets, Hedge Funds and the Perils of Financial Innovation*. Hoboken, NJ: John Wiley & Sons.

—— and Jacob, David P. 1986. "The Composite Hedge: Controlling the Credit Risk of High Yield Bonds." *Financial Analysts Journal*, vol. 42, no. 2, pp. 25–36.

Bridgewater Associates. 2009. "The impact of securities lending on credit creation." *Bridgewater Daily Observations*, February 19, pp. 1–7.

Brinson, Gary, Hood, Randolph, and Beebower, Gilbert. 1986. "Determinants of Portfolio Performance." *Financial Analysts Journal*, vol. 42, no. 4, pp. 39–44.

Brunnermeier, Markus K. and Pedersen, Lasse Heje. 2005. "Predatory Trading." *Journal of Finance*, vol. 60, no. 4, pp. 1825–63.

Cairns, Ann. 2009. "A Bankrupt Insolvency System." *Wall Street Journal Europe*, May 14.

Campbell, John Y., Lo, Andrew W., and MacKinlay, A. Craig. 1997. *The Econometrics of Financial Markets*. Princeton, NJ: Princeton University Press.

——, ——, and Viceira, Luis M. 2005. "The Term Structure of the Risk-Return Tradeoff." *Financial Analysts Journal*, vol. 61, no. 1, pp. 34–44.

Campbell, Rachel, Koedijk, Kees, and Kofman, Paul. 2002. "Increased Correlation in Bear Markets." *Financial Analysts Journal*, vol. 58, no. 1, pp. 87–94.

Cauchi, Marietta. 2009. "Funds of Funds Sell Stakes at Discounts." *Wall Street Journal*, May 6.

Caulfield, Jon. 1998. "Timberland Return Drivers and Investing Styles for an Asset That Has Come of Age." *Real Estate Finance*, Winter, pp. 65–78.

Chacko, George. 2008. "Liquidity Risk in the Corporate Bond Markets." In H. Gifford Fong (ed.), *Innovations in Investment Management: Cutting Edge Research from the Exclusive JOIM Conference Series*, pp. 155–72. New York, NY: Bloomberg Press.

Chicago Board Options Exchange. 2003. "VIX CBOE Volatility Index." Chicago IL: CBOE.

Clarke, Roger G. 2006. "Trends in Portfolio Structuring." In Rodney N. Sullivan (ed.), *Global Perspectives on Investment Management: Learning from the Leaders*, pp. 177–95. Charlottesville, VA: CFA Institute.

Commodity Futures Trading Commission. 1995. "Order Instituting Proceedings Pursuant to Sections 6 and 8a of the Commodity Exchange Act and Findings and Order Imposing Remedial Sanctions, CFTC Docket No. 95–14." July 21.

Conkin, Paul K. 2008. *A Revolution Down on the Farm*. Lexington, KY: University Press of Kentucky.

Cui, Carolyn. 2009. "Computer-Trading Models Meet Match." *Wall Street Journal*, April 19.

Cvitanić, Jaksa et al. 2004. "Optimal Allocation to Hedge Funds: An Empirical Analysis." *Quantitative Finance*, vol. 3, no. 1, pp. 28–39.

Dacorogna, Michel M., Gençay, Ramazan, Müller, Ulrich A., Olsen, Richard B., and Pictet, Olivier V. 2001. *An Introduction to High Frequency Finance: Theory and Application*. San Diego, CA: Academic Press.

Daniel, Kent, 2009. "Anatomy of a Crisis." *CFA Institute Conference Proceedings Quarterly*, vol. 26, no. 3, pp. 11–21.

de Silva, Harindra. 2006. "Modern Tactical Asset Allocation." *CFA Institute Conference Proceedings*, vol. 23, no. 4, pp. 1–10.

Derman, Emanuel. 2004. *My Life as a Quant: Reflections on Physics and Finance*. Hoboken, NJ: John Wiley & Sons.

DiBartolomeo, Dan, Gold, Richard, Baldwin, Ken, and Belev, Emilian. 2005. "A New Approach to Real Estate Risk." Unpublished manuscript available at http://www.northinfo.com/documents/191.pdf.

Dorsey, Alan H. 2007. *Active Alpha: A Portfolio Approach to Selecting and Managing Alternative Investments*. Hoboken, NJ: John Wiley & Sons.

Duarte, Jefferson, Longstaff, Francis A., and Yu, Fan. 2007. "Risk and Return in Fixed Income Arbitrage: Nickels in Front of a Steam Roller?" *Review of Financial Studies*, vol. 20, no. 3, pp. 769–811.

Dusak, Katherine. 1973. "Futures Trading and Investor Returns: An Investigation of Commodity Market Risk Premiums," *Journal of Political Economy*, vol. 81, no. 6, pp. 1387–406.

El-Erian, Mohamed. 2008. *When Markets Collide: Investment Strategies for the Age of Global Economic Change*. New York, NY: McGraw-Hill.

Ellis, Charles D. 1975. "The Loser's Game." *Financial Analysts Journal*, vol. 31, no. 5, pp. 19–26.

Elton, E. and Gruber, M. 1977. "Risk Reduction and Portfolio Size: An Analytical Solution." *Journal of Business*, vol. 50, no. 4, pp. 415–437.

—— and ——. 1994. "Multi-Index Models Using Simultaneous Estimation of All Parameters." In *A Practitioner's Guide to Factor Models*, pp. 33–58. Charlottesville, VA: The Research Foundation of the Institute of Chartered Financial Analysts.

Engle, Robert F. 1996. "The Econometrics of Ultra-High Frequency Data." *Econometrica*, vol. 68, no. 1, pp. 1–22.

—— and Rangel, Jose Gonzalo. 2008. "The Spline-GARCH Model for Low-Frequency Volatility and its Global Macroeconomic Causes." *Review of Financial Studies*, vol. 21, no. 3, pp. 1187–222.

Erb, Claude B. and Harvey, Campbell R. 2006. "The Strategic and Tactical Value of Commodity Futures." *Financial Analysts Journal*, vol. 62, no. 2, pp. 69–97.

Fabozzi, Frank J., Focardi, Sergio M., and Kolm, Petter N. 2006. *Trends in Quantitative Finance*. Charlottesville, VA: The Research Foundation of The CFA Institute.

Fama, Eugene F. and French, Kenneth R. 1993. "Common Risk Factors in the Returns of Stocks and Bonds." *Journal of Financial Economics*, vol. 33, no. 1, pp. 3–56.

Feldstein, Martin and Green, Jerry. 1983. "Why Do Companies Pay Dividends?" *American Economic Review*, vol. 73, no. 1, pp. 17–30.

Fraser-Sampson, Guy. 2006. *Multi Asset Class Investment Strategy*. Chichester, UK: John Wiley & Sons.

——. 2007. *Private Equity as an Asset Class*. Chichester, UK: John Wiley & Sons.

Fridson, Martin S. 1994. "Do High-Yield Bonds Have an Equity Component?" *Financial Management*, vol. 23, no. 2, pp. 82–84.

Fung, William and Hsieh, David A. 2001. "The Risk in Hedge Fund Strategies: Theory and Evidence from Trend Followers." *Review of Financial Studies*, vol. 14 no. 2, pp. 313–41.

Glosten, Lawrence R. and Jagannathan, Ravi. 1994. "A Contingent Claim Approach to Performance Evaluation." *Journal of Empirical Finance*, vol. 1, no. 2, pp. 133–60.

Goldman Sachs. 2004. "Asset Allocation and Manager Selection: Theory *vs.* Practice." Occasional paper available at https://360.gs.com/gs/portal/?st=1&action=action.binary&d=6036018&fn=/document.pdf.

Greenwood, Robin and Schor, Michael. 2007. "Hedge Fund Investor Activism and Takeovers." Harvard Business School working paper no. 08-004, available at http://hbswk.hbs.edu/item/5739.html.

Greer, Robert J. 2004. "What Is an Asset Class, Anyway?" *Journal of Portfolio Management*, Winter, pp. 86–91.

——. 2005. "Commodity Indexes for Real Return." In Robert J. Greer (ed.), *The Handbook of Inflation Hedging Investments*, pp. 105–26. New York: McGraw Hill.

Grinold, Richard C. and Kahn, Ronald N. 2000. *Active Portfolio Management: a quantitative approach for providing superior returns and controlling risk*. New York, NY: McGraw-Hill.

Hagan, Patrick S., Kumar, Deep, Lesniewski, Andrew S., and Woodward, Diana E. 2002. "Managing Smile Risk." *Wilmott Magazine* (online), November 18.

Haldane, Andrew G. 2009. "Rethinking the Financial Network." Speech delivered at the Financial Student Association, Amsterdam, April. Transcript available at http://www.bankofengland.co.uk/publications/speeches/2009/speech386.pdf.

Harvey, Campbell R. and Siddique, Akhtar. 2000. "Conditional Skewness in Asset Pricing Tests." *Journal of Finance*, vol. 55, no. 3, pp. 1263–95.

——, Liechty, John C., Liechty, Merrill W., and Müller, Peter. 2004. "Portfolio Selection with Higher Moments." Working paper available at SSRN: http://ssrn.com/abstract=63414.

Hechinger, John and Levitz, Jennifer. 2009. "Battered Nonprofits Seek to Tap Nest Eggs." *Wall Street Journal*, February 11.

Henriksson, Roy D. and Merton, R. C. 1981. "On market timing and investment performance II: statistical procedures for evaluating forecasting skills." *Journal of Business*, vol. 54, no. 4, pp. 513–33.

Hodson, Jennifer. 2009. "Life-Settlements Business Gets Boost amid Crisis." *Wall Street Journal*, February 4.

Horwitz, Richard. 2004. *Hedge Fund Risk Fundamentals*. New York, NY: Bloomberg Press.

Hsu, David H. 2004. "What Do Entrepreneurs Pay for Venture Capital Affiliation?" *Journal of Finance*, vol. 59, no. 4, pp. 1805–44.

Inklebarger, Timothy. 2009. "Alaska blazes new trail in risk-based investing." *Pensions & Investments*, June 1. Available at http://www.pionline.com/apps/pbcs.dll/article?AID=/20090601/PRINTSUB/306019981&crit=Inklebarger.

Investors Diversified Realty. 2008. "Debt Market Presentation." PowerPoint presentation, November.

Javaheri, Alireza. 2005. *Inside Volatility Arbitrage: The Secrets of Skewness*. Hoboken, NJ: John Wiley & Sons.

Jetley, Gaurav and Ji, Xinyu. 2010. "The Shrinking Merger Arbitrage Spread: Reasons and Implications." *Financial Analysts Journal*, vol. 66, no. 2, pp. 54–68.

Jones, Charles P. and Wilson, Jack W. 2004. "The Changing Nature of Stock and Bond Volatility." *Financial Analysts Journal*, vol. 60, no. 4, pp. 100–113.

Kahn, Ronald N. 2006. "Asset Growth and its Impact on Expected Alpha." In Rodney N. Sullivan (ed.) *Global Perspectives on Investment Management*. Charlottesville, VA: CFA Institute.

Keating, Con and Shadwick, William F. 2002. "An Introduction to Omega©." Finance Development Centre research paper.

Keehner, Jonathan and Kelly, Jason. 2008. "Harvard-Led Push to Sell Private Equity Stakes Hits LBO Values." *Bloomberg Online*, November 30.

Keynes, John M. 1964. *The General Theory of Employment, Interest and Money*. New York, NY: Harcourt & Brace.

Kirschner, Sam, Mayer, Eldon, and Kessler, Sam. 2006. *The Investor's Guide to Hedge Funds*. Hoboken, NJ: John Wiley & Sons.

Kishan, Saijel and Burton, Katherine. 2009. "Hedge Funds Get Earful from Clients about Fees, Withdrawals." *Bloomberg Online*, April 3.

Kocagil, Ahmet E. 2004. "Optionality and Daily Dynamics of Convenience Yield Behavior: An Empirical Analysis." *Journal of Financial Research*, vol. 27, no. 1, pp. 143–58.

Kochard, Lawrence E. and Rittereiser, Cathleen M. 2008. *Foundation and Endowment Investing: Philosophies and Strategies of Top Investors and Institutions.* Hoboken, NJ: John Wiley & Sons.

Kovacs, David and Turner, Robert. 2004. "Asset Capacity Study for Turner's Stock Portfolios." Occasional paper available at http://www.turnerinvestments.com.

Krapels, Ed. 2001. "Re-examining the Metallgesellschaft affair and its implications for oil traders." *Oil & Gas Journal*, vol. 99, no. 13, pp. 70–77.

Krishnan, Hari and Nelken, Izzy. 2003. "A Liquidity Haircut for Hedge Funds." *Risk*, vol. 16 no. 4, pp. S18–S21.

Kritzman, Mark and Page, Sebastien. 2003. "The Hierarchy of Investment Choice: A Normative Interpretation." *Journal of Portfolio Management*, vol. 29, Summer, pp. 11–23.

Lerner, Josh. 2007. "Yale University Investments Office: August 2006." Harvard Business School Case 9-807-073. Boston MA: Harvard Business School Publishing.

——, Hardymon, Felda and Leamon, Ann. 2005. *Venture Capital and Private Equity: A Casebook.* Hoboken, NJ: John Wiley & Sons.

Lhabitant, François-Serge. 2004. *Hedge Funds: Quantitative Insights.* Chichester, UK: John Wiley & Sons.

—— and Learned, Michelle. 2002. "Hedge Fund Diversification: How Much Is Enough?" *Journal of Alternative Investments*, Winter, pp. 23–49.

Ljungqvist, Alexander, Hochberg, Yael V., and Lu, Yang. 2005. "Whom You Know Matters: Venture Capital Networks and Investment Performance." Working paper available at SSRN: http://ssrn.com/abstract=631941.

Lo, Andrew W. 2004. "The Adaptive Markets Hypothesis." *Journal of Portfolio Management*, vol. 30, special 30th anniversary edition, pp. 15–29.

——. 2008. *Hedge Funds: An Analytic Perspective.* Princeton, NJ: Princeton University Press.

—— and Hasanhodzie, Jasmina. 2009. *The Heretics of Finance: Conversations with Leading Practitioners of Technical Analysis.* New York, NY: Bloomberg Press.

——, Mamaysky, Harry and Wang, Jiang. 2000. "Foundations of Technical Analysis: Computational Algorithms, Statistical Inference and Empirical Implementation." *Journal of Finance*, vol. 55 no. 4, pp. 1705–70.

——, ——, ——. 2004. "Asset Prices and Trading Volume under Fixed Transaction Costs." *Journal of Political Economy*, vol. 112, no. 5, pp. 1054–90.

Loomis, Carol. 1966. "The Jones Nobody Keeps Up With." *Fortune*, April 1966, pp. 237–47.

Madigan, Peter. 2008. "Don't Follow the Herd." *Risk*, vol. 21, no. 9, pp. 88–90.

Mainelli, Michael. 2007. "Liquidity: Finance in Motion or Evaporation?" Gresham College Commerce Lecture, Transcript available at http://www.gresham.ac.uk/even.asp?PageId=45&EventId=640. September 5.

Malkiel, Burton and Saha, Atanu. 2005. "Hedge Funds: Risk and Return." *Financial Analysts Journal*, vol. 61, no. 6, pp. 80–88.

Mamarbachi, Raya, Day, Marc and Favato, Giampiero. 2008. "Evaluating Art as an Alternative Investment Asset." *Journal of Financial Transformation*, vol. 24, pp. 63–71.

Mamudi, Sam. 2009. "Morningstar to Take Fresh Look at Funds." *Wall Street Journal*, February 24.

Mandelbrot, Benoit. 1962. "Sur certains prix spéculatifs: faits empiriques et modèle basé sur les processus stables additives de Paul Lévy." *Comptes Rendus*, vol. 254, pp. 3968–70.

—— and Hudson, Richard L. 2004. *The (mis)Behavior of Financial Markets.* New York, NY: Basic Books.

May, Robert M., Levin, Simon A., and Sugihara, George. 2008. "Ecology for Bankers." *Nature*, vol. 451, February 21, pp. 893–95.

McDonald, Linda. 2007. "Investing in Infrastructure." Occasional paper, available at http://www.rogerscasey.com.

Meerkatt, Heino and Liechtenstein, Heinrich. 2008. "Get Ready for the Private Equity Shakeout." Boston Consulting Group occasional paper, available at http://www.bcg.com.

Merton, Robert C. 1981. "On Market Timing and Investment Performance I: An Equilibrium Theory of Value for Market Forecasts." *Journal of Business*, vol. 54, no. 3, pp. 363–406.

——. 2008. "A New Generation of Pension Fund Management." In H. Gifford Fong (ed.), *Innovations in Investment Management: Cutting Edge Research from the Exclusive JOIM Conference Series*, pp. 1–17. New York, NY: Bloomberg Press.

Michaud, Richard O. 1989. "The Markowitz Optimization Enigma: Is 'Optimized' Optimal?" *Financial Analysts Journal*, vol. 45, no. 1, pp. 31–42.

Miller, Claire Cain and Fabrikant, Geraldine. 2008. "Beyond the Ivied Halls, Endowments Suffer." *New York Times*, November 26, 2005.

Miller, Merton H. and Modigliani, Franco. 1961. "Dividend Policy, Growth and the Valuation of Shares." *Journal of Business*, vol. 34, no. 4, pp. 411–33.

Mitchell, Mark and Pulvino, Todd. 2001. "Characteristics of Risk and Return in Risk Arbitrage." *Journal of Finance*, vol. 56, no. 6, pp. 2135–75.

Montier, James. 2002. *Behavioural Finance: Insights into Irrational Minds and Markets.* Chichester, UK: John Wiley & Sons.

Moskowitz, Tobias J. and Vissing-Jørgensen, Annette. 2004. "The Returns to Entrepreneurial Investment: A Private Equity Premium Puzzle?" *American Economic Review*, vol. 92, no. 4, pp. 745–78.

Nantamanasikarn, Porntawee. 2008. "The Global Investable Universe." *CB Richard Ellis Investors Investment Research Quarterly*, Fourth Quarter, p. 11.

Needham, Paul. 2009. "Endowment Falls 25 Percent." *Yale Daily News*, January 12.

Newell, Graeme and Peng, Hsu Wen. 2008. "The Role of U.S. Infrastructure in Investment Portfolios." *Journal of Real Estate Portfolio Management*, vol. 14, no. 1, pp. 21–33.

Nielsen, Kasper Meisner. 2005. "The Return to Pension Funds' Private Equity Investments: Another Piece to the Private Equity Premium Puzzle?" Financial Management Association working paper, available at http://www.fma.org/SLC/Papers?KMN_private_equity.pdf.

Nuttall, John. 2000. "The Importance of Asset Allocation." Unpublished paper available at http://publish.uwo.ca/~jnuttall/asset.pdf.

Page, Sébastien. 2006. "Optimal Hedge Fund Allocations: Do Higher Moments Matter?" *CFA Institute Conference Proceedings Quarterly*, vol. 23, no. 3, pp. 26–33.

Patterson, Scott. 2008. "October Pain was 'Black Swan' Gain." *Wall Street Journal*, October 3.

PricewaterhouseCoopers. 2008. "Behind the Numbers: Medical Cost Trends for 2009." PricewaterhouseCoopers Health Research Institute occasional paper, available from http://www.pwchealth.com.

Pulliam, Susan and Strasburg, Jenny. 2009. "Brokerages Tighten Hedge Fund Financing." *Wall Street Journal*, February 19.

Rahl, Leslie. 2000. "Risk Budgeting: The next Step of the Risk Management Journey." In Leslie Rahl (ed.), *Risk Budgeting: A New Approach to Investing*. London, pp. 3–26. UK: Risk Books.

———. 2001. "Capital Market Risk Advisors NAV/Fair Value Practices Survey Results." *Journal of Alternative Investments*, vol. 4, no. 3, pp. 55–58.

Reddy, Girish, Brady, Peter, and Patel, Kartik. 2007. "Are Funds of Funds Simply Multi-Strategy Managers with Extra Fees?" *Journal of Alternative Investments*, vol. 10, no. 3, pp. 490–561.

Reilly, Brian, et al. 2009. "Hedge Fund Intelligence—February 2009." Barclays Capital research publication.

Rothman, Mathey S. 2008. "Quantitative Equity Asset Management: Reassessing, One Year Later." Lehman Brothers research presentation, August.

Seides, Ted. 2008. "Understanding Hedge Fund Fundamentals and Trends." *CFA Institute Conference Proceedings*, September, pp. 45–53.

Shawky, Hany A. and Li, Liuling. 2006. "Optimal Asset Size for U.S. Small-Cap Equity Funds." *Journal of Investing*. Spring.

Singer, Brian D. 1999. "Risk Analysis: A Geometric Approach." *Risk Management: Principles and Practices*. Charlottesville, VA: Association for Investment Management and Research Conference Proceedings, pp. 7–19.

———, Staub, Renato and Terhaar, Kevin. 2003. "An Appropriate Policy Allocation for Alternative Investments." *Journal of Portfolio Management*, vol. 29, Spring, pp. 101–110.

Soe, Aye M. and Dash, Shrikant. 2009. "A Tale of Two Benchmarks." Standard & Poor's occasional paper. June.

Soramäki, Kimmo, Bech, Morton L., Arnold, Jeffrey, Glass, Robert J., and Beyeler, Walter E. 2006. "The Topology of Interbank Payment Flows." Federal Reserve Bank of New York, Staff Report no. 243, March.

Statman, Meir. 1987. "How Many Stocks Make a Diversified Portfolio?" *Journal of Financial and Quantitative Analysis*, vol. 22, no. 2, pp. 353–363.

Stefanini, Filippo. 2006. *Investment Strategies of Hedge Funds.* Chichester, UK: John Wiley & Sons.

Swedroe, Larry E. and Kizer, Jared. 2008. *The Only Guide to Alternative Investments You'll Ever Need: The Good, the Flawed, the Bad, and the Ugly.* New York, NY: Bloomberg Press.

Swensen, David F. 2000. *Pioneering Portfolio Management: An Unconventional Approach to Institutional Investment.* New York, NY: Free Press.

——. 2009. *Pioneering Portfolio Management: An Unconventional Approach to Institutional Investment,* second edition. New York, NY: Free Press.

Taleb, Nassim N. 2007. *The Black Swan: The Impact of the Highly Improbable.* New York, NY: Random House.

Tam, Pui-Wing. 2009. "Venture Capitalists Chart a New Course." *Wall Street Journal,* March 13.

Timberlake, Jeanene. 2009. "Hedge Fund Admins Bite Separate Account Bullet." *Operations Management,* vol. 15, no. 2, p. 1.

Tokat, Yessim and Stockton, Kimberly A. 2008. "A Primer on Tactical Asset Allocation Strategy Evaluation." Occasional paper, Vanguard Investment Counseling and Research, October.

Vara, Vauhini. 2005. "Photo Agencies Scour the Web for Copyright Violations." *Wall Street Journal,* October 14.

Vaughan, Liam. 2009. "Deal Spreads Widen as Investors Grow Fearful of Prospects." *Wall Street Journal,* January 12.

Viceira, Luis M. 2006. "Developments in Asset Allocation Modeling." In Rodney N. Sullivan (ed.), *Global Perspectives on Investment Management: Learning from the Leaders,* pp. 145–157. Charlottesville, VA: CFA Institute.

Wade, Adam. 2009a. "U.S. Venture-Backed Liquidity Reaches Lowest Point in 5 Years, Down 58% to $24.1 Billion in 2008." Press release, Dow Jones VentureSource, January 2.

——. 2009b. "U.S. VC Investment Slips 8% to $28.8 billion in 2008 as Year Closes with Slowest Quarter since 2005." Press release, Dow Jones Venture-Source, January 17.

Wilmott, Paul. 1998. *Derivatives: The Theory and Practice of Financial Engineering.* Chichester, UK: John Wiley & Sons.

Wright, Christopher. 2009. "Score Wars: Do Consultants add Value to the Manager Research Process?" *CFA Magazine,* March/April, pp. 34–40.

Wright, Colby, Banerjee, Prithviraj and Boney, Vaneesha. 2009. "Behavioral Finance: Are the Disciples Profiting from the Doctrine?" *Journal of Investing,* vol. 17, no. 4, pp. 82–90.

Wu, Jinglian. 2005. *Understanding and Interpreting Chinese Economic Reform.* Mason, OH: Texere.

Zerolis, John. 1998. "Picturing Volatility and Correlation." In *Derivatives in Portfolio Management* (ICFA Continuing Education Series), pp. 49–64. Charlottesville, VA: Association for Investment Management and Research.

Zhou, Zu-Shen and Dong, Ming. 2004. "Can Fuzzy Logic Make Technical Analysis 20/20?" *Financial Analysts Journal,* vol. 60, no. 44, pp. 54–75.

Index